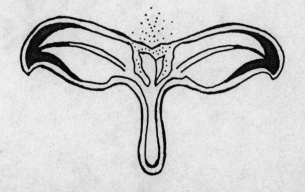

Gay Talk

(formerly entitled *The Queens' Vernacular*)

A (Sometimes Outrageous)
Dictionary of Gay Slang

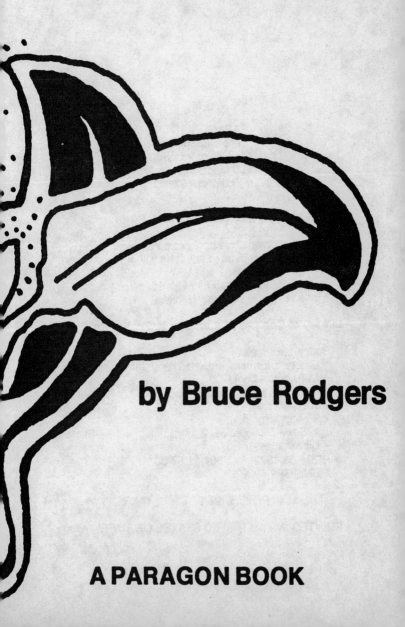

by Bruce Rodgers

A PARAGON BOOK

PARAGON BOOKS
are published by
G. P. Putnam's Sons
200 Madison Avenue
New York, New York 10016

This is an authorized reprint of an edition originally
published by Straight Arrow Books.

Library of Congress Cataloging in Publication Data

Rodgers, Bruce.
  Gay talk: formerly entitled The queens' vernacular.
  (A Paragon book)
  Reprint of the ed. published by Straight Arrow Books,
San Francisco.
  Bibliography: p.
  1. Sex—Dictionaries. 2. English language—Slang
—Dictionaries. I. Title.
HQ9.R63 1979   301.41′57′03   79-13972
ISBN 0-399-50392-7

First Paragon Printing, 1979

PRINTED IN THE UNITED STATES OF AMERICA

In memory of
April—
who more than anyone else
wanted to see this book
& to Billy's House (you too, Phil L.),
Chris Bundance, Crystal, Dwah,
Giuseppi, Jim & Mary &, John
(a svelt Wisconsin mist), Lauracita,
Luther, Mammy Blueballs, Peaches.
Ron-Ton Sisters, Snooze, Sunshine,
Trees, Witch Dee, Yrral.
also:

Dear Bruce,

By wonderful strange coincidence, a month or so ago I was telling our linguist about your dictionary. He had been sending a research assistant out collecting slang. He was quite interested, and I told him that I didn't know when, but that I would be hearing from you. So: congratulations all over the place! Send the university a copy by all means, and send me an inscribed one.

I am deeply honored to have a dictionary dedicated, in part, to me. It's an opportunity that comes to few. Do it. Just don't mention my name. . . .

f you accept cultural anthropologist Franz Boas' dictum that "Language *is* culture," then you'll agree that *The Queens' Vernacular* is not only first-rate lexicography, but also an important contribution to the history of American culture.

Having made that pronouncement, let me quickly add that this book is not "scientific" or "scholarly" in the academic sense; nor is it definitive or objective. Its author does not even draw any conclusions about his work, except to say that it is "linguistically nonapologetic."

It *is* an admittedly random, passionately gathered and meticulously collated compendium of the current "slanguage" of a very large group of people who are members (part- or fulltime) of the homosexual community. It is the result of years of interviews with hundreds of informants whom Bruce Rodgers sought out in bars, steam baths, dance halls, public johns and on street corners. He did not have at his disposal a team of field workers or researchers or editors, nor did he have a foundation grant to underwrite his labors. He had only his own energy and uncommon zeal. This book is the impressive result.

The most felicitous speech in our language often goes by the cliche "The King's English." A play on words might have suggested we call this book "The Queen's English," but what we have here is not a dictionary of proper speech but rather, a lexicon of *actual* speech: the vernacular, the street language; rough crude and vulgar, but also witty, self-deprecating and pointedly revealing in the way that only the common speech of a traditionally oppressed minority can be.

There is an easy but sound parallel between the gay subculture and the black subculture, and between the use of the words "nigger" and "queen" or "faggot." I remember a book published in the late 1950s called *A Jazz Lexicon,* which purported to be a lexicon of the vernacular of jazz musicians. It was an interesting and worthy effort, for it documented for the first time many of the slang words associated with the use of marijuana, cocaine, heroin and other drugs; street terms such as "motherfucker"; and a variety of other now familiar slang words. As one critic pointed out at the time, however, it was actually a lexicon of black language. If the author had been a jazz musician or had been personally involved with the people whose language he was documenting, he might have called his book something like "Nigger Talk: A Partial Lexicon of Black Speech." What he in fact compiled was the vernacular of the alienated black subculture as it surfaced among jazz musicians, black and white. Since the book appeared, however, our consciousness of (and respect for) the separate life and language of the majority of black people has risen considerably.

The same historical changes will probably be true of the gay subculture. Many people would no doubt agree with Merle Miller's observation that the Gay Liberation Movement is presently at about the same point as the Civil Rights Movement in, say, 1957: Still oppressed and heavily discriminated against both legally and socially, but also a highly fractionalized movement, parts of which (like their middle class black counterparts in the '50s) would prefer to forget that there are any differences between gays and straights. They are opposed by the more militant gays who insist that they be accepted without necessarily being assimilated. I was impressed when reading *The Queens' Vernacular* by the large number of homosexual slang terms—many of them now part of the general slang—which were coined in the 1950s. It was a decade during which a great many gays "came out," acknowledging their homosexuality at least among fellow homosexuals. It was also a period which saw the rapid growth of gay bars and ghettos in many of the larger American cities, and of a recognizable private language with which this new community identified.

There is a great deal of ambivalent feeling among gays about what is or is not a part of their culture, and that ambivalence is reflected in their language. The word "queen" for example, was originally coined by heterosexuals as derogatory slang for the more outrageously effeminate homosexual; the grand, haughty, often comic "screaming queen" who is still the Stepan Fetchit of the gay community. The term has, over the years, become as important a part of the gay vernacular as has the word "nigger" among blacks, and it reflects the same historical linguistic process: The proud adoption of a pejorative as the badge of membership. As with nigger, the term remains loaded. It is all right for one homosexual to call another a queen, but it is definitely not all right for a straight person ignorant of the gay subculture to use the term in front of gays.

The Queens' Vernacular is unlike any published work on the subject of homosexuality. It is a book about words, those previously agreed-upon symbols for recognizing things and actions. The more private the words, the fewer the number of people who previously have agreed upon their meanings. And the deeper the recognition. All of us speak English. But how many speak Southern American or black, junkie or gay? How deep is our recognition of "good ol' boy" or "oreo cookie," "pusher" or "bull dyke"?

This is also a book about oppression, for words are a means by which the oppressed deal with that condition, and with the pressure and tension that results from living a "secret" life. Much of it is more vulgar, barbaric, cruel, racist and sexist than any speech you will ever encounter, and it will shock and perhaps infuriate. But it says a great deal about quite a large part of our society which you probably do not know very much about and which you probably have a strong prejudice *against*, whether you are straight or gay. We believe it will enlighten you. Just as blacks have come to recognize that no matter what their income, neighborhood, diction or hue, they will remain "niggers" so long as white society clings to its racial cliches, so every homosexual who has even one foot out of the closet knows that no matter what he says or how he acts, he will continue to be branded a "queen" and a "faggot" by straight society (and the oppressor by nature has a different meaning for his words than the oppressed). His life—including his language—will continue to be as schizophrenic as straight society insists it be.

We use words to give expression to our thoughts about our experience. *The Queens' Vernacular* demonstrates the imagination, subtlety, humor, self-pity and downright masochism with which gay people have forged the common language into a means of communicating their experience. It deserves your attention if only because it will enrich your own language and experience immeasurably. However, it is a lexicon; it is *not* meant to represent the everyday speech of the majority of gay people. One would be hard put to find someone who speaks *any* slang all of the time.

"When *I* use a word,' Humpty-Dumpty said to Alice in a rather scornful tone, "it means exactly what I choose it to mean, neither more nor less. . . . But when I make a word do double duty, I always pay it extra."

Douglas Mount
Straight Arrow Books

he principal aim of this book is to make available a dictionary of homophile cant. Previously gay slang has been explored only in slight, dated glossaries or in booklets, not much more than glossaries themselves. I found that many entries were faulty simply because the authors, too far removed from the gays' community, didn't really know what they were hearing; they weren't using slang themselves and so were simply wrong. They would even label some words as vulgarisms, "best left undefined."

In essence, this is the book of my childhood. My early fondness for philology led me to conceive a book recording the street poetry of queens, those lively stereotypes forming yet another subculture within the homosexual minority. Linguistically, the book is nonapologetic. It records, without meaning to shock or anger, overheard pieces of living, fascinating slang.

Slang flourishes in the ghetto. Those who struggle to leave the ghetto shake off its language first and then decry its message. Slang is secretive, a form of protest and an expression of social recognition. Secret, because it leaves outsiders where they usually are. Yet this secretiveness is not restrictive or snobby; Anyone interested can break the code. Slang is a tricky piece of pun acrobatics; the more subcultures one contacts, the more meanings slang words project. When the secrecy in slang becomes an object in and of itself, at that point slang stops being primarily a form of communication.

Slang is social protest, used to deflate the hypocrisy of nice-sounding labels that mean nothing to the people who use them. Slang is also the expression of the underdog—it is always aimed against the establishment.

Because the people who use slang words most frequently in their everyday speech are the economically oppressed—blacks, chicanos, hippies, ex-convicts, prostitutes—slang also records their desire to obtain what they do not have. At the same time, it is a means of identifying other members of the same group, *eg,* going up to a group of long-haired young people and passing around a "joint" is more apt to identify you as a member of their group than is suggesting that they share a marijuana cigarette. And the relevance of slang to culture is also evident in this example: A narcotics officer would ask for a "joint" with the full knowledge of the implication of the word. Slang moves from the specific to the general; from the regional to the national. Words move up and out of usage within a group and are promptly replaced by new terms.

It is, of course, unwritten, and even the compilation of words in this dictionary/lexicon is only an approximation of what is currently being spoken by gay people. Hearing another person's language—the essence of slang—is one of the few ways we can "get into his head."

Gay slang, like black slang, enriches our language immeasurably. "Camp," "straight," and "vibrations" were once solely gay inventions that are today part of every hip vocabulary. Gay slang was invented, coined, dished and shrieked by the gay stereotypes: The flaming faggots, men who look like women, flagrant wrist-benders, the women who don't shave their legs, all those who find it difficult to be accepted for what they feel they are even within the pariah gay subculture. And they stereotype others because they themselves have been labeled offensively: They see all Italian straights as members of the Mafia, and they speak of Yiddishe Mamas with a knowing smirk. They overdramatize words to make up for the plainness they find in their own lives; to them life is a stage with all the lights going and the audience constantly clapping for more. It's Vegas every minute! They jeer because they have been mocked; they retaliate with a barrage of their own words which ridicule women, male virility, the sanctity of marriage, everything in life from which they are divorced.

Since they are outlawed from the comfort of most religions as well, they have imparted a decidedly sacrilegious quality to their slang: "bullshit" = bishop, "May Miss God strike you dead!" *etc.* Gay slang also borrows freely from other languages. In the Southwest, for example, Mexican-Spanish borrowings add variety and richness.

Many gay militants are avidly opposed to this contrived lingo with which the oppressed faggot makes himself understood, and then only to a "sister." They consider the jargon yet another link in the chain which holds the homosexual enslaved. If this is true, then its widespread use and complex, subtle vocabulary would seem to indicate that liberation has not yet occurred.

It is my hope that this book will be more than a study of sex behind the English laboratory; that it will spur further study of homosexual slang patterns. No study can ever be conclusive; it can however, point the way to further research and more advanced analysis.

Bruce Rodgers
June 1972

Explanation

The entry styles in this lexicon take three forms. Most entries are structured as follows:

main entry (pronunciation key, where known, date, derivation; however, see also alternate possible derivation) **1.** first definition and possible example followed possibly by synonyms related only to this meaning.
2. second definition and example, *etc.*
Synonyms related to the whole entry.
Followed by related terms, definitions, examples and synonyms.
Followed by subentries formed from the main entry, definitions, examples, synonyms, antonyms.
Also see other pertinent entries.

However, some of the more substantial entries are arranged in a "story" format. These include entries such as **armed forces,** for which the homosexual community has its own special vocabulary, or entries such as **prison terminology,** which is the special vocabulary convicts and their keepers have for homosexuals and homosexual practices. The form is as follows:

❡ **heading** is explained in a story with **slang** interspersed throughout and defined only when doubtful. Followed by related terms not in the story, definitions, examples and synonyms.
Also see pertinent entries.

In other cases, both of these styles are blended together:

main entry (pronunciation key, where known, date, derivation) Definition and possible example followed by any related synonym, followed by story, with **slang words,** explaining themselves usually by the tale's context.

Abbreviation

Ans = answer
Ant = antonym
camp = sex reversal, strictly humorous, self mocking
cent = century
cf = compare
colloq = colloquial, well known regionally
dated = dates the user
dial = dialectal
= = equals
eg = for example
etc = and so forth
fr = from
// = from previous derivation
hetero = heterosexual
ie = that is
kwn = known in
les = lesbian usage
lit = literally
* = look up main entry alphabetically
med = medical terminology
narc = narcotic usage
naut = nautical
obs = obsolete
orig = originally
pej = pejorative
pl = plural
? = perhaps
+ = plus
pros = prostitute
sl = slang
SM = sado-masochistic
usu = usually
var = variant
vul = vulgar

Sources

Am = American
AS = Anglo Saxon
Aus = Australian dialect
Brit = British
carnival/carny sl = pig-latin whereby syllables are camouflaged by "e(a)za," *eg* house = hezouse.
Chin = Chinese
Du = Dutch
E = English
Fr = French

Ger = German
Gk = Greek
Gullah = S Carolina Black dialect formed from English and African Gold Coast languages.
Haw = Hawaiian
Heb = Hebrew
Ir = Irish
It = Italian
Jap = Japanese
L = Latin
La Creole = Louisiana Creole
M = middle, *eg* ME = Middle English
Mex = Mexican
O = Old, *eg* OFr = Old French
Pach = pachuco Spanish
Parlyaree cant = largely composed of Italian words salvaged from Lingua Franca.
Russ = Russian
Skt = Sanscrit
Sp = Spanish
Yid = Yiddish

Locations

Arg = Argentina
Ariz = Arizona
Cape Town = Capetown, South Africa
Chi = Chicago
Ill = Illinois
LA = Los Angeles, California
LV = Las Vegas, Nevada
NYC = New York City
PR = Puerto Rico
SF = San Francisco, California
Wis = Wisconsin

Parts of speech

adj = adjective
adv = adverb
exclam = exclamation
imp = imperative
interj = interjection
n = noun
pron = pronoun
v = verb
voc = vocative, name-calling

Pronounciation

(for those sounds that might give the reader trouble)

ə = about

a = map

ā = cape

ä = father

au = now

e = bed

ē = machine

g = always hard as in
  good lover

hw = why

i = tip

ī = fly

kh = German Buch;
  Spanish jota

o = knot

ō = beau, hole

ö = French feu

o͞o = boot

oi = join

u = butt

ū = unique

zh = French je, rouge

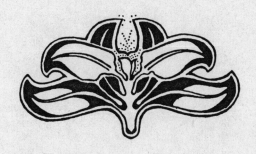

abareskin (*camp*) embarrassing.

abdicate to leave a public toilet because of possible interrogation by an attendant or vice squad officer "Time to abdicate the throne; hither cometh the vice-man."

Abigail nickname awarded to a middle-aged homosexual whose approach to life and love is conservative. *****Aunties, *closet queens** and *****piss elegant faggots** are also Abigails, but see their entries for the subtle differences in meaning.

abort to shit soon after being ass-fucked. Some queens erroneously believe that this is a wise-ass practice to prevent VD; others, however, are more concerned with the practice's camp value: "Ooh, I'm in love with my abortionist!"

accoutrements (a-kōō′-tra-ments, *fr* Fr *accoutrement* = bizarre attire) **1.** male genitals; see *****balls 2.** any gadget, especially a mechanical device whose name is unknown, unfamiliar or too technical to remember.
    Syn: **crown jewels** ("What's with all the crown jewels [locks] on your door . . . expecting Raid to drop in?"); **do-hickies.**

AC-DC see *****bisexual.**

ace gear (mid '60s, *fr* black sl *ace* = first-rate, as in *ace boon coon* = a best friend) sexually talented homosexual, one who is adept at everything.

acrophobia (*fr* GK *acros* = at the top + *phobia* = fear of) fear of smoking marijuana. The medical term for fear of heights reaches a new high (and meaning) in gay slang.

action (late '50s-mid '60s) **1.** one's ideology, philosophy of living "What's his action?" **2.** sexual preference. In a leather bar, for example, "What sort of action do you dig, man?" is often delivered as a sexy challenge **3.** general term for one who is sexually promising and exciting; also **piece of action** "There's always action on Greenwich Avenue, even when it snows."

active partner man who fucks in anal intercourse as opposed to the one who is fucked
    Syn: **ánus[biscuit, bun, keester] -bandit** (prison sl); **back-door man; bang artist** (late '60s); **bodyguard** (*kwn* Calif, mid '60s); **boretto man** (*dated*); **bottle opener** (*cf* sl *the bottle* = male prostitution); **boy-fag** (*kwn* LV, mid '60s); **brown artist; brown hatter** (Brit naut sl); **brownie king [BK]; bucket[*bunny cake] queen; buey** (bwā, Mex *fr* Sp *buey* = ox); **bugger** (*kwn* Brit sl, *fr* ML *bulgarus* = a heretic Bulgarian, and by extension a sodomite); **buggerantoes** (*rare, fr* character in 1684 production of *Sodom* reputed to John Wilmont, Earl of Rochester); **bum-fugger** (Brit); **bummer** (Brit, *fr bum* = ass); **bunger** (*dated*); **deadeye dick** (the *dead eye* being the anus); **dirt tamper** ('40s); **eye doctor** ('40s); **forty-niner** ('40s, ?*fr* rhyming sl for *miner* reflecting the activities of women-starved 19th cent Calif miners); **gander** (late '50s, ?*fr* variant **gooser;** but *cf* Hindi *gaundhu* = one who abuses an ass); **giver** (prison sl); **gonif**

(gun'-if, *rare*, *fr* Yid *gunnif* = thief // Heb *ganar*); **gooser** (*rare*: "The bi's motto is, 'What's good for the goosed is good for the gooser!' "); **Greek*; **gut-reamer[-stretcher, -stuffer]** (prison sl); **hip-hitter** (late '60s); **humper and a pumper** (*kwn* SF, '70, *hump* and *pump* are two well-known slang verbs for copulation); **inspector of manholes** (Brit); **jocker** (prison sl); **king** (*kwn* San Diego, late '60s); **knight[of the golden grummet]** (*rare*, so called because knights had *lances; also, grummet*, var of *grommet* = metal loop through which rope is passed and securely fastened); **miner** (mid '60s); **pit bull** (*kwn* LV, mid '60s: *fr* the man who practiced heterosexual anal intercourse); **pratt-hunter[-man]** (*rare*); **punker** (prison sl); **rear specialist; rider; ring snatcher; tom fucker** (*dated*, Brit sl); **top man; turd packer** ('40s); **turk** (19th century Turkish soldiers were reported to insult their dying enemies by anally abusing them); **tusk** (prison sl); **wheelman** (prison sl); **wildeman** (*fr* a Walter Winchellism coined from Oscar Wilde's surname).

actress (*camp*) homosexual character who hogs the limelight—egocentric but the life-of-the-party as well.

Also see **star*.

ad graffito, usually on a gay frequented washroom wall, stating the sexual desires of the writer. The scrawl often includes the time and place for oral and anal adventures.

Adam the first man with whom one has had homosexual relations.

Adam's P.J.'s nudity "He was wearing Adam's P.J.'s" = he was nude.

a-dollar-an-inch man (hustler sl) one who claims he's so large he could charge cocksuckers a dollar an inch and still come out ahead of what his rivals charge.

Adonis (*fr*.Gk *Adōnis* = proper name of a beautiful youth) flawless specimen of male physique.

advance a storm (*kwn* SF, black gay sl, '70) to work up a sweat from dancing or other forms of exertion "I'm advancing a small storm, girl; this Funky Penguin is too much!"

adventure (*fr* Fr *aventure*) love affair.

advertise 1. to dress in a sexually provocative manner. A gay maxim runs: "It pays to advertise!" **2.** (*camp*) to pluck and then paint the eyebrows.

advertising bar (early '60s) bar frequented by male prostitutes and their clients.

advertising pilgrim (mid '60s) sexily dressed straight man, unaware of the rise he's getting.

Also known simply as **pilgrim**.

affair 1. illicit extracurricular relationship. Among gay die-hard romantics, the word carries the strength of three months. To the majority, however, the word often represents five minutes in the bushes **2.** (Brit gay sl) one's current lover of uncertain duration "Ques: 'How old did you feel my affair was?' Ans: 'Probably much less!' "

afghan (mid '60s, *fr* the implied need of old age for a shawl, a knitted *afghan*) middle-aged homosexual who sometimes wears the regalia of a woman.

Agnes vocative implying that the person addressed is gay "Agnes here was in the army—she was the enemy!"

agreeable consenting to a homosexual act, especially used of someone new to the game.

A-hole (abbreviation of **asshole**) the rectal opening; anus.

Syn: **alleyway** (late '50s); **anus** (med *fr* L for "ring," usu in compound form, **anus bandit**, *etc*); **Arschloch** (ärsh'-lōkh, *fr* Ger = asshole); **back door** ("Must be the milkman knockin' at my back door"); **bird cage** (mid '60s; **blind eye; brown** ('30s-'40s); **brownie** ("You'll need a wide-angle lens for that brownie"); **brown lips; bung[hole]** (ME, fr sl bung = a cork for the mouth of a cask); **cooze** (kwn LV, late '60s); **crapper; culo** (fr Sp cola = a tail; cf Sicilian cula/gula also meaning the tail); ***cunt; cut** (an abbreviation for cunt or a comparison with slit); **dirt road[run]** (see *hobo slang); **ditch; dot** (obs); **exhaust pipe; eye** ('40s); **gee-gee[hole]** (gē-gē, kwn Wis, late '50s, fr vul sl gig = the vagina; cf La Creole, gigi, a child's favorite toy // Gullah gri-gri = a voodoo doll: "I'd be willing to bet money that Jim has a tight little gee-gee); **gonga** (obs, cf Sp ganga = a kind of prairie hen with the incubating rump of a brooding hen); **Hawaiian eye** (late '60s); **Hollywood uterus** (kwn LA, late '60s); **hymie** (late '30s, fr hymen); **inner-sanctum; jam-pot** (particularly when licked by a *rim-queen); **kiddie** (mid '60s, fr kidney); **kootch** (kwn LV, mid '60s); **kwazakoo** (kwä-zä-kōō', kwn NYC, black gay sl); **leather** (obs, '30s: comparing the texture of the tissue immediately surrounding the a-hole with leather); **lips; manhole; mustard pot** ('40s-'50s); **nooky** (?fr Swahili kunuka = to stink; cf *fish); **old-rip** ('30s-'40s: "No more hot peppers for me, Gracie, or old rip will be throwing it up on my face tomorrow"); **pan** ("He wanted to deep fry some sausage in your pan"); **poon** (kwn SF, '70s, fr sl poontang = black harlot // La Creole putaine = whore: "Put this in your poon and smoke it!"); **poop-hole** ("Why ask me for money . . . Fort Knox isn't up my poop-hole"); **poopoo** (fr baby talk = feces); **pussy** ("Marriage isn't all pussy and mouth, you know"); **quim** (obs, '30s: variant pronunciation of *queen); **recky** (short for rectum: "Why can't you sit down, your recky fall out?"); **rinctum** (fr black sl); **ring** (fr L anus = ring: "Have you found a ring to fit your nose yet?); **rosebud; round brown; round eye** (obs); **scratch** (rare: "You must be part Kraut . . . your scratch is pretty sour"); **shitter** ("There ain't no dick up his shitter? Man, o man! A vacancy in Shangri-La!"); **slick and slim up the old dusty road** (Prison sl); **slop[poop-, shit-] chute** (late '60s); **slot** ("Nice slot if you can get it, and you can get it if you try"); **snatch** ("Your snatch just blew me a kiss" = to fart); **split** (rare); **tan track** (fr hobo & prison sl: "His tan track was as lit up as Vegas"); **thrasher** ('71); **toilet** (prison sl); **tunnel** ("Divinity student or not, he had it right up my tunnel"); **twat[-arooney]; vault** ('71: "He once gave me the combination to his vault, and, man, was that ever a number!"); **wazoo** (wă-zōō', kwn western US: "Whew! You've been fingering the compost heap again; now you'll have to keep scratching your old wazoo to get rid of that aroma"); **web-center** ('30s, fr misconception that spider silk is stored rectally); **wing-wang** (late '60s: "His wing-wang was filled with throbbing cock, and he loved it.")

Related terms:

biting dog (late '50s, fr pros sl) the anal sphincter muscle as it contracts during anal intercourse. Syn: **snapping turtle[pussy] brown berry** (mid '60s) virginal asshole Syn: **flower** ("I was the first to pluck his flower"); **prune** (prison sl, late '60s: "Pull down your briefs, sweetheart, an' I'll show you how to stew a prune.")

bull ring anus of a rugged he-man, usually never having been explored by a cock. Syn: **jock hole**.

dingle-berries (late '50s-late '60s) dried globs of feces clinging to the anal hairs of an unfastidious person "Harvest your dingle-berries, Repunzel, and I'm sure someone will be along to irrigate your ditch." Syn: **cranberries** (late '60s).

glass asshole (kwn SF, '70) hairless anus free from bumpy hemorrhoids or anal warts.

natural breech (mid '60s-'71) the rectal tunnel that affords an unstrenuous entry during ass-fucking "He has a natural breech" = an ability to take on size with little or no hardship.

porthole sailor's asshole.

puff pussy (late '60s) swollen hemorrhoid tissue—specifically as the reward engendered by a careless homosexual.

Also see *grapes, *pussy tightener.

airtight said when all the body orifices (as opposed to the cock) are in sexual use "At the gang-bang, the blond one was sure airtight: some dude was even dorkin' him in the ear."

alice 1. common euphemism for the uniformed law, see *Lily Law **2.** (*kwn* SF, late '60s) LSD-25; acid "Alice dropped by here last Tuesday" **3.** (*kwn* SF, late '60s) acid-head **4.** (*kwn* SF, '71, *fr Alice in Wonderland*) a liar, storyteller "Alice, Alice, full of malice!"

alley affair 1. quick sexual encounter in dark, deserted public place **2.** one who is sucked off in an alleyway **3.** any sordid act of sex "You make sex with Tim sound like an alley affair!" Syn: **alley job[number].**

alley queen one who enjoys and seeks out sex in alleyways.

all-night movies someone who spends all night making love. Syn: **all-nighter.**

almost there (*kwn* LV, early '60s) just about to be led to the bedroom.

Amanda (*camp*) gay nickname for Andrew "Keep lifting weights, Amanda, and you'll look like Boulder Dam on legs."

ambidextrous see *bisexual.

ambiente (äm-bē-en'-tā, Mex *ambiente* = atmosphere; *cf* Ger translation "the airy packages" = homosexuals) a male homosexual. Plural: **los de ambiente** (those of the air).

amyl amyl nitrite gas inhaled because of its aphrodisiac powers. Generally, a nasal inhaler containing a crushed amyl nitrite ampoule or cotton saturated with liquid amyl nitrite sniffed during sex. Amyl nitrite is used medically to revive heart patients, but if inhaled during sex, the experience seems to last longer and feel more intense. It has become, in a manner of speaking *the* gay drug.

Until the late '60s, homosexuals as a group religiously avoided pills and other drugs though they would continue to use amyl. Paraphrasing the Bible's injunction "Gag at a gnat and swallow a camel" pre-hippy fairies would "gag at a joint and swallow an inhaler." Syn: **sniff.**

—queen an inhaler addict "He's such an amyl queen—he'd go home with the first druggist he met!"

Related terms:

amies amyl nitrite ampoules. Syn: **banana splits** (*fr* the pungent odor of overripe bananas emitted by breaking the ampoule); **crackers** ('70s); **pearls; poppers; Rice Crispies** ('70s: suggested by the other amyl nitrite sl names' relation to the "snap, crackle and pop" of the cereal); **snappers.**

inhaler 1. a commercially sold nasal inhaler used as the bedside container for amyl nitrite **2.** a noncommercial inhaler, usually metal, made solely for the purpose of amyl nitrite inhalation "That's not a mezuzah George is wearing around his neck . . . it's an inhaler."

joy juice (*kwn* SF, SM sl, '72) liquid amyl nitrite.

plug in the neon (*kwn* SF, '72: *fr* the effect of sniffing amyl) to inhale amyl nitrite while balling.

anal virgin boy or young man who has never experienced passive anal intercourse "Not even the twelve-year-olds in Hank's neighborhood are anal virgins anymore."

Syn: **canned goods; cherry** ("The closest you ever get to being cherry, Tramp, is by baking pies for Washington's birthday"); **crumpet** (*kwn* LA, mid '60s; *cf* Brit *bit o' crumpet* = sexual achievement with a female: "Man, was that crumpet tight— I had 'a use a whole jar of vaseline t' get it in"); **muffin** ('40s-early '50s: "Muffins have *their* prices too, but it's never too dear if you're a dedicated gourmet"); **turkish delight** (*fr* sl *Turk* = an active pederast); **virgin; Virginia** (*camp, kwn* SF, late '60s: "Getting laid, Virginia, is something like shitting backwards").

Related terms:

bonbon anal virginity "I've been in the life for thirty years . . . and in all those years, I've still kept my bonbon."

break[cop, get] a cherry to be the first to fuck an anal virgin "If this bus hits one more bump, it'll get my cherry." Syn: **pick a rosebud; pop a cherry; pop somebody open** ("He pops 'em open like there's no tomorrow"); **pop the cork.**

cherry picker homosexual seeking those who have never experienced it up the ass. If the homosexual is a tough who forces timid heterosexuals into anal submission—"counting coups" with straight boys as it were—he is said to be a **scalp hunter** ('40s).

tight ('40s) used to describe virgin asshole.

anekay (ă'-nē-kā, *fr* Haw gay sl // Haw *kane* = man) a heterosexual man; a masculine man. Some Hawaiian homosexuals resort to pig-latin to go undetected. These Hawaiian queens will sometimes speak to one another in a pidgin composed of Hawaiian, English, Chinese and Japanese: "Anaka no anekay; anaka mahu-lani, like watashi-me" = You're no man; you're a queen, like me.

angel any homosexual male. Angel, to some, mends the crumpled wings and pride of the denigated fairy.

Angelina sorority ('40s) the young homosexual's world.

angel with a dirty face (obs, mid-'30s, *fr* motion picture *Angels with Dirty Faces*) homosexual who is too timid to participate in homosexual acts.

Also see ***closet case.**

Angie (*voc*) preferred every now and then to the actual baptismal name of the listener "Say, Angie, how do you manage it, considering your age and all."

animal 1. sexually aggressive person "That girl's a real animal once she gets goin'!" Syn: **beast 2.** (*kwn* LV, mid '60s) one with a voracious appetite.

antique dealer young man interested in landing an elderly and wealthy man.

Syn: **gold-digger.**

anybody we know? a ***gay** line asked of one who sniffs his hands.

appetizer the first sexual partner of many encounters in the same day. Mainly heard in jocular context rather than in serious conversation "He wasn't big enough for an appetizer."

Aquarian (*kwn* SF, '70, *fr* the Age of Aquarius highlighted in the musical *Hair*) **1.** broad-minded, willing to make sexual allowances without jealousy "He's not as Aquarian as he thinks —he still gets uptight whenever his lover looks at another guy" **2.** free-love enthusiast.

arch it (*fr* archway) to solicit from an alleyway.

are you for real? question hinting at the possibility of overexaggeration "Five paddy wagons are lined up outside that gay bar!" Ans: "Are you for real?"

are you ready? means the same as "are you prepared to accept and believe this as fact?"

armed forces soldiers are keenly eyed by gays but should be avoided as indicated by the term **army style** (mid '60s: beating the cocksucker after the act). However, temptation being what it is, any serviceman is spoken of as being **Miss USO** (*camp, kwn* SF, '70) or a **uniform** ('40s).

Being drafted into the army = **rounding up the meat** (a cattle drive for slaughter); terrified homosexual draftees who are loathe to join the service willingly when greeted by **Uncle Samantha's meat call**; some will simply **mark the X** (check the little homosexual tendencies box on the questionnaire).

The boys in the barracks are called **dog food** (*kwn* SF, '72, *fr* army sl *dogface* = a private), **government-inspected meat** (late '60s), **khaki pussy** (*kwn* LV, late '60s: "They gave a medal to that khaki pussy for killing men, but they gave me a dishonorable discharge for kissing one"). A young soldier who services others on base with his ass provides **comfort for the troops.** On leave, a squadron of soldiers are defined as **campfire girls** (*camp*), while one lonely soldier is a **girl scout** (*camp*).

The Marine's overemphatic version of masculinity is an object of gay derision. After all, anybody *that* manly has *got* to be making up for something. Two popular graffiti to this effect state: "Sucking is better than fucking—hmmm, must be a Marine!" and "A Marine will suck you and let you suck him/he'll fuck you and let you fuck him/but don't ask him to kiss you/because that's queer!" Marines, with their crew-cut reputations, are designated as the **Marionettes** (reducing their drill to a Radio City Music Hall dance formation), **the mary ann[ie]s, military mary-annes** ("Stop eating your heart out over that military mary-anne—his bayonet's made out of rubber"), **murdering butches** (*kwn* LV, mid '60s) and **murines** (*camp*). When in combat, he, along with other soldiers, is spoken of as being a **killer queen** (late '60s).

The Navy, on the other wrist, is fantasized as full of young, doll-like boys who have signed up at seventeen [**chickens-of-the-sea, gobettes,** and **yeomanettes**]; when out to sea, boredom is relieved by **boring a bud** (short for *buddy*) and playing **drop [pick up] the soap.** Swabbies, in their tapered bell bottoms [**tuna tins**] and white **squid lids** (*fr* naut sl *squid* = sailor) worn rakishly **on nine hairs** (cocked) continue to set gay hearts and else throbbing. Sailors in general are known as **seafood** ("Danish seafood! Well, you know what they say, 'What a difference a Dane makes!' ") or **luimas** (lōo-ē'-măz, *fr* Haw).

A drunk sailor leaned up against an alley wall and quickly sucked off in a **short-order shrimp,** while the more fastidious cocksuckers feel that they need **salt in their diet** which may be found by unwrapping some **salt-water taffy** (a sailor's cock) at barnacle-encrusted dives like San Francisco's Embarcadero Y. After swallowing the **gob's goobers,** a typical **sailor queen** may attempt **naval combat** (to fuck a sailor).

If the sailor is gay, he is **aggie** (*rare, ?fr ****fag** minus the initial letter), **blueberry pie** (late '60s), **Neptune's daughter** (*camp*), **a piece of Navy cake, sea pussy, squib** (*kwn* SF, late '60s, mispronunciation of naut sl *squid* = a sailor) or a **Wave** (*camp*). If his homosexual tendencies have surfaced while he sails for his country, he has acquired a **service-connected disability** and is prone to unfastening all thirteen buttons on his **draperies, ding-dongs** (*fr* naut sl), **ND's** (short for NDBB = Navy Denim Bell Bottoms), **sea legs** (*kwn* LA, late '60s) and willing to do it **Navy style** or enjoy a **sailor's cup of tea** (*dated,* stooping over to accept a cock anally) Groaning with pleasure **on deck duty** (fucking), he can be heard to **sing the sailor songbook** (make appropriate sound effects).

An impecunious young sailor, bored and restive, will sell himself to **pier angelies** (*camp, kwn* SF, '70, = **sailor queens**). If he sells only his penis, he is a **salt-seller, shore dinner** or **tuna** (a delicious sea product); a **lobster pot** (the *pot* signifying the upturned rump) offers to sell his ass to those wanting to **bait the hook** (fuck).

Foreign sailors are not neglected here in America: **ice-cream sundaes** (*kwn* SF, late '60s) are French sailors whose caps are topped with a red cherry-like pom-pom; lithe Japanese seamen are **water chestnuts** (*kwn* SF, '71); **water lilies** (*kwn* LV, late '60s) represent able-bodied British crews.

If **Tina Tuna** (*camp, kwn* SF, '71; nickname for any sailor) gets too out-of-hand, the **jumper** (*obs,* hustler sl, mid '60s) is thrown into the brig by the naval MP's [**sea-lions, sea-wolves, sharks**] and, if caught *in flagrante delicto* with another man, he is given a dishonorable discharge (**donald duck,** in general, but a **blue discharge** when handed down by the Army and a **green discharge** when arranged by the Naval department).

The air force, the newest branch of the military arts, produced only one term for its men: **angel food** (*kwn* SF, late 60s). Evidently there's not enough to go around.

Related terms:

seacow girl with a sailor boyfriend.

shrimp in a basket (*kwn* LV entertainer sl, mid '60s) a sailor standing out like a sore thumb in a crowd.

armoured trucks cockroaches, for the clattering noise made while scampering across the linoleum.

Syn: **kaka-roaches** (see ***kaka**).

artiste (är-tēst′, *fr* Fr) well versed in all aspects of lovemaking "I'm not a queer, you moronic prig; I'm an artiste par excellence!"

Syn: **pro** (*fr* professional).

Art Nuevo (*kwn* Calif, '71: play of words on Sp *nuevo* = new + Art Nouveau) a style of decorating in bright, unmatched colors. Mass-produced oriental rugs, gaudy ceramic crockery, paper tiffanies, etc. are all considered Art Nuevo.

Syn: **decorated by Cost Plus** (*kwn* SF); **Mexican Nightmare; Schlock Mexican** (*schlock fr* Yid = defective merchandise // Ger *Schlag* = a blow).

ass the posterior with the exception of the anal opening (***a-hole**), unless preceded by the prepositions *up* or *in* "He takes it *up* the ass" describes anal intercourse; I'll kick your fuckin' ass *in*!" does not **2.** one who is desired for anal intercourse; also **piece of ass** "There bobs some really fine ass"

Syn: **Arsch** (Ger cognate of *arse*); **arse** (Brit); **bakery goods** (mid '60s); **back porch; backs** (prison sl: "Give me some backs, kid"); **beauns** (būnz, a form of *buns*); **beautocks** (bū-toks′, *fr* beauns + buttocks); **beauts** ("Sit on your beauts; maybe that'll stop your hole from flapping"); **beauty** (bū-tā′, *dated, early '60);* **biscuit[s]; bonbons; boody** [**booty**] ("Set your booty down on my new chaise an' I'll set my hounds on you"); **bottom; broad** (since this part of male anatomy most resembles a woman's curves: "His head says 'no,' but his broad really wants that dick"); **bucket; bum** (Brit); **bun[s]** ("What bunderful buns you have, Grandma; you should have them bronzed for posterity"); **bun-bun; bunt; butt** (*colloq,* short for buttocks);

caboose (the trainmen's car at the end of a train); **cakes, can; canetta; canister set; change-machine[register]; cheeks; chips; chundini** (chŏŏ-dē'-nē, *fr* Pach); **copper penny** (*kwn* Midwest, late '50s); **cozy drop** (*kwn* LA, early '60s) **cupcakes; cushion; derrière** (Fr = behind); **dokus** (*rare, fr* Yid tokhes = the rump); **drop** (*kwn* Calif, late '50s); **duff; duster; fanny; fesse** (*fr* Fr = the buttocks: "Fesse up"); **flip side** (mid '60s: "Turn the flip side over and see if it fucks"); **fundillo** (fŏŏn-dē'-yō, PR Sp); **gates** ("Did Dave ever open his pearly gates for you?)); **gazeet** (gə-zēt', *?fr* It); **ham; hill-lock[s]; hernandies** (mid '60s, *fr* song "Hernando's Hideaway"); **hips; hot pockeroo [potcharooney]** (mid '60s, *?fr* Anglicised *puka,* Haw = hole, or *?*pertaining to jeans' back pockets where teenage boys tuck their hands); **jam-blocks** (*kwn* SF, early '60s); **kazoo** (kä-zŏŏ', *kwn* Southwest, mid '60s); **keester** (*fr* Rom *kistur* = to ride a horse); **labonza** (*rare,* = posterior); **loaves** ('71); **male tale; moon; money-maker** ("Kick her on her money-maker!"); **motor, nachas** (nä'-chäs, *fr* Pach: "I don't care if he gives you the eye, just as long as I get the nachas"); **naka-naka** (nä'-kä-nä'-kä, *fr* Jap *naka* = mid- as the mid-section of the body reinforced by the onomatopoetic knock-a-knock-a = the swinging of walking hips); **ninan** (nēn-yän', *fr* Salvador Sp *nina* = girl); **okole-mas** (ō-kō'-lä-mäs, *fr* Haw); **paddies [patties]; pellin** (pä-yēn', *fr* Pach); **piece of luggage** (*kwn* Midwest, mid '60s); **popo** (pō'-pō); **pound-cake** ('40s); **pratt** (*dated*); **puss** ("Move your puss, hon, run-away shopping cart coming through"); **rolls; roscas** (rōs'-käs, *fr* Pach // Sp *rosca* = roll); **rosey** (*fr colloq* rosey red cheeks: "Here's a posey for your rosey" accompanied usually by the extended middle finger); **rum** ("Jim, why don't you fasten a speedometer to your rump and clock how many strokes you mile?"); **set of cakes[pears]** ("My poodle licks my set of cakes while I watch the tube; after an hour or so I shoo him away"); **sitzbein** (sits'-bīn, *fr* Ger = sit-bone); **sizzlers** (*kwn* Southwest late '60s); **south-end** ('40s); **spare tire** (*kwn* Midwest, mid '60s *fr* the spare tires fixed to the back ends of cars); **tail; taquitos** (tä-kē'-tōs, *fr* Mex Sp = little tocos); **tokus[tooky]** (to'kəs, *fr* Yid = the rear-end; a camp anglicization of the Yid *Kush mir on tokhes* = kiss my ass is **Cashmerian togas!**); **twin-hills.**
—**business** prostitution.
—**fucking** anal intercourse.
—**games** (SM sl, late '60s) anal erotic practice with gadgetry such as *dildos, enemas, belts, etc.
—**hound** attracted to asses. Not as common as: **ass queen.**
—**y** (*adj*) see *bitchy.*
   Related Terms:
baker's dozen group of young, attractive men.
the baker's is closed adamant statement denying anal approach.
crack the crevice between buttock cheeks. Syn: **crease; foul line** (early '50s); **valley.**
cracker ass a flat ass. Syn: **flat tire; western patio** (*kwn* Southwest, mid '60s).
cupcakes small but rounded buttocks, most temptingly found on narrow hipped boys. Syn: **English muffins; honey rolls; hot cross buns** (*fr* former religious connotation; *?*connected with **blessing,** an ass-fucking); **love buns** ("Watch that you don't fall on your love buns . . . the ice is murder"); **smallers** (*kwn* SF, '71); **sugar cookies.**
dutch dumplings nicely shaped, firm and fully rounded ass. Syn: **rounders** (*kwn* SF, late '60's: "Ask that kid with the rounders if he'd be interested in joining in an ancient Greek

initiation rite"); **royal buns; rumpus delecti** (late '60s); **yeast-ful buns a plenty** (*kwn* SF, black gay sl, late '60s); **having European accentuation** to have a jutting rump. Syn: **bunder-ful; just coming out of the oven** (*kwn* SF, black gay sl, late '60s); **rear[rose] window** spreading the cheeks of the ass wide apart for a ***rimmer's** easy access. Syn: **dingle-berry pie** (early '60s); **salad bowl** (late '50s).

rock ass trim muscular rump. Syn: **solid gold.**

satchel ass[butt] abundance of buns; lard ass. Syn: **barrel** ("I let her have it both barrels; I sat on her"); **battleship hips; big buns; cookie jars** ('71); **tankers** ("There's enough tankers there to stock up for the winter"); **wedding cakes** (*kwn* SF, black gay sl, late '60s).

Also see ***a-hole, *booty shot, *hilltop drive, *little surprise, *six inches of daylight.**

auntie (*pej, fr* sl *aunt* = old prostitute; perhaps reinforced by Fr *antique* = old thing) middle aged homosexual "I do wish these old fuckin' aunties would leave the tearoom alone for the groovy numbers." To the younger homosexual, an auntie often translates as anything over thirty having lived too long with nothing to show for his age. Youth is the premium in the real world, but it is the criterion in the gay world. It is synonymous with sex and vitality. Old age is viewed as the loss of sexual attractiveness, leaving only the pleasures of a lady in retirement, visited like Grandma and feeling just as sexy.

Syn: **aging actress; aunt Mame; aunt Mathilda; chin-strap and wheelchair set** (*cf* sl Geritol set); ***dirty old man; fallen star** (also used of a has-been); **flea[fleet]bagger** (*kwn* Midwest & Southwest, late '60s, *fr* pros sl *fleabag* = a dangerously old whore); **fleadum** (flē'-dum, *kwn* LV, late '60s); **grandma** ("Either the plot's beginning to thicken or I'm sitting on some of grandma's denture glue"); **gray lady; grimm's fairy** (a quarrelsome old goat); **old girl[hen, one, thing, queen, queer]** (*pej:* "Is it true that old queens have to *gum* their food before swallowing?"); **prune person; rancid flower** ("Toss the rancid flowers out of the john, Lillian!"); **soiled senior citizen.**

An auntie with money is a ***sugar daddy.**

—queen young man who seeks the companionship of older men "I have just the man for your auntie queen . . . I do hope my friend is senile enough for your's."

Related terms:

wrinkle room a drinking establishment where the gay oldtimers meet "Streisand hangs in the Wrinkle Room like myrrh." Syn: **crow's nest; mustache bar** (*kwn* NYC, mid '60s); **rest home; white-haired bar** (*kwn* NYC mid '60s: "In a white-haired bar, every cloud has a silver lining").

Also see ***mother, *turkey.**

aussie-ola (*n & adj, kwn* SF *fr* Cleveland, '70; ?*fr* Osceola, famous Seminole chief; *cf* Sp *ocioso* = idle + bigot's idea of what a Negro is supposed to be like) black "Cleveland's been getting very aussie-ola lately."

Syn: **aussie-pa** (os'-ē-pä: "A lot of aussie-pas do their dancing there").

available open for sexual consideration "Is that pretty thing available tonight?"

Syn: **catchable; fuckable; haveable; in circulation; on the make; suckable; up for grabs.**

ayuga (ä-ū'-gä, *kwn* LV, late '60s, *fr* the signal made by a submerging submarine; etymologically, it is strange that a nautical term should be used so far inland; *cf* Dakota *wayuga* = he

separates something from its covering) exclamation referring to *going down on an attractive man usually purred nasally when excited or agreeing with a comrade "Ques: 'Care to
drop by Miss Chris' place and get high?' 'Ans: Ayuga!'" but
also "Ayuga! Dig the hunky number with the surfboard!"

baby (1900) **1.** sweetheart "You're my baby and nobody else's"
2. (*kwn* SF) a teenager, see *chicken **3.** (*kwn* SF, late '60s)
first person singular pronoun "Baby want go bar" **4.** (*kwn*
SF, late '60s) at times used to mean the second person singular "Does baby want to play with fire?" **5.** (*voc*) a lover or
close friend "The show will continue, baby, but with a slight
change in cast."

baby butch (*kwn* NYC, les sl, mid-late '60s) boyish, adolescent
lesbian.
   Syn: **camper** (*kwn* LV, les sl, late '60s); **camp truck** (*kwn*
LV, les sl, late '60s); **dinky dyke** (*kwn* SF, '71-'72); **semi-diesel.**

Baby Crockett (*camp, kwn* SF, '71, *fr* Davy Crockett) gay nickname
for a would-be woodsman; a pseudo-cowboy.

baby discovers (*exclam, kwn* SF, late '60s) said when reacting
with the same awe-stricken expression as that of an infant
"A new kind of pill? Baby discovers!"

backstage 1. uncouth, wicked, rude "That remark was *so* backstage" **2.** unpretentious, unrehearsed, genuine.

bad case of the tins (*fr* pros sl, '30s) **1.** a continual dread of being
raped **2.** fear in general; paranoia; the jitters.
   Syn: **stage fright.**

bag 1. (*fr* O Norse *baggi* = sack) the scrotum "The bar was
shut down because some hungry faggot copped a feel off
of some plainclothesman's bag" Syn: **grand bag** (= a large
scrotum; handful); **jewel box** (*fr* relationship with sl *family
jewels* = testicles); **purse** (*camp*); **sack 2.** (*obs, fr* douche
bag) cruelly used by one male homosexual for another. Syn:
douche bag.

bagpipe (*rare*) med, *coitus in axilla* = to copulate the armpit of a
partner until an ejaculation is reached; considered peculiar
to the homoerotic subculture "He's a real case for bagpiping
guys with big hairy arms."
   Related terms:
   pit job the copulation of a lover's armpit—the hollow underneath the arm is either licked or has semen ejaculated into
it.
   pit queen homosexual with an armpit fetish.
   thumb holsters armpits.

bags 1. the testicles, see * **balls 2.** pair of baggy, loose-fitting
trousers "When *you* were a little girl, *everybody* wore bags·

to school." Syn: **fat pants.**

bait attractive, young male, in league with the police or criminal element to entrap homosexuals into performing an act of sex in a public place "Be careful of that tearoom; there's usually some bait positioned around the throne-room."
Syn: **come-on boy; decoy[er]; fairy hawk.**
Also see ***dirt.**

ball see ***fuck.**

ballad poor excuse, a fib "Don't sing me that ballad—you could have showed up and you know it."

ballad bar a ***gay bar** whose jukebox selections are primarily slow love-songs; bar whose dining room atmosphere discourages loudness.

ball gown (*camp*) a man's suit.

ballroom (*fr* sl *ball* = to copulate) the bedroom.

balls (O Norse *böllr* = globular object) the testicles "Hit the dude in the balls, then you'll know if he's S or M."
Syn: **bags** ("Don't let that basket fool ya—it looks like he's got a long schlong, but it's only big bags"); **diamonds** (*camp*); **ding-dongs** ("No, these levis are too tight—there's no room for m'ding-dongs t'breathe"); **dusters; eggs [in the basket]** (*cf* other languages where eggs = testes: Heb *betism*, Sp *huevos, etc*); ***family jewels; gadgets** ("My gadgets itch; maybe my crabs are givin' a show down there"); **goatees** (*kwn* LV, late '60, *fr gonads //* Gk *gonē* = seed); **gongs** (*obs*); **nuts** ("Ah, Christmas, with the smell of roasted nuts, poppers and A-200 filling the air"); **orbs; rocks** ("Is it okay if I go out and look at some rock formations?"); **scalloped potatoes** (=sunburned testes); **stones; velvet orbs** ('71).
—y gutsy, forward, possessing *chutspah.* Syn: **bold** (Brit gay sl); **cheeky** (Brit).

B&D see ***SM.**

bang-bang-bang (*interj*) quick sexual act with little or no tenderness "I couldn't, even if I was face to face with the last man on earth, have sex—bang-bang-bang—just like that." Syn: **slam[wham], bam, thankee ma'am!**

bar (*kwn* SF, '70, *fr* comparison with sl ***gay bar**) any public locale, such as a park, crowded with men congregated there for sexual purposes "This beach used to be such a camp until it became too well-known—now it's a bar."

bargain basement any place where it is easy to locate a sex partner.

bar handles fleshy sides of the waist; a spare tire "This mad dyke danced off her bar handles."
Syn: **fuck handles** (*kwn* NYC, late '60s); **goodyear; love handles.**

bar hustler male prostitute who solicits his customers in bars.

barracuda (*kwn* LV, mid '60s) predatory, shrewd individual capable of stooping to devious tactics; a hunter par excellence.

basket the overly emphasized bulging outline of male genitals crammed into too-tight pants; nature accentuated by tight pants "Did he have a basket! It was like walking into Safeway!"
Syn: **box; canasta** (*fr* Sp = basket or crate); **laundry; lunch** (Aus gay sl); **lunch-meat** (*kwn* NYC, '71); **meat case** (=expensively wrapped basket); **packet** (Brit gay sl); **showcase.**
—days the warmer seasons when the wearing of basket-revealing pants is unencumbered by coats or jackets "Oh, Mary! the rhododendrons are blooming. Basket days are coming, so burn your furs and bleach out the blue jews!"
—eer one who ogles male crotches. Syn: **basket-watcher** ("The

motto of basket-watchers is, 'Tis better to conceal than to reveal.' ")

—ful of meat the male genitalia.

—lunch blow-job performed without completely removing the pants.

—party (*kwn* Hollywood & NYC, mid '60s) man with large genitals.

—picnic leisurely spending time looking at crotches. Syn: **basket-shopping; playing canasta.**

—weaving wearing tight pants.

bat 1. large penis 2. (*pej, fr* colloq *old bat* = mean old woman) a fellow homosexual "If that bat brings one more trick here, we'll have to change the porch light to red."

—boy cross-country hitchhiker or young soldier who will allow a homosexual driver to suck him off in exchange or trade for a ride.

Also see **road queen.*

—ter a man who has a anatomically large organ "Batter up, three strokes, you're out!"

batch night (*kwn* SF, late '60s) scheduled evening set aside by two homosexual lovers for separate cruising; a night-long vacation from the spouse. Straights call it "a night with the boys" or "business trips."

Syn: **trick night.**

baths gay Turkish baths where the bathing is not as popular as the sex, orgy-style. Often the baths endeavor to compete for the trade with novel decors, a bigger orgy room [**pig room**] or other gimmicks to attract the gay clientele. Queens are funny: bathing before going to the baths is *de rigeur.*

Syn: **church** (*camp*); **den [of sin]** (*camp*); **flesh factory** ("My see-through briefs were designed in early flesh factory" = my underwear is sexy); **hygiene hall** ('71: "Can't keep a hope chest in a hygiene hall, girl"); **skin room; the tubs; whorehouse** (*camp:* "What? Another freeze-dried whorehouse?").

Related terms:

Bathsheba (*camp*) frequenter of the baths "All that good clean fun has stewed Bathsheba's brain." Syn: **our lady of the vapor[s]** ('40s).

crib (*fr* pros sl = apartment) cubicle rented out to a customer at the baths for more private fun.

Dorothy Lamour terry-cloth mini (*camp*) small bath towel.

ghost (*rare,* late '50s) homosexual wandering the halls of a bath.

sarong large bath towel, particularly when tied suggestively about the bath patron's hips.

steam daddy[queen] middle-aged homosexual spending most of his time in the cloudy steamroom of a baths "Lettin' a steam daddy out into the daylight is like takin' a fish outa water." Syn: **sweat-room fairy.**

batter (Brit gay sl) to work as a male prostitute "I did batter around a bit when I was a bit younger."

batts (Brit gay sl, *fr* Brit cant *bats* = pair of worn, shoddy boots) shoes "What lover batts, dearie—did yer shush 'em from a client, then?"

baubles jewelry.

Related term:

ear-baubles a pair of earrings.

BD 1. Bette Davis; La Lupe herself 2. anyone imitating her. **To pull a BD** = to imitate Miss Davis "Do *all* fags have to pull a BD when they get the least bit polluted?"

be (bē, *interj, kwn* SF, '70) farewell, bye-bye. Almost always shouted in a high falsetto.

beach bitch homosexual who sets up a cruisy camp on the beach-heads during the balmy summer months.

Syn: **sea-fairy** (*pej, fr* seafarer); **shell queen** (*obs, fr* sl *shell* = bikini bathing suit); **sunflower** (= young man tanning himself on the beach); **tailgator** (*dated,* Florida hetero sl, late '50); **tansie** ('40s).

Related terms:

diners' shore (*camp*) beach frequented by homosexuals.
tansie's formal (*camp,* '50s) scarlet red bikini worn by a gay boy.

beads the inner awareness of being gay. Beads represent an imaginary string of pearls worn by all homosexual men; thus the clutching mannerism so common to effeminates. Others believe that beads distinguish certain circular erogenous zones of the body—the breasts, genitals, buttocks. The word is never used alone but appears in phrases.

Related terms:

bust the beads 1. to beat somebody **2.** to make an endeavor.
drop the beads[cookies, load, plate] to be shocked, stunned, surprised "She almost dropped her beads when she saw you locked in face drag."
explore the beads 1. to fondle another's body "Continue exploring my beads, Silas, and you'll run up quite a bill!" **2.** to find out, usually by literally feeling out, what a partner prefers sexually. If a homosexual wants to fuck, he'll gently finger his partner's ass; if no move is made to suppress this fondling, it is likely that anal intercourse will be enjoyed.
in the beads in the cards; left for Fate to determine "It won't work between Chuck and Irma; it's not in the beads."
rattle the [giddy] beads 1. to chatter on endlessly **2.** to rake somebody over the coals "There seems to be a certain amount of needle between those two—first Ned rattles his beads at Simon, then Simon rattles his at Ned."
read the beads to chastise somebody; punish by tongue-lashing "Those Sagittarius girls are always readin' somebody's beads—only *they* regard it as a service well rendered."
shake the beads to dance "C'mon, let's go shake our beads!"
wear giddy beads to celebrate, have a good time.
wreck somebody's beads 1. to beat somebody up **2.** to shock, startle a person "The Pope's Jewish?—that wrecks my beads!"

bean juice liquid found around the anus of one who constantly breaks wind.

Syn: **fart slime.**
—**queen** see **rim queen.**

bean oil (*fr* sl *beaner* = Mexican + hair pomade) hair oil, especially when used to lubricate the penis before copulation.

bean queen (*fr* sl *beaner* & *chile bean* = Mexican) **1.** Mexican homosexual. Syn: **Carmen[cita]** ("Do any of you Carmencitas *blow* in el inglé's?"); **freejack [cat]** (*kwn* Tex *fr* Mex *frijole* = bean); **hot enchilada[tamale]; joto** (khō'-tō, *pej, fr* Mex = fag); **Mexicali Rose** (=a gay caballero); **Miss Morales** ("Just cause Miss Morales paints her nails is no sign that she doesn't know how to point her johnson"); **señoreater** (*fr* Sp *señorita* + sl *eat* = to suck cock); **Spanish Rose** ("And God knows that that Spanish Rose did her best to pour herself into an early grave"); **south-of-the-border tart** (*kwn* SF, late '60s); **Tijuana queen** (said of one especially trashy) **2.** anglo who sticks to Mexican boys. Syn: **Miss Tijuana** (makes many "business trips" to Tijuana); **taco queen; tamale-pie eater.**

beard (*kwn* LV, mid '60s: *fr* a beard = virility symbol)   **1.** a woman who dates homosexual men to help them socially   **2.** to date a woman to prevent suspicion of being homosexual "Are you bearding tonight or is that your lesbian mammy?" Syn: **flinking** (Brit gay sl).

bearded lady 1. (*dated*) any homosexual who has a beard   **2.** a homoerotic hippy. Syn: **beaded lady.**

beatnik suitcase (*kwn* LV, late '60s, *cf* prison sl *Oklahoma suitcase* = a cardboard box) a paper bag used to carry personal items.

beat off see*jack off.

beauty an attractive *you*   "I call that beauty 'Moon River' . . . 'cause his is wider than a smile."

beauty bar vanity or dressing table used by professional *drag queens; a make-up mirror and table   **2.** *gay bar decorated with wall-to-wall mirrors.

bedbug hypersexual; thinking of nothing but sex.

bee bites man's nipples.

bee cups [B-cups] large pectoral muscles. Beecups may be muscular and quite attractive, but usually the breasts spoken of are flabby and unappealing   "Why go to the baths—you'll never find a towel big enough to hide those B-cups." Syn: **cups; pecks.**

beef 1. see *cock   **2.** a masculine man, such as a Texan ranch-hand or a member of the armed forces "So he married a real girl, huh? Well, I guess he preferred fish to beef." Syn: **piece of beef.** Related term: **beef jerky** (*camp*) a punchy, off-balance football player.

beefcake 1. masculine sex appeal. Syn: **MQ** (=masculine quotient); **X-appeal** (*camp*)   **2.** photographs of nude men in sexy situations "And to Culligan, I leave my entire collection of European beef-cake." Syn: **cheesecake** (*camp*). —**king** popular muscleman in physique magazines and pornographic snapshots "Some fag-mags have more beefcake kings in 'em than chicken."

belch a hymn to sing a song.

bella (Cape Town gay sl) a real bash.

belle (*obs*, '30s)   **1.** another homosexual   "Just how many belles *did* you invite to my party, hon?" Since the word belle was popular in the 1930's, some homosexuals are opposed to letting the word slip in their speech for fear of revealing their age. Some middle-aged homosexual men will call one another belle as a reminder of when they were strapping youths.   **2.** (*pej*) employed to point out fading age and loss of sexual attractiveness.

belly-fucker[-queen]   1. homosexual attracted to lean, trim stomachs   **2.** one who rubs his penis on his partner's stomach until ejaculation. Syn: **rubber; rub freak.** Related terms: **college fuck[style]** (late '50s) the act of rubbing the penis against the flat stomach muscles of a partner until orgasm. It was alleged that college men, wanting to explore homosexuality, would refuse to actually penetrate one another for fear of turning queer; so, they turned to a position which most resembled heterosexual coitus. Syn: **hump** (*kwn* SF, belly-fucker sl).

bench 1. (*rare*) to sit down "Let's bench here for a few min-mins my feet are killing me." Syn: **park the biscuit** (late '50s)   **2.** (*kwn* LV, hustler sl, mid '60s) to wait for someone in a public place "I benched for that asshole for two hours—he never showed."

bend over to be passive to anal eroticism "Mention 'dick' and that one bends right over and touches her toes."

benny house (*fr* pros sl) bordello featuring young boys for its homosexual customers.

Syn: **boy's smoking house; fag factory** (prison sl); **flower house** (*rare,* said to be a translation *fr* Chin).

bent 1. angry, furious "He was really bent when he found out that his professional guest split with all the grass" **2.** (Brit gay sl; *cf* criminal sl *crooked* = queer) homosexual "Is he bent?"

benzadrina (ben'-zä-drē'-nä, *camp*) **1.** amphetamine **2.** gay nickname for a habitual user of amphetamine.

Syn: **benny** (*fr* narc sl).

Betty shits her dress (*kwn* SF, '72) statement mocking a homosexual who is shabbily dressed. In the same way, if one is caught in tattered shoes, he will be described as "Betty shitting her shoes."

Beverly (*kwn* SF, '71, *fr* beverage) beer "Every Sunday afternoon this one has a mad date with Beverly" = he drinks beer on Sunday.

BF (les sl, mid '60s, acronym for boy friend) the lesbian who assumes the male role in a partnership romance. But **real BF** = man dating a woman.

big J simultaneously fucking and sucking the sex partner; a **shrimp job** ("Shrimp jobs ain't too easy unless the boy on the bottom is a Texas longhorn.")

Big Legs (*fr* pros sl; *cf* the monicker *High Pockets* = tall man) a rich man; sport carrying a wad of bills.

big woman 1. a very effeminate man. **2.** (*camp*) tall man.

Bill 1. Masculine male homosexual "Tote that bag, lick that Bill!" **2.** sarcastic title for one who claims to be masculine "Get you, Bill, in that butch marine drag" **3.** (*kwn* LV, les sl, mid '60s) banter term between mannish lesbians "Hey, Bill, who was that redhead in your bed this morning?"

bindle boy see *hobo slang.

bird circuit sightseeing the gay bars with the purpose of becoming better acquainted with their patrons and locations for future visits.

Syn: **the circuit** ("Once we get to know the circuit we won't have to watch late shows on the tube allatime.")

bibbing using items (towels, contraceptives, vaseline) or taking extra precautions (locking the door, turning on soft music, more vaseline) during carnal activity "It's practically impossible to do any bibbing at ten o'clock at night up in the park. If you find a guy with a humpy arse, all you can do is throw your coat on the ground and tool up with spit."

the big beast (*kwn* LV, mid '60s) sex as a compelling habit "Balling's okay, but it's becoming the big beast in your life. Take it easy for a couple of hours."

Syn: **the bear** ('72: "Gotta feed the bear!")
Related term:

have the big beast going for one to be attracted to somebody "He has the big beast going for anybody in duck-levis."

Big Bertha (*camp*) gay nickname for any tall, heavy-set man, especially if effeminate "Tommorrow's my birthday . . . I sure hope Big Bertha has the guest list started."

big dick from Boston (*pej, fr* pros sl, '30s) puritanical at home but everything goes outside or away from it; a loudmouth tourist.

big game one who is stalked for future seduction "The paperboy's going to be my biggest game; I'll wait till he stops to collect the money, then I'll invite him in for cocoa."

bird in a gilded cage man's crotch clothed in expensive trousers.

bird's nest visible pubic hair extending from the crotch to the navel;

pubic hairs *per se.*

bisexual (bī-seksh'-wəl, *fr* L prefix *bi* = two, *lit* meaning hermaphroditic) sexually interested in both men and women "He's
bisexual—he digs both men and boys." Many gays feel that bisexuals brag about their superiority to homosexuals. They re-
assure one another that bisexuals are but repressed faggots who
simply refuse to admit defeat ("Nobody can dance at two wed-
dings, dear; you're either one or the other!")
    Syn: **AC-DC; acey-deucy; ambidextrous; ambisextrous; am-
bisexual; bi; bicycle [rider]** (*kwn* LV, jazz musician sl, mid
'60s); **convertible; double-gaited; double-life man** ('40s); **flippy**
(also used of a homosexual who is able to fuck or be fucked);
gate-swinger; gray cat (*kwn* SF, hip gay sl, late '60s: one whose
sex life is gray, *ie* unclear); **half-and-half; half bent** (Brit gay
sl); **sidesaddle queen** (*kwn* LA, late '50s: "Get lost! Sidesaddle
queens were all the rage *last* week"); **switch-hitter; two-way
baby** (early '60s).
    Related terms:
bi-lingual orally bisexual, *ie* gratified by sucking either a man
or a woman.
dabbler (les sl) suburban housewife giving lesbianism a try.
gillette blade (les sl, early '60s, *fr* double-edged Gillette blade)
bisexual woman.
go both ways to be bisexual. Syn: **play both sides of the fence;
wear bifocals; wear two [pairs of] shoes** (*fr* pros sl, '30s).
half-husband married man with a homosexual liaison on the
side; he has one foot upon dry heterosexual land and the other
in hot, gay water.
on the fence bisexual; able to dry off with either a *his* or *her*
towel. Syn: **caught between the pointers and setters.**

bitch (*fr* AS *bicce* = female of the canine family) **1.** (*pej*) insolent,
resentful homosexual "That butler bitch looks like something
you'd find under a wet sock" **2.** (Brit gay sl) man preferring
the passive role in anal intercourse **3.** gay vocative "You're
screaming up the phone bill, bitch!" Syn: **heifer** (black gay sl)
4. to complain, criticize, nag. Syn: **hagmouth** (mid '60s: "Don't
hagmouth me—I'll finish the dishes later!"); **pitch a bitch.**
—ed up gussied up; frilly, overdecorated. Syn: ***tra-la-la.**
—es' Christmas Halloween "They were singing 'Don us all in
gay apparel' on Bitches' Christmas." Syn: **queens' Christmas.**
—es' blinds heterosexual wives of bisexual men.
—queen ('70) one who finds fault with everything; spiteful ton-
gued shrew. Syn: **cobra lady.**
—'s curse 1. misfortune which supposedly befalls the robber or
killer of a prostitute or homosexual **2.** (*kwn* Southwest, mid
'60s) minor's revelation of a homosexual seduction to the authorities. Often used by blackmailers or spiteful youths "Remember that boy Ed used to ball? Well, the punk's sic'ed the
bitch's curse on him."
—y slanderous, critical, snide, vindictive "Don't get bitchy with
me, Rose, just because you lost some number to an old auntie."
Syn: **assy** (*dated*); **bitey; catty; cunty; evil; fierce; flip[py]** (Brit
gay sl, *fr* flippant); **vichyssoise** (vi'-she-swaz', *camp*, '71, *fr* Fr
= potato soup); **vicious** ("How did that vicious bitch get her
nappies so clean—Ultra Brite?").

bite to contract and relax the sphincter muscle during anal intercourse.
    Syn: ***snap.**

biting daddy male homosexual who takes sadistic pleasure in biting nipples, shoulders and buttocks.

biting their nails describing homosexuals who use coded gestures
in public places to meet other homosexuals "The End is

getting to be a bit TM—everybody spends time biting their nails but nobody sucks cock."

BJ see *blow job.

black widow (*kwn* SF late '60s) male homosexual who habitually takes away the love-mates of other homosexuals.
Syn: **burglar; dragon lady; spider lady.**

blank (*adj*) conservative, dull "Don't be such a blank—this is a glory hole!" "That was really a blank drink—I didn't get anywhere on it!"

blind see *unsliced.

blow to suck a penis "That old queen blew me three times in a row."
Syn: **blow the whistle** ("If that cute cop doesn't stop hanging around with gay kids, he'll find his whistle being blown some dark, foggy night"); **brush the teeth** ("He finished brushing Harry's teeth five seconds before Velma waltzed in") **catch it; chew** (but **chew it** = unfriendly command to be still); **cop a bird[cock, doodle, hot one, joint]; cuff a carrot** (prison sl); **do** ("Don't do anybody I would"); **drop on it** (*kwn* SF, SM sl, '71); **eat** ("That one cruises the girlie shows eating horny sailors while they're watching the flicks"); **eat it all up; faire** (fãr, *fr* Fr = to do, make "Faire me well, dearest!"); **fix somebody up; flute** ('30s "Fluting doesn't give you cavities, just syphilitic tonsils"); **French** (*fr* WWII sl; the French, having no love lost between the Germans, will sometimes speak of homosexuality as *l'amour allemand*); **gam** (Brit; also used is the command **give us a gam!** = blow me); **get a facial; get it off; get punked in the head[mouth]** (*pej*, prison sl = to be forced into sucking cock); **give head** (late '60s: "He's weird, he'll lay on his belly, but he won't give head"); **give pearls** (*kwn* SF, black gay sl, '70; pearls, in this instance refers to teeth); **gobble [the goop]** ('40s); **go down for whomp; go down like white on rice** (*kwn* SF, black gay sl, '70: to enthusiastically suck a white man's cock; *cf:* soldier's simile of a fist fight: "Man, I was all over him like stink on shit"); **go down on it** ("C'mon, go down on it, I haven't got all day"); **grab a hot one** ('50s); **gunch** ("He gunched me a little until he got it hot"); **have some cream sauce; hum a tune [on the flute]** ('30s); **inhale the oyster; kiss it** ('40s—late '50s); **kneel at the altar** ('40s: "Honey, ain't no time to be thinkin' 'bout bathtub water when you kneelin' at the altar"); **knock somebody off** (SM sl, '71; *cf* '20s sl *knock him off* = kill him & *knock off a little* = to have carnal knowledge of another: "I came down into the pit t'get knocked off"); **lay the lip** ('40s); **lick** ("First lock gate, then lick mate"); **mamar** (mä-mär', *fr* Sp = to suck: "Mamar yo quiero!); **perform** ("When will Mr. Magnificent Seven let me perform?"); **picnic up on it** (mid '60s); **plate somebody** (Brit sl); **play a tune** ('50s, connected with *piccolo* and *flute* both = cock); **play bugle boy** (early '60s, hetero college sl: "I let some fag play bugle boy, but I didn't do one thing to help *him* come . . . I'm not queer"); **play musical arrangements [on the flute]; play the flute [horn, organ]** (*fr* Brit sl: "Why don't you prove you're a music lover by playing my horn for me?"); **polish the knob; puff on some tubing** (*kwn* SF, '70); **pull some peepee** ('60s); **root** (prison sl, *fr* root = to poke or grub about with the nose); **scarf [scorf] up on a bod** (*kwn* LV, mid '60s, *fr* black sl *scarf* //hobo sl *scoff* = eat); **service** (to be the receptacle for a piece of trade); **sit on a face** (*camp*); **speak Low Genitalese; stoop for it; suck** ("He probably sucked his way to the top"); **suck a bondini** (*dated*, mid '60s); **swallow a sword; swing on it** (early '60s);

swing on some flivver (late '60's); **take it in the mouth; take somebody on** (late '50s); **wean** (*obs*, late '50s: if *fr* weenie, the word should rightly be spelled ween); **whistle** ('30s: "It's not true that gay boys can't whistle!" "Whistle while you jerk!"); **whomp down on it; whomp it up; woof up on it; worship at the altar** ('40s: "I'll be worshipping at the altar when Johnny comes marching home"); **wring it dry** (to get the last drop); **yummy down[up] on it** (mid '60s—extended to food: "You really yummied down on that burger—the poor dear didn't stand a chance.")

—job act of sucking the penis until ejaculation. Syn: **ai** (Ī, *fr* Haw gay sl, mid '60s: "First we honi-honi'ed, then we do ai"); **bird** (*kwn* NYC, '70, *fr* sl *bird* = cock: "Hiya, kid, wanna bird?" = want to get sucked off?); **BJ** (initials for blow job); **blue jay** (*rare*, mixture of past tense *blew* + initial of *J* in *job*); **French art[s]** ("Are you well versed in the French arts?"); **French job[love, way]; head job; job** (short for blow job; perhaps one of the few euphemisms in Masculinese: "I used to let some queer give me a job whenever things got dull—he would pay me plenty for eatin' it"); **knob job** (early '60s); **kowtow chow** (=kneeling and sucking); **mouth job; quickie** (hustler sl: when a buyer does the sucking); **shot upstairs** (*fr* pros sl: "It's five for a shot upstairs"); **skull job; snow job** (early '60s: *fr* blow job); **tongue job** (*rare*).

—off see ***come** (*v*).

—off steam (les sl) experience orgasm.

—out the candles (late '60s) to upset the apple cart; ruin anothers plans, dreams "You bitch! Who gave you the right to blow out my candles . . . now I'll never see him alone!"

—the head off (mid '60s) to ejaculate large amounts of semen while being blown "Cup-and-a-half Jones about blew my head off." Syn: ***drown somebody.**

—some dirt to gossip, talk idly about others, backbite "C'mon over an blow a little dirt.".

Related terms:

do somebody for a trade to suck the penis of a man who refuses to return the compliment. The gentleman who is done for trade does not think of himself as being gay, since he does not suck cock.

hum job (mid '60s) an act where the sucker hums to heighten pleasure since humming gently vibrates the head. Syn: **dinner music; whistling while working.**

ice job (late '60s) sucking with ice cubes or ice cream in the mouth.

LBJ (late '60s) a presidential blow job; a long-lasting blow job.

self-service auto-fellation.

sissy-suck (*kwn* LV, mid '60s) timid, poorly executed blow job.

what can I do you for (*camp*) What can I do for you with a humorous suggestion of payment in exchange for getting blown.

blueballs aching in the testes triggered by an inability to copulate **[lighten the load]** "Know what the sure cure for blueballs is? Scratch them until they're red!" Syn: **love nuts** (= swollen testes); **stoneache.**

blue jews (blue jeans + connection with the Heb *Levi* = popular Jewish surname take *fr* Biblical son of Jacob) pair of blue denim levis, usually tight.

Syn: **poke pants; pokes** (late '50s, *fr* cowpokes).

Related terms:

duck levis (*kwn* LV, mid '60s) tight, white levis. Syn: **western pearls** (*kwn* SF, late '60s).

levis lady 1. one who bleaches his levis until they are sexy: faded in the crotch and ass **2.** (*camp*) homosexual cowboy, though, more often than not, a cowboy homosexuals wish were gay.

levis queen homosexual with a jeans fetish.

ruggies (*kwn* LV, early '60s, *fr* rugged) old pair of faded, torn levis.

blue movies pornographic films "Star, my ass! The only thing you ever starred in was a chain of blue movies sent to Red China to make them lose interest!"

blue stockings (Brit) strange, queer, odd "We always felt that she was a bit blue stockings, but imagine our shock when we found out that she married another woman."

bod the body "It's a mystery that Tony has such a fantastic bod, but doesn't pull any tricks."
Related term:
one's bod oneself "To where are you dragging my bod?"

body body beautiful; an attractive physique "You could pose for body magazines if you left out half of your body."

body job carressing the body as foreplay to more torrid sex "First he gives 'em a body job, and then he turns 'em over."

body queen the homosexual man who is an aficionado of firm, muscular physiques **2.** muscle-builder.

bold (Brit gay sl) impudent, cheeky. nervy "Pinching a London bobby upon the arse would be bold!"

bonar (Brit gay sl *fr* Parlyaree // It *bona* = good) attractive, beautiful "He really has a bonar bod, small wonder he's on the game."
Syn: **bonaroo** (bon'-ə-rōō, prison sl = wonderful, excellent).

bonbon (*fr* Fr *bon* = good) physically beautiful "He was very bonbon, but not gay."

bonbons l. erogenous areas of the male body which normally appear in dual number: nipples, testes, buttocks **2.** one's common sense "She lost her *bonbons* over *that* piece, hon!"

boner see *hard-on.

boob[ie]s 1. prominent female breasts "her boobs were so big that she could balance a beer mug on 'em without spilling a drop." **2.** (*camp*) padding worn beneath a *drag queen's gown to give the appearance of a bosom "What am I going to use for boobies?"
Syn: **barbettes** (usually said of a young girl's breasts); **bazooms** (bə-zōōmz'); **jubes** (Brit gay sl, ?*fr* rhyming sl = boobs); **jugs; knockers** ("Stomach in, knockers up, and into battle"; however, "Knockers up" = chin up, don't let it get you down); **maracas** (especially when in movement as when dancing or running); **melons; memories** (*kwn* SF, '71, *fr* mammary glands); **milk cans[wagons]** ("Puttin' on a bra is like hitchin' up the team to the milk wagons"); **mollies** (Brit gay sl); **piggies** (especially used of rubbery, sloppy breasts of an obese woman).
Related terms:
juicy sewer (*kwn* Wis, early '50s) nickname bestowed upon a large-breasted woman.
nylon milk pails (*camp*) a bra.

boobless (*voc, fr* YID *bubeleh* = an endearment) darling.

boogedewa on out (bōō'-gə-dē-wä', *kwn* LV, mid '60s, *fr* car club sl, ?*fr* boogie) to leave, make an exit "Let's boogedewa on out of here, before he offers me another beer!"

boogie ('72) to work hard, to slave.
Syn: **push; *scuffle.**

boom-chee-chee (*interj*) an onomatopoetic imitation of the erotic swaying of the buttocks when walking "Check out those buns on that angel food—boom-chee-chee; boom-chee-chee!"

boost (*fr* criminal sl, early 20th cent) **1.** to shoplift "Ma Parker taught me how to boost in drag" **2.** broadly, to steal anything.
Syn: **liberate; mop** (*kwn* SF hustler sl, late '60s: "I mop only the *prime* cuts from Safeway"); **u-haul** (*kwn* SF, '71: to steal something on a grand scale).
Related terms:
benny (mid '60s, *fr* criminal cant) overcoat or raincoat used for shoplifting "I need a new benny or I'll never acquire a good library."
clip (*dated*, hustler sl, '50s) to rob a homosexual partner as he sleeps it off "That little fuck clipped me of my rent money!" Syn: **shush** (Brit gay sl, *fr* colloq *shush* = shhh, a command to be quiet especially made to children).
clipping days (*dated*, hustler sl, '50s) period of prostitution and stealing to stay alive or maintain a drug habit.

booty-shot snapshot of an attractive bottom "I get most of my booty-shots on Powell and Market, where the cable cars turn around. Everybody thinks I'm just another tourist taking pics of the cables."

bop (*kwn* SF, late '60s-'72) to amble.
Related terms:
bop in! = come in!
bop on over! = come on over, to go visiting "I bopped on over last Thursday, but I guess nobody was home—except 'us rats'!"

bo-peeps eyes "Just focus your bo-peeps on *that*!"

boss (*fr* black sl) marvelous, remarkable, wonderful.
—queen beautiful, sexually talented homosexual.
—trick (*fr* pros sl) prostitute's customer who pays well.

bottoms passive anally.

bow low to leave for one's own advantage, to depart from a gathering "Get ready to bow low; here come the queen who hates your crown."

bow tie (*kwn* SF, '70) bus-boy "I buy most of my grass from the bow tie who works at Fosters."

boy any homoerotic man. Based upon the theory that homosexuals have not sexually matured as did their heterosexual playmates.
Related terms:
the boys a homosexual group; the subculture of the male homosexual "You've been seeing a real woman—what will the boys think?" Syn: **the kids.**

bracelet a lover to show off.

braces on the brain (borrowed *fr Auntie Mame*) a metaphorical expression implying inability to comprehend or apply intelligence.

brain bowl a motorcycle helmet.
Syn: **skid lid** (Brit sl).

brain-burners amphetamines taken by needle.

brand name 1. slang term for a sexual position "Well, like 'zigzagging' is another brand name for 'sixty-nining,' you know" **2.** a nickname; an alias. Syn: **trade name.**

break like a shotgun vagina "He wants a break like a shotgun an' none of your shit—literally!"

break one's face (*kwn* SF, black gay sl, '70, *fr* black sl *break a face* = to punch somebody in the nose) **1.** to startle, surprise **2.** to be taken aback "I don't have to say a word, all I have to do is stand in line by the checkout counter and I break faces right and left."

break one's shit-string see *fuck it rotten.

break one's wrist loose and effeminate hand movements "Look at that nelly thing breaking her wrists while she decorates that soldier."

Brenda Starr (*camp*) any reporter, but particularly if *he* happens to be gay.

brilliant successful, prosperous, and therefore socially popular "Please don't bring any of your brilliant PE chums to my little bash. I couldn't take their cute remarks about my quaint furnishings."

bring on to excite "Not too many nellies bring butch numbers on when they swish around."

bring off to cause orgasm "He brings me off the best when he lets me pound his popo."

bring one out to introduce to homosexuality by either acquainting him with other gay people or by seduction.
   Syn: **break somebody in[out]; present a debutante to the court; teach school** ("Where did you teach school, Professor, the third glory hole from the right?")

broad (*rare*) male homosexual "Aw, c'mon, give the old broad a little of your time."

broadwalk the sidewalk of any main street used as a promenade.

brother mannish lesbian who is befriended by blatant homosexuals "Me ball with her? Don't be silly, we're brothers."

brown see *a-hole, *fuck.

browned off angry "Mister Jane's going to be browned off at you if you don't take his lover with you to Mountain Nowhere."

the Brown Family (*dated*, '40s) the homosexual subculture.

brownie anus "Did you hear the one about the blonde boy scout who was nearly trampled to death when he tried to sell his last remaining brownie to a house full of camps?"

brownie queen see *passive partner.

bruise the fruit to pinch a fellow homosexual. Heard as a jocular reprimand to stop fooling around in a bar "Stop bruising the fruit or the price will go down!"

BT (les sl) the initials stand for "bare titty" "I don't mind if my fluff runs around the house BT when I'm at home, but she better cover up when some of those wolves I know come over."

bubble gum dinner (*kwn* SF, '70) a toothsome repast of foods such as snack cakes and Coca-Cola.

bubble-gum machine (*obs*) a condom-vending machine found inside men's lavatories.

buckaruby (*kwn* SF, late '60s, *fr* Sp *vaquero* = cowboy) **1.** homosexual cowboy, be he genuine or out of a drugstore **2.** any cowboy.
   Syn: **cowgirl** (*camp*); **Dale** (short for Dale Evans); **the levis lady of shady Spain** (*camp, kwn* Ariz, late '50s, *fr* song title "Naughty Lady of Shady Lane"); **poke** (*fr* cowpoke: "Some of those pokes throw a mean fuck first, and a mean fist later"); **ranchera** (rän-chä'-rä, *camp, fr* Sp = female ranch owner).
   Related terms:
   cowboy drag (*camp*) cowboy costume, particularly when worn by a homosexual.
   ranch queen homosexual spending his vacation on a dude ranch busily seducing the cowboy staff "Ranch queens don't wear 'chaps,' you sil, they wear leather culottes."

bud to blossom forth into puberty "He's still too young—wait 'till he starts to bud; then he'll really be something."

buddy (*euphem*) the homosexual love-mate of a man.
  Syn: **good buddy** ("There they go, buddies to the end. . .and I do mean *end* of each other.")
buffle (*kwn* Boston gay sl) to rapidly tickle the tummy of a lover with one's mustache while mumbling "Buffle, buffle, buffle!" The intended effect is to please and amuse.
buff-light (*fr* sl *boff* = to copulate) **1.** nightlight, usually red or blue **2.** the dim lighting in a gay steamroom "My dear, when the vice came they turned up those buff-lights and you could hear the sighing all through the tubs."
bugger see *active partner.
buggery (Brit gay sl) hell fire, damnation. Applied facetiously "Oh, buggery! I've lost my wallet!" **Go to buggery!** = go to blazes!
bugskin (*camp*) imitation leather, naugahide "How d'ya like my bugskin couch, Grace?"
bulb (*fr* pros sl) **1.** a douche bag "Whew! But your breath is really rank! want to borrow my bulb?" **2.** (*camp*) enema device. Syn: **ginger-ale purse.**
bull ('40s) **1.** the obvious, aggressive lesbian "My ex-boss was a bull; everytime she laughed the windows would crack" **2.** (prison sl, *fr* bulletin) note, letter "Here's your bull—what's it say?" **3.** (*adj*) masculine "Is he bull or cow when it comes to the sack?"
  —**dagger 1.** the burly lesbian who dresses more like a truck-driver than a PTA member; lesbians who assume the male role in lovemaking **2.** girlish homosexual man who will conduct himself in a two-fisted fashion "Why you coming on like a bull-dagger, dear; trying to impress a piece of sweet ass?" Syn: **bull bitch[dyke].**
  —**dicker** (*fr* sl *dick* = cock) the active lesbian whose extended clitoris enables her to fuck in a face-to-face position imitating heterosexual coitus.
bullets splotches or gobs of semen "After he shot his wad for only the fourth time, he said that he ran out of bullets."
  Related terms:
  lose bullets to ejaculate sperm by masturbation.
  shoot bullets to experience a climax by discharging semen into a mouth, anus or vagina.
bull-ring camp 1. a brothel of male prostitutes "He goes to the bull-ring camp where he gets to fuck anybody butcher than him." **2.** any place in which a goodly amount of virile men are to be found, such as a gym, etc. Syn: **bull pen.**
bum see *ass.
bumper-to-bumper 1. tribadism, i.e. rubbing vulvas in a face-to face position "Not all gay women do it bumper-to-bumper; some prefer sixty-nining instead" **2.** close, intimate dancing or standing close together, vagina to vagina "Okay, gang, no bumper-to-bumper dancing in this bar—or out you go; we run a clean place here!"
bumping pussies the embarassing of two homosexual men who find themselves too passive, active, or in other ways too similar to create a sexual situation 'He thought that you and I were carrying on together— what would we do, bump pussies?"
buns see *ass.
burners (*kwn* NYC, '71) cigarettes "Set the burners on high" = to smoke many cigarettes.
burnies sideburns "He really looks sharp in those burnies. . .even if they are his mother's!"
bushie moll ('40s-mid '50s) male homosexual who thrills to the

danger of having sex in a park or other public areas "The bushie moll recalls his childhood fantasies of how much gay fun he had when he played cops and robbers."

Syn: **Earl Stanley Gardner** (camp, fr gardener = somebody hired to tend the yard); **green queen; park-mouth [queen]**.

bust see *police.

bust some suds to drink beer.

busy 1. booked solid with dates **2.** on the trail of an attractive male "She's one busy girl—each time I bump into her she's chasing something gorgeous—away!" **3.** occupato "I got to hang up, toots, I'm, er, busy!"

butch (fr sl butch cut = man's severely cut hair style) **1.** lesbian with masculine characteristics, see *dyke **2.** ('40s) nonhomosexual man whose virile appearance both draws and repels the homosexual (repels because of the danger of the violence if the butch is enraged by a gay proposition). Syn: **all man; butch number; hesexual** (rare); **kane** (kä'-nā, fr Haw = male: for further secrecy; Haw gays disguise this word with piglatin anekay); **RM** (acronym fr real man = virile, skirt-chasing, beer-drinking he-man); *stud **3.** (adj) manly in speech, in fashions and in bed; submission impossible "He's strictly butch —he wouldn't roll over for a gay apostle." Syn: **big** ("I like 'em big"); **boonch; bootch; butz** (böts, a lisped butch: "But I am butz; I am. I am!"); **chesty; masc** (short for masculine: "That one's so masc. all the world to him is one big fix-it palace!")

—**as Kong** (Brit gay sl, fr movie ape King Kong) very, very masculine; hulking.

—**er** (pej) to *fuck, especially to deflower a young man "If they're old enough to bleed, they're old enough to butcher."

—**er boy** (dated, les sl, '30s) homosexual who has sexual relations with a lesbian.

—**er shop** used in statement "**the butcher shop is closed!**" denying the requests of a cocksucker "Stop manhandling your sister— the butcher shop is closed for repairs."

—**fluff** (les sl) masculine courtesies performed by an active *dyke: opening car doors for a date, lighting another's cigarette, etc.

—**it up** warning to act manly in the presence of friends who "don't know" or the police who do "Butch it up, Mae, Tilly's got us spotted." Syn: **BIU; clean [it] up** (kwn LA, '70).

—**queen** homosexual man whose virile activities and responsibilities make him hard to detect. The only distinction between the gay boy who is butch and the butch queen is that the latter will get fucked. Effeminate men will sometimes say that the butch queen is nothing but a *big woman ("You can't tell a nooky by its cover.") Syn: **crew-cut queen; hairy mary** (kwn LV, mid '60s); **roarer** (Brit gay sl).

—**school** (kwn LA, les sl, late '50s) any place, but usually a private home where effeminate public personalities are taught how to act manly.

—**stone** (camp) boulder "It's difficult lifting these butch stones, dear; my brand-new marble pumps keep slipping."

butt see *ass.

butterfly ring 1. a coterie of effeminate homosexuals **2.** an inexpensive ring with paste setting worn on the little finger.

buy queen a homosexual man who has a desperate compulsion to buy furnishings for the home constantly.

buzzed excited; roused up and raring to go "His talking about the baths got me buzzed for trashin'" **2.** artificially energetic through amphetamines or caffein, etc. "Don't pay him any mind, he'll rattle on for at least another hour—he's still buzzed from breakfast."

cackle 1. to laugh wickedly at another's misfortunes "Cackle on, dearie, my day will come" **2.** to chatter, gab. Syn: **cluck** ("You go with Floyd; Greg and I are going to cluck about antiques.")

cacky (*fr kaka* = shit, reinforced by tacky) repulsive, ugly.

cage (*fr pros sl*) dismal hotel room or apartment.
    Syn: **crib.**
    Related term:
queen's gilded cage (*kwn* SF, late '60s) apartment of a hip gay boy.

call it (hustler sl) **1.** to hold a business discussion with a paying customer. The hustler calculates the amount he expects to receive from the customer for the sex acts desired "This dude said that he wanted to fuck me, so I called twenty and told him to take it or leave it" **2.** to tell in what position to pose. "You didn't call it yet, man; am I supposed to pose in the nude or with these sailor tights on?"

call Ripley (*exclam*) expression of disbelief meaning "can you honestly believe that?"

call Wardrobe (*exclam*) statement of complaint.

Camille homosexual who goes from one tragic love episode to another. Most often sarcastically directed at one who over-exaggerates and therefore, perhaps, delights in his misfortune "That one's a real Camille, never has one happy thing to talk about."
    Related term:
pull a Camille to lapse into deep, sullen melancholy; to "suffer," usually alluded to one feigning illness; to gain sympathy. Also those who pretend to have financial or personal injuries to delay paying bills or fulfilling obligations.

camp (*fr* theatrical 16th century England *camping* = young men wearing the costume of women in a play // Fr *campagne* = the countryside [where strolling mime troops entertained]) one of the most famous and used of all homosexual slang words, camp became celebrated linguistically in 1968, when pop culture discovered the word: overnight everybody knew what it meant. Only they really didn't. Camp firmly remains homosexual slang.
    What is camp? Camp is burlesque, fun, an ability to poke a jocular finger at one's own frustrations and guffaw at the struggles of other pathetics, homosexuals or famous, influential people. A cripple is not camp unless he has a mordant sense of humor. A bit actor who works in commercials is camp; a

politician who tries too hard is also camp. Camp personalities are sometimes loved because they are unpretentious, real. They make no excuses for their actions or words. The funny thing about a camp is that the more seriously he or she takes himself, the campier he becomes. Batman became camp because his purpose in life—crime-fighting—became so serious it grew absurd. Items are also camp if they are so ostentatious they're considered good taste. So bad they're good. Some, such as pop posters, were once camp, but here comes the rub: as soon as an object is advertised as such, it no longer is camp.

Camp is discovering the worthiness in something seemingly without value; finding the genius in something that flopped once upon a time; beauty in the grotesque. Camp is nostalgia, a carefree exhumation of the good old days, bringing back a lighter nonsense when things get dull. It is the means, the bridge, by which elaborate and necessary foolishness is briefly reclaimed. With personified Hollywood figures, it is also canonization. Women who are camp have donated, whether they know it or not, courage and bits of wisdom to the homosexual effeminate who often imitates them. It must be pointed out that in a world of heroes that come and go, it is also natural for their names to disappear from the camp roster. Except, that is, for the old standbys. Today's camp is not necessarily tomorrow's. Also, today's generation of homosexuals is not as eager to emulate camp personalities as their predecessors. In a nutshell, camp is remember when, mixed with a jigger of let's pretend.

1a. a fellow homosexual who is witty and well-liked "That camp keeps the measuring tape in the bedroom" **b.** who is beginning to take himself too seriously "Oh, Henrietta, stop being such a camp!" **c.** who is *not* funny or who is not even trying to be funny "That gorilla is such a camp! He just broke that guy's neck!" **2.** (Brit gay sl) effeminate male homosexual **3a.** enjoyable, causing laughter "That queen's such a camp!" Syn: **campy b.** obnoxiously effeminate "Stop coming on so camp, bitch!" **c.** dear to one's heart "Her films are really camp, ya know?" **4a.** to mimic the opposite sex knowingly or not; flamboyantly displaying effeminate mannerisms "Did you see the linen salesman camping with the elevator boy?" **b.** to be aggressively girlish with a group of fellow homosexuals "See that sign, girl, it says "No Camping!" Syn: **bend; camp it up; camp up a storm; fluff it.** Ant: **butch it up 5.** to be witty, clever, whimsical "Once he starts camping, you can't stop laughing" **6.** to mix with homosexual friends frequently. Used of a heterosexual man. When a heterosexual friend or couple visit homoerotic friends, they are **setting up camp** "Are Wayne and Martha setting up camp here tonight or staying with the Joneses?"

—as a row of tents (Aus) unquestionably homosexual.

—it off to shrug it off, laugh off insults "Camp it off—it's wawa off a quack's back."

—names girls' names exchanged for boys' names and vice versa. Burt becomes Bertha. Georgette turns into George, and Jo-Anne equals Joe on Christmas packages. Sometimes camp names are nicknames which have stuck or parodies of famous individuals: Bubbles McGoo (a nearsighted queen); Mae Murray (a Mr. Murray who idolizes Miss West), *etc*. Other camp names are used to point out faults or attributes. Grace for somebody who lacks it, Maud for a heavyset person or one with a haglike personality, Irene for anybody who is given the gate ("The party's over, Irene!")

—voice a falsetto "Don't use a camp voice if Tilly stops you."

Syn: **nance voice.**

—walk parodying the walk of the opposite sex. A camp walk of a boy would be an exaggerated swing of the hips, while a girl's would be an exaggeration of a manly stride. Syn: ***mantee [nance] walk.**

—y possessing the qualities of ***camp** "That dyke's such a campy thing with her diamond cufflinks sparkling on her denims" **2.** enjoyable, nifty, humourous; loosely, anything pleasurable or anyone who makes light of troubles "Please God, give him my cold; he's campy, he'll enjoy it." Syn: **giddy** ("Keep this giddy country clean—don't litter the desert with any more dead Indians").

can 1. the toilet "I gotta hit the can; don't fly far, I'll be back" **2.** the behind, see ***ass.**

cancel the act to break a date "Cancel the act and then you turn up and see if he's with anything you know."

candy maker homosexual who masturbates his partner and then swallows the spillage as a grand finale.

capello (ka-pel'-lō, Brit gay sl, *fr* It = hat, cap) a hat.

card-reader homosexual prophet; always the first to shout "I told you so" when misfortune arrives.

Syn: **bead-reader.**

car-hop (*fr* pros sl) to solicit cruising drivers from the sidewalk. Also used of one who solicits in such a style "Vegas is one of the worst towns to car-hop in."

Carlotta (*camp*) names often hurled at hassling heterosexuals "Kiss it, Carlotta!" & "Suck it, Carlotta!" are more offensive than "Eat dick," *etc.*

carry on 1. to be homosexual, flamboyant, to ***camp** "It's a miracle you haven't been eighty-sixed from the library the way you carry on with your friends" **2.** to talk, simply, to hear oneself chattering "You *do* carry on, don't you, dear; does anybody ever listen?" **3.** to last, to endure; to continue to the point of becoming irritating "That pot of boiling water really carried on." When superlatives like **for days** or **like Faust** are added, the comparisons suggest eternity and infinity. "The spearmint in my gum carried on for days" "The chlorophyll coating on your teeth is carrying on like Faust. Don't you ever douche out your mouth?" **4.** unrestrained hilarity and commotion "It was mucho difficult trying to listen to Mae's lines at the premiere of *Myra Breckenridge* with all those queens carrying on as if they were white." **5.** one who carries on, becoming exhausting; one who thinks he is the life of the party.

—with to have a homosexual affair.

carve them out ('72) to taper a pair of pants.

carwash sexual carryings on within an automobile "We had a car-wash after we left the bar."

Related term:

have a carwash to sexually soothe a motorist "When that hustler doesn't have a room to ball in, he has his client's car washed under the desert moon."

case one who is, according to his acquaintances, in need of psychiatric aid.

Syn: **head case** ("No, dear, Miss Cliff was not part of the set—they don't let head cases into South Bend"); **patient.**

cash-ass (*fr* cautious) cynically applied to ***hustler** who feigns coyness until assured of material gain "He's not shy, he's cash-ass; mention money and watch his cheeks light up!"

Cash Flagg (*camp*) second rate movie actor; a B-grade hero in western reruns on TV "Let's cuddle up by the fire and watch a film with Cash Flagg and Nola Nobody."

cash rack (hustler sl) area such as a park or frequented bus stop

where male prostitutes gather to meet their public.
Syn: **hustlers' row.**

casting couch used by a movie or television director to audition (= seduce) young men and women who want to make their way into acting "I've heard of gay old Hollywood and her casting couches."

castratos (kä-strä'-tōs, It = those deprived of testes) deballed choir boys of medieval Italy. Each boy's voice had tenor volume plus a soprano range (castration for Jesus?). Homosexuals are often portrayed as being castrated creatures with words like **banty** (fr bantam rooster), **capon, eunuch,** and by saying "it's a **neuter!**"

catalogue queen homosexual who collects physique magazines for masturbation purposes.

catty see *bitchy.

CFD (kwn SF, black gay sl, '70) **1.** cock for days! and/or cute for days! **2.** cakes for days, ie an attractive behind.

cha-cha palace 1. dance bar **2.** dancehall.

change one's luck 1. to go to bed with a black man for the first time "Ray's changed his luck; he's shacked up with a cute brown betty on the side" **2.** to perform a homosexual act for the first time "I'll tell you when I changed my luck, it was when I discovered that boys looked just like girls from the back."

change over 1. to adapt to or discover a different sexual pattern, eg heterosexuality to homosexuality **2.** to go through a medical sex change "He wants to change over, but isn't fifty-two just a wee bit late?"

Chanukah snow (khä'-noo-kä-snō', fr Heb Chanuka = Jewish holiday) candle wax.

charity case (pej) one who has a hard time finding a trick due to untidiness or a questionable mental condition. One sleeps with a charity case out of pity rather than out of desire.

charity goods [stuff] male prostitute who doesn't get paid for his service; a *hustler who gets hustled.

Charlene (camp) gay nickname for Charles "Charlene, I've never noticed that you have brown eyes—no wonder you have a shitty outlook on life."

charm bracelet list of ex-lovers; "little black book" "Did you ever add that hung stud to your charm bracelet?"

charming having a magnetic personality, sexually attractive "He's such a charming hunk of man!"

chastise one to scold in the presence of others; to shut someone up by shaming him "He chastised me in front of all those fags. I was wrecked to say the least—which I won't."

chastity case singularly faithful; one who finds promiscuity distasteful; chaste to the point of neurosis.

check (fr black sl) to look at something "Check those cheeks!"

check out to die "He checked out during the night."
Syn: **finally split** (kwn LV, '70); **sign off [out]; turn the teacup over.**
Related terms:

final curtain 1. death **2.** obituary. Syn: **grand finale; last call** (fr the last call for alcohol = announcement closing bars for the night).

go to the river to commit suicide. Used in mock disappointment: "Tim didn't call and the beans burned—I think I'll go to the river." In San Francisco, bridge is substituted for river. Syn: **Take a Drano cocktail** (kwn LV, mid '60s).

cheese smegma; cheezy ooze caked beneath an unclean foreskin, or about the unwashed labia minora of a woman "Once you get past the stench of cheese, you've got it licked!"

Syn: **cock[head] cheese** (when found on the male); **duck-butter; rag-cheese** (when found in the female: "Anybody here for a rag-cheese sandwich?"); **smentana** (smen-ta'-na, *fr* Yid = sour cream // Pol *smietana*).

—scraper knife carried for self-defense.

—sy having the foreskin lined with smegma; stale and musky smelling "That sailor was so cheesy that I felt like asking him where he hid the crackers."

Related term:

zucchini a "green" penis, *ie* an unclean prepuce.

cherry 1. see *anal virgin 2. (*kwn* SF, teen sl, late '50s) a conservative, follow-the-crowd person; an unworldly "square."

cherry flip (mid '60s) a cock in the mouth "She wants a pink lady, but I'll settle for a cherry flip if you don't mind."

cherry splitter (*kwn* LV, early '60s) long, needle-like cock "Cherry splitters are the best things in the world for breaking in a new set of buns."

chew see *blow.

chew foreskin (*camp*) to chew gum "Stop chewing that spearmint foreskin on stage, diz!"

chibby-chase (*kwn* SF, late '60s, *fr* sl *chippy* = loose woman) 1. an unfaithful lover 2. to cheat on a lover.

chic (shēk, *fr* Fr) stylish. The latest craze is chic. Cruising the busy streets after the bars close is chic. Getting invited to an orgy is chic. Sucking men off in a public john is not chic. Wearing pearls with gray flannel is not chic either, unless one is serving tea in a closet.

chicken (*fr* naut *chicken* = a young recruit // sl *spring chicken*, usu in negative context as "You're no spring chicken") 1. any boy under the age of consent, heterosexual, fair of face, and unfamiliar with homosexuality "So many chickens were flapping around that I thought we were touring Colonel Sander's plantation" 2. juvenile, youthful, young-looking. Syn: **chicken-looking** ("You're chicken-looking enough to pose for Maypo cereal boxes); **tender** 3. (*rare, kwn* LV, mid '60s) to fuck a pretty boy.

Syn: **babette** (*kwn* SF, '70, *fr* sl *baby:* baby-faced teen who appeals to the paternal side of the mature homosexual "I'm a big city queen, but if there's a lot of babettes in Nevada, I'm sure I could adapt"); **baby** (*kwn* SF, late '60s: "Lookit that sweet hippy baby selling papers"); **beauty** (early '60s: "Turn on 'Adam 12,' and you'll see some streamlined beauties running around"); **candy** (late '50s: "Stop picking up on those young tricks—don't you know that candy rots your teeth?"); **chicken-little** ('70: "I think I'll go run some chicken-littles out of their roost"); **cluck** [-**cluck**] (*kwn* Denver, mid '60s: "Don't count all your cluck-clucks until they hatch"); **cutie** (*rare,* prison sl); **faunlet; fawn; flower** (*kwn* LV, early '60s) **fragile number** (*rare,* '30s, *fr* sl *fragile* = breakable, therefore virgin: "Lay off the fragile numbers, or you'll bring the heat down on us"); **fuzz face** (*rare,* usu hobo & prison sl: boy with a peaches & cream complexion); **god-forbid** (*fr* Cockney rhyming sl = kid); **lifesaver** (*kwn* LV, early '60s: *fr* the Lifesaver candy ad, "the *candy* with the *hole* in the middle"); **missy** (*camp, kwn* LV, mid '60s: any teenage boy, gay or straight: "Hi, missy, wanna come over and have a completely unique experience in depth?"); **nymphette** (late '60s: "I can't promise lining you up with a nymphette; I'm not in charge of central casting"); **peach fuzz** (*rare,* mainly prison sl); **peeper** (?*fr* *peep-peep* = sounds made by baby chicks); **pig meat** (*fr* black sl = sexually inexperienced but willing girl); **pio-pio** (pē'-ō-pē'-ō, Mex Sp for *peep-peep,* the cheeps of a chick: often inserted into stories to whet the listener's appetite and to pass on a clue divulging the ***trick's** tender age, *eg* "So when I took off his shirt so that I could rub his chest—pio-pio—he was so smooth!"); **precious** (presh'-us, also pres'-sē-us', *kwn* SF, '70); **pretty** (mid '60s; *cf* fairy tale witch who addresses all children as "my little pretty": "I shudder to think that I might have to backtrack in the snow to find myself another pretty if you don't work out"); **pumpkin pie** (*kwn* LV, mid '60s, *fr* prison sl ***punk:** "Honey, I'm Alabama bound—think of all that pumpkin pie with nuthin' t'do but slop hawgs"); **piece of hot pumpkin pie** (a boy who gets cornholed); **piece of pumpkin pie a la mode** (a boy who gets blown); **punkie** ('40s-early '50s, *fr* prison sl ***punk** + diminutive: "That punkie's solid spinach—everything he touches turns to rigor mortis"); **puppy flesh** (*kwn* LA, mid '60s: generic for pubescent young men just beginning to melt off their puppy fat "Red Wings are *tres* puppy flesh"); **puss** (*fr* sl *doll puss*); **sexteenager** (curious about homosexuality); **slat** (*rare*, *fr* naut sl *slat* = a fun-loving sailor; *cf* also cowboy sl *hit the slats* = to go to bed: young man seen as a sex object); **sweet thing, teeny [bopper]** (*fr* black sl for a white, middle-class teen who thinks himself sophisticated); **tender stuff; twent** (*kwn* SF, '70: a young man in his early twenties); **twinkie** (*kwn* SF, late '60s: an attractive straight boy); **young action [YA]; young stuff** ("He's not stuck someplace outside of Memphis, honey; he's stuck in some young stuff right here in town"); **zip gun** (early '60s, *fr* sl *zip gun* = homemade pistol used in teenage street wars: a youthful loud-mouth); **zit** (late '60s, *fr* sl *zit* = a pimple: boy with Pepsi consciousness, *i.e.* nothing going on between the ears).

—coop any place filled to the brim with nubile young men; basketball games, etc.

—dinner sex with a teenager.

—feed see ***prison terminology.**

—freak elderly man with a voracious appetite for young roosters; one with a psychotic need for young men; frequently, he can't experience orgasm with any save young men. It is widely believed that chicken freaks were seduced into committing homosexual acts when they were children. Syn: **boy-eater [-kisser -lover]; bronco-buster; chicken hawk; chicken hunter** (Brit gay sl); **chicken queen; coke-roller** (*kwn* SF, '70); **hawk** (= older man whose lustful peculiarities are shared solely with young, unjaded boys); **kid fruit [KF]** (prison sl); **pumpkin eater** (*kwn* LV, mid '60s); **uncle** (prison sl); **youth worker.**

—house coffeehouse catering to young homosexuals too young for taverns "It's just another princess sitting in the chicken house waiting to be discovered." Syn: **gay milk bar** (mid '60s: a **milk maid** is a waiter in such an establishment); **pimple joint [palace].**

—on a spit a youth who is literally the center of attention in a ***three way** (being fucked by one while sucking the other's cock).

—plucker man who enjoys "deflowering" young boys.

—pox (*kwn* LV, mid '60s) the urge to have sex with younger men.

—rustler (*rare*, mid '60s) homosexual placed in charge of boys, who abuses that trust by seducing members of the group.

—with-a-basket (pun made upon ***basket** and the chicken-in-a-basket lunch) teenager who fills out his jockey shorts.

Related terms:

butchered chicken boy who recently lost his anal virginity; "he walks like a butchered chicken" = he walks bowlegged or stiffly with the legs apart.

fountain of youth (*kwn* LV, mid '60s) said of one who is able to reach several orgasms in one day.

fried chicken suntanned boy.

gay chicken a homosexual teenager. Syn: **brunster** (*dated*, '30s, hetero *brunser* = a homosexual+youngster); **bud** (esp used of young latent homosexuals: "The buds are coming out earlier this Spring"); **chit** (Brit *chit* = a silly girl // ME *chitte* = kitten or cub: delicate boy who chits and chats); **daffodil[ly]** (hetero sl); **princess** (*camp,* one who is not mature enough to be a *****queen); **queer pup** (*kwn* LA, mid '60s).

head and heels (*kwn* SF, '70: describing physical allurement despite extreme youth, but too young or small to know what to do in bed: he must be helped by someone more experienced who will clasp the boy by his head and heels to lift him onto the cock); **jail tail** (late '60s) any boy below the age of consent with whom sex merits a possible stretch in the pen. Syn: **jail house pussy** (so named because a taste of that kind of pussy could land one in jail).

poultry dealer man who pimps boys to interested homosexuals.

pluck some feathers to make love with a young boy, especially anally. Syn: **rip off a drumstick** (late '60s); **skin some chicken** (*rare:* = to force a boy to come across).

quail migratory bird: a delicacy to chicken hawks.

student prince sexually congenial college student.

token chicken ('70) the newspaper boy   "Tell the token chicken that I'd like to make a deposit."

Venus in blue jeans (*camp, fr* song recorded in the early '60s by Bobbie Vinton) attractive high-schooler.

     Also see *****cornflakes, *****anal virgin.

chillette (*kwn* SF) chilly, brisk   "It was a bit chillette outside."

chippy bread pancakes, because they're quick to fix.

chip the lips ('71) to speak evilly of somebody   "Don't chip the lips about someone you can't afford!"

chiva (chē'-vä, Mex gay sl *fr* Sp *chiva* = female goat) a heterosexual woman, often bleated "Es una ch-h-h-i-i-i-va-a-a!"
     Related term:

look chiva (Mex-Am gay sl) to look very good   'Ooo, you look so chiva!"

Christina (*camp, fr* narc sl *crystal* = methadrine) methamphetamine in powdered form.

Christine (*camp*) gay nickname for Christopher   "Well, Christine, we're either in Shangri La or Cost Plus!"

chrome 1. clear nail polish   **2.** cheap facial makeup allowing the nose to shine   "Don't dent my chrome, you uncultured lump!"

chrome-plated (late '50s) dressed up in new or costly attire.

chuck a slob (*obs,* teen sl, late '50s) to kiss   "Sure I'd let some fag go down on it, but I ain't chuckin' no slobs with the cat, man."

chunk (*kwn* SF, '71, *fr* colloq *chunky* = stocky) an overweight person.

ciao (chou, *fr* It = "Hi!" & "Bye!") bye-bye, see you later. A favored farewell because of the continental flavor and because "Ciao!" lacks the finality of "goodbye!"   "Ciao, for now, Jimmy, call me tomorrow!"
     Syn: **hasta lumbago** (pun made upon Sp *hasta la vista* = until we meet again); **keep the queen's peace; later** (*fr* black sl); **latori** (lā-tō'-rē, *camp,* mid '60s, *fr* L *Laetare* = rejoice ye); **see you in bed.**

Cinderella [Cindy] (*camp*) **1.** burly-framed man who acts years younger than his peers; one who looks better at night (by candlelight)   **2.** older queen who has to be in by twelve before her face falls off   **3.** (*kwn* LV, mid '60s) young, gay gadabout; a silly effeminate.

cinny (Brit cinema) **1.** a movie, film   **2.** a movie theatre.

circle a homosexual's group of friends; a queen's Christmas card list   "I can't afford to be in Lester's circle."
     Syn: **the group; the set** (*fr* colloq *set of friends*).

circle jerk group masturbation, see ***jack off.**

circus (fr pros sl) **1.** professional orgy for a paying audience, including normal and abnormal performances **2.** any grand scale orgy.
   Syn: **gazoopy** (rare, '40s).

circy (sur'-kē, fr med sl) a circumcision operation.

cissy variant spelling of ***sissy.**

civvies men's clothing without that special flair.
   Ant: ***cruising clothes.**

Clarabella [**Clarabelle, Clairabell**] (camp) gay nickname used to form compound names: **Clarabella Camp** = a real card, a laugh-a-minute man; **Clarabella Clown** = a dolt, nitwit; **Clarabella Cow** = large and sloppy man; **Clarabella Starr** = a cop.

class a code of honor, more often criminal than not; savoir-faire; style; couth "He has class—he'd never tell the cops nuthin'." Also used tongue-in-cheek: "He died? That's not featuring much class, is it?" "That's real class, taking a leak under the picnic table in high drag."

classic[al] (cf bebop sl classy chassis = well-developed body) **1.** beautiful, exquisite, well-built "That number had the most classical body I've ever laid hands upon" **2.** wonderful "She bought a classic pair of jeans."
   Syn: **major** (kwn SF, '70).

clean queen (late '60s) homosexual who does his wash and cruising at the laundromat "That Miss Oklahoma is such a clean queen! She'd wash and dry a bloody hanky for two hours, until she turned a trick."
   Related term:
   bubble palace any laundromat.

cleavage (camp) imitation but realistic-looking ***drag queen's** cleavage formed by taping the breasts together before slipping into a gown.

clever 1. handsome, charming, bewitching "Who's your clever little friend, darling?" **2.** fashionable "Oh, how clever, he opens his mouth and shows us his asshole!"

click (interj, '71, fr sound made when hanging up a phone receiver) slipped good-naturedly into a phone conversation when an insult has been made and clearly understood.
   Also see ***flush.**

click and clack (mid '60s) to prattle, especially if under the influence of pep pills.

clip one's wings 1. to deflate one's ego; to let the air out of one's bubble "He clipped my wings when he told me that my laugh marks were crows feet" **2.** to settle down; get married "I know for a fact that George is out to clip your wings, I even smelled the cigar band."

clit (fr L // Gk kleitoris) clitoris; primary organ of erotic sensation in the female "I want me a dong, princess, not some exaggerated clit like that thing you've got" "I've got to go pick up a book on clit disorders."
   Syn: **button** (**push the button** = fingering the clitoris until orgasm); **dot; jointess** (camp, fr sl joint = cock; the clitoris becomes erect like a penis when stimulated) **little boy in the boat** (fr L naviculans = clitoris // navicula = boat).
   —**closet** ('71) hotel which rents rooms to prostitutes and their ***johns.** Syn: **hot-sheets hotel** (pros sl, '70).

clique bar a bar where small groups of gay friends meet to gossip, discouraging those outsiders who try to strike up a conversation; a neighborhood ***gay bar,** not appropriate for someone intent upon finding a sex partner.

clock (kwn SF, hip gay sl, fr underworld sl clockin' = casing a joint; timing a victim's daily routine) to scrutinize, size up "Did you clock that joint? It was a real lulu!"

closet case [queen, queer] (*pej*) **1.** homosexual who denies his sexual longings. A closet case is resented by his fellow homosexuals for being a gay Uncle Tom—servile to the heterosexual majority "There is bound to be at least one closet queen working for the FBI in San Fran" **2.** (*rare*) a latent homosexual "Of course, he's noncommittal—what did you expect from a closet queer?"

Syn: **canned fruit** (late '50s); **cedarchest cissy** (*kwn* Midwest, late '60s); **crushed fruit** (late '50s-mid '60s: because he is crushed by society's mores); **dry queen** (*kwn* Albuquerque, late '60s); **hidden queen; pink tea** (= the after-hours homosexual); **undercover fag[man, punk, sissy]** ('40s-mid '60s).

Related terms:

closet dyke lesbian who isn't candid.

closeted [in the closet] refusing to associate with known gays for fear of being discovered.

closet name pen name used by gay author of obviously homosexual works. Don Cory, writer of many works with gay themes, is a closet name formed from Corydon (euphemism for gay man used by Roman poet Virgil).

come out of the closet to admit to being gay.

cover up to pretend being heterosexual, expecially in one's own environment.

clothing queen (mid-late '60s) a gay clotheshorse. Queens decorate themselves with hundreds of dollars of casual sublimation and womanishly complain of nothing to wear, while a virtually endless wardrobe hangs in the closet collecting dust and rust.

Related terms:

delicate-assen (late '60s) pants store.

lace outlandishly ornamental fashions designed for today's modern man.

novelty clothing (late '60s) outrageous clothing worn especially for fun; fad clothing. Syn: **fish-net shifts.**

peacock palace a gay clothier's. Syn: **fag factory** (*kwn* SF, '70).

Slavonian army (*fr* Al Capp's mythological country Lower Slobbovia) Salvation Army resale stores where one may purchase janitorial kick-offs (*kwn* SF, '72: = second-hand clothing). Syn: **Miss Sally's** (*fr* hobo sl *Sally* = Salvation Army).

strapless (*camp*) tank-top.

voyeur clothing (late '60s) see-through clothing. "Looking at me in my voyeur clothing will be the best beauty treatment you'll ever receive."

walk a dress (*camp*) to wear a new outfit in front of somebody for the sole purpose of showing off; to model a new ensemble.

CO cock odor.

cock (*fr* 16th cent Brit) the penis, the 16th male organ of reproduction and urine elimination "A rolling stone gathers no cock!" (said of a *walker).

Many syn for cock come under the category of food terms, male names, and tearing implements (weapons, some tools):
bagaga (*fr* It *bagaglio* = baggage); **baloney** (one Las Vegas boy was nicknamed Tony Baloney because of his large organ: "Then what's phony baloney—a dildo?"); **banana** (?sprang up in relation to *monkey = vagina); **bar** (*rare*); **beef** ("He stood in the back playing with his beef"); **bird** (late '60s: "How's your bird?" serves as a comic homosexual greeting, but "do you wanna bird?" = do you want to be sucked off?); **black jack** ('40s: a black man's penis): "I'm tired of pink sausage; I'm going to get me a black jack"); **bone** (*dated*: "There's not a shy bone in your body—yet"); **boy toy** ('50s, especially when manipulated by a masturbator); **butcher knife** (one of the weapon

words); **candy cane; cartso** (Brit gay sl, *fr* It *cazzo* = penis); **chingus** (*dated, ?fr* Sp *chingar* = to fuck: "Lithen, Mith LaTour, don't come on so big and butch with me; there ain't a chingus between us"); **chopper; chora** (chō'-rä, Mex); **chota** (chō'-tä, Mex, '40s); **clyde** (*rare:* "C'mon, show us how big clyde has grown"); **corpuscle** (rhyming pun on muscle); **dagger; dang** (not as common as dong); **dangle** (since it just hangs there); **dark meat** (= a black penis); **dick[y]** (*colloq*, short for **Richard:** "Eat dick, Tracy!"); **ding-dong** (It must've been a rerun of Ding-Dong School—every urinal was in session"); **dingus** (*dated*); **dink** (see ***small meat**); **dolly** (*fr* the old joke where a father tells his inquisitive daughter that his penis is a doll. One day he awakes from a nap and sees his daughter crying. When asked what happened, she replies that she was playing with the dolly with the greatest fun, until it squirted her in the eye!); **dong** ("Wait till you see the dong on him—you'll want him to measure your throat with it"); **dork** ("Your dork is so short that if you cut it off you'd have a scar on your ass"); **drill; dummy** (largely used in the phrase **beat the dummy** = to masturbate: perhaps the old-wives' tale of feeble-mindedness resulting from masturbation is at play here); **fag[got's] toothbrush** (*pej, kwn* Southwest, late '50s, said especially of fellated penis: "Oh, pard-*on*! I didn't know you were brushing your teeth!"); **flute** (late '50s: "may I play your flute?" = open invitation to a blow-job); **front porch** (cock and balls as opposed to the *back porch* = ass); **fuck pole; fun bone; gadget** ("Are you the guy with the two-headed gadget?"; **gong** (*dated, fr* sl *kick the gong around* = *jack off); **gun** an Army chant teached: "This is your rifle, this is your gun; one is for killing, one is for fun"); **hamilton wick** (*fr* Brit rhyming sl = dick); **hammer; handle** ("That ain't no cock—that's just the handle they use to turn you over with'); **hang-down** ("Check out the hang-down on *this* baby . . . he oughta be in pictures"); **hank; honk[er]** ("His hinker must be half-a-block long!"); **hose** ("Watch the heels, Mae, you might step on my hose"); **hot dog** (*fr* the similarity between frankfurters and penises: "Hot dogs and buns—get 'em while they're hot!"); **hot rod** (*fr* black sl); **human enema** (*kwn* Ariz, early '60s: penis as an anal probe in anal intercourse); **hunk of meat; ID** (early '60s, *fr* identification); **it** (one of the most common euphemisms: "You're offering two for one today . . . what'd you do, graft it back on?"); **jakey** (les sl, mid '60s: "Don't lean on jakey—it can't breed!"); **jock** (*fr* jock-strap); **johnson; joint** (hip sl, late '50s, *fr* joint = large cut of meat with the bone still intact: "I bet a ham sandwich tastes just like Wyatt Hurts' joint." By extension, man as a sex object: "The library's no place to look for a joint"); **joy stick** ("Man, oh man! Here's where I shift my joy stick into high gear"); **jungle meat** (*pej*, though used by those who don't intend a derogatory meaning: black man's penis); **kidney wiper; knitting needle** (early '60s: "He wanted to know what my knitting needle could do, so I crocheted 'Home Sweet Home' all over his arse"); **laka** (lä'-kä, *kwn* LA, mid '60s, *fr* Haw); **lance** (weapon word); **lanoola** (Brit, mid '60s); **leg** (*fr* sl *short leg* = cock); **licorice stick** (black penis, by extension a black man: "The licorice sticks almost burned LA down"); **light [white] meat** (penis of a white man as opposed to that of a black man); **lipstick** (*kwn* Hollywood, early '60s: *fr* analogy with lipstick which rises out of its tube when dialed); **lob** (*dated*); **lollipop** (penis as implement of desire to cocksucker); **longfellow; longhorn; love-rod; meat** ("Women are cunts! And besides that they have small meat!"); **Mickey** ("Mickey Spillane—private dick!"); **Mr. Wong; muscle; nightcrawler** (*kwn* Midwest teen sl, late '50s); **old crank case** (the masturbated penis); **old faceful** [**faithful**] (early '50s, the cock when pumped for ejaculation); **pecker** (*lit* = something that pecks, *ie* makes a hole; rapidly becoming *obs* and considered adolescent: "Lookin' for a little pecker tonight, soldier?"); **peculator pecker** (hot, throbbing cock); **peeny** (*fr* L *penis:* "Teenies have big peenies!" is chanted like the grade-school taunt, 'Na, na, na, na, na! Janey's got a boy friend!"); **peep** (*kwn* LV, mid-late '60s, short for **peepee:** "He put rouge on his peep and he went to the party as a hot dog"); **peepee** [**pipi**] (*fr* baby talk: "Don't shake your peepee at me . . . unless you mean it"); **peeper; penis** (pen'-us, *camp,* means the same thing as it does in standard English; only the pronunciation has been altered: "Are we going to flash a little pen-us for the camera, kids?"); **peter** (considered childish by sophisticates: "Milpitas? What's that mean . . . a thousand peckers?"); **piccolo** (*dated,* the cock as viewed by a fellator); **piece of meat** ("He may be a nice guy, but I really did his piece of meat"); **pinga** (pēn'-gä, Mex); **pipe; pisser** ("Tell him to go slow if he screws ya, cause that ain't no pisser he got danglin'—that's a killer'); **piston rod; pizzle**[**r**]; **pogo stick** ("Why did you turn Jerry down—is his pogo stick made out of styrofoam or something?"); **poker; pole; pork** (mainly black and southern sl); **pork enema; prick** (considered corny, *fr* ME *prikke* = sharp projecting part: "Then he balanced those horn-rim glasses on his prick an' said, 'look aroun', Big Boy, an' see if you missed anything!'"); **prong** (*fr* ME *pronge* = slender pointed or projecting part, such as the point an antler: "Prawns, you dizzy queen, not prongs."); **pud** (found in the expression **pound the pud** = to masturbate; *fr* L *pudend*[*um*] which in a general sense means the genitals of either sex, though many limit the meaning to apply only to the female); **pump-handle** (especially when stroked); **pup** (*fr* sl *pup* = frankfurter); **rammer; ramrod** ("Looks like Sabrina's ramrod just gave its death rattle"); **raw meat** (poised before the fellator's lips: "All your analisp will deliver is a diagnosis that you return to your diet of raw meat"); **rib** (*fr* Genesis where Eve was created by God from one of Adam's ribs); **rig** (Brit gay sl); **roger** (Brit: "Roger, roger everywhere, and not a drop to drink" = in the midst of a straight group); **root; rupert** (Brit); **salami** (usu relegated to a large penis); **sausage** ("Well, you and that Polish sausage weren't playing jacks"); **scepter** (*camp;* **scepter and jewels** = cock and balls); **schlong** (*fr* Yid // Ger *Schlange* = snake: *cf* sl *snake*); **schmuck** (*fr* Yid // Ger *Schmuck* = ornament: *cf* sl *family jewels* = genitals); **schnitzel** (*fr* Yid // Ger *Schnitzel* = a chip, cutlet); **schwantz** (shvänts or shwants, *fr* Yid // Ger *Schwanz* = a tail: *cf* sl where *tail* = hindend, then *cf* L *penis* related to *cauda* = tail) **sewing maching** (*fr* sewing seed[s]: "I'll have that stiched up in no time with my sewing maching"); **silver penny** (*kwn* Midwest, early '50s: *cf* sl *copper penny* = ass, calling attention to the coloring of fecal matter); **skin flute; slug; smoked meat** (*kwn* Canada, late '60s: a black penis); **snake; spear** (weapon word); **spout; steak** (late '50s: the cock when sucked); **stick**[**er**]; **stud** (*kwn* SF, SM sl, '70: "He made me suck his stud dry, man"); **sugar stick; sweet meat** (an attractive man or the penis thereof); **swipe** (*kwn* Chi prison sl, mid '60s: *fr* swipe = to hit with a sweeping motion); **sword** (weapon word); **tan-trouser**[**ed**] **snake** ('70); **thumb; tiki-tiki** (tē'-kē-tē'-kē, *fr* baby talk *tiki* = to urinate); **tom-tom** Usu in the expression **beat the tom-tom** = to masturbate; **tool** (early '50s: duck-tailed schoolboys rhymed "Keep a cool tool, fool; I'm wise to the rise in your levis"); **vegetable stick** (early '60s, *cf* sl *rabbit* = fellator: a cock before the fellator's lips); **voorsch** (vo͞orsht, *fr* Yid // Ger *Wurst* = sausage: "The voorsch in Vienna vas wunderbar"); **wand** (camp, since all faries carry one); **wang** (not as well known as **wong**); **water pistol** (SM sl: the urinating penis); **weener** [**weenie, wiener**] ("I wish *I* had Oscar's mile weener"); **weewee** (*fr* baby talk = a puddle of piss: "Pour a Pepsi on his weewee an' watch it come alive"); **wheezer** ('70s, largely straight usage: "Would half an order of wheezer be cheaper"); **whelp** (*rare*); **white owl** (= white man's cock); **wire**; **wishbone** ('70) **wong** ("Give him enough wong and he'll hang himself"); **worm; ying-yang** (early '60s, most likely *fr* sl *yank off* = masturbate & not *fr* Chin concept of yang-ying = male-female; *cf* however sl *up the ying-yang* which refers to either anal intercourse or to anything in great abundance: "I had Indianhead pennies up the ying-yang, but my mother accidentally threw them out").

Related terms:

accordion (late '60s) unexciting unexcited cock which expands to a much greater length when aroused. Syn: **hidden magic; surprise package; tomato surprise** (*kwn* LV, mid '60s: one gets more tomatoes than he bargained for).

cinnamon stick the cock immediately after anal intercourse. Syn: **tar brush.** Both are rare and used mainly in jocular context.

club[bed] foot ('40s) slightly bent or curved cock.

dead rabbit penis incapable of erection. Syn: **bent stick; dead stick; sleeping beauty** (= twelve inch softie won't get lofty).

eye[pee]-hole opening in the *glans penis*.

glut[ton for punishment] ('40s) one who continues to suck even after his partner has ejaculated. Since the *glans penis* is ticklish and somewhat sensitive immediately following orgasm, the glut is more of a nuisance than the sexual godsend he believes himself to be.

midweight (*adj*) portraying the average sized penis (roughly six inches); **heavyweight** refers to large genitals and **under par** is what's left "He might have a heavyweight's chest, but believe me, it's all midweight below the navel."

spitter a cock at the moment of orgasm.

Also see *hard-on, *size queen, *small meat.

—and balls (*camp*) bacon and eggs.

Related terms:

Adam and Eve on a raft—wreck 'em (*camp, fr* lunch counter sl) two scrambled eggs on toast.

Christ and two apostles (*camp*) ham and two eggs.

—bath licking the penis, usually as a prelude to licking the entire body of a partner.

—ettes (late '60s-early '70s) trope of long-haired San Francisco Thespians. Columnist Herb Caen once called them "the wildest drag show in town."

—hound (*kwn* SF, '72) a Cockette disciple.

—sucker [CS] **1.** fellator "It's as cold as a cocksucker's knees in the Klondike." Syn: **acorn-picker** (early '60s, translation of L *glans* = acorn as in *glans penis* = the uppermost end of the cock); **band-member; BJM** (teen sl, early '60s: = blow job man); **bone queen; cannibal; cock-eater[-lover]; come freak** (early '60s: "That come freak looks positively bloated"); **crunch queen** ('71: nibbles with his teeth); **dick-drink; dick[y]-licker[-taster]** (*pej*); **face artist[pussy]; flute player** ('40s-'50s); **fluter** (prison sl); **fly trap** (*kwn* LA, mid '60s); **gobbler** (note the riddle "Why is a gay bar called a turkey club? Because there's a gobbler on every stool"); **goop-gobbler** ('40s); **head artist [hunter, queen, worker]; hot brains[head]** (prison sl); **icing expert** (*dated*, coined in CCC camps during '30s); **iron jaws** (late '50s: the dedicated cocksucker); **jaw queen; jock-warmer** (prison sl); **knob polisher** (*fr* 19th cent Brit where maids polished the master's silver knob on his walking stick); **licker** (*pej,* usually reserved for a lesbian); **mamon** (mä-mōn', *fr* Sp, shor for *mamon de verga* = sucker of cock); **maneater; mouth queen**[worker]; **nibbler** ('40s-'50s); **peepee-puller** (*kwn* SF, '70); **peter-eater; piccolo-player** (late '50s); **prick-licker; protein queen; rabbit; roundmouth** ('70); **Schwanzesser** (shvants'-es-ser, *fr* Ger = penis-eater); **skillful skull** (mid '60s); **skull pussy, smoker** (early '60s); **snake charmer**[tester] ("Bet that snake tester can't eat just one"); **suck-cocker; suckster; trapeze artist** ('40s); **whistler** (*fr* naut sl; "Only two people are allowed to whistle aboard ship—queers and bo'suns": sometimes sailors catching somebody whistling tease him for being gay); **wormeater; yo-yo mouth** ('71: "He has the mouth of a yo-yo, it goes up and down") **2.** a fellator's mouth. Syn: **face pussy; hole** ("Shut your hole, bitch!"); **skull pussy** ("Here, shove this ham sandwich into your skull pussy").

—suckerish (*adj, kwn* LV, mid '60s) **1.** homosexual "I hear that new bar is cocksuckerish!" **2.** lou̇d, gaudy, sȧid of clothing, makeup, etc. "Is my new tie a tish cocksuckerish, Queen?"

—tease to arouse sexually and then refuse gratification; to lead somebody on and then fail to deliver. One who **cock-teases** is called a **cock-teaser,** a **CT, prick-teaser, PT, teaser, witch.** The young and beautiful are prone to this practice though the term can be hurled angrily by anyone who missed getting a trick. The ones that got away are either *****messes** or **teases.**

cod (Brit gay sl, *fr* sl *cod* = to hoax) vile "I *do* beg your's, you huffy cod bitch!"
   Related term:
   just for cod just for laughs, something to do "Just for cod, name me two Hollywood stars who aren't *that* way."

coffin queen 1. one who finds the usual business of death—corpses, caskets, and funeral wreaths, *etc*—erotic **2.** (*camp*) any mortician "There's a school for coffin queens in the next block" **3.** one who takes sexual interest in corpses. Syn: **casket freak; Morticia** (*camp*); **necrofellow** (*fr* necrophile = lover of dead bodies // Gk *nekros* = corpse + *philos* = loving); **pork packer.**
   Related term:
   Smiley Schultz ('40s) any corpse.

cognoscenti people in the know; homosexuals united with congenial heterosexuals forming a hip underground.

cold wind [from the North] high chilling "Ooh!" made when one recognizes a bitchy remark.

collect interest to have sex with a person as payment for past debts "After all the stuff Moris gave Jeff, I hope there'll be a time when he can collect interest."

Comanche (late '60s) man who uses cosmetics.
   Related term:
   paint back like an Apache[Comanche] to completely cover the face in cosmetics—mascara, pancake, erase on the lips, and the like "If they painted the Parthenon back like a Comanche, an' put in some flocked wallpaper, they'd have a swingin' night club."

come [cum] **1.** (*n*) semen "Can't hear? Then take the come out of your ear!" Syn: **baby paste; ball-bearing oil** (particularly when used to masturbate the partner); **beef gravy; cocoa butter** (= black man's come); **comings** (Brit); **cream; cum-cum; doll**[y] **spit; face cream** (= a cocksucker's reward); **french dressing; fruit juice; gism** (jiz'-m: "We could market this gism if you put some vanilla in it"); **goo** ('40s); **hot lead** ("C'mon baby, fill me full o' hot lead"); **hot milk' jelly; jizz**[um]; **juice; liquid hairdressing** (*fr* theory that semen contains large quanties of protein which helps to curb baldness); **love juice** ("He's busy studying some love juice under the microscope"); **mahu-pol** (mä'-hōō-poi', *rare, fr* Haw gay sl // Haw *poi* = a fermented, eatable paste of taro root whose whitish color resembles semen); **man oil; maria** (Brit gay sl: "Maria's on your tweeds, dear"); **mayonnaise** ("Just slap some meat and mayonnaise down on these buns, girl!"); **meco** (mä'-kō, *fr* Pach // brand of green chile sauce: **meco en tu boca!** = bullshit, **mecotero** = a comer); **oyster** ('40s: gob of semen); **pearl[drop]** (mid '60s: drop of semen); **protein** ("We all need our protein—some of us get it from vegetables, and some of us get it from behind the greeneries in the park"); **rice pudding** (*kwn* NYC, '40s: in India rice symbolizes male spermatozoa); **rich cream sauce; royal jelly** (the substance upon which *queen bees survive); **sauce** ("La 'sauce' c'est vous!"); **scum** (*fr* black sl); **snake venom; snowstorm** (= a great deal of semen ejaculated all at once); **soul sauce** (= the semen of a black man); **spunk** ("No sense in cryin over spilt spunk"); **starch** (comparing the odor of semen and laundry starch); **sticky** ("There's sticky all over my new sailor poster"); **turnip seeds** (*rare, fr* sl *turnip* = *glans penis:* "Been planting turnip seeds in my back porch?"); **vitamins** ("A busy bee needs her vitamins"); **whore's milk.**

Related terms:

French fried ice cream (*kwn* LV, black gay sl, mid '60s) smooth, creamy semen.

French fried ice water (*kwn* LV, black gay sl, mid '60s, lumpy semen forming a tapioca-like consistency) Syn: **Spanish rice; tapioca pudding.**

sour cum acrid, bitter semen. Syn: **goat's milk**

2. (*v*), to experience an orgasm. Used of either sex, but homosexuals often limit the meaning to male ejaculation "The only way Roberta can come is by whipping last women." Syn: **bang it; blow off** ("He sure knows how to give good head . . . I blew off almost immediately"); **get one's balls[gun, nuts, rocks] off; happen** ('70: "Didn't you happen yet?"); **jizz** (late '50s: "Hey Tony, can I jizz in your ass?"); **shoot [a load]** ("He shot off in my mouth"); **spit; spurt.**

—**back** a reentry into gay society "I've been out of town for an entire month nursing a wounded heart, so warn the kids that their mother's goin' to stage a grand comeback like they've never seen . . . by the by, bring your own bottle!"

—**balloon** a diaphragm.

—**clean** to be unaffected by a veneral disease "Come clean with your lovers—don't pass on the clap."

—**drum** (*fr* pun made upon *come* + the *cun-* of British Colonel Cundum, 17th century inventor of the prophylactic) a cundum or condom. Syn: **bag** ("First ya put a bag on, and then you fuck her legs clean off"); **envelope** (short for **love envelope**); **pecker glove** (*kwn* Southwest, late '50s); **protective; raincoat** (*fr* black sl); **rubber** (perhaps the commonest word for a condom); **rubber goods** ("You're here because of weak rubber goods, Bovina!"); **safety** (early '50s).

—**fuck-me's** (mid-late '60s) overly tight pants. Syn: **bun-pressers** (*kwn* SF, '71: fit snugly about the buttocks); **capris** (*camp*); **leg-crushers** (*kwn* SF, '71: fit especially tight about the calves and thighs); **pegs** (*dated:* pair of pegged pants); **pipes** (*dated*); **riders** (so called because they ride up the crack of the ass: levis that ride are chic . . . undershorts that do are not); **skinny pants** (early '60s); **skins** (because they fit tightly like a second skin); **slims** (mid '60s); **soundproof pants** ('70: so form-fitting that the wearer can't hear *it* sloshing around); **training pants** (late '60s: one's very first pair of tight pants).

—**on** to direct, invite erotic encounters by looking deep into another's eyes "I didn't believe that so many salesgirls would come on while working." Syn: **come on strong with someone.**

—**on like** (late '50s-early '60s) to affect the style of something or someone: **come on like confetti** (frivolously); **come on like gangbusters** (to be enthusiastic); **come on like Garbo** (to covet solitude, be retiring); **come on like King Kong** (aggressively); **come on like Mata Hari** (to hide the facts behind a smile, to keep secrets).

—**on over to the S & M side** (mid '60s, fr the cigarette commercial, "Come on over to the L&M side!") jocular reference to give sado-masochism a try

—**on picture** (early '60s) alluring photograph of a sensual naked man "The covers of most fag-mags are come-on pics with little action inside."

—**out** to become aware of one's own homosexuality "Ruth came out when she was thirty-five—that's a long time to wait." Syn: **debut** ("Haven't you debuted in cocksucking yet?")

—**tosis** (camp, blending of come + halitosis) stale semen on a cocksucker's breath "The Binaca's for the afternoon cometosis." Syn: **bed breath** (camp).

commercials 1. old tired excuses used by *hustlers: "I hustle 'cause I need the money to pay the rent" and "You were really nice, and I hate to ask you for money, but . . ." are two well-known lines **2.** personal build-ups to interest a possible buyer "I'm blond and hung and loved to get fucked, if that's your bag" **3.** ads run by male models in underground newspapers.

communist M and M's (mid '60s, fr M&M candies) ambars: peppills with a red candy-coated shell.
Syn: **M and M's.**

competition 1. rival in romance; one who represents a threat; that scoundrel who would compete for the same *trick "I'm not one to dish, but your best friend is also your best competition" **2.** any threatening female "Pick out your man, girls, and rush him to your dens 'cause here comes some of our competition."

contact (exclam, kwn Cleveland, mid '60s) to make known that there is a sexy man in the vicinity. To avoid arousing suspicion, the command may be murmured offhandedly while paging through a magazine "Don't break your neck, precious, but, contact! Over towards the right!"

cooch 1. (fr vul sl cooch = vagina) any woman "I was twenty-four before I knew that a Bloody Mary wasn't a cooch in her period" **2.** generic for odds and ends; extra attachments as in **all that cooch** = all that stuff.
Also see *snap.

cookie crumbs 1. come stains lining the trouser leg. Syn: **decorations. 2.** traces of effeminacy.

cookie duster any mustache, but usually the bristles found on the upper lip of some women charged with being lesbians "A Van Dyke is a bull-dagger with a cookie duster."
Syn: **muff tickler; pussy duster; womb broom** (fr black sl).

coolie an unwise move; action without forethought.
Related term:
pull a coolie to blunder, to fuck up "Rotten Rodney pulled a coolie when he made a u-turn on the freeway."

cool off some dude (kwn SF, '71) to pick a *trick's pocket.

cooze-cola (camp) carbonated soda.

cop a squat ('50s) to sit down to urinate.

copy (camp) yesterday's stale coffee "Wanna cup o' copy?"

corkle (blending of quarter + nickle) imaginary denomination denoting cheapness "Hey, whore boy, got change for a corkle?"

Related term:

pick up pennies to be fucked for a mere pittance.

cornflakes (*kwn* Southwest, late '60s) **1.** loveable, big, dumb farm boy "It was sure easy to lure that cornflakes into my faggoty hayloft!" Syn: **cream of the crop[wheat]** (*camp*) **2.** generic for the clean-cut, all-American naive youth.

Related terms:

honeysuckle vine slim, lanky makeable Southern farm boy "Pull any honeysuckle vine while down in Tennessee?"

RFD queen (*dated*, '40s, *fr* Rural Free Delivery) small-town homosexual unfamiliar with urban ways, gay hick. **Come on like a RFD queen** = to understand little.

Syn: **lily of the valley** (*camp*); **pasture woman.**

cornhole see *****fuck.**

cosmetic intuition ('71) homosexual's sixth sense about danger.

couch audition (*fr* Hollywood of the '40s) obtaining a job by sleeping with the prospective employer "The stage manager took one peek at that boy's basket and decided to hold a couch audition—all noon."

countess well-to-do effeminate, usually older than his companions. Since countesses act their age, the title is not derogatory like *****auntie** "Hang on some glass, countess; let people know that class does well."

court 1. see *****circle 2.** group of admirers.

cousin the hands-off lover of a gay friend (*****sister**).

Also see *****incest.**

cow 1. any woman, but especially one with big tits "How'd that cow ever get into the movies—she must've worn her dentures thin by the hundredth director." Syn: **bossy, bovine 2.** homosexual encumbered with one or more of the following: excess weight, clumsiness, social offensiveness, bad breath "Who does that leather queen think he is, stepping all over my feet—the cow!" **3.** (*dated*) coy.

cowboy see *****buckaruby, *****hustler, *****SM.**

cowboy it to swagger, strut.

Also see *****butch it up.**

crabs (*fr* ME *crabbe* = crab // OE *ceorfan* = to carve) crab lice infecting the pubic areas "The wind is strong enough today to blow away my dead crabs." Syn: **crotch crickets** (late '60s); **family** (*fr* pros sl, '40s: "Sleep with that pig and you'll probably end up with a family to feed"); **love bugs [lice]; social dandruff.**

Related terms:

A-200 brand name of a popular crab disinfectant.

crab souffle crotch crawling with lice.

crack[steam] crabs applying disinfectant ointment to the crotch area.

one on a motorcycle or an entire army phrase used to determine how advanced the infection is "I won the title of 'Yellow Rose of Texas' when I caught infectious hep from one on a motorcycle."

Trixie (*camp*) one crab pulled off and quickly pulverized.

what you see is what you get! (*kwn* SF, '71, *fr* Flip [Geraldine] Wilson) shrieked when seeing lice on a lover.

crapper-dick 1. vice-squad officer on the washroom beat, see *****vice 2.** an extortionist who poses as a vice-squad official to extort a "bribe" in exchange for forgetting about a sordid incident.

cream see *****come.**

cream one's jeans (late '50s) to become climactically excited "I knew this one case who creamed his jeans every time he rode the roller coaster."

creature (*kwn* SF, hip gay sl) drug-taking, long-haired erratic homosexual; a weird-o.
    Syn: **creature of the night** (hip night-owl).

crepe wrinkled skin tissue found around the eyes, jaw, and/or elbows of maturing adults.
    —**suzette** *crepe in general, but particularly when located in the neck region, the most difficult area to cover up.

crib (*fr* pros sl = room rented for sexual purpose) **1.** an apartment, see *cage **2.** private cubicle rented at a baths.

crown 1. (*camp*) any sort of tiara worn by a *drag queen **2.** the head ". . . and after she finally shaved all her hair off, we got to see what the queen's crown looked like."

crown jewels 1. jewelry worn by a *drag queen "Girl, you're wearing so many crown jewels that somebody's going to mistake you for a carnival ground and charge you rent." **2.** (*camp*) male genitals, see *family jewels.

crud dried semen stuck to the body or clothing.
    —**catcher** (*kwn* LV, mid '60s) homosexual who masturbates his sex partner and then rubs the semen all over.

cruel (krōō-wel') see *bitchy.

Cruella (krōō-el'-lä) gay nickname for one who thinks of himself as a femme fatale; a heartbreaker; a homewrecker "How could Cruella turn him down after all those nice gifts?" French-sounding surnames such as LaCruel, LaBiche and La-Tease often complete the fantasy name.

cruise (*fr* Du *kruisen* = to cruise // L *crux* = cross) to search for sex; to find a need and fill it "Cruisin', boozin', and snoozin' —ever since old Ronny got you on welfare, that's all you've been doin'."
    Syn: **bash[do] the beat** (Aus gay sl, '70); **camp** (Aus gay sl); **cat** (*dated*, largely hetero sl, *fr* prowling tom cats: "Let's go catting around"); **hunt** ("Honey, you know it's the hunt that brings home the meat—the barfly just buzzes roun' somethin' dead"); **on the bash** (Brit gay sl, *fr* Brit sl *bash* = cigarette); **on the game** (Brit gay sl, *fr* pros sl = streetwalking); **on the make[turf]; shop** (Mother does most of her shopping at the Y"); **stalk** ("A person who persists in stalking game in a place where there is none may wait forever without finding any," *fr* the *I Ching*); **whore; work** ("He works 42nd and 8th.")
    —**y** used of a location favorable for good cruising.
    —**ing clothes** skintight clothing accentuating the lower extremities and hopefully attracting others to these areas "I'm getting so low on funds that I may have to hock my cruising clothes to a desperate lesbian." Syn: **gay uniform[s]; scandal clothes; sin suit; working clothes; whoring clothes.**
    Related terms:
heavy cruising looking for sex partners seriously: no time to chit-chat with acquaintances met on the street "Don't get your face into an uproar—maybe he didn't say 'Hi' because he's doin' some heavy cruisin'."
the hunting season (*kwn* Chicago, late '60s) April through October, the months when the park washrooms are left unlocked at night.
john cruising looking for agreeable men in public toilets.
shopper (*kwn* SF, late '60s-'71) one who rarely makes out—he spends most of his time looking for the unattainable Mr. Right.
    Also see *walker.

crush infatuation; hero-worship.
    Syn: **crushies; crushvilles** (*dated*).
crushed fruit (mid '60s) homosexual who has been physically assaulted "Get your machine going, girl, if you don't want to be a puddle of crushed fruit."
crystal lady (*kwn* SF, hip gay sl, late '60s) amphetamine-using homosexual.
cubans (*camp*) heavy-duty boots "He won't be able to lift his foot to the curb for the cubans he's wearing."
    Syn: **cuban pumps** ("He's so dizzy he wears cuban pumps to the dancing bar")
cucumber queen homosexual who enjoys pushing phallic-shaped vegetables up his ass "That cucumber queen tosses a salad in the most *un*orthodox way."
culo see *ass.
cum see *come.
cunt 1. (*pej, fr L cunnus* = wedge) the female sex organ "Some women believe that they can rule the roost just because they have that golden cunt between their legs" **2.** (*pej*) woman as a sex object "Why should you have to give that cunt alimony—she can earn a living on her back like she used to do before she married you" **3.** (*camp* but *pej*) insult aimed at anybody held in low esteem **4.** (*camp*) homosexual's ass "Move your cunt—Mama wants to sit down!" **5.** (*camp*) a cocksucker's mouth "Close your filthy cunt; I don't want to hear any more about it!"
    Syn: **coin-slot, cookie** ("I'm only twee and a ha'f years old, an' already I have hair on my cookie"); **cooze[y]** ("Does that dull dyke really love that girl, or is she just talkin' through her cooze?"); **crack** ("Put your teeth back in your crack, I can't understand a word you're saying"); **cream catcher** (*fr* sl *cream* = semen); **crease; crooney** (*kwn* LV, les sl, mid '60s); **crunt** (*kwn* SF, late '60s-71); **cunker [kunker]** (*kwn* SF, black sl: "Man, that skirt's so mini you can count the hairs on her cunker"); **cuntie** ("Let's get us a petition going to keep cunties off the street after twilight"); **gash** ("Turn up your gash; I'm colder'n Hell!"); **hole** ((shut your hole! = shut-up); **katoka** (kä-to'-kä, Haw gay sl: "Did he marry her just for that katoka?"); **knish** (k'-nish', *fr* Yid = dumpling: "She's doing the Can-Can? It looks more like she has ants in her knish"); **merchandise; nooky [nookie, nookey]** (see *ass); **noose; puka** (poō'-kä, *fr* Haw = hole: "There's room enough in her puka for an entire Army"); **quiff** (*rare*); **scratch** (*dated*); **shmoya** (?*fr* Yid); **slit; slot; snatch** ("Why's your hair so white, Snatch; is it frostbitten?"); **twat** ("I love the ground that twat hobbles on": **twat hair** = beard); **yawn** (*rare*); **zosh** ("The skinny old zosh has been gaining some weight—it's all behind her now." "That dumb zosh has so many streaks of light pouring through her wig that she looks like a Hallmark Christmas card.")
    —y 1. possessing the qualities of a woman; womanish "Imagine *me* cooking for my old man—that makes me feel so cunty!" **2.** frilly "This ballroom is too cunty, why don't you spill some coffee on the carpet to butch it up!" **3.** see *bitchy.
Cup-and-a-half title much like Mr. for one who ejaculates copiously "There goes Cup-and-a-half Wilson into the john; I bet he tickles some lucky queen's tonsils."
cupcake (*rare*) young girlish boy, though not necessarily gay.
cup to feed you with (*kwn* Southwest teen sl, late '50s) friendly taunt accompanied by a clutching gesture indicating the speaker's cock. However, some maintain that the sentence "This is the cup to feed you with" = "shut up and start sucking!"

curb service 1. pedestrian homosexual who cruises passing motorists **2.** shouted from the sidewalk at a motorist and meaning "I'm available."

curbstone cupcakes ('70) dog droppings.
> Syn: *****dogey-doo; ghetto gumdrops** ('70).

cure ('50s) to renounce homosexuality through psychiatric assistance.

curlies (Brit) pubic hairs.
> Syn: **curls** ("Don't you tell me that you haven't been cheating—there's crud in your curls."); **short and curlies.**
> Related term:
> **have one by the curlies** to be in an awkward situation "He has me by the curlies, luv, what can I do but pay the bugger his filthy blackmail money?"

curtain calls subsequent sexual visits "I brought him home from a waterfront bar, and let me dish you, Bess, he's been back for curtain calls—knows a good thing when he feels it, I guess."

cushion one's jewels to press up close to behind in a crowd; to practice frottage.

cute 1. puckish, said of the fresh-scrubbed countenance of a little boy **2.** small, lithe "He sure does have a cute little body on him."
> **—ness 1.** good-looking youth "Here comes some cuteness, Vampira, drag out your net!" **2.** handsomeness "Cuteness reigns, dearie; and that's the reason you should abdicate!"
> **—thing** comely man, especially when boasting of an ex-*****trick** "That cute thing I had last night was built like a brick shithouse—and not one brick was out of place."

cuts (fr pros sl) the streets.

Cy (dated, late '50s) homoerotic in the choice of bed partners "Isn't he kinda Cy?"
> Syn: **Sy.**

Cynthia (adj) synthetic.

daddle (les sl, ?*fr* sl *diddle* = to fuck; *cf diddle-daddle,* killing time, with sl *fucking off*) to practice tribadism (*fr* Gk *tribein* = to rub: bumping in a face-to-face position, both vaginas touching.)
Syn: **dry fuck** (*kwn* Calif women's prison sl)**; flat fuck** (les sl).
daddy older man who shows affection for his younger male lover with gifts "Some of these young, clever queens latch onto a daddy for as long as their beauty holds out."
Also see ***sugar daddy.**
daddy-o (*fr* black sl, '40s) **1.** synonymous with ***daddy 2.** butch, often sarcastically applied "We all know how big and butch you are, Daddy-o; you'd rather plow broads, but can't tell the difference between the real thing and a screaming boy in the dark."
Dahlia dyke (*kwn* SF, '71) saleswoman in a clothing store.
dainties 1. woman's undergarments when worn by a male transvestite **2.** (*camp*) men's underwear (jockey shorts, etc) "Which drawer do you keep your dainties in?"
dainty daddy homosexual who affects the mannerisms of woman and takes the active positions sexually; the *cow* that jumps into the *moon.*
Syn: ***empress** (*kwn* LV, late '60s)**; pretty daddy.**
dairy queen 1. gay milkman "Are you sure that your sweet petunia hasn't been having an affair with the dairy queen?" **2.** an obese person "I've heard of excess poundage, but that dairy queen is an escapee from a sideshow" **3.** gay farmer **4.** (*kwn* SF, '71) early morning liaison "Get a good start, have a dairy queen in the morning!"
daisy 1. short for ***daisy chain** "Let's turn this family reunion into a daisy, gang!" **2.** the man at the end of a ***daisy chain 3.** (*kwn* LV, late '60s) the person who sexually entertains more than one man at one setting "Let's have a party—who'll be daisy?"
Syn: **link-sausage [queen].**
daisy chain (early '50s, *fr* an analogy with a woven chain of daisies) an orgy of men; men linked anus-to-penis, anus-to-penis simultaneously.
Syn: **chain gang; floral arrangement; ring around the rosey.**
Related terms:
fugitive from a chain gang ('40s) one of the links in a daisy chain.
lamma hutching an orgy where everybody has his mouth full.
daisy ring a small gathering of homosexuals in a public park for nothing more important than chatter; an unlinked ***daisy chain.**
Syn: **bouquet [of pansies]** (*rare,* '40s)**; *butterfly ring.**
dally (*adj, fr* sl *dilly-dally*) hospitable, kind. lovable.
dalmation queen (*fr* dalmation dog = the mascot of the firehouse) any fireman "I must be growing up . . . I've become a dalmation queen."
damaged goods (*n* & *adj, fr* hobo sl, early '50s) former virgin.

dance to strut, to swagger, to stroll in a carefree manner "Dance up to that stud an' ask him if he has the time." **Too much dancing** is said of too many people cruising in a park.

dancer's belt (*fr* entertainment sl) jock-strap worn by a male dancer to protect his genitals. The same gismo is used by a ***drag queen** who wishes to hide his penile bulge when masquerading as a woman.
   Syn: **gaff** (?*fr* gaff = pole supporting a fore-and-aft sail).

dancey [*var:* **doncey**] (*kwn* LV, black gay sl, mid '60s, *fr* danceable) wonderful, splendid.

dangle queen 1. gay exhibitionist "Johnny was a dangle queen; he used to get busted for showing his schwantz to little old ladies in the vestibule." Syn: **dangler** ("A dangler without jewels is like a night without stars") **2.** man who wears tight trousers in order to show off his crotch contours **3.** (*kwn* SF, '72) homosexual who wears long, dangling earrings.

dangles long-hanging earrings.

Danny Debonaire proper name for a smooth-talking ***hustler.**

darling (*fr* OE *deorling // deore* = dear) **1.** sweet, treasured "Fire Island was just *too* darling, Lovey" **2.** form of address, may be friendly or elaborately malicious "Howevah have you been, darling?" but also "Discounted by servicemen, darling?"

darling Daisy Dumpling (*kwn* SF, '70) the epitome of middle-class femininity; legally wedded wife "I do hope he doesn't bring his darling Daisy Dumpling with him, or we'll have to admire the pink booties she's been knitting for the last two years."

dash (?*fr* "dashing" or sl *dash* = a tiny bit) **1.** latent homosexual **2.** willing to give homosexuality a try "On the exterior he looks happily married, but he's dash around the edges."

daughter (*kwn* LV, les sl, late '60s) homosexual adopted by a lesbian clique.

days (var: **DAZ,** dē'-ā-zē') (*exclam*) affirmative, translated to mean you said it! "He's so pretty." "Days!"

dazzle dust 1. face powder **2.** (*camp*) flour.

dazzle the audience to startle nonhomosexuals; to wreck people by exhibiting exaggerated homosexuality.

dear (dēr or dē'-ä) same as ***darling** in all senses "Having a wonderful time, dear; glad you're not here!"

dearest superlative of ***dear** "Oh, dearest, how lovely for us that you could bring your father."

dearie low, common, coarse; not dear "Why, dearie, is yer lip bleedin' or is that last night's lipstick leftover?"

debut (*fr* Fr = beginning, coming out) first crack at homosexual behavior "Oh, don't tell me that that nelly thing hasn't made her debut yet?"

debutante one becoming familiar with his homosexuality "Watch your vulgar tongue—that's a debutante, strictly virgin in the ears."

deckers (*dated*, late '60s, *fr* deck pants) pair of white clamdiggers, longer than knickers, and often tapered to emphasize the crotch.

de dulce (dā-dōōl'-sā, Mex hetero sl) homosexual "No es de dulce" = he's not queer; comparable to colloq *sweetie* = someone sweet.

deep (*kwn* SF, '70) crowded "It's pretty deep in that bar; let's wait until some people leave."
   Syn: **mussy.**

degenerate (*pej*) **1.** (hetero sl) a ***queer,** since he does not procreate **2.** homosexual lacking the respect of his peers "That degenerate comes from the wrong side of the Nile" **3.** contemptuous word for any person who is erotically aroused by perverted sex acts—the eating of feces, necrophilia, bathing in urine, *etc*

"That degenerate will put us *all* back ten thousand years with her foul deeds at Butt's Crematorium."

degenerate bar affectionate term for a gay bar where *anything* goes "There's this one degenerate bar on Miracle Mile with cock-sucking in back and ID checking in front."

delicious delectable, tantalizing, desirable "Doesn't that one have a simply delicious smile?"
   Syn: **delish** ("Your capris are just *too* delish!").

deliver a baby (*kwn* LA, early '60s) to remove the pants and expose a hard-on.
   Syn: **take the meat out** [of the basket].

Denise gay nickname for Dennis or Dana "Don't bovver Denise, she's busy reading—the walls."

depress-o (*kwn* LV, late '60s) despondent, feeling low, dejected "Don't feel depress-o—you're not worth it!"

desparate hours 1. the '50s decade **2.** closing time at your local gay bar, see *panic.
   Related term:
   desperation number one still around at this time.

destroy somebody to appall, horrify; to get the best of an opponent through startling, unexpected means "You really destroyed him, Rose, when you told him point blank that you were queer."
   Syn: **destroy somebody's mind.**

dethroned forced to leave, usually by police order, a public toilet one has been *cruising "Lilly Law *finally* dethroned that tired old faggot—now *I* can occupy the empress bench."

develop one's talent to work at becoming adept at a specific erotic craft, such as cocksucking "He started developing his talent when some stud told him he didn't know how to give good head."

dew oily sweat secreted from the anus "Rhapsody in dew!"
   Syn: *bean juice; soup.

DG (dē'-jē, *kwn* LV & SF, '70) degenerate "Only somebody as DG as you could find that funny."
   Syn: **deegy.**

diamonds 1. (*camp*) paste jewelry, sequins, rhinestones **2.** (*camp*) metal studs found upon leather jackets.

dick see *cock.

dicky bird 1. phallic charm of winged genitals, usually worn about the neck. Syn: **flying angel 2.** a fool, idiot child, "dodo".

diddle see *jack off.

did I say that (*kwn* SF, '71) said after saying something bitchy.

dig (*fr* black sl, ? // Ir *tuigim* [tig'-um] = I understand) **1.** to be fond, to like, to enjoy, to take pleasure in **2.** to look, to see "Dig that fine-lookin' dude comin' out of th' Tool Box" **3.** to comprehend, to perceive, to interpret correctly "Did you dig what that guy said?"
   Related term:
   dig somebody fat righteously (*kwn* LV, late '60s) to love somebody.

dike see *dyke.

Dilbert Dildo (*fr* Army sl *Dilbert* = one having the brains of a dill pickle) a prick, a sap "Why, it's Dilbert Dildo and his Darling Daisy Dimple—*again!*"
   Syn: **herkle;** **prune** (= a stooge); **Ricky Recruit** (*fr* Army sl).

dildo (*fr* sl *diddle* = both to masturbate or copulate and pass the time idly and leisurely) artificial cock-like implement of plastic, hard rubber, *etc.* Used by women to masturbate and by queens anally for many purposes "Ques: 'Why is this dyke's suitcase so heavy?' Ans: 'It must be her dildo collection.' "
   Syn: **dill doll; dingus** (*fr* Ger *ding* = thing); **johnson bar** ("I knew this one lez who would strap a johnson bar to her head—

like if it was some sorta hat—every time she took the garbage out to the can"); **potato finger** (*rare*); **prop; training bar; woman's home companion** (*camp*, mid '60s).

Foreign syn:

France: **bientateur** (bē-ye'-tä-tōōr' = do-gooder); **consolateur** (kon'-sō-lä-tōōr' = relaxer); **godemiche** (gō-də-mēsh' = I enjoy myself).

Germany: **Phallus-Phantom** (fä'-lōōs fän'-tōōm = spectre penis). Italy: **passatiempo** (pä-sä-tē-em'-pō = pass-the-time).

Related terms:

decoy dildo worn beneath the pants by a *drag butch or a homosexual to give the appearance of a larger basket. Syn: **gay deceiver** (mid-late '60s).

double dildo two-headed dildo.

snap-on [tool] dildo strapped to the pelvis of the active lesbian as she assumes the male position for coitus.

dillpickle (*kwn* SF, '70) affectionately applied to Bob Dylan.

dilly (Brit gay sl) Picadilly Circus, a favorite cruising area of homosexuals and *hustlers (in this area called **dilly boys**).

Syn: **the circus.**

[a] dime-a-dance (les & hust sl, SF, '68, *fr* a torch song revived during '50s) male homosexual.

dindin baby talk for dinner "Sandpaper your hansies, girl: dindin's most ready."

dindins 1. food, groceries "We have to go shopping an' get next week's dindins" **2.** (*rare*) nipples "He moonlighted by making pasties for strippers' dindins."

dine in to entertain sexually at home "Too rainy to go out and cruise? Call a model and dine in tonight."

dine out opposite of *dine in, to dawdle or cruise around a park in search of sexual sustenance "Don't wait dindin for me: I'll be dining out tonight—all night."

ding (surfer sl = a chip or mar in a surfboard) hole, chip or trace of damage. Used by homosexuals who deal with antiques "I'll sell it for only twenty, since it has a slight ding in its base."

—one to be astonished "That show dinged me all the way through."

dinge queen [*black*] (*pej, fr* dingy = dirty-colored, ? // dung + -y) a black man "My Gawd, but there certainly are a lot of dinge queens in her tonight—did the bar on *their* end of town burn down?"

Syn: **African queen; begonia** (*pej,* black gay sl); **Beulah** (black gay sl); **black angel; black bitch** (*pej,* used by both black & white homosexuals); **boogaloo** (bōō'-gä-lōō, '70, *fr* ironically enough a black dance step popularized in '60: using the word confirms the bigot's maxim "They're inferior, but they sure got rhythm"); **boong moll** (*dated fr* Aus sl *boong* = aborigine); **brown Betty** (mid '60s); **buck** (= black man as sex object; stud); **chocolate bunny; Clareen Coon** (*kwn* SF, black gay sl, late '60s: "What's up, Clareen Coon, besides the usual twelve inches?"); **dark meat** ("Even though it ain't Thanksgiving, I prefer dark meat to white"); **ditsoon** (dit-sōōn', *kwn* Chi, late '50s: usually used in the pl); *effeminative; **Georgia peach; Gertrude Brown** (*kwn* NYC, black gay sl, late '60s: often used to address oneself as when looking into the mirror and commenting "Why, Gertrude Brown, you look good enough to eat!"); **jungle meat; kabuki** (*kwn* NYC, late '60s); **Lena** (black gay sl, vocative for a black Afrodite: "Lena, your wig's so dirty that there's little things walkin' 'roun' up there with picket signs"); **Lu** (black gay sl, vocative formed *fr* Luther, common black name: "Forget him, Lu; love is just a forty-dollar word to that one"); **[Miss] Mabel** ("Who callin' the kettle black, Miss Mabel?"); **Moor** (*cf* colloq

Ger *Mohr* = Moor; also meaning Negro: "I'm dreaming of a dusky Moor sweeping me off my feet and onto his Cadillac); **mulengian** (mōō-len-jän', *pej, kwn* Midwest, late '60s-71, *fr* Sicilian // It *melanzana* = eggplant: "A couple of mulengians made me donate my brand-new watch"); **Nigerian; Nubian** (reflecting the bygone slave days of ancient Egypt and imperial Rome: "Class is when you're carried into the shitter with two big beautiful Nubians on either side"); **Osceola** (see *aussie-ola); **princess of the Nile [river]; rughead** (*pej*, mid '60s); **schwartze** (shvärt'-sə, *pej, fr* Yid *schwartz* // Ger = black; unquestionably derogatory since the word carries the connotation of an unskilled darkie shuffling about the kitchen); **Shadrack; Sheba; skillet queen** (*kwn* SF, black gay sl: black man freshly arrived from Dixie); **smoked meat** (*kwn* Canada); **snowflake; soul sauce; spade** (*fr* spade = one of the four suits of playing cards); **sunkist queen** ("That park's too dangerous for this sunkist queen; I shop where it's safe"); **watoo** (wä'-tōō, mid '60s, *fr* Watusi); **Zulu princess** (young, beautiful black man).

Related terms:

begonia broom (black gay sl) black domestic worker.

chuck-lover (*pej*, black gay sl, *fr* black sl *Charley* = the white man) black man who prefers white sex partners. Syn: **snow queen** (*kwn* SF, black gay sl, '71); **snow-shoveler** (prison sl); **Uncle Ben** ('71).

dinge palace bar frequented by black homosexuals.

dressed [up]] like a spade hooker decked out in some pretty fancy duds; dressed fit to thrill and kill.

graham cracker (black gay sl, '72) crumbling Uncle Tom.

Leroy (*camp*) a black *hustler.

paleface (*dated*, black gay sl) generic for white homosexuals. Syn: **Uncle Ben's converted white rice** (= white lover).

smoked ham (black gay sl) black public figure, especially in entertainment.

spadena (spā-dē'-nä, *fr* sl *spade* = black + feminine suffix -*ena*) a black lady, particularly if lovely.

dinge queen [*white*] white homosexual who prefers black men· sexually. White gays will sometimes state that dinge queen is not meant to be derisive, but black homosexuals reinforce the term with a stinging double entendre such as: "Why do I hang aroun' wif only my black sistuhs? Why, Sugah, you *know* I'm a *dinge* queen at heart!"

Syn: **Beulah-lover** (black gay sl); **chocolate lover** (late '50s); **coal burner** (prison sl); **midnight queen** (*kwn* Midwest, hustler sl, late '60s: "You'll never get him—he's a midnight queen an' you're not even near seven-thirty"); **negrera** (nä-grä'-rä *pej fr* Pach // Sp *negro* = black + feminine suffix -*era*); **Sheena** (*fr* dated comic book character Sheena, Queen of the Jungle).

dinge-rim queen (*pej, kwn* Southwest, mid '60s) **1.** any white who inserts his tongue into the ass of a black. Used as a bigot term for the loss of caste **2.** white who brown-noses blacks; one who is subservient (in the eyes of other whites) to a black person. **Dinge-rim queen** = nigger-lover "Why did you break my locket? You faggot! You ugly cocksucker! You . . . you dingerim queen!"

dingy (din'-ji, *adj*) **1.** Negroid "Why don't you do your hair dingy—you know, with those cute little pickaninny top curls?" **2.** feeling horny enough for a black man, said of whites who are not usually erotically inclined towards blacks "I have *nothing* against the boy cruising me—I just don't feel very dingy tonight" **3.** (*rare, pej*) coarse, unrefined "Belching again? Honestly, your manners are just too dingy!"

Syn: **boogaloo; dinge** ("You'll go there despite its being a tish dinge? Why Louella, how absolutely *big*ot of you!"); **gamey; nubian** ("The bride wore porcelain on the nubian side of town"); **schwartze** (*rare, fr* Yid: "That jacket is so schwartze . . . don't you have anything else to wear"); **spade** ("It's easier to dance to spade music"); **sunkist.**

dink see *small meat.

dinky 1. the cock when shriveled up by the cold **2.** having an unnaturally small cock "He's so dinky you have to be careful not to bite it off by mistake."

diplomat queen 1. tactful homosexual who keeps the peace among quarrelsome acquaintances **2.** one who charms lovers into bed; a soft-soaper, a flatterer **3.** (*rare*) homosexual in politics "That black tie makes you come on like a diplomat queen."

dirt 1. gossip; the low-down "Give me all the dirt on Walter's latest fiasco. Syn: **blunt dirt 2.** generic term for those who cause homosexuals trouble. Two examples are the rip-off hustlers and pack-traveling bands of straight youths out to get the "queers" "That hunky dirt took my clock radio last night while I was taking a leak" "It's good that they check IDs: keeps the dirt out of the gay bars." Syn: **beats** ("Cross the street; this looks like beats coming"); ***faggot beaters; filth; fish** (*obs,* early '60s, *fr* young hoods' leather jackets looking like shiny fish scales); **grief** (heterosexual Torquemadas adding more faggots to the blaze); **trouble** ("There's been a lot of trouble at the beach lately"); **TP** (*kwn* LV, mid '60s: = teenage punk[s]).
Related term:

gay dirt admitted homosexual who robs or betrays fellow homosexuals.

dirty (durt'-ē or durt'-rā) lewd, vulgar, pornographic "Your mind needs changing—it's dirty!"
Syn: **piggie** ("Did things get piggie after ten?"); **smutty; trashy** ("Oh, you're such a trashy thing—I *love* it!"); **wanton** (*camp*).

dirty old man [DOM] 1. one who leches after bodies years younger than himself "He might be only twenty-nine, but he's still a dirty old man:" **2.** *auntie who chases prospective partners away from each other by his presence "DOMs should know better than to come to the tubs and fuck it up for the rest of us." **3.** (les sl) any heterosexual man, but especially one who keeps trying to bed down with a lesbian.
Syn: **soiled senior citizen.**

dirty pee on one (*kwn* LV, mid '60s) to get the best of; to have the last laugh "She really dirty pee'd on you! Maybe now you'll think before you tear into anybody."

dirty sex 1. low-down and *good* "I'm in the mood for dirty sex; let's split to that new grope bar." **2.** referring to one who looks to be exciting in bed: virile, potent and game enough for all hell to break loose "Ooh, how I love that man! He's dirty sex: I can tell just by smellin' his sweat when he eats."

dirty thing 1. naughty, impure, unchaste, but affectionately "Dirty thing, you knew how cruisey this john was *all* along, but you never let on. You never told *me* about it too." **2.** unclean genitals when clowning around and feigning ignorance "You want *me* to put that *dirty* thing in my *mouth?*" **3.** any woman who poses a threat "What's she doing in here? Can't the dirty thing get enough cock from straight bars?"

discover gender to understand and finally accept one's own sexual desires "Wait till that rock star looks down some morning an' sees that fine pussy of his: then he'll discover gender."

disdig (hip sl, SF, late '60s) to dislike, but apologetically "I don't disdig it even if I said I didn't care for it that much."

dish 1. (*fr* sl *dish it out* = admonish) "We're just dishing about the new drag Lillian Law slipped into". Syn: **dish the dirt [to one]** **2.** to insult, to slander, to be overly critical; to attack verbally, to put down "In add-dishing to that, I have this to say." "Never dish another queen or she'll dish you right back—and she may· be better at it than you." **3.** sexually attractive man "What a dish! I'd love to be his jockey shorts on Friday night."

—**one 1.** to relate the entire incident to someone "Why don't you stop on by and dish me what you did in the park" **2.** to get in a dig; to speak evilly of another "The movie critics dished the film for days; it should be really good."

—**y** (?*fr* sl *vishy* = vicious) critical, and verbally able to express it "Being dishy and bitchy goes hand in mouth."

—**queen** a critic who runs others down ruthlessly "That Ericka is such a dishy queen. That's probably why so many fags chum around with him; they're out to pick up a few hints on viciousness."

divine (*adj*) used to make a point more emphatic, but done to death by women and effeminates "Isn't that man just too divine?"

dizzy ('30s) **1.** foolish, silly, *meshuga* **2.** scatter-brained, ridiculously indecisive, usually heard in affectionate motherly context "You'll never score in this bar if you continue being so dizzy! Stop grabbing with your sisters all the time!" Syn: **cracky** ('72, *fr* crackpot); **dingie** (ding'-ē); **silly; twinky.**

—**lizzy** (*camp*) slow-thinking, dim-witted lesbian.

—**queen 1.** one who lacks common sense, especially on how to behave in public "I wonder if that dizzy queen could talk that fast with a dick up his mouth." **2.** a dimwit; nincompoop "Girl, you are the dizziest queen I've ever had the misfortune of meeting." Syn: **diz** ("What's takin' that diz so long? Is he dabbing A-200 behind his ears?"); **dingle faggot** (early '60s); **Dora [Dim, Dumdum]** ("And who do you think got a double page spread? Dora Dumdum, of course!"); **Doreen; Dumb-o [The Flying Asshole]; Ma Bell** ('71, *fr* sl *dingdong* = a nut); **Myrna** (*pej*); **sil** (short for silly); **twink** (*rare*); **twit** ("That twit's brain must be the size of a pea's piles").

Also see ***Dilbert Dildo.**

do see ***blow.**

doe eyes large and expressive eyes, especially if accented with makeup.

does it wink inquiry about an uncircumcised cock "Remember that humpy number you met at the Varsity? Well, tell me, does it wink?"

dog fashion[style] see ***fuck.**

doggy-do 1. dog droppings on the street "Shit, Madge, it's doggy-do!" **2.** bad-tasting food "I can't eat this doggy-do. Call the waiter and tell him to sweep it away!"

dog water urine.

do it any particular style of sexual activity "She doesn't do it that way, Sam."

doll a person whose appearance excites the onlooker "How can you keep your hands off all those dolls you live with, Richard?" Syn: **muñeco** (mōōn-yā′-kō, Mex gay sl *fr* Sp *muñeca* = doll).

doll racket (Ill women's prison sl, '60s) female homosexuality within prison. Syn: **chick[girl] business.**

doll-tits (black gay sl, '60s) **1.** euphemisim for the absence of large breasts **2.** vocative for a friend or another homosexual "Gimme a beer, will ya, doll-tits?"

dolly 1. penis, see ***cock 2.** attractive, popular; having a magnetic personality "One side of the beach is filled with nothing but dolly studs." Syn: **dolly-looking 3.** referring to oneself "Is that ciggie-poo-poo for Dolly?"

dolly domestic homosexual *hausfrau;* a homebody "You've become a regular dolly domestic since you and Seymour started living together. And you used to be such a campy thing."

dolly pals male lovers.
    Syn: **chuff chums** (*dated*)

do me a favor (*interj,* Brit gay sl, '60s) keep quiet!

dong see ***cock.**

Donna (*camp*) Don "What was that book you were reading Donna, Gullible's Travels?"

don't be so naive (*exclam*) retort to one who claims never to have heard of such a thing "Ques: 'Is it true that Tom's peddling his ass?' Ans: 'Of course it's true. Don't be so naive!'"

don't spare the boy child (*exclam*) an exhortation of encouragement or to be generous "Fuck me hard an' fast, Daddy, an' don't spare the boy child neither!"

doodoo (*fr* baby talk) to shit "I gotta go doodoo."

do one some dirt 1. bring another grief through gossip or lies "He's never going back to that bitch. Did you hear about the dirt she did him?" **2.** tell some juicy morsel of news "Do me some dirt, girl!"

doorbell trade (*kwn* SF, '70) having a regular stream of sexual visitors "He doesn't have to go out on the streets to cruise for numbers: his doorbell trade is so strong, there's always somebody in the sack with him."

doorbell trick [DBT] (*kwn* Boston, '60s) an ex-***trick** who returns but is not welcome.

Dora (Cape Town gay sl) wine "All we want to do is dora time" = to get drunk.

Dorian (*fr* L *dorius //* Gr *Doris,* a region in Greece) homosexual, used as medical euphemism, and preferred to labels like "faggot" *etc.*

Dorian Gray (*fr* Oscar Wilde's *The Portrait of Dorian Gray*) one fearful of old age.

dorian grays (*rare*) acne.

Doris [Day] 1. nickname of an imitator or admirer of Doris Day **2.** name for one who aspires to be the girl next door.

dorky absurd, peculiar, strange.

Dorothy (*rare*) vocative used before a lecture, comparable to the "Buster" of an irritated New York cab driver.

Dorothy and Toto 1. gay boy and his dog **2.** dominating effeminate homosexual man with his paid-for escort **3.** extended to any male couple whose effeminate partner is in command "When's Dorothy and Toto getting here with the chest of drawers?"

do-sei-ai (dō'-sā-ī' *// kwn* SF, *fr* Jap = same sex love) homosexuality, heavily used by non-Japanese.

do social work (*kwn* SF, '70) to date a member of another race; to strive to be instantly *hip* by showing one's broad-mindedness

dos tortillas (dōs-tōr-tē'-yäs, *kwn* S Calif, '60s, *fr* Mex = two pancakes) gay couple.

do the thing be an active homosexual "Doug Crudley doesn't do the thing, but yet he's no prude."

Dottie vocative used for euphony "Damn it, Dottie! I've misplaced my beaded handbag again."

double-barreled broad real female woman.

double-barreled ghee (gē') homosexual.

double entry 1. kissing two people simultaneously **2.** see ***fuck.**

double-time hurry one's pace "Let's double-time, Mary. I want to get a better look at that doll ahead" and also in "Double-time, girl, there's grief close behind!"

douche 1. to take an enema before and/or after sex "Oh, go

douche out your pussy: get rid of those old loads before they remember Mama!" **2.** bathe or shower "Everybody was so clean . . . they must have all super douched."
—**in** to skid to a stop, to slide, to slip.
—**out one's mouth 1.** to wash out a mouth with soap, a jocular threat "If you don't stop that swearing, we're gonna have t'douche out your mouth" **2.** more conventional forms of oral hygiene "Ugh! your mouth is really icky. Why don't you go douche it out?"
—**powder** bathroom cleanser.

doul (do͞ol, fr Gr doulos = slave; cf misspelling of doll) exceedingly young gay boy.

dowager any affluent elderly homosexual, but extended to apply to any gay man who has retired; not an unkind word, but **dirty dowager** most assuredly is.

downer (black, hip, narc sl, '60s-72) any form of barbituate or tranquilizer, especially in pill form "Mixing booze and downers killed that dizzy faggot."

down payment (hustler sl) money given to a *hustler for standing still while his wares are being sampled.

downstairs (kwn SF, '60s) the beach at Land's End; the crowded upper parking lots are **upstairs.**

do you have the time ice-breaking question used when cruising, usually meaning "Do you have the time to have sex with me?" Other ice-breakers include "Do you have a match?" and "Funny, but you look familiar."

do you mind (imp) a rude pardon me "Do you mind? After all, he's my friend, or should I say was?"

draft ('50s) to force young boys into performing homosexual acts. The bully (usually a straight young tough) is a **drafter**, and the victim of **draft age** is the **draftee.**

drag (fr 19th cent Brit theatrical sl = petticoats worn by male actors playing female roles) **1.** clothing of opposite sex **2.** (camp) any robe or uniform worn as a costume "Pope Joan just hated leaving all that drag behind after she was exposed as a woman." **3.** (camp) clothing in general "You're in different drag today. What happened? did your tanktop finally sink?" Syn: **drag clothes; drags** (Haw); **hems** (fr pros sl, '20s); **velvets** ('20s).
   Most of the following terms apply equally well to men and women:
—**bag** tote-bag containing beachwear; overnight case.
—**ball 1.** a pageant where men wear their best evening gowns **2.** social affair attended by men in dresses and, to a lesser degree, by women dressed as men. Syn: **costume party; grand ball; pansy ball** (pej, hetero sl, '20s).
—**body** underpadding worn by a man to give the illusion of a more feminine shape. Syn: **props**
—**butch** woman masquerading as a man. Syn: **drag king; dragster; mack-truck; masquerader** (les sl); **MI** (= male impersonator, usu an MC for a *drag show).
—**eyes** large, expressive eyes, especially if they give the appearance of being made up. Syn: **cow eyes; *doe eyes** ("Don't let these doe eyes fool you; I'd rather fuck than swish.")
—**face** man dressed, oddly enough, as a man but whose face has been made up like a woman's "Hand me the eyebrow pencil, will ya, sis? I want to put on a drag face for the audience at Times Square."
—**hair 1.** woman's wig worn by a man **2.** wiglet used to build up a transvestite's coiffure. Syn: **frosting** ('50s); **hair** ("Hair is to the drag queen what the angel is to the Christmas

tree"); **piece** (black gay sl, early '60s, *fr* hairpiece); **switch** (mid '60s, *fr* Victorian use of *switch* = false hairpiece).

—**hustler** (late '60s) male homosexual who dresses and solicits like a female whore. These prostitutes perform fellatio only, since anything more would reveal their deception.

—**lips 1.** a man's lips heavily coated with lipstick **2.** woman who doesn't apply lipstick correctly. Syn: **Joan Crawford ate here.**

—**mags** (late '60s), magazines devoted to transvestites and their problems, sometimes sensationally depicted. Syn: **drag confessions.**

—**mustache 1.** false moustache "One scene in *Sunset Boulevard* shows Gloria Swanson wearing a drag moustache and aping Charlie Chaplin" **2.** (*camp*) the moustache of an effeminate boy "Do you feel that drag moustache on your lip makes your cock any bigger, Queen?"

—**picture 1.** a photograph of one in *drag **2.** (*camp, kwn* LV, late '60s) snapshot of a soldier relative, proudly displayed.

—**queen [DQ] 1.** man who dresses as a woman "To a drag queen, it's 'how many more shopping days till Halloween'" **2.** (*pej*) a female impersonator **3.** (*kwn* LV, hairdresser sl, '60s) a vulgarly overdressed woman "By the time *that* cheap bitch left my shop, I had her looking like a real drag queen." Syn: **drag darling** (*pej, kwn* hetero sl, SF, late '60s): **drag fag** (*pej*); **madame joy** (*kwn* SF, '71); **mad masquerader** ("That mad masquerader looks pretty authentic on stage, but will she hold up under closeups?"); **mahu-holoku** (mă'-hōō-hō-lō'-kōō, Haw *mahu + *holoku* = dress); **queen of the gown** (late '60s); **rapid transit.**

—**race** (early '60s) clearance sale on dresses.

—**show** nightclub act featuring men dressed as women.

—**store** a department store patronized by smart women shoppers.

Related terms:

debutante one who gets up in drag for the first time.

go in drag to go dressed as a woman. Syn: **drag up** (Brit sl); **dress up** (mid '60s); **halloween** (*kwn* LV early '60s: "Miss Thang got her giddy ass thrown into the pokey for Halloweenin' in the casinos"); **hem it** (pros sl, '20s); ***masquerade.**

pass off (*fr* black sl) to look so much like the opposite sex when in drag, that even the experts are fooled.

zip wax hair remover, depilatory. Syn: **wax** "Can I fruit some wax from you? Tomorrow night's my big debut in drag."

Types of Drag:

casual drag a frowsy housedress.

comic drag exaggerated dress to provoke laughter.

full[heavy, high]-drag woman's complete outfit worn by a man: everything from sables to nuts "My mama done tol' me/When I was in high drag . . . "

lazy[low]-drag just wearing a few pieces of women's clothing; just a sweater on, a pair of shoes, eye makeup, *etc.* Ant: **full drag.**

legal drag 1. man who wears a dress when masquerading is permitted by law (Halloween, Mardi Gras, *etc*) "I'm a legal drag until midnight—then I change back into a Marine". **2.** (*kwn* LV, mid '60s) real woman "She's a legal drag, not some two-bit washed-up star with tinsel tits like you!"

drain the lizard to urinate, said of men.

draped uncircumcised.

draped shape clothed body.

draw drapes uncircumcised cock whose foreskin may be pulled back "The first thing you should do for your spring cleaning is get rid of those draw drapes: they're chokin' up the atmosphere."

dream[**-boat, -boy, -lover**] attractive man. Ironically: "You're a dream—that's polite for nightmare!"

Syn: **wet dream** ("He's my favorite wet dream—even with his clothes off.")

dream whip (*fr* the dessert topping, '70) **1.** nocturnal emission **2.** semen

Dresden china false teeth "It's really campy the way he keeps losing his Dresden china in the soup."

Syn: **diner's card** ("He needs some form of identification? Show him your diner's cards"); **typewriters** (especially when they clatter).

dried fish sterile seed.

drip queen one who emits precoital fluid.

drop a dime on someone inform.

drop a pearl (*fr* Jean Genet's *Our Lady of the Flowers*) to break wind, fart.

drop a whole string of pearls fart rapidly and in succession "She's such a mess! She thinks nothing of dropping a whole string of pearls in a crowded movie theater."

drop five[**four,** *etc*] **at the tubs** (*fr* gambling *sl*) to spend the price of admission to the Turkish baths "It's a gamble for me to spend the money for the tubs; I don't think I can afford to drop five tonight."

drop hairpins[**beads, pearls**] leave broad hints about one's homosexuality "You must really have wanted him to know: you certainly dropped enough hairpins."

drop one's petals (*obs, fr* pedalpushers and a pun on *sl flower* = gay boy) lowering one's pants, leaving the ass bare for sex in a vertical position "Back up to the glory hole an' drop your petals so he can give you a good browning."

drop your camera (*imp*) focus attention below "Yes he has pretty hair, but drop your camera: there's where the excitement is!"

drove up sexually excited, "hot to trot."

drown one to ejaculate so much ***come** the cocksucker chokes and splutters.

dry charge keep in reserve for a later appointment "He's making it with Cliff now, but he sure has some cute ivy-pie in dry charge."

dry date 1. a platonic date "Yeah I went out with him once, but I still don't know if he digs goin' down. He was a dry date" **2.** any nonerotic appointment "You have a dry date today, Queen: with the dentist" **3.** sexy photographs "If she doesn't get any ***cock** in the park, she'll pound her pud at home over a dry date."

dry hump see ***fuck.**

dry rub wrestling with strong erotic undercurrents "When I used to rub with my brother, we both got the strangest feelings!"

dry run 1. dancing or some other close contact, with thighs rubbing together **2.** fucking without ejaculating.

duchess (*pej*) one who falsely assumes grand airs, see ***piss elegant faggot.**

duck to be the passive partner.

ducky vocative often directed at one being put down "Listen, ducky; the only cotton I'm pickin' is jockey shorts."

Syn: **ducks** (Brit).

dude (black, hip, les *sl*) any man.

dugout jaded, saturated with experience "The trouble with dugouts is that they come on hipper-than-thou."

dump to injure or hurt, usually physically "We found her in the alley, and man, had she been dumped!"

dumper sadist.
dung palace 1. outdoor toilets for construction workers and in picnic areas **2.** untidy living quarters "The only way to clean up this dung palace is to toss a match into the middle of it."
Syn: **donniker** (carney sl).
dunk to charge something; to use credit cards.
dyke (*fr -dite* in hermaphrodite) **1.** the mannish, swaggering, cigar-puffing lesbian **2.** (*pej*) any gay woman "You'd turn queer too, if your mother was a dyke."
Syn: **amy-john** (*kwn* Calif, late '50s, *fr* Amazon); **Apache** (*obs*, '30s *fr* pros sl); **brother-girl** (Jap *fr* Eng); ***bull dyke; big diesel** [dyke]; **cat** (*kwn* Calif, pros sl, '30s-'40s, *fr* black sl *cat* = a man); **collar-and-tie** ('40s); **dagger** (*cf* sl *dagger* = cock); **dandysette** (*rare,* hetero sl, '40s: "That dandysette was sure embarrassed—she even swallowed her golf ball"); **derrick** (*kwn* LA, les sl, early-mid '60s: lesbian with a masculine face); **diesel** [dyke] ("You butch? Don't make me laugh—a diesel has more hair on her chest than you do"); **dike** ("Man, is she heated up—she's a leaky dike."); **Dutch girl** (play on words relating dike with the dikes of Holland); **fellow** (*camp,* "You better worry about one of the fellas stealin' away your old man if that falsetto is real"); **gal-officer** (*dated*); **girl kisser** ("So the girl kisser is writing about her sex life . . . what's she doing—a punch line?"); **goudou** (gōō-dōō', *fr* Fr argot); **gougnotte** (gōōn-yōt', *fr* Fr argot); **grousse** (grōōs, *fr* Fr argot); **he-she** (*obs*); **horsewoman** ("You must have been a horsewoman in your last life 'cause you're sure a nag now"); **jasper** (*kwn* NYC, late '60s: "Go ask the precious jasper in the bermudas what time it is"); **jota** (kho'-ta, Mex); **king**[stud] (les sl = lesbian potentate); **lady-lover** ("Mirror, mirror, omit the clutter—who's the baddest lady-lover?"); **lasser** (*rare, fr* dial *lass* = girl + suffix -*er*); **lesbo** (*pej*), hetero sl, *fr* lesbian: "It looks like the Les Bo' Game!"); **major** (hetero sl, '40s, *fr* Phys. Ed. major = woman excelling in sports); **mal-flor** (mal-flor', *fr* Pach // Sp *marimacho* = tomboy; but *cf* Sp *mal* = bad [masculine] + *flor* = flower [feminine], a linguistic castration of the lesbian just in case she should have balls?); **manflora** (man-flo'-ra, *fr* Pach: "Que bato tan manflora!" = "what a tomboyish fellow!"); **manny** ("What say, manny; how's the broads been treatin it?"); **mantee** ('40s); **marimacho** (mä-rē-mä'-chō, Sp *fr* Maria = Mary + *macho* = masculine; insensitive title for a tomboy); **mason** (*dated,* hetero sl, '40s, because she lays bricks = homely gals); **no-nuts** (*camp, kwn* LV, '70: "What'll it be tonight, No-nuts, the usual Scotch on the rocks?"); **pansy without a stem** (*camp,* mid '60s); **pantalonuda** (pan-ta-lo-nōō'-thə, *fr* Pach *pantas* = pants // Sp *pantalones* = pants: a pants'-wearing tomboy); **penis-envy queen** (*camp*); **polone-homi** (pō-lō'-nē-hō'-mē, Brit gay sl *fr* Parlyaree // It *pollone* = sprout or // Sp *pollo* = chicken; *cf* sl *pullet* = young lassie & It *uomo* = man); **poppa** (les sl); **pot** (= cooking pot: there exists a gay Du expression, which translates into English as "there is a lid for every pot!" Figure that out!); **queer bird** (*pej* hetero sl *fr* sl *queer* = homosexual + *bird* = woman); **queer queen** (*camp,* mid '60s: "No, no Larry, you misunderstood—not 'dear' queen, as in Ted—'queer' queen, as in Alice"); **Sapphist** (*fr* Sappho, Greek poetess and lover of women); **she-male** (hetero sl); **she-man** (hetero sl); **shesexual** ("That shesexual has a gut as large as the Ponderosa Spread"); **shim** (*dated,* '40s): blending of the two pronouns she + him); **slacks** (*obs,* les sl, '40s); **Tom** (les sl); **top sergeant** (late '50s: "We call her the top sergeant because she takes command of the girls' privates"); **tortillera** (tor-tē-yä'-rä, Mex = tortilla maker); **truck dyke** (les sl); **vegetable**

(*camp:* because they're not known as fruits); **vot** (*kwn* Calif women's prison sl, *fr -vert* in pervert: "What happened to the vot's twelve-inch chest expansion?"); **vrille** (vrēl, *fr* Fr argot form of *vrille* = manly, virile; but *cf* Fr *vrille* = gimlet or vineyard tendril); **wolf** (= **vot**); **woman-lover** (hetero sl: "Yeah, dey's a couple o' dem wimmen-luvvers alivin' over dere in de canyon.")

—city 1. relating to female homosexuality "That bar is strictly dyke-city during the weekend" Syn: **dykesville** (Let's split, this place is too dykesville for your mother") **2.** (*camp*) rugged, salty. Levis are usually spoken of as being dyke-city when faded in just the right places.

—daddy 1. a straight man who credits himself with being messianic—chosen to possess *the* cock with which to save misled lesbians **2.** lecherous man who pesters women in gay bars. Syn: **dyker; john; malecher** (*kwn* LV, les sl, mid '60s, *fr* male = lecher); **square john** (this one, however, doesn't want to make it with a dyke, he just wants to bar-hop with them.)

—queen 1. homosexual who associates primarily with lesbians **2.** (*camp*) straight man who digs licking vulvas.

—queer (*kwn* LV, mid '60s) homosexual who imagines his partners as lesbians "I made it with a dyke queer in August; he wouldn't shoot until I told him that I'd take hormone shots in his honor."

—s a lot! (*camp*) expression of gratitude.

—ing (*camp*) **1.** tribadism, see ***daddle 2.** used of two homosexuals who rub against each other's oiled body, also **dyking it.**
Related terms:

dicky broad (les sl) aggressive lesbian who possesses a clitoris the size of a small, relaxed penis. Syn: **stallion- [stud-] broad.**

dove (*kwn* NYC, les sl, late '60s, ?*fr* sl *bird* or past tense of ***dive**) the aging lesbian. Syn: **grandpa** (*kwn* Ill, les sl); **old tom.**

dragon female with masculine qualities though not necessarily gay.

dump truck (les sl, *fr* pros sl *dump* = to beat) **1.** the masculine-type lesbian who wins arguments with muscle instead of wit **2.** (*camp*) a wrestler of either sex **3.** (*camp*) an effeminate who is more growl than bite; toughey-wuffy.

homo's lesbian (*kwn* SF, les sl, '70) **1.** a tee-hee way of saying dyke **2.** lesbian who is so masculine that she is often mistaken for being a gay boy "Anybody got an extra nickel for a coffee-drinking homo's lesbian?"

mantee ('40s) *adj* found primarily in the two terms: **mantee voice** (a deep bass) and **mantee walk** (swagger).

pick-up truck (*kwn* LA & LV, mid-late '60s) lesbian who makes pickups in the street, a not too common practice. Syn: **battle cruiser; hawk** (short for the hawkeye who never misses spotting a new chick).

to be frank the aggressive partner in a lesbian encounter "Honey, I want to be frank with you tonight. . ." "No, no, I'm Frank tonight; you were Frank *last* night."

village overtones (late '50s, *fr* New York City's Greenwich Village, retreat for the avant garde) said of a woman who has strong masculine features.

wear boxer shorts (*fr* pros sl, '30s) to take the active role in a lesbian relationship.

Also see ***baby butch, *butch, *drag butch, *lesbian, *molly dyke, *muff-diver, *van dyke.**

early bird the fellator who always seems to get to the best cruising spots before anybody else. A gay proverb bitterly states: "The early bird gets *all* the worms."

Earl Stanley Gardner (*rare, kwn* SF, '70) a **park queen.**

Easter queen ('70) homosexual who ejaculates prematurely—he comes as quick as a rabbit.

Syn: **dry meat** (*kwn* LV, mid '60s).

easy make ('40s) a man easily persuaded to participate in a homosexual act "Don't let those butch shoulders throw you, he's an easy make!"

Syn: **easy mark[meat].**

eat see *blow.**

eat dick in the ear (late '60s) **1.** to act in a stupid way **2.** to be worthless "Wow, man, the alarm didn't go off! This fuck-me clock eats dick in the ear!"

eat it all out see *rim.**

eat it, lady (*exclam*) teasing or threatening command to drop dead. Often emphasized by extending the middle finger of either hand.

ecaf (Brit gay sl *fr* backward sl, new word formed by reversing an existing word's letters) the face Mary: "I think all that lifting will give me a hernia!" Betty: "It already did—your ecaf!"

eclair queen (Mid '60s) a rich homosexual.

Also see *piss elegant faggot.**

Edna (*camp*) Ed(ward) "Has Edna been pleading with you to pay her bust bills again?"

eerquay (*dated,* hetero sl euphemism *fr* pig latin '30s-'40s) homosexual "I saw him go into one of them eerquay arbays."

effeminative (ē-fem′-a-nā-tiv, *kwn* SF, '70) a black gay boy.

effie (*dated,* hetero sl, '30s, *fr* L *effeminatus* = an effeminate boy) stereotype effeminate homosexual. The straight world ignorantly equates homosexuality with feminacy and cowardice as many of the following synonyms, largely heterosexual in origin, show. Effeminate gays form a small group within the homosexual community, frequently the most colorful and most noticed; however, they are the ones who are keeping the slanguage alive.

Syn: **Angelina** ('40s); **bender** (because he bends over); **bent-wrist; birdie** (*pej,* hetero sl, '40s: "Little birdies might be able to fly over the rainbow, but not old buzzards like you"); **birl** (*kwn* LA, hustler sl, late '50s: boy + girl); **bitch** (Brit gay sl); **bunter** (*pej,* hetero sl, '30s, *fr* Brit *bunter* = woman rag picker = a whore); **buttercup** (hetero sl, '30s); **butterfly [boy]** (hetero sl, late '50s); **camp bitch** (Brit gay sl); **chirujo** (chē-rōō′-khō, *pej,* Mex hetero sl: "Hey, chirujo, I wanna take a picture of you . . . bend over and smile!"); **cissy** (variant spelling of *sissy); **cooch** ("I've got news for you, Cooch, men aren't after *your* saggers—they're after your husband's");

cookie (*pej*, hetero sl: "Yeah, some cookie asked me if he could suck my dick"); **cot betty** (Brit); **cow** (*dated* since early '50s); ***cupcake; daffodil[ly]** (hetero sl); **dainties** (hetero sl: male homosexuals collectively portrayed as affected and precious); **dandy; darling** (*pej*, hetero sl: "He's a regular little darling, isn't he"); **duchess** (prison sl); **duck** (*kwn* LV, teen sl. mid '60s: taken *fr* limp-wristed afternoon TV cartoon character; also *cf* ***gay as a goose**); ***fag; *fairy; fay** (*fr* Scotch-lr // Fr *fēē* = fairy); **feigele** (fā'-gə-lə, *fr* Yid = birdie, variant spelling **fagola**: "Such a nice looking boy, Mrs. Fox's son. Too bad he's such a feigele already"); **fellow** (hetero sl); **femme** (late '50s-early '60s, *fr* Fr *femme* = woman); **filly** (because a filly can be *mounted*); **finocchio** (fē-nō'-kē-ō, *fr* It = fennel seed: see **Finn's** under ***place names**); **fish queen** (*dated*); **flame; flame artist[thrower]** ("I hope the flame thrower doesn't take a load off her mind here. . .we ran out of Airwick"); **flamer; flaming bitch[faggot, lady, queen]; flapping fag; flicker** (*pej*, *fr* Du); **flit** (hetero sl: "Almost all them toe-dancers is flits"); **flossy one; flower** (hetero sl: "When a flower speaks, it's like listening to a music box"); **flutterer** ('30s); **flying faggot** (*pej*); **freak[of nature]; *fruit; fruitcake** (*pej*, hetero sl: "They're both a couple of fruitcakes, if you ask me"); **fu** (fōō, *fr* Haw gay sl, mid '60s); **fuff** (*rare*, *?fr* mispronunciation of **fluff**); **gay girl** (*camp*); **giddy woman** (*camp*); ***girl** (*camp*); **glitter girl** (*camp*, late '60s: usually said of a dandy); ***hair fairy; lacy lad** (hetero sl); **laddie** (hetero sl: "That laddie has a big laddle"); **lily[white]** (*dated*, '40s: what the straight "good guy" used to call the gay "baddie"); **limpwrist** (graffito: "Christ was a limpwrist: the nails did it"); **lisper** (hetero sl, '40s: "That lisper played a mean upright organ"); **little dear** (*pej*); **loca** (lō'-kä, *pej*, Mex hetero sl = crazy girl: "The chotas took all of loca's jacks in the raid"); **maricon** (mä'-rē-kōn', *fr* Sp); **mariposa** (mä-rē-pō'-sä, Mex sl *fr* Sp = butterfly); **mavis** (Cape Town gay sl); **milksop** (hetero sl, also used to belittle a coward); **milquetoast** (hetero sl, *fr* term used for timid or apologetic person // the early cartoon character Caspar Milquetoast: "I never thought that milquetoast had it in him, but he did: he had mine in him, Tom's in him. Harry's in him. . ."); **min** (Brit gay sl); **mince [meat]** (hetero sl, '40s); **mintie** ('40s *cf* ***hint of mint** = a flavor of homosexuality); **miss boy** (*camp*); **mollycoddle** (a mama's boy); **muffie** (Haw gay sl *fr* hetero sl *mutt* = hermaphrodite: "This muffie just loves rimming yesterday's onions"); ***mujerado** (*fr* Sp); **nance; nancy boy** (Brit gay sl); ***nelly; neon-sign [carrier]** (*kwn* LA, mid '60s) **niceling** (*dated*); ***nicht** (*fr* Du); **painted willy** (*pej*, hetero sl, '40s, *fr* Willie Sutton, prim bankrobber who wore pancake before pulling a heist); **pansy** (*pej*, hetero sl, '40s-'50s: "Anyway that's how a little pansy got the goods on Goliath"); **panz** (*rare*: "Even Nero was a panz—which ain't sayin' much"); **papaout** (pä-pä-ōōt', *fr* Fr argot); **patapouf** (Brit); **pato** (pä'-tō, PR Sp, *fr* Sp = duck); **pee willy** (*pej*, hetero sl, '40s); **Percy [Perthy]** (hetero sl: "Now it's time for Percy to chop wood and lose the ballgame for us"); **petal** (*rare*, variant of *flower*); **pix** (*rare*, hetero sl reinforced by use of the slur ***fairy**: "Where'd that pix get his license—out of a Wheaties box?"); **pood** (Brit); **poof[ter]** (*pej*, Brit); **pouf** (*pej*, Brit hetero sl, *fr* Fr *pouf* = cushioned ottoman, *cf* with puff of Am sl **powder puff** = sissy); **punta** (pōōn'-tä, Mex hetero sl *fr* Sp *puta* = whore); ***queen** ("God save the queens!"); **queenie** ("Queenies are thought of as weaklings, but I've never met one who couldn't lift a bushel of rhinestones"); **quin** (*dated*, *?fr* queen + quim, the latter being hetero sl = vagina);

quince (Aus hetero sl); **red lip** (*dated:* the cosmetic-wearing effeminate); **red one** (*dated, fr* the bright color of red as a vib-
rant, eye-catching color); **screamer; screaming-bitch** [-faggot,
-fairy, -mimi, -queen] ("I had no idea that he was such a scream-
ing-mimi—and with muscles!"); **screecher** (late '60s); ***sis**[sy-]
queen; sister boy (*fr* Jap *sista-boi //* English); **Squeaking fag;
squealer** ("That squealer's been around—only eighteen and his
curlies are stone gray," not to be confused with underworld
definition of *squealing* = informing); **sugar sweet** (*kwn* NYC,
'40s); **sweet boy** (hetero sl); **sweetheart** (hetero sl); **sweetie**
(*pej,* hetero sl: "I asked some sweetie if he ever got pregnant,
and he said, 'How should I know, do I have eyes in the back
of my head?"); **sweet William** (hetero sl, '40s); ***swish**[er];
tapette (tap-et', *fr* Fr argot / Fr *tapette* = a gentle tap,
a swat); **tauatane** (tä'-wä-tä'-nä, *fr* Samoan); **tender lily** (*kwn*
NYC, '40s: a cry-baby); **tit-face; toots** (hetero sl, '40s); **torch**
(variant of *flame*); **tripper** (*kwn* San Diego, teen sl, mid
'60s); **triss** (*dated*); **tweener** (*dated,* hetero sl, '40s: one whose
sexual identity is between male and female); **twinkle-toes**
(*kwn* SF, SM sl, late '60s); **twit** (Brit hetero sl); **twixter**
(hetero sl, '40s; another between [*twixt*] the two sexes); **uffimay** (uf'-fē-mā, Haw gay sl, *fr* pig-latin rendition of *muffie:* "This uffimay like to honi-honi"); **waffle** (= man with
the stamina of a crepe suzette); **whoopsie boy** ('40s: *fr* the
flamboyant manner in which homosexuals sometimes greet
one another); **Willy** (?hetero sl, '40s); **winny** (?*fr* a horse's
whinny duplicating a falsetto); **yoo-hoo boy** ('40s, = **whoopsie
boy:** "That's not quite like hometown yoo-hoo boy 'makes
good'—it's more like rich man's kid makes better.")
egg (*kwn* SF, '70) a male child too young to be sexually developed and therefore considered neuter.
  Syn: **bibette** (*kwn* SF, late '60s-70); **peepee meat** ('40s);
yo-yo (*kwn* Midwest, late '60s).
  Related terms:
  egg-sucker (*pej*) a cradle robber; man who likes very young
  boys. Considered repugnant and poor taste to the gay majority.
  Syn: **peepee lover** (*pej,* '40s: "Anything older than ten is over
  the hill to a peepee lover.")
  ready to crack [**hatch**] **open** said of a boy on the verge of
  puberty.
  Also see ***chicken.**
Egyptian queen (*kwn* SF, black gay sl, late '60s) any black homosexual man, particularly if stately and proud.
eh-eh (ə'-ə, *kwn* LV, les sl, mid '60s, *fr* Ger-Yid *eh-eh* = baby's
word for feces, comparable to *doodoo, poopy*) 1. the anus,
especially when speaking of male anal intercourse: "With a
jakey up his eh-eh he lit a cigarette and blew the smoke
into the other guy's face." 2. (*adj*) said of a subject considered foul or tasteless in any way: "That flick was just
too eh-eh for the price of admission." Syn: **icky; ishy.**
eight pagers pornographic comic booklets, originally eight pages
of erotic cartoon drawings "Hey, get a load of Plastic Man's
dong in this eight paper."
eighty-six (*fr* '40s tavern sl = to refuse to sell drinks to a disorderly customer or have him bounced // rhyming sl *86* = nix)
to ostracise a nuisance from a primarily gay bar, bath, washroom, movie theater, *etc* "Adam and that giddy Evette
were eighty-sixed from Eden at about the same time Clifford
was first coming out!"
-ele (*fr* Yid diminutive, early '60s) suffix of endearment attached
to a word, usually monosyllabic, in order to confuse "I have
some *pot*ele in my *bag*ele."

Variant spellings: **-ala, -ola.**

electric queen (*kwn* SF, hip gay sl, late '60s-'70) homosexual following hippy lifestyle.

Also see ***shrink shocker.**

elegant   1. luxurious, expensive   "That bar is okay if you want to be seen; but personally, I can't stomach elegant taverns"   **2.** exclusive, wealthy   "The upper East Side is nothing but the elegant ghetto of New York." Syn: **richly** (*camp:* "Wanna go halfsies on a richly ice-cream sundae?")   **3.** frequently, elegant is interchangable with ***piss elegant** which tries to approximate true elegance "An elegant motorcycle is one painted orchid with white trim"   **4. *smart.**

Ella (short for ***Cinderella**) one who demands sympathy for trivial misfortunes; a crybaby "Aw, did Ella stub her toesie-poo?"

empress   1.(*kwn* SF) the annual winner of what seems to be a Miss America Pageant of the San Franciscan gay set   **2.** (*kwn* Southwest, mid '60s) a femme homosexual who takes the active role in anal intercourse   **3.** (*camp*) the President of the US.

—affair (*kwn* Southwest, mid '60s) love affair between two effeminates.

—bench (*kwn* Southwest, mid '60s) toilet seat located in a public washroom favored by ***toilet queens** "They're putting new lids on the empress benches—one of you chuspanels wore out the last set."

—Josephine piece (*kwn* SF, '71) especially large and ostentatious rhinestone necklace.

—towel (mid '60s) large bath towel.

encore queen (*fr* Fr *encore* = yet, still, just once more) one who revisits ex-lovers.

Ant: **oncer.**

The End see ***place names.**

endowed see ***well hung.**

enforcer (*fr* pros sl) ***dyke** who manages and controls female prostitutes without pimping.

English martini (*kwn* SF, late '60s) tea, especially when spiked with gin.

English method see ***Princeton style.**

entertain to ball; especially said of cocksucking "His peckerooney entertained my cavities for hours!"

entertain royalty to host a group of obvious queens "Don't your ossifers know when they're entertaining royalty, Sergeant O'Toole? You better tell them to treat ladies with more respect!"

enthroned ('40s-early '50s) squatting on a public toilet in order to cruise men on their way to urinate "That skinny faggot's been enthroned in there so long, she'll probably get the bends if she tries to leave."

equipment   1. male genitals   **2.** anything which helps create a sexual image: tight clothing, well-groomed hair, a solidly structured body, clean teeth, *etc*   "Well, it's time to build up the equipment; I've really started sliding into fat!"

erector-set queen a gay construction worker   "I'd really dig it if that humpy erector-set queen whipped up a miniature bedroom for just us two!"

Syn: **bull-in-boots** (*kwn* LV, mid '60s); **hard-hatted hanna** (*kwn* SF, '70).

Erma (*n* & *adj*) a well meaning fuck-up "She's not so Erma, she knows exactly what's coming off!" But **my friend Irma** = the person talked about "I'm not one to dish, but my friend Irma is going to Europe on company funds."

Esther the Queen (*fr* the Biblical heroine, Esther, who became queen of Persia and saved her people from extermination) any Jewish "homosexual, even though a Jewish adage pronounces "There are no Jewish homosexuals!" "What do you mean Esther's taking the first offer. . .who's offering?"

Syn: **chewess** (pun made upon *chew* = to fellate + Am-Yid pronunciation of Jewess); **Goldie Chanuka** (*camp*, '71, *fr* Goldie Hawn + Goldberg = Jewish surname); **he-blew** (late '60s, *fr* Hebrew + past tense of *blow; comparable to *Hebe*); **kosher boy** ("My second lover was a nice kosher boy"); **Rachel** (*fr* Heb *rakhel* = ewe, in the Bible the younger of Jacob's two wives: "They got Rachel right where it hurts—in the jewel box.")

Related terms:

gefillte fish (*fr* Yid = stuffed fish reinforced by gay sl *fish* = woman) Jewish woman. Syn: **gold fish** (sl *fish* + Goldberg = surname.

Also see *Jewish complement; *kosher.

ethnic what is understood as in-humor to one group while remaining evasive to another, example: a Puerto Rican tells a story in English that only other Puerto Ricans find funny. This ethnic in-joke goes over the heads of non-Puerto Ricans. The same is true for homosexuals who are able to share bits of wit, leaving outsiders confused "That was ethnic joke number five, Grace; you've been leaving the rest of the guests out of the party!"

European accentuation a tapered body with jutting buttocks "That cowboy may never. see Paris, but he certainly has European accentuation."

evil (ē'-v'l *or* ē-vil', mid '60s) hostile and vindictive "Don't get evil with *me*, No-Taste, or I'll rip out your green contact lenses with my teeth."

Also see *bitchy.

evil belch ('71) a fart.

exchange (pros sl) a telephone dispatch system.

exchange loads to transfer semen through passionate kissing after sixty-nining.

Related term:

snowballing per performance of load-exchanging. Syn: **boule de neige** (bo͞ol'-də-nāzh', Fr translation of *snowball*); **white Russian.**

exchange slobs to kiss passionately "The cop shined his spot on us while we were exchangin' slobs in the doorway."

Syn: *chuck slobs; exchange spits; *French kiss.

excreech (*fr* excretion) 1. feces 2. shitty.

exotic (mid '60s) outside of one's usual sexual preference; exciting because of differences (opposites attract) "Black Beauty's hair isn't kinky, dearest, it's exotic!"

exotic remnants ('71) 1. antiques 2. fancy word for junk.

Syn: **things gorgeous** (*kwn* SF, '71).

expensive stuff handsome, well groomed man often working as a professional model "Throw some expensive stuff on the cover of next month's mag, and I guarantee that they'll sell like hotcakes."

express queen 1. one who combines cruising with hitchhiking along freeway offramps, see *road queen 2. (*rare*) one who wastes time. 3. (*rare*) one who hurries to nowhere in particular.

eyeball (*fr* black sl, early '50s) to look something over; to see.

—palace (*dated*, mid '60s) gay bar full of young men who prance about admiring themselves and compare clothing and hairdos. Very little cruising occurs; one goes to an eyeball palace to be noticed, idolized, and finally worshipped.

—queen 1. voyeur, see *watch queen **2.** (*camp*) anybody who stares.

eye fuck (late '60s) **1.** to undress somebody visually **2.** to stare holes through someone.

eyeliner woman (*kwn* Southwest, '70) **1.** homosexual who applies cosmetics to enhance his beauty **2.** (*camp*) the local Avon representative "If anybody ever blows Reagan away, it'll put the eyeliner woman out of business."

eyewash cheap champagne; by extension, any cheap liquor "Here, try revivin' the cow with some eyewash!"
    Syn: **mouthwash; wash** ("Who dropped the acid in the wash?")

fab fabulous, fantastic "Whatever did you drop into my martini to make it so fab?"
    Syn: **fabby; fantabulous** (fantastic + fabulous); **frabjous** (*camp*, '50s).

face freak[queen] one whose head is turned by a pretty face; homosexual who equates sexual ability with the handsomeness of his partner.

fag[got] [*var:* **agfay; faggart; faggert; faggit**] (*pej, fr* WW I *sl fag* = cigarette, because cigarettes were considered effeminate by cigar-smoking he-men; *fr* Brit schoolboy *sl fag* = inferior to older students; *fr* ME *flaming faggot* = heretic burned alive; *?fr* Charles Dicken's character Fagin in *Oliver Twist* = man who teaches boys how to be dishonest) male homosexual "That faggot is such a dirty thing—she's always looking up mens' dresses."
    Syn: **fagocite** (*kwn* NYC, '40s).

—got beater hostile heterosexual man whose anti-homosexuality is sometimes violently expressed; the homosexual's bogeyman; Attila the Heterosexual. This term is almost always used in the plural since such types usually band together in packs to attack lone homosexuals "Beneath the exterior of every faggot-beater beats the heart of a screaming queen." Syn: ***dirt; faggot-killer** (*rare*); **night crawler** (*kwn* LA, late '60s: "Either that guy running after me was a night-crawler or madly in love").

—gots' finishing school a federal prison.

—got-killer (*kwn* LV, late '60s) any inanimate object that might cause injury: faulty elevators, runaway cars, half-buried water sprinklers, *etc* "You won't catch *this* girl skipping through M'sieu le Parque, not with all those gay faggot-killers in the grass waiting to upset my act."

—gotry male homosexuality "Today's movie industry offers a side order of faggotry."

—goty effeminate; pertaining to male homosexuality "Your mouth really looks faggoty when you say 'worm.' " Syn: **faggy** ("Do you think this shade of lipstick makes my lips look faggy?")

—**hag** heterosexual woman extensively in the company of gay men. Fag-hags fall into no single category: some are plain janes who prefer the honest affection of homoerotic boy friends; others are on a determiend crusade to show gay boys that normal coitus is not to be overlooked. A few are simply women in love with homosexual men; others discover to their chagrin that their male friends are charming but not interested sexually. No matter how you cut it, fag-hag has an ugly ring to it. Syn: **faggot-chaser** (*pej*).

Also see *****fruit fly, *queen bee.**

—**joint** (hetero sl) homosexual bar.

—**workers** male-prostitutes who prey upon their male patrons "Miss Law's more upset with the fag workers than she is with the kids."

Syn: *****rough trade.**

faire (*fr* Fr = to do, make, create) **1.** to last, endure   "A dildo cast from papier-mâché ne'er faires out!" **2.** to suck cock, see *****blow.**

fairy (*pej*, '40s) a homosexual man, particularly if feminine   "Oh, Mary! A fairy! Make a wish before rigor mortis sets in!"

—**around** to endulge in nonproductive activity; to kill time "I'm tired to going to the bar and fairyin' aroun'; let's take in a tearoom this weekend instead."

Syn: **cooch[pansy] around.**

—**breath** overpowering odor of semen upon a cocksucker's breath.

Also see *****cometosis.**

—**fur** false eyelashes.

—**godmother** one's homosexual mentor and, occasionally, protector.

—**gown** frilly, floor-length ball gown as worn by a *****drag queen 2.** (*camp*) robe of any person in authority, such as a judge or priest.

Syn: **drag[royal] gown.**

—**hawks** those who take pleasure in harassing and terrorizing homosexuals.

—**hunt** the prowl of fairy hawks.

—**land 1.** any social environment sympathetic to homosexuals **2.** public park frequented nocturnally by homosexuals.

—**nice** (*camp*) very good, just great   "Your sofa's fairy nice."

—**pants** (*camp*) a dress, particularly an evening gown.

—**'s day** (note: L *galbanati* = homosexuals who chose green & yellow as favored colors // *galbinus* = greenish-yellow; *cf* Roman's political choice indicated by colours of his favorite chariot team) Thursday; according to American folklore, any man wearing yellow or green on Thursdays is displaying his homoeroticism.

—**'s day off** (*camp, fr* the fact that gay men cruise even in torrential downpours and hazardous blizzards) never   "When will I stop talking cock? On a fairy's day off, that's when."

—**'s phone booth** (*camp*) toilet stall occupied by a homosexual who is bathroom cruising. Syn: **fairy's photomat.**

—**'s wings** the arms, see *****wings.**

—**wand** any phallic staff carried by a homosexual. Fairy wands include cigarettes stuck into rhinestone-studded cigarette holders, umbrellas carried when there is no possible chance of rain, pencils, long-stemmed American Beauty roses or even joss sticks. The hand holding a fairy wand usually performs wildly exaggerated gestures.

Syn: **pixie stick.**
—**wheel** the ferris wheel "Don't go on the fairy wheel with Twiss; she'll rock the gay seat, an' lemme dish ya that you may have wings but just try to fly."
—**woman** (*camp*) mature homosexual man who behaves in a womanly fashion.

fallen angel male homosexual. A reminder of Judeo-Christianity's moral condemnation.

fall off the roof 1. to menstruate "She can't answer your call tonight, buddy! She fell off the roof las' night" **2.** to be irritable, cranky, overly sensitive **3.** to have problems which interfere with one's sex life.
Syn: **be on the rag.**

falsies 1. a padded bra giving the outward impression of a larger (or real) bosom "Why dearest, didn't you know that most teenies turn queeah the moment they reach down an' grab a han'ful of falsies?" **2.** padding harnessed to parts of the body which need more shape or weight, see *drag body "Without her falsies, she weighs almost ten pounds" **3.** (*camp*) false teeth. Syn: **mouth falsies.**

fam 1. family "Maybe I'll go straight someday and raise me a fam" "Sundays are bad for park cruising—all the picnic tables are overrun with fams" **2.** the whole shebang; a bunch.

family 1. close-knit group bound together by friendship rather than by blood-ties and usually living together "It's family night at the tubs again—everybody's shootin' off at the mouth rather than just plain shootin' off" **2.** (*adj*) trustworthy "Go ahead, you can talk in front of Tommy—he's family" **3.** (*fr pros sl*) pubic lice, see *crabs.

family jewels (because they are a man's most precious possessions) male genitals, see *plumbing.

fan 1. to wiggle the posterior in order to be noticed "That go-go boy is just TM! He's on the other side of the room, but he's fannin' my soup clear over here" **2.** (*rare*) to parade about flagrantly to be noticed and possibly admired.

fanny bellhop (early '50s) gay bellboy working in a hotel, who, when solicited, stretches his duties to serving as a prostitute to homosexual guests.
—**queen of the air** (*dated*) gay elevator boy "I had a quickie with a fanny bellhop, queen of the air! She stopped her machine between floors just long enough to seal the deal."

fart in somebody's face (*kwn* SF, '71) to throw an adversary into confusion "Don't you go fartin' in my face, boy!"

fat on top 1. intellectual **2.** intoxicated.

fat righteous (*adv*) **1.** a lot "I dig you fat righteous" **2.** really, truly "Do you fat righteous want to loan me the bread."

faule flicker (faul'-lə-flik'-ər, *fr* Du) dirty queer.

featherdusters hands.

feathers body hair.
Syn: **down.**
Related terms:
featherless possessing smooth, hairless body "What I really dig about young guys is cute featherless butts sticking up in the air."
feathery hairy "You'll never make it as a drag hustler, Bertha; you're much too feathery."
have the feathers fall (*kwn* NYC, black gay sl) to have a shocking disappointment "Chile, when he tol' me dat, my feathers fell *rat* off."

feature 1. to spotlight; to emphasize as the main attraction "Mr. Diana loves to feature her monkey fur—even on her knees in the johns" "Don't you think it's about time you started featuring a mouthwash?" **2.** to figure "That's the one. Can you feature him and Doug making it for the past two reels?"

feed somebody's monkey (*fr* sl *monkey* = vulva) to go to bed with a woman.
   Syn: **milk a cow** (*pej;* "Everybody should milk a cow at least *once* in his dairy daze.")

feed the sack (*fr* sl *sack* = scrotum) to eat protein-producing foods; to renew one's vitality and sexual reserves.

feelsie 1. petting, see *grope **2.** (*kwn* Wis. teen sl, late '50s) the last hand in strip poker "Let's not play for pennies tonight, let's play for feelsies instead."

felch (*jocular,* late '60s) complicated erotic process of sucking out the come one has ejaculated into an ass and returning it orally.
   —freak[queen] one who likes doing this.

Felicia 1. (*camp*) gay nickname for Felix "We call her Felicia because she cats around" **2.** fellation, see *blow job.

fellatio (fe-lā'-shē-ō, *fr* L *felare* = to suck) **1.** sucking cock "I'm more intrigued with his fellatio-fees than his philosophies." Syn: **fellation 2.** (*camp*) Italian surname "Here it is, Friendly Fellatio's Used Cars!"

fellover (*camp*) **1.** bar-fly suffering from the wages of sin "Would one of you kids ask the rest of the fellovers to move down a seat?" **2.** any man.

femme (*dated, fr* Fr *femme* = woman; but *cf* fem, short for feminine) **1.** passive homosexual. Syn: *nelly **2.** (les sl) passive lesbian, see *molly dyke **3.** (les sl) any feminine woman "She's a super femme: she can clean a house, mend socks, bake cakes, and talk on the phone all at the same time."

fetish freak (*fr* Fr *fetiche* = artificial and descriptive of primitive charms // L *facticius* = factitious) any person who has a strong sexual attachment to articles (boots, leathers, brass knuckles, jockey shorts) or to specific parts of the body (nipples, tattoos, toenails).

FI female impersonator, often professional.

fifi ('40s, *fr* pros sl = one who enjoys being blown) **1.** anybody who derives pleasure from mutual fellatio or cunnilingus, see *sixty-nine queen **2.** fussy; offensively ornate.

fifi-bag (*kwn* LV, late '60s, *fr* Fr sl girl's name *Fifi* = a tart) homemade masturbation utensil made with hot towels and vaseline or a well-lubricated slit sponge tucked into a baggie.

fifth wheel single heterosexual in a homosexual gathering.

fifty-fifty 1. a split bill of ass-fucking and cocksucking; taking sexual turns with one another.

fifty-nine (*camp*) mutual cunnilingus, see *sixty-nine ("I guess you take ten points off for lack of cock.")

fig (*rare*) posing strap.

film for the brownie (late '50s) toilet paper.
   Syn: **ragpaper** (*rare*); **sandpaper** (reinforced by '50 sl *sandbox* = toilet); **wipe** (short for colloq *ass-wipe*).

fine (*fr* black sl) good-looking, shapely; presentable.
   —peein'-last (*kwn* LV, black gay sl, mid '60s) the best, supreme, irreplacable "My fine-peein'-las' man was as happy as a gay bar."

finger to manipulate the clitoris "French dip is what you get when you finish fingering your girl friend."
   —artist (les sl) lesbian who masturbates her lover "Tell the finger-artist to stop using my coffee for a nail-softener." Syn: **fingerer.**
   —fuck to ease the middle finger into the rectum and move it in and out in sham coitus; usually done simultaneously with sucking cock "He wouldn't let me fuck him, but he sure climb-

ed the wall when I finger-fucked his cherry."
—**paint** nail polish.
—**somebody out** (*camp*) to figure somebody out; to make sense
of a remark "I cunt finger you out; bare ass me again."
—**wave 1.** medical digital probing to massage swollen pros-
trate gland **2.** (*camp*) finger-fucking.
fire queen (*kwn* SF, '71) militant homosexual.
first dramatic role the initial homosexual experience; one's giant
step into active homosexuality.
first lady of the land (*kwn* SF, early '60s) one who puts on airs
"Look at her—she thinks she's the first lady of the land with
her salvaged fire-sale chandeliers and all."
fireworks orgasm "Some fireworks, huh, kid?"
fish (*fr* belief that the vagina has a piscine odor) **1.** the vulva
2. a straight woman; any woman "I can't talk to a fish
unless I think it's a boy in drag" "We call it fish, darling,
because it absolutely *smells* like one—a dead one" Syn:
Gerties (Cape Town gay sl); **GG** (=genetic girl); **one of those**
(*camp:* "It was one of *those* asking for Ted"); **pancake**
(*dated*, '40s, *fr* the facial cosmetic: "Whew! I thought for a
minute there that daddy had married a pancake"); **real girl** ("He
married a real girl—suddenly last summer"); **RF** (=real fish); **RG**
(= real girl; "He's bi—he opens doors for Hollywood hustlers
and RG's"); **three-ring circus** (the three rings symbolizing
anus, mouth, vagina) **3.** newly sentenced prisoner, see
*****prison terminology 4.** (pros sl) semen, see *****come** "Don't
you even have the decency to wash the fish out before you
take *me* on?" **5.** (*fr* pros sl, '30s-'40s) man who *****muff dives**
while playing with himself. Syn: **fish queen 6.** (*v*) to *****muff
dive.** Syn: **chew[eat] fish 7.** (*adj*) limp, heady, drooping,
giddy "When that butch number touched me, why, I just went
fish all over." Verb forms **to be[go] fish** = to become coy,
fluttery; to react to a situation as would an average teenager
8. troublesome youths, see *****dirt.**
—**dinner 1.** sex with a woman **2.** any female "Miss Dwayne
is having his first fish dinner; he finally met a broad who
can talk football." Syn: **brain food.**
—**pond** vagina.
—**queen** (*dated*) **1.** one who sucks cunt **2.** (*pej*) any heterosexual man.
—**tank 1.** the vulva "Don't tell me one of Boom-Boom's
sequins got lost in her fish tank again" **2.** dowdy, cheap,
descriptive of vulgar costume jewelery.
    Related terms:
fish-tank boa stole or length of cloth used in a stripper's
act.
fish-tank jewelry trinkets worth about as much as the sparkling pebbles at the bottom of an aquarium of Piscean pets.
—**y 1.** crowded with women **2.** by extension, tasteless "She'll
never look charming, dear; her with her fishy tastes for
clothes."
    Related terms:
smell something fishy to suspect that some vixen is behind
some poor boy's gullibility.
fist fuck the extended process of inserting a fist to the elbow
anally.
    Syn: **shake hands with the baby** (*camp*).
    Related terms:
FFA (*kwn* SF, SM sl, '71) **1.** fist fuckers of America, *ie* those
who practice fist-fucking **2.** the act of fist-fucking "He's
bottoms in our FFA's."
fit-up (Brit gay sl) **1.** starring in one-night performances in dif-

ferent theaters   2. a one-night stand.

five and a two (*exclam, kwn* Cleveland, *fr* pros sl = five dollars for the room and two for the body) squealed upon sighting an attractive man; often worked into an open proposal.

Syn: **seven and a three; twenty and a ten** (inflation?).

five-geared (*kwn* LV, hip gay sl, mid-late '60s) hypersexual; eager to couple with anything; able to mount men, women, children, beasts and knot holes.

Syn: **trisexual** (because he'll try anything).

five minute's worth 1. two cents' worth   "Here hon, let me give you my five minutes' worth"   **2.** thrown together: shabby   "Put on your five minutes' worth of sandals and let's vamoose."

flag (*dated, fr* pros sl) to signal to another, usually by a friendly waving of the hand.

flamingo (*kwn* NYC, '70) opulent dresser; a dandy who struts around like a peacock.

Syn: **looking-glass people** (*kwn* NYC, '70); **pose queen** (*kwn* SF, late '60s); **statue queen** (*kwn* SF, late '60s).

flame [it up] to overemphasize, often deliberately, all girlish traits attributed to the effeminate   "You should see those kids flame after the boss leaves for vacation."

Syn: ***camp it up; flap** ("The makeup just makes you look like a demented flower child—add one eyelash more, though, and you'll start to flap"); **turn up the flame** ('72).

flange (*rare*) the corona of the penis.

flap 1. to babble; talk aimlessly; ramble   **2.** to sass back. Syn: **flap off at the face**   **3.** to gesticulate wildly with the hands, see ***windmill**   **4.** to act effeminate, see ***flame.**

flash 1. tidings, news scoop   "Didn't you get the latest flash on Chris' party? It petered out!" Syn: **fat flash; the large news** ("I have *the* large news for you, Bertha; you've just been drafted")   **2.** flashy jewelry of poor workmanship; **going the flash** = wearing cheap jewelry   "Don't you feel that seventy-seven is a bit too old to go the flash?"   **3.** to breifly expose oneself.

flashlight obvious homosexual who is approached to find out the hot spots in an unfamiliar town.

Syn: **key.**

Also see ***push button.**

flash queen (*fr* narc sl *flash* = jolt brought about by drugs) gay drug user   "A flash queen wears her best necktie around her arm."

Syn: **Miss Flash.**

flawless ('71-'72) handsome.

fleece pubic hairs

Syn: **patch** ("When you dye your hair, do you dye your patch to match?"); **pelos** (pā'-lōs, Mex *fr* Sp *pelo* = hair).

Related term:

Jason's golden fleece blond pubes

fleece market (*kwn* SF, '70) high-priced flea market.

flesh corset [FC] dieting by plastic surgery   "It isn't Grape Nuts that keeps her trim, m'dear; she puts down a few thou to wear a flesh corset."

flick freak (*fr* sl *flick* = movie) homosexual who cruises movie houses,

Syn: **movie queen.**

Related term:

play checkers[chess] switching seats often to locate prospective sex partners.

flight (*fr* locomotion of a fairy's wings) homosexual outing or excursion.

flighty piece fickle gay boy.

flip 1. (*fr* hairdresser sl) hair styled to fall over one eye, especially when accidentally occuring after some form of exertion Syn: **gilda** (*fr* '40s movie *Gilda* with Rita Hayworth) **2.** one who is out of his mind. Syn: **flip artist** (= a professional madman: one whose habit is supported by the state).

flip-collar fairy clergyman with an eye for altar boys "Forget about what that blonde flip-collar fairy preaches from the pulpit; what counts is what he preaches *behind* the pulpit later on."

> Syn: **Mary of the cloth** ("I used to think that *all* Marys of the cloth were named 'Bing'"); **gugusse** (*dated*, Brit gay sl, *fr* Fr Auguste = Augustan priest: "That bald gugusse must have been a big hit around Easter.")
> Related term:
> **steeple** a minister's cock.

flip queen Filipino homosexual.
> Syn: **bini boy** (bin'-ē-boi).

flippy lovable unpredictability.

flip the wig (*fr* black sl = to become furious, to get enraged) to be aroused, to fall in love "He flipped his wig over that butch Marine"

floater 1. (*fr* hobo sl = migratory worker) transient hustler **2.** *gay bar **3.** male who prostitutes himself as he travels across the country, see *road queen **4.** a prostitute's client, see *john.

float like soap 1. to be chaste, sweet **2.** to be sexually naive, spotless "His little buns are so clean, they float like soap."

flower lounge (*fr* hetero sl *flower* = sissy) coffeehouse or gay bar attracting a young statuesque clientele.

fluff 1. effeminate homosexual, see *effie **2.** (*kwn* Texas, les sl, late '60s) elaborate mannerisms "I can't *stand* that big dyke; she's always makin' with that butch fluff like openin' doors for me an' lightin' my cigarillos" **3.** elaborate hairdo **4.** pubic hairs **5.** (*camp*) reference to one's own sex organs, especially the ass "You don't have to tell me how many inches you got: fluff knows, she's my radar you see" **6.** (*camp*) used fur coat or tattered jacket "Hand me fluff, will you?"

> **—it up 1.** to work up an erection "A lot of hustlers fluff it up before they hit the streets, so that their meat will really cop the trick" **2.** to raise a passive partner's ass higher into the air by placing a pillow beneath the tummy "He was cherry, so I fluffed it up a little before I tunneled through."

flush (*fr* teen sl, late '50s = to evacuate toilet-wise) to reject; to cancel; to eliminate "Jim wanted to fuck, but Larry wanted to suck: so that flushed their relationship" **2.** (*exclam, kwn* LV, late '60s) impossible; not worth continuing. Syn: *click; the party's over.

flutter (*rare*) **1.** sex partner obviously thinking of someone else **2.** to *mince about "Stop fluttering, girl; sit in the back seat an' keep your wrists out of sight."

flutter[er]s false eyelashes.

fly (*fr* another analogy to fairy wings) to travel at a fast pace "Honey, as soon as I told him there was extra money involved, that cabbie flew his gay taxi to my doorstep."
> Related term:
> **fly, girl** (*exclam*) encouragement "I saw the way he eyed you! Fly, girl, don't let it get away!"

flyers (*kwn* SF, '70) opening statements; ice-breakers used when cruising.
> Related terms:

fly[post] flyers to make a proposition "I posted a few flyers, but I guess he doesn't know how to read lips." Syn: **hit somebody up; prop somebody** "He wasn't out of the shower before he was propped by the fucking buddies."

fly jockey man who copulates without removing his pants.

fly picking [time] 1. in the habit of nervously fidgeting with one's hands; talking with the hands "I don't mind listening to her insane stories—it's all her fly picking that drives me to distraction" **2.** (*pej*) slightly crazed. Syn: **fly-time** ("Have you ever noticed the way Sydney cracks his neck? I think he's fly-time!")

Follies' beauty (*camp*) man who thinks of himself as a sex symbol.

follow queen (*kwn* SF, late '60s) homosexual who shadows his intended for what seems like *miles* before bolstering up enough courage to say "hi."

food generic for men as sex objects "What foods these mortals be."

foo-foo 1. (*fr* baby talk) excretion. Syn: **big potty** (*fr* baby talk) **doo-doo** (*fr* baby talk); **kaka** (*fr* Sp baby talk: *cf* other languages using *kaka* = feces, *eq* Yid *alter kocker* = old shit); **number two** (*fr* children's sl); **poopy** (*fr* baby talk) **2.** disgusting **3.** (*exclam*) oh crap "Foo-foo! I've lost my date book!"
Syn: **poopoo nasty** (*kwn* LV, mid '60s); **poopy** (*kwn* LV, mid '60s); **foo-foo dust** (*kwn* LV & SF, mid-late '60s, *fr* Gullah *fu-fu dus*' = fine powder used in *Voudon* recipes calling for desire) any powder: baby powder, antilouse powder dusted upon new prisoners, chalk dust, *etc*.
Syn: **pixie dust.**

fool around (hetero teen sl) to experiment with homosexuality.

for days (*adv*) **1.** for a long period of time "This letter goes on for days; I'll finish reading it later" **2.** busy, ornate "That picture frame goes on for days" **3.** pleasing to the eye "He has buns for days" **4.** plenty for everybody; unlimited supply; won't quit "He has biceps for days" **5.** galore; a lot, usually used in exaggerated statements "He has teeth for days" = he has a lovely smile **6.** an affirmative, see ***days.**
Syn: **forever** ("Honey, I dig paleface—but his white skin goes on forever.")

foreigner (black sl) a homosexual, see ***queer.**
Syn: **skippy** (black sl)
Related term:
speak in a foreign tongue (*fr* sl *French* = sucking cock) to have oral intercourse with either sex.

fork (*rare*) to have the penis awkwardly reach an erect state in public "He's one of us—it started to fork when that cute piece stood up."

formula eighty-six (*camp, kwn* SF, '71, *fr* gay sl *86*) an imaginary brand of hair spray guaranteed to make the hair fall out.

for real[serial, sure, true] 1. factual "Is Arnold moving out for real?" **2.** truly, seriously "Are you for serial or just camping it up?" **3.** an affirmative "Ques: You're tired of having to pay for it, right?' Ans: 'For true!'"

fountains of Rome (*camp*) urinals in a men's room.

four doors (*kwn* SF, late '60s) **1.** carload of young men intent upon finding and beating a gay boy **2.** (*fr* the advice to "run when you hear the sound of four car doors slamming") quick warning to leave the immediate area "Four doors! Let's angle on to the exit quietly but rushingly!" **3.** mean; liable to turn against a gay boy "I don't trust him—he looks too four-doors."
Also see ***dirt.**

fourth sex (*fr* Jess Stern's *The Grapevine*) female homosexuality.

foxy (*kwn* SF, hustler sl, *fr* black sl = well built) clever; on the ball mentally, physically, and financially. Used of either sex.

frame 1. (*fr* black sl) the body "I'll let you in just as soon as I drape the frame" = as soon as I dress **2.** (*rare*) man who possesses certain characteristics which appeal to homosexuals though he may not be gay himself.

freak 1. (*fr* sl *freak of nature*) a homosexual **2.** one with very abnormal sexual interests. Syn: **sick faggot[thing]; twist 2.** suffix used to form compounds, *eg* **horn freak** = one who is drawn to the brass section in a band. Note: young gays prefer using **-freak** as a suffix-word, while the elderberries continue their habit of ***-queen** "Caution: speed freak smoking!" **4.** to be delightfully uninhibited; to have an uproarious time at a party "You really freak when you dance, did you know that?" Syn: **freak out** (but not to be confused with hip sl = having a bad drug experience) **5.** to have the libido lifted by a pretty face; to be entranced with another's body "His nose freaks me" "Big pecks on a man freak a pap-nibbler." Syn: **send** ("He sends me.")
—**around 1.** to kill time, like strolling through the park; to just be your gay self **2.** to window shop "I freaked around in McDonald's until it was time for the movie to start."
—**it up 1.** to be unquestionably gay **2.** to attend an orgy, enjoying it to the fullest **3.** to be unfettered by social restrictions **4.** (*exclam*) a command to advance: "Charge!" Also used like the "Io Saturnalia!" greeting of old Rome "Freak it up, girls: there's plenty of men for everybody."
—**look** (*kwn* LV, mid-late '60s) **1.** a double-take; to look at something with disbelief **2.** a rude-stare; a hate-stare. Syn: **geek-look** (*kwn* LV, mid-late '60s: more intense stare).
—**looking** (*pej*) **1.** of a strange or unusual countenance **2.** said of a man who looks more like a woman than a man "You freak-looking bitch!"
—**scene** (late '50s) **1.** an orgy, especially professionally performed, which delivers the bizarre, *eg* a *menage à trois* featuring a man, a boy and a duck **2.** homosexual party ending up as an orgy.
—**trick** (*fr* pros sl) man who prefers unusual practices to standard positions.
—**us** (*kwn* LV, mid '60s) vocative reserved for the bohemian homosexual.

freda 1. (Cape Town gay sl) frustrated "The mavises living in this town are all jessie and freda" **2.** (*camp*) gay nickname for Fred "You always come across, Freda; but you never excite" **3.** (*rare*, mid '60s) a female prostitute.

French to practice any form of oral copulation, see ***blow, *muff dive.**
—**artist 1.** a fellator, see ***cocksucker 2.** a pornographer.
—**bathe** (*fr* 18th cent France) to employ perfumes as a deodorant in lieu of bathing.
—**by injection** said of a first-class cocksucker; having gone to the source itself to learn the trade. Often a comeback answer to the question of nationality: "I'm Irish by birth and French by injection."
—**dip** (*kwn* SF, '70) vaginal precoital fluid "Stop sloshing around in the french dip an' come answer this phone!"
—**embassy** (mid '60s) YMCA with homosexuality running unchecked.
    Related term:
—**ie** a fellator, see ***cocksucker.**
    Syn: **French lady; French language expert; Frenchwoman** ("What you askin' me for the KY for—you *know* that I'm a Frenchwoman.")
—**kiss** to kiss passionately; to probe another's dental cavities

with an amiable tongue "They're too young to neck. When they French kiss, their braces hook together."

Syn: **mouth wrestling; pass secrets; throw the tongue.**

—**kiss filter** any filter-tipped cigarette "Hand me my French-kiss filters, will ya, doll?"

—**language training** teaching, with patience and an ample supply of bandages, an oral virgin how to fellate a penis skillfully.

—**photographer** homosexual photographer who aims at cocks "You can tell that the guy was a french photographer: there's not one butt in this portfolio."

—**postcard** a handsome devil who has the look of exciting sex about him.

—**prints** unusual heterosexual pornography.

—**revolution** (*camp*) the revolution for gay rights as advocated by Gay Liberation.

—**stuff 1.** gay Frenchmen **2.** pornography **3.** (pros sl) unusual sex activity.

—**tickler** condom with protuberances on the top and along the sides to increase the tingling sensations in a woman during coitus.

fresh fruit a newcomer; a stranger.

Syn: **new faces; strange piece.**

freshly killed[butchered] recently introduced to ass-fucking "See how bowlegged that chicken walks—looks like he was freshly killed in the hayloft."

fresh meat 1. inexperienced homosexual **2.** someone new to have sex with to nip boredom in the bud.

Syn: **fresh one[piece].**

frilly-dilly (*camp, fr* joke: "What's a frilly-dilly? That's a cock circumcised with pruning shears") circumcised penis, clipped after adolescence, having scars around the *glans penis.*

Syn: **gone through the Civil War** (*adj*).

frog queen (*pej, kwn* Seattle, *fr* sl *frog* = Frenchman // WWI sl *frog-eater*) French-Canadian homosexual; also has the connotation of having halitosis.

front marriage social or economical marriage of convenience in which one or both of the partners are homosexual. Most commonly used as a cover device by famous celebrities.

Syn: **twilight tandem** (late '50s).

front page spectacular "He gave me a front-page sampling of his corkscrew."

front step (mid-late '60s) one who goes along with the crowd; a social butterfly with little individuality.

Syn: **social queen, sosh** (*fr* social).

frozen fruit frigid homosexual.

frufru (frōō′ frōō) dainty, lacy, flowery.

fruit 1. (*pej*, hetero sl, '30s) any male homosexual, but especially a cocksucker "That curly hair style makes that fruit look like a fat Victorian cherub." Syn: **banana** ("That banana acts as if he were five going on four") **2.** (*adj*) homosexual "That boy will drive me out of my fruit mind before the evening's up." Syn: **bananas** ("Loving you has made me bananas!"); **fruitsy; fruity[as a fruitcake]** (*pej*) **3.** (*camp, kwn* LA, early '60s, *fr* the carelessness of many young effeminates with the possessions of others) to borrow money without any intention of paying it back "Can I fruit some coin off you, Martha, till my welfare check comes?"

—**boots** (*dated*) throughout the '50s, fruit boots were white tennies or white suede shoes. Into the '60s, the term became the Beatle boots or any Italian-made sharp-toed shoes which heightened the so-called effeminization of the American youth.

Since almost everyone wears fruit boots, the viciousness behind the term is all but lost.

—bowl queen 1. gay football player **2.** homosexual sports
fan **3.** one who digs (and sucks) football players "He's such
a Fruit Bowl Queen. I honestly expect him to someday wear
a ribbon that says 'Miss Pasadena '69'."

—fly (*pej*) woman who enjoys the company of gay men.
Syn: **drosophila** (drō-săf'-ə-lă, *camp*).

—jars (*camp*) dumbbells, weights used for body building
"Shut up, or I'll use your padded bra for fruit-jars."

—picker one who blackmails or robs homosexuals.

—salad 1. large gathering of homosexuals; a gay crowd or
audience **2.** multi-colored gown **3.** (*rare, camp*) a hand
made quilt.

—'s machine male genitals.
Related term:

work [out] on a fruit's machine to suck cock.

fu (fōō, *fr* Haw gay sl) **1.** stereotype effeminate, see ***effie 2.**
(*rare, exclam,* mid '60s) fie! "Fu, girl, your face is so white
it hurts my teeth!"

fuchsia queen (*obs*) lovely woman.

fuck (*?fr* naval commanders in the early 19th cent who ab-
breviated For Unlawful Carnal Knowledge in their logbooks
as FUCK; however *cf* Du *fucken* = to breed; Gk *futueva* =
to plant seeds; L *futuere* = to strike [*var frig fr* Ger *ficken*
= to strike]; Sanscrit *ukshan* = bull; Cantonese *fook* = hap-
piness) **1.** a person as a sex object "Was Tyrone a good
fuck?" Syn: **piece [of ass]** ('20s) **2.** (*v*) to insert a cock
into a vagina, mouth, or anus "I wouldn't mind fucking Mick
Jagger if he kept his mouth shut!" Syn: (all refer to anal
intercourse except where noted) **back scuttle** (*dated,* '30s,
fr scuttle = to sink a ship by drilling holes in its bottom);
bag (*rare, fr* bagging big game: "Tonya finally bagged that
blonde who hangs out at Bob's Broiler"); **bake potatoes**
(*kwn* NYC, '30s); **ball** (*fr* '30s black sl = party: "I haven't
balled any ass since I left the military academy"); **bang;
behind [the behind]** ("We're all behind you goddess!"); **bend
somebody over; bend some ham** (mid '60s); **BF** (*kwn* Southwest,
early '60s, acronym for butt fuck: "I've never BF'ed anybody before, man"); **bless** (*kwn* NYC, black gay sl, late '60s:
"Honey, he blessed me!"); **bore** (early '60s: "A bored girl
is one not bored"); **broaden somebody['s outlook]** ("Prison
will broaden your outlook, my boy"); **brown** ('30s, *fr* brown =
anus: "The Unbrownable Molly Sink!"); **buff** (*fr* teen & hustler
sl, mid '50s // buff = polish a surface); **bugger** (more common
in Brit than in US, *fr* ME *bougre* = a sodomite ML, *Bulgarus,*
= heretic Bulgarian and by extension a sodomite: "Why were
you defrocked? Were you caught buggering the altar boy?");
bum a load (Brit sl); **bump** (*kwn* Texas, late '60s); **butt-bang
[-fuck]** (mid '60s); **charva** (Brit sl); **coat** (*dated*); **cochar**
(kō-khär', *fr* Mex: *el 'sta cochado* = he's been fucked); **coger**
(kō-khär', *fr* Mex // Sp *coger* = to seize, grasp); **come in
an ass[hole]; cop [an ass]** (cool sl, mid '60s, *fr* copulation:
"Let me cop ya, man: I'll ease it in real easy-like."); **cornhold**
(*rare*); **cornhole** (considered silly, '20s, *fr* dried corncobs as
ass-wipers in the days of the outhouse); **coucher** (kōō-shā'
fr Fr *coucher* = to lay down: almost invariably camp-queens
will answer the question "Can you speak French?" with
Voulez-vous se coucher avec moi? = do you want to go to
bed with me?); **culiar** (kōō-lē-är', *fr* Mex *culo* = the ass:
!Quisiera yo culiarlo! = I'd love fucking him); **dick somebody;**

diddle (*rare*, usu connected with masturbation and pitching woo); **dig a ditch** (*fr ditch* = an anus); **dig boy ass** (*kwn* LV, mid '60s; *fr* "digging something out" of a nook: a popular joke campingly shouted back and forth between lesbians and queens was "Do you dig boy ass?"); **do a brown** (*dated*, '20s); **dork** (teen sl, '60s ?*fr* dial *dornick*, // Ir *dornog* = a stone, fig, a testicle; ?*fr* sl *dork* = a penis, possibly *dick* + cork: "Somebody was even dorkin' me in the ear!"); **dot the "I"** (the anus is the "dot," while the "I" symbolizes the penis: "He forgot to dot his 'I'"); **drill** ("F'crissakes, man, whatcha tryin' t'do . . . drill me a new hole?"); **dry clean a rear** (*rare*, early '50s); **dry hump** (*kwn* LV, early '60s: as opposed to the wetness of a vagina); **dust somebody off** (black gay sl, late '50s, *fr* sl *duster* = the buttocks); **flip one over** (gently or with pressure turn a partner over onto his belly); **fork** (*camp*: "Fork you, Rose, we're doing it *my* way!"); **fuck in [up] the ass** ("Fuck me in the ass? Why, how can you speak of love at a time like this?"); **fuse together** (cool sl, late '60s); **get into some ass; get it up there [where the air is rarefied]** (*kwn* SF late '60s, an import from the enchanting Midwest); **get one** ("Hon, I'm not out to *get* nobody. . .I'm the one who wants to get *gotten*!"); **goose** (*dated*); **go to press** (prison sl, '30s); **greek** (*rare, fr* Greece's Golden Age when pederasty was in vogue: "He'd rather greek than freak"); **groove** (cool sl, early '60s: "Man, I don't wanna groove ya, all I want is a cup-o'-coffee); **hit the round brown; hump** (*rare*, mainly prison sl: "She's not so elegant! She was humping some polish cunt in Milwaukee); **jog[joog, jook, jug] [up some buns]** (hustler sl, mid '60s, *fr* Gullah *jook* = to poke); **knock off a little** ('30s); **lay** ('30s: "Sure, I'd like to lay you—lay you out!"); **lay some pipe** (black sl); **lay the leg** (*kwn* black & prison sl); **make** ("Soldiers should be made and not heard"); **make babies[piggies]** (early '60s); **open up the ass; oscarize** (*dated*, Brit sl, *fr* Oscar Wilde's name); **oso-oso** (ō'-sō-ō'-sō, *kwn* LA, mid '60s, *fr* Haw gay sl); **pack fudge** ('40s); **pack some mud** ('50s, *fr* gay sl *mud* = feces: "Some night Jack the Stripper is goin' t'slip in 'tween the lily-whites an' pack your mud!"); **paint the bucket** (mid '50s); **part somebody's cheeks; perve** (*kwn* Aus & Brit hetero sl, *fr* pervert); **pitch** (prison sl: "If you pitch, sooner or later you'll catch!"); **plank somebody** (late '60s: "Who cares if he's a sparkling conversationalist—all I wanna do is plank him"); **play dump truck** (*fr* gay joke: "Let's play dump truck—you back up and I'll put the load in"); **play leap frog** (?*fr* naut sl: "Don't play leap frog with him—he doesn't jump high enough."); **plow; plug** ("Boy, did I *ever* get *plugged* in Hawaii"); **pop it in [-to the toaster]** ('20s); **pound one's popo** (*kwn* SF, late '60s: "Admit it! You wouldn't mind pounding Greg's popo!"); **powder someone's cheeks** (*kwn* SF, '70); **pull a boy[onto the dick]; pump someone; punk in the ass** (see *punk); **push** ('30s); **put a hurtin' on an ass** (*kwn* NYC, black gay sl, late '60s); **put it to somebody; queer a person** (hetero sl); **ram** (*rare*); **rectify** (*rare*: "Girl, you done been rectified!"); **ride** ("Did you ever ride Chris?" Syn: **ride a bull** = to fuck a virile man); **ride the deck** (*dated*, '50s); **roger a bud[-bum]** (Brit naut sl, *bud* = buddy, *roger* = cock); **roll somebody over; rosquear** (ros-ka-ar', *fr* Pachuco Sp: ?*Te gusta rosquear, ese?* = do you like fucking, man?); **rump the cula** (*obs, fr* Am soldiers stationed in Panama where *cula* = ass); **saddle it; screw[some ass]** ('30s: "Fifty dollars to screw you? What's your ass made out of. . .gold?"); **service** (hustler sl = to fuck a customer); **sexualize** (*rare*, hetero sl, mid '60s = standard coitus);

shaft one in the bum (Brit hetero sl); **shtup** (*fr* Yid // Ger *stupsen* = to push: "Shtup you!"); **skewer a shish-kabob; slide [slip] it in[up]** ("My love life is slipping, Cap'y—right into you"); **snag** (*rare*, "Snag onto any cute Greeks while you were stationed around the Cobaltic?"); **split some buns; spread somebody [apart]; stir fudge** (mid '60s); **stir somebody's chocolate** (late '60s); **surf** (early '60s, LA pun on sl *ride* = fuck + ride the wild surf); **third way** (*fr* pros sl: 1st way = standard coitus, 2nd way = fellatio); **thread somebody** ('mid '60s, *fr* the penis depicted as a needle: "He'd give up his new metallic suit just to thread me"); **tom-fuck** (*dated*, Brit sl); **vegetable** (*dated*, *kwn* LA, early '60s, ?*fr* take-off on cornhole); **wheel down** (*kwn* LV, teen sl mid '60s: "Did you wheel down las' night?); **work somebody** (cool sl, late '50s: "I worked that one until those white thighs changed color"); **yentz** (*fr* Yid) **3.** to function, work "Turn the record over and see if it fucks!"
—able 1. willing to be ass-fucked "Get Chris away from his fish friend and you'll have a fuckable man on your hands" **2.** possessing a desirable ass. Syn: **prattable.**
—a-buck (*rare*, not as common as shortened *var* **a-buck**) fucking position: laying with legs thrown over the head "A-bucking we will go. . ." The passive partner who bucks his legs into the air to better expose his rear-end is said to have **helium legs** (*kwn* SF, mid '60s) with his feet **glued to the ceiling** (early '60s). Syn: **family style** (mid '60s, *fr* standard heterosexual position); **V for Victory** (late '60s, the two outstretched legs form the "V"); **vis-a-vis** (vēz'-a-vē', *fr* Fr = face to face).
—ing anal intercourse. Syn: **guy-fucking** (hetero sl, '70); **hot-dogging** (*kwn* SF, late '60s: an analogy made upon *buns* = ass + *hot dog* = cock); **ninety-nine** or **sixty-six** (the numerals 99 and 66 serve as ideographs in showing the whole story of two men going at it); **RE** (*kwn* LV, mid '60s, acronym for rear entry); **seventy-one** (late '60s, an advanced ***sixty-nining**); **shot in the back door; stern approach[job]** ('30s); **tender love** (mid '60s, *fr* gay joke: "What is tender love? It's two Greeks with hemorrhoids.")
—ing and sucking uninhibited lovemaking, especially at an orgy. Syn: **knitting [one] and pearling [two]** (*kwn* Southwest, mid '60s: "There was some *wicked* knitting and pearling going on after his straight relatives left.")
—in the face[head, mouth] mouth fucking (med = *irrumation*), as opposed to cocksucking "He grabbed hold of my ears, honey, and fucked me in the head! I loved it." Syn: **fuck the teeth.**
—me 1. sex-symbol; sexually attractive person. May be most effective when said sarcastically "Sure Tom Jones is a fuck-me; that's why so many people pay to watch him sing" **2.** (*kwn* LV, late '60s) damned, dad-blasted, *etc* "I arrive on the fuck-me plane at nine, so be sure to have a limousine waiting."
—movies pornographic films. Syn: **skin flicks.**
—one rotten to .fuck hard and fast "He fucked that little bitch rotten—she's still going through traction." Syn: **break one's shit string** (*kwn* black sl, late '60s: to fuck so violently that the anus bleeds afterwards); **burn some buns; bust a cap in an ass** (= to overpower, especially by filling the fallen opponent full of hot lead); **cowboy** (*kwn* Ariz, late '50s; sug-guested *fr* prison sl *bronco-busting* = riding, fucking a struggling boy; "He got cowboyed in the john before he knew what hit 'im"); **curl the tail** ("She may be the grand BQ, but

if she lets Al curl her tail, she'll have to have the gay doctor crochet her hole back together again"): **drive[cram] it to home base; give one a stab** (prison sl) **lance it in** P*kwn* LA, early '60s, *fr* sl *lance* = cock); **rasgar** (rās-gār'-/-kar, *fr* Am-Sp sl. late '50s // Sp = to rip); **raw-fuck** (hetero sl, mid '60s, usu descriptive of prison rapes or fraternity initiation rites); **screw somebody to the chicken wires** (*kwn* SF, '70: the chicken wires in this instance refer to a baths where the "roof" of each cubbyhole is made of fence material); **spear it in** (*fr* sl *spear* = cock: "You're not worth the spit I use to spear it in!"); **throw a mean[wicked] fuck; wreck a rectum** (serviceman sl, '70: describes ass-fucking as something detrimental, Ant: **soft-fuck**); terms for men who fuck hard and fast are amazingly complimentary, even though the practice is not always greeted favorably: **humper-and-a-bumper; pile-driver** (because the sudden shift into overdrive can result in hemorrhoids: his theme song is "The Shadow of Your Piles"); **plunger; rammer.**
    Related terms:
backswing (late '50s) perhaps the most common position for anal intercourse where the passive partner lies on his belly. Syn: **bottom's[sunnyside] up** (Now we all know what "Keep your sunnyside up" meant.)
boy-scout queen (*kwn* SF, '70, *fr* sexually experimenting boy scouts who fear giving a response) one who pretends to snooze as he is fucked or sucked off. Another unlikely excuse is: "I was drunk, man, I didn't know what he had in his mouth, er, I mean, mind!"
breakthrough (early '60s) farting while being fucked. Most unchic.
dog fashion 1. heterosexual coitus with the female on all fours, a la canine, while the man mounts her from the rear **2.** homosexual anal intercourse conducted in such a manner. Syn: **dog[gy] style[ways]**.
double entry two men enjoying the same passive partner simultaneously. It should be noted that this style of anal copulation is rare due to its difficulty.
drown the ass in baby oil (*rare,* late '60s) to ejaculate so much semen when fucking that the ass literally overflows.
force-fuck (late '60s) to rape a man's anus; used mostly of prison gang-bangs. Syn: **barrel** (*fr* having someone literally over a barrel); **break and enter; hit and run.**
goosey (*adj, rare,* mid '60s) **1.** having rounded hips and full buttocks which encourage ass-fucking "You wouldn't have believed some of the goosey little butts on some of those guys" **2.** happily going to pieces when the ass is being played with.
ice-cube sandwich (late '60s) the insertion of ice cubes into the passive partner's anus before actual intercourse (talk about head colds!)
Roman engagement (late '60s, *fr* alleged It custom of keeping safe while keeping the boys content) anal copulation with a virgin girl who wishes to remain a technical virgin.
shortcake (*kwn* Northwest, mid '60s) quick, brief act of anal intercourse "He had to catch a plane, but he did have enough time for some shortcake."
stand up job ('50s) anal entry done in a standing position. Syn: **wall job**
stuff a turkey (*kwn* SF, '71) to fuck an old man.
fudge baby turd.
fudy [futy] (*dated*) same as *cunt in all senses.
fufu funnel a pampered, powdered ass.

full face man's face covered in cosmetics.

full focus 1. undivided attention "At the mental health meeting, they put full focus on us homothekthuals" **2.** (v) to look at "Full focus on that crotch, hon!"

full house public rest room with every urinal, toilet seat, sink and mirror occupied by a homosexual man "I bet it's a full house today—packed to the rafters with hungry salesmen."
Related term:
full up (adj) packed.

fumigate to take an enema before and after anal intercourse.
Syn: *douche.

fun fun-filled. Most often said sarcastically "Get out, kids, we've arrived at Fun City!"
Syn: *mad.

funch (fr *fag + lunch) brief sex act accomplished at noontime; a midday *quickie "Where do you disappear to have your funch?"
Syn: **matinee [trick]** (fr Fr matinée = morning // L matutinus = of the morning // Matuta = goddess of morning, akin to L maturus = ripe, mature); **nooner.**
Also see *morner.

funky [fonky] (adj, fr black sl // funk or fungus, but cf Swahili, funga = close or familiar) **1.** sticky with perspiration after good clean fun, work, sexing; musky, odoriferous "Go throw your funky self into the shower before you come to my bed!" **2.** unpretentious, basic, earthy, down-home **3.** downtrodden, inferior, in bad taste.

funny-paper trick an ex-lover now considered a fool.

fur[s] 1. one's outer attire, such as a topcoat **2.** young man's wrap for outside wear "Which one of my furs shall I wear to the beer bust, Kym!" Syn: **furpiece; mink; peltz** (fr Yid = a pelt) **3.** pubic hairs coating the vulva "He won't leave now . . . his girl friend has her fur in his face."
Related terms:
clean up the furs (camp) to pick up loose clothing at an orgy; to pick up after others.
drag the fur[mink] to drag a sweater or coat along the floor as if it were a train.
fur-lined foxhole wealthy homosexual.

furnished apartment (fr pros sl, '30s-'40s) **1.** clothed body. **2.** uncircumcised penis; left whole.
Related terms:
go as a furnished apartment to dress, wear clothing.
unfurnished apartment the naked body.

furniture (fr pros sl, '30s-'40s) vantage points; money-making portions of a harlot's body "Teeth are furniture to a Frenchwoman like the schlonger she swings on is furniture to the trick.'
Related terms:
move furniture 1. to fondle, see *grope **2.** to disperse mobs, break up a crowd "Here comes Tilly to move furniture—let's start hikin'!"
new furniture padding, see *falsies **2.** false teeth
the furniture needs repainting said of one with an as yet untreated venereal disease

futch (kwn Southwest, les sl, late '60s, fr sl *femme + *butch) a gay AC-DC; not strictly active nor totally passive but arises to whatever the occasion may demand.

future-ex-old-man (kwn LV, late '60s) ex-lover who can't be gotten out of the blood "No, I can't say we really go together anymore; he's my future-ex-old-man."

fuzzies (fr sl fuzz = female pubic hairs) **1.** strip teasers **2.** photographs of vaginas.

GAA Gay Activists' Alliance, gay liberation group.

gaff 1. (*fr* pros sl = sex organs) the open lap of a seated man especially when his genitals are clearly outlined **2.** protective device for a dancer's genitalia, see ***dancer's belt.**

gaggy (*kwn* LV, mid '60s, *fr* pros sl) **1.** sordid, unsavory, in the worst possible taste "Not another one of the dictionary's gaggy jokes?" **2.** filthy, revolting "He's not a real man unless he has *the* gaggy rosebud" **3.** (*rare*) boring, dull, square "Is he bringing his gaggy cousin with him again?"

Syn: **frumpy** (late '60s); **pukey** ("Kissing a drunk man is pukey, as is spending a night in jail"); **pusy** (pus' ē, "How pusy! Beer with eggs!"); **shitty.**

Also see ***gross, *mess, *rank.**

Gail (Cape Town gay sl, *fr* abbreviation of gay language) the contrived slang of Cape Town's gay community "Tell us in Gail!" Gail draws strongly from other girls' names to stock its vocabulary: **dora** = a sot, **wendy** = white, *etc*. This practice is, to a lesser degree, also to be found in the USA: **beverly** = booze, **nell** = girlish, *etc*.

gallant (*kwn* Cleveland, mid '60s, *fr* ME *galaunt* // MFr *galer* = have a good time) attentive to the queen; gentlemanly; a more considerate version of ***butch** "This girl tipped on up to me so gallantly that I thought I was going to be married for lunch."

Also see ***elegant.**

gal pal any homosexual's female friend. This word lacks the vulgarity of ***fag hag, *fruitfly** or ***queen bee.**

game (*cf* colloq *game of love*) teasing while cruising, leading somebody on; playing hard to get "Phil, tired of the games on Polk, rode the Fruit Stripe Run out to The End, and found out that they game there too" **2.** to be choosy, picky, waiting for prime put teasing ground beef "All this hip shit is just a front—these young faggots are still gaming."
—er one who is overly critical of others while cruising; a coy cruiser. Syn: **game player.**
—ey 1. flirtatious with one but going home with another **2.** selective.

Related term:

in the game being a homosexual "Being in the game has its ups and bottoms."

gang-bang[-shack, -shag, -shay (*fr -cher* in Fr *coucher* = to lay down) -splash] **1.** several men taking turns fucking one who is held down; mass rape. Usually used of prison assaults **2.** (*camp*) homosexual orgy. Syn: **GB** (*kwn* SF: "Pack your toothbrush, Cherie, it'll probably turn out to be an all-night GB."); **round-up** (wild west version).
—ing the gums to be loquacious.

gang fairy (prison sl) man who is forced to sexually entertain many others at one session   "By the time they get that fairy buried, he'll be a health hazard."

gangrene contest one of those days; a time when someone looks his worst   "Having a bad one, hon? You look as though you just won the booby prize in a gangrene contest."

Ganymede (Trojan boy who in Gk mythology was the cupbearer to Zeus; cf It non fare il ganimede, don't play Ganymede = "act your age"—said to old man trying to act young) younger partner in a pederastic relationship "You're going to get into hot water with his parents if you keep havin' that Ganymede sleep over at your place everynight."

gape (gāp) to sit with the legs spread far apart.

garage door the pants fly   "He opens his garage door, honey, an' a big black Cadillac comes out, honkin' for orders."
   Syn: **hinge on a barn door; shop door.**
   Related term:
   open for lunch said of an unzipped fly.

garbage-can gray (camp) bad job of frosting the hair "The next time you want silver pubes, go to a specialist an' you won't have the garbage-can gray you have now."

garbage-mouth somebody 1. to backbite   **2.** to heckle, rebuke somebody "Petunia Pig started to garbage-mouth me, but I set her head to reeling when I handed it right back."

garconniere (gär-son-âr', fr Fr garcon = boy + suffix -ière = storage room) **1.** the apartment of a *kept boy   **2.** an apartment kept solely for sexual purposes
   Syn: **fuck-flat; set-up** (Brit gay sl).

garter party (les sl, late '60s) lesbian game with the following rules: initiator calls out "garter!" when she sees another's garter-snaps and so wins a chance of introduction and further socializing.

gay (fr 16th cent Fr gaie = homosexual , man; cf Brit sl gay girl = whore) **1.** one who is homosexual. Sometimes used of only the active member of the homosexual community, ie one who speaks the slang, buys homophile literature, is homosexually sociable, etc "Gays march on Washington!" "Hate that gay? Blow it away!"   **2.** (adj) homosexual; associated with homosexuality "Gay is as gay does!" "Blow Tilly a gay kiss!" Syn: **happy** ("Tired of the run-of-the-mill numbers? Phone the Happy Miller at Exbrook 2254"); **jolly.**
   —abandon brash unconcern exhibited publicly between two homosexuals.
   —as a goose[rose] (kwn SF, late '60s) said of a man who presents no doubt as to whether or not he is overtly homosexual.
   —bar a drinking establishment frequented by homosexuals. The biggest complaint among gays about gay bars is that it's the same scene week-in week-out. Syn: **boite** (bwät, fr Fr = box); **country club** (late '60s); **floater** (kwn LA, mid '60s. bar running a high risk of being closed by the police and moved to a new location); **fruit bin[market]; hangar** (because fairies fly in and out); **homo haven; pansy-palace[-perch]; quaint bar** (kwn LV, late '60s); **queens' church** (pej); **the bar gay** ("So this is the bar gay—so, this is being grown up!"); **trap; turkey club** (camp).
      Related terms:
   fluff parlor (kwn LA SM sl, '70) tavern catering to the effeminate crowd. Syn: **swish joint** ("The owner of that swish joint must've been born under the sign of Prices.")
   truck stop (kwn SF, les sl, '71) bar for lesbians. Syn: **birdie**

joint (*pej,* hetero sl, '40s).

—boy [**-cat, -guy, -lad, -man**] the homosexual man, regardless of age. Syn: **blade** (*kwn* San Diego teen sl, mid '60s, used by those who fancy themselves "in" with the local deviates: "Knew this blade once—wonder what ever happened to 'im—maybe something he swallowed killed 'im"); **gray boy** (*rare,* gay + neutral color of gray); **joy boy** (Aus sl); **masisi** (Haitian Creole); **one of us** ("He's one of us, it's safe to camp"); **passion fruit** (*kwn* Hollywood, '40s); **warm brothers** (E translation of Ger gay sl *Warmbrüder*).

—chick[**-woman**] a lesbian Syn: **madivinaise** (mä-dē'-vi-nāz, Haitian Creole = my divine one: actually, a voodoo priestess who is a lesbian); **mermaid** (*fr* Gullah from the idea that one rarely hears of mermen).

—deceiver 1. a *dildo,** especially when worn beneath the pants in an attempt to round out the crotch **2.** (*kwn* Cleveland, mid '60s) man who convincingly masquerades as a woman **3.** (*fr* Joe Solomon's film *The Gay Deceivers,* late '60s) heterosexual feigning homosexuality in order to escape military obligation.

—dirt homosexual who robs his partners "That LA is just crawling with gay dirt—they'll pull down your panties, suck you off an' pick your pocket all in one blow."

—dom homosexual subculture with respect to the standard norm "Julius Caesar was no stranger to ancient gaydom; he was a mad fuck to the King of Bythynia, at least." Syn: **gay life**[**world**] ("Little did he know that he took a giant step into the gay world when he became a fashion designer"); **gray world** (the ungay world of the homosexual).

—dude (hip gay sl) an aware homosexual; gay following the hip philosophy.

—er (teen sl, late '60s) homosexual "You're a gayer? You don't *talk* like a gayer."

—Liberation radical political movement.
Related term: **pink panther** gay libber.

—lines (*fr* theatrical sl *lines* = the spoken parts in a play: "Stop stealing all my best lines!") clever dialogue for filling gaps of silence and raising grins; theatrical sentences which reflect homosexual humor; memorized cliches found in the speech of the gay populace. The cream of the crop are those lines which one thinks of on the spur of the moment. Others are taken from song and movie titles. The following are but a few examples:

"Alone at last!" (*kwn* SF, '72: said when there is a lull in the party)

"He's so good looking he should be hanged!" (*kwn* LV, late '60s)

"My hips are alive with the sound of music!" (*kwn* SF, late '60s)

"Spread your sunshine all over my face!" (reflective of the verb *rim**)

"He took to it as naturally as to wearing high heels!" (= he had no problem in adapting.)

Related term:

throw out gay lines 1. to fish verbally with gay puns as bait in order to find out if one is indeed homosexual **2.** to speak gay slang.

—marriage an agreement between two members of the same sex to live together as man and wife, *ie* active (drinking the beer) and passive (buying it).

—lingo[**-talk**] the homosexual jargon "Does he know any Italian gay talk?" Syn: **buff-talk** (*rare,* hustler sl, mid '60s, *fr* sl *boff* = fuck); **fag-lang** ("Fag-lang is spoken by three people in Trenton, New Jersey"); **faglish** (***fag** + English:

"Did you see the sign above the glory hole that said, 'Faglish understood here?'"); **show[stage-] talk; tramp talk** (*rare: vulgarisms found in gay slang*).

Related term:

jargon (*kwn* SF, '72) to be acquainted with the local gay slang "I can't jargon that!" Syn: **know the words and[to] the music** ('40s).

—wedding serious or mock ceremony in which a couple of the same sex exchange vows before a minister, witnesses and guests.

—woman 1. (*camp*) mature homosexual "A gay woman should know better than to spend all of her money on one face." **2.** (les sl) a lesbian.

geeky terrifyingly abnormal, unethical, smacking of villainy, fun "*Marat-Sade* was positively geeky!"

Syn: **geekish.**

gender found only in the expression **discovering gender** = becoming aware of one's own homosexual desires, see *come out "Someday that Jones boy will discover gender after he looks down and sees that pussy swinging."

gentlewoman (*camp*) tasteful, well educated gay man "Larries and gentlewomen!"

George (hetero sl) male homosexual "Oh, George, you're gorgeous!"

Syn: **Bruce; Cy; Oscar.**

Georgina of the Jungle (*camp, kwn* SF, '70 *fr* television cartoon program "*George of the Jungle*") homosexual whose living-room looks like "Green Acres"; a plant fancier.

German marching pills (*kwn* Texas, late '60s) amphetamines, especially methedrine.

get a distance reading able to see for blocks.

get burned (pros sl) to be cheated out of money.

get gone (narc sl, *fr* black sl) to become elated through the effects of narcotics, alcohol or pure love "I wants t'get *gone,* honey; so pass me that funny cigarette" "One look at that child's basket an' I was *gone!*"

Syn: **get high; get jacked up.**

get her (*exclam, dated,* '40s) command to take a gander at someone who is trying his damndest to be charming and witty but winding up a fiasco. Equivalent to "who does he think he is?"

—bar tavern frequented by gossipy homosexuals who tend to live in the past.

get in on some action to conveniently chance upon some horny young stud in a restroom.

get in tune (*kwn* SF, '71) to make a hissing noise while smoking marijuana.

get next to somebody 1. (*fr* black sl) to pay court to a sweetheart **2.** (*kwn* SF, black gay sl, '70) to bother, annoy, irritate, vex "It sho'nuff would get next to *me* if my bossman'd buy liquor with *my* money."

get off my case (*imp*) a demand to stop interfering. Equivalent to: "Keep your nose out of my business!"

Syn: **get out of my life.**

get off my face (*imp*) = get out of my sight!

get off the weed (*dated, imp,* late '50s) a command to stop daydreaming "Get off the weed, Mae; he wouldn't look at you in an open-coffin funeral."

Syn: **Get off it!**

get one's lunch (lunch *fr* lumps) to be battered, roughed-up, beaten.

Syn: **catch one's lunch.**

get one's nerves together (black gay sl) to build up one's courage, to become nervy "Madame mayor finally got her nerves together an' told off that big woman in Washington."

get on somebody's case to pick on somebody, get on one's nerves "I quit working there when they started to get on my case."

get out of budget dresses (*kwn* SF, '71) to step out of the everyday humdrum routine "My honey got me out of budget dresses" **2.** to hobnob with high society "Hi, there, fella, wanna get out of budget dresses?"

get out of somebody's face[life] to leave another's presence "I'll get out of your face just as soon as I finish douching out my mouth."

get out the lavender[pink] spot to shine an imaginary spotlight upon a loud queen "Get out the lavender spot! Andrew's starting to get into her number!"

get real (*exclam*) stop playing dumb "Get real! We saw the two of you trashin' it up in the balcony."

get somebody 1. to succeed in seducing somebody **2.** to beat somebody in a contest of wits "I finally got the company."

giddy (*fr* ME *gidy* = mad, foolish, frivolous) **1.** gay, in every sense of the word **2.** elaborately decorated; crammed, busy "Austrians, statues of countless gods, fountains spewing God-knows what—you certainly do have a giddy place here in the mountains."

Gina (*camp*) gay nickname for Gene "Oh, my word! Look who's riding across the screen—Gina Aubrey!"
  —LaSalsa (*camp*) gay Italian.

girl (*fr* pros sl *girl* = whore) **1.** a fellow homosexual "Any girl that loves leeks that much must be a golden shower queen at heart" **2.** gadget (likening object to naughty child), see ***accoutrements** "You brought the salad—we'll set the girl right over here next to the radishes" "I just can't seem to clean these girls" (*ie* sunglasses) **3.** used to form pronouns: **that girl** = him, he; **this girl** = I, me.
  —y (*kwn* SF, late '60s) girlish, womanish "Having long hair made me feel *so* girly." Syn: **pussy** ("Apricot brandy toothpaste? How absolutely pussy of you!")

give a double dig (*fr* black sl) to look at something a second time "Give a double dig, girl; he's not as plain as you think."

give birth to a monkey to defecate.

give head to suck cock.

give it flint (*imp, kwn* SF black gay sl, '70) give it hell! Yelled to somebody dancing up a storm. Equivalent to "work it out!"

give one a gay knock (*kwn* Cleveland, mid '60s) to attack a person, either physically or verbally "Give that shitass a gay knock, Ronny; tell him that you have the clap *after* you fuck him."

give over (*imp,* Brit gay sl) shut-up! "Give over! I'm not forty-three, I'm only forty-one."
  Syn: **give way** (giv hwī).

give somebody a ride (*dated*) to lie; stretch the truth.
  Syn: **take somebody on a ride.**

gladiola seedlings (*kwn* Haw gay sl) youths blossoming into homosexuals.
  Syn: **buds.**

glitter (*kwn* SF, hip gay sl, late '60s) methedrine in powder form.

glitter girl (*camp*) costly dressed homosexual.

glom [onto] someone (*fr* hobo sl *glommer* = hand) to be over-possessive of a lover "Don't glom me; let me out by myself once in a while!"

glory hole a hole drilled or carved between the partitions of two toilet stalls in a men's room and used for sex ("That's the glory of love.") Glory holes are attractive to those who wish anonymity mixed with the sensation of danger.

Syn: **suck hole** ("They were a happily married couple until a suck hole came between them one gloomy afternoon").

Related terms:

Christmas caroling (*kwn* SF, '71 *fr* parody of Christmas message "Gloria in excelsis Deo!" = Glory to God on high!) testing out all the new glory holes in town.

suck factory 1. men's room with at least two glory holes **2.** a men's washroom with potential.

go (*dated*) to deliberate in a homosexual's bedchamber "Do you think he'll go?" = will he have sex?

—it alone to masturbate.

go chookin' (*kwn* Texas, *fr* Am-Sp *pachuco* = Sp-Am teddy-boy) to go slumming, especially used of a hip gay who makes the rounds of all the straighter, swankier places.

God help us all and Oscar Wilde (*proverb*, Brit gay sl) quick prayer for the earth's poor gay souls with an additional indulgence for Mr. Wilde.

go down to suck a cock, see ***blow.**

go foot-tappin' to seat oneself in a public toilet and tap the foot as a signal of availability; to cruise a washroom in such a manner "Draw up the divorce papers—I went foot-tappin' last night and recognized my husband's shoes in the booth next to mine."

go for yourself (*imp, fr* black sl) believe in yourself (because ain't nobody gon to believe it for you.) A cry of encouragement shouted to musicians, dancers and anybody having the time of his life.

Syn: **do it on for yourself** (cause ain't nobody dying for you but yourself).

go groupie on somebody (*kwn* SF, hip gay sl, '70) to carnally know a famous personality, especially a rock performer "I know I'm gay, but I could sure dig goin' groupie on Tina Turner."

go Hollywood (*obs*, '40s) **1.** to mingle with gays. . .socially or bareback **2.** (*rare*, even then) to be showy "Has he gone Hollywood? Mary, he's the only man I know that has an escalator in his garage."

go home with the garbage-man[milkman, trucks] (*kwn* SF, late '60s) to go home tired and frustrated after having cruised all night long.

Related term:

close Polk Street (*kwn* SF) to be the last person left cruising Polk Gulch.

golden boy ('70) young man in the prime of his youth "The golden boy looks as though he has a promising future ahead of him in the insurance business."

golden shower a stream of piss.

Syn: **champagne fountain** (mid '60s); **golden champagne** (mid '60s); **orange ade** (*kwn* SF, '71: "He was pouring orange ade all over the fire hydrant."); **warm beer** (*kwn* SF, SM sl, late '60s): "Do you like warm beer? = Do you like being pissed on? Do you drink urine?

—queen an urolagniac (*med fr* Gk *ouron* = urine) a urine fetishist who enjoys being pissed on: "Boy, are you ever sucking up the suds—do you have a hot date with a golden-shower queen later?" **2.** (*camp*) one who has disregard for the feelings of others; one who pisses on people.

Syn: **golden queen** (*rare*); **piss queen** ("There's no telling what a piss queen will dunk his doughnuts into next"); **tinkler-belle; yellow-stream queer** (*kwn* SF, '72).

Related terms:

golden screw anal intercourse with urine instead of semen released into the rectum.

water sports (*kwn* SF, SM sl, late '60s) urolagnia, erotic interest given to urine "You into water sports, man?"

gold fish (*rare*, lunch-counter sl) sliced peaches.

go mad 1. to get carried away with decorating "Didn't Montessa absolutely go mad with these curtains?" **2.** to be uninhibited; to enjoy life "Go mad with the wine, dear; that's what it's there for."

gone (*fr* black sl, '20s-'30s, revived for a laugh) **1.** unable to keep a straight thought due to excessive doping or drinking; too far gone; ***high** "That was righteous grass, man; I'm gone on one hit." **2.** handsome, striking "He's *so* gone; all the bitches turn their heads when he walks in, and they sweat their makeup off until he splits."
   Syn: **out-of-sight.**
   —on somebody in love "He's gone on some Capricorn piece."

gooboos (*adv, kwn* LV, mid '60s, *fr* Fr *beaucoups* = gobs of) plenty, a lot "We're having high tea with gooboos of grass."

good fuck sex praise from both sides.

good head man who excels in cocksucking.

goodness (*exclam*) mild-mannered, feminine oath used to express surprise. Equivalent to the stronger: "Oh, Christ! I shot my load!"

goodrich queen one who passes bad checks—they bounce.

goo goo stuff (*dated*) excessive romanticism; mush.

goose ('40s) playfully poking the finger(s) into another's ass; pinching the ass "Did you get your Christmas goose yet, Liebling?"
   Syn: **backhand drive; sneak attack.**
   Related terms:
   shfriend (shfrend, *kwn* LA, mid '60s) goose's warcry: to startle a friend by quickly thrusting an extended finger in between his buttocks while shouting "Shfriend!" "We'd shfriend each other in study hall."
   weenie-dog (*kwn* Wis, teen sl, late '50s) to off-balance a man by thrusting the hand in between his legs from the rear so as to reach in far enough to easily clutch his balls.

go over to join the ranks of the homosexual.

gopher tits the flat breasts of a man.

gorgeous [gorjesus] (gōr′-jus, gōr-jē′-zus) **1.** attractive, becoming "I did this gorgeous hippy at the park" **2.** well built, robust, manly "He has such a gorgeous bod!" **3.** magnificent "What a gorgeous sandwich—it was like nibbling ambrosia on rye."

go rest (*kwn* Texas, late '60s) to go to the bathroom, particularly to move the bowels "I gotta go rest, kiddies, but keep the campfires going 'til I get back."
   Syn: **go biffy** ("Why don't you go biffy first, Diz; *then* we'll cut the cake"); **go up the stairs** (Brit).

gorilla it down (*kwn* SF, '71) to devour a large amount of food rapidly.

gorilla salad thick, hairy pubic area.

go that route (hetero sl) to be a practicing homosexual.
   Syn: **be that way; go Wilde** (late '50s).

go to cathedral (*kwn* SF, '71) to smoke hashish.

go to the veins (*fr* black narc sl) to inject drugs into the bloodstream; to mainline.

grab at the pearls (*camp*) to clutch at the throat with the fingertips when surprised, taken aback, or absent-mindedly pondering a question "You can't tell me that one's straight—didn't you see him grab at his pearls just then?"

Syn: **grab for pearls.**

Grace (*camp*) allotted to those who are not graceful "Way t'go, Grace; why don't you spill the rest of the bourbon?"

gracious (*exclam*) another weak expletive stolen from the vocabulary of housewives "Gracious! Look at the basket that one is showing!"

grand 1. haughty, fashionable "A grand person nevah carries a purchase home—he has it delivered" **2.** grandiose, showy **3.** (*camp*) extensive "He might be my interior-decorator sister, but he'll never be able to mask the grand damage that his Victorian features."

Grand Canyon loose-fitting anus, as complained about by an active partner "Talk about the Grand Canyon: her ass is as wide as the natural wonder itself."
Syn: **Lincoln Tunnel.**
—Suite noisy, sloppy-sounding intercourse ("Skoosh, skwish, slap, shwop, slurf.")
Related terms:
bum fuck one whose anus is no longer tight. Syn: **hobo-sexual** (*camp*); **Miss Arizona; Miss Grand Canyon; Miss National Park.**

Grand Central Station (*fr* narc sl *tracks* = needle-marks) scarred arm of a die-hard heroin addict.

grand entrance an impressive entry; an arrival "Let's make our grand entrance a year from now—you know it's chic to be tardy."

grand exit 1. departure made with chaotic commotion and general ribaldry **2.** the act of being bounced "He was given the grand exit for taking off his clothes and jumping onto the bar."

grand finale death.

grassy-ass (*interj, camp, fr* Sp *gracias*) an expression of gratitude. Syn: **mercy** (*interj, camp,* black gay sl, *fr* Fr *merci*).

grapepicker one who scratches his posterior as though he were plagued by itching hemorrhoids "The grapepicker must be going to the movies—he's already picking out a seat."
Related terms:
piles hemorrhoids. Syn: **goose-eggs** ("He's got goose-eggs? I guess that doesn't make him the 'perfect asshole' any more."); **Henries; lilies of the valley** (*camp*); **rhoids.**
small vineyards bad case of anal warts.

grapes any unsightly conglomeration stuck to the anal hairs or found adhering to the anal tissue itself: **dingle-berries, venereal warts** and **hemorrhoids** are all classified as grapes "Rimming him is totally out of the question—grapes give me gas."

gratis (*kwn* SF, late '60-'70) **1.** a gift from——— "This brass candelabra, gratis Miss Linus, is my most precious jewel in the house" **2.** stolen from——— "The clock is gratis Sears."

gravy sweat.
Syn: **gravy for the meat.**

gray queen (*kwn* SF, '70, *fr* gray flannel suit) the conservative, Wall Street career-type queer.

grease any manufactured lubricant used for a tight squeeze by an anal copulator "There ain't nuthin' no good without the grease!" (quote from Tina Turner). Two favorites are Vaseline and KY; spit is not considered grease.
Syn: **bean oil** (= hair oil, *fr* sl *beaner* + *greaser* = Mexican); **cocktail oil** ('72); **crisco; pimpo** (pēm'-pō, *fr* Pach = pimp); **shmear** (*fr* Ger *Schmiere* = grease); **slip-ins** (prison sl); **veenershlicker** (*camp*); **weenerslider** (*camp*); **wishbone salad dressing** (*fr* sl *wishbone* = cock).
—d up having some form of lubricant smeared about the anus to insure an easy intromission "He goes up to the park at night all greased up an' rarin' t' go." Syn: **pregreased.**

great beauty moviestar type of person; rave material; someone to write home to mother about   "A pink belt in karate doesn't make you a great beauty."

Great Lakes (*camp*) the urinals; the big boys' room   "Here's your ticket to the Great Lakes—another beer!"

Greek (*fr* Old Greece where pederasty was fashionable) **1.** the active pederast   "A Greek is somebody who gets a little behind in his work." **2.** to practice anal eroticism, see ***fuck.**

  —love[**—way**] pederasty (*fr* Gk *paid* = boy + *erastes* = lover) **1.** love expressed by an older man for a boy **2.** anal intercourse. Syn: **Dorian love; pig sticking** (hetero sl: "There was plenty of pig sticking in the royal families, let me tell you!")

  —side the posterior, see ***ass**   "If he slaps you on the cheek, turn him the Greek side—maybe you gave lousy head."
    Related term:
  athenian active pederast.

green ('70) menthol; a mentholated cigarette   "I want a ciggie-poo without any green in it."
  Syn: **peppermint stick.**

Greta [Garbo] **1.** sobriquet of a loner **2.** (*rare*) among astrology buffs, nickname for one born under the sign of Virgo **3.** (*kwn* SF, '70) important; when used of a person, however, the importance becomes an idle wish outweighed by self-esteem   "Come off the throne, you're not as greta as you stink."

grief merchant (*kwn* SF, late '60s, *fr* sl *grief* = complications) **1.** newspaper vendor **2.** on-the-minute reporter. Syn: **Brenda Starr 3.** (*camp*) a gossipy busybody.

grief up on 1. to watch the daily news on TV **2.** to watch soap operas **3.** to beat somebody up, see ***dirt.**

grime material (late '50s) **1.** cardholding member of the levis-and-crud set **2.** a model citizen from Skid Row   "Wanna touch some grime material and catch a new disease?"
    Related term:
  skin some grime to bathe, feed and fuck a derelict.

grinders sharp or broken teeth.
    Related terms:
  snaggle puss chip-toothed cocksucker. Syn: **snaggle-tooth fairy.**
  grind some meat to be careless while cocksucking; to bite. Simplified to mean merely sucking a man's organ   "Gosh! Did someone grind your meat or did you get it caught in the revolving doors at Bickfords."

groceries 1. genitalia   "I'm surprised that the accident didn't deball him completely—there were some pretty busy casts on his groceries." **2.** (*kwn* LV, late '60s) found in the expression **carry the groceries** = to room and board a lazy friend. Syn: **carry somebody; pull somebody's boat** ("I don't mind pullin' my sweetie's boat; but I sure as shit ain't gonna pull her sister's too."

groove on (*fr* black sl, '50s-70) to enjoy   "He grooves on Victorian houses."

groovy [**grooby**] (Oregon pronunciation: **grovey**) (*fr* black sl, '30s, *fr* sl *in the groove* = current, with the times) popular catch-all adjective for describing that which is pleasing; jim dandy   "We had such a groovy time with Doug and Carol; they're such groovy people and they always have such groovy food." Sadly enough, it has become a loose shoe appearing in even the jargons of the nongroovy.
  Syn: ***boss; tough** ("He has such tough buns.")

grope ('40s, *fr* ME *gropen,* akin to OE *gripan* = to sieze) to fondle another person's clothed genitals   "You shouldn't grope—didn't your mother ever tell you it wasn't polite to play with your food!"

Syn: **cop a feel** (early '60s: "Hey, Mister, can I cop a feel? I haven't eaten in a week"); **eat with the hands; feel [somebody up]** ("Mary, you jumped as though you just got felt up by a wet fish."); **fist it** (= to seize another's erection, particularly in a public restroom); **give somebody a grope; honk** (*kwn* LA, '70); **read braille; reef** (Brit gay sl); **take somebody's pulse.**

—**bar** crowded gay bar were groping occurs. Syn: **pinch palace.**

—**y** said of an establishment which is conducive to groping "That bar doesn't get gropey 'till Sunday afternoons."

gross unbelievably vulgar, foul "That magazine is the grossest thing I've ever paid good money for" "Gross is when you kiss your grandmother, and she slips you the tongue."

A gross description of an acne problem: "When he smiles, his face runs."

Gross proposition: "Hi, kid, wanna shit better?"

—**somebody out** to morally offend; to shock by being coarse "Mighty Mouth here grossed out every guest at the party with his offensive lines."

ground round 1. accident victim "Do they package all the ground round at the emergency ward" **2.** cock bearing the scars of a "snaggle puss."

grow some wings 1. to come alive; perk up "You should see him grow some wings whenever he hears Neil Diamond" **2.** to conduct oneself in a flamboyant manner. Syn: **grow tits** ("The longer he chatters, the bigger his tits grow") **3.** to run, flee, escape "Grow some wings, girl, here come some uptight hicks—and that ain't love in their eyes."

G-string jockstrap or posing brief, see ***joys** "I want him in some real action shots, not this G-string crap."

guest star 1. a visitor **2.** a pickup who strips upon entering the apartment pantomiming the entire score of his favorite musical comedy. Guest stars are not easy to befriend.

gum job blow job given by a toothless old man ("fuckin' teeth just get in the way anyhow.")

Syn: **slob-job; velvet job** (*kwn* SF, early '60s).

Related terms:

gum it to death to remove the choppers before sucking.

gummy 1. any homosexual with false teeth **2.** one who sucks his partner only after removing his dentures. The word is neither complimentary nor derisive. Grafitto: "Have gums, will travel—The Prairie Fairy."

hachi [**hatchi, hotchy**] (ho'-chē, GI English, *fr* Jap *hachi* = eight + pun made upon sl *ate* & *hot:* used by GI's with native women: "Me likee numbah one hachi") homosexual soldiers, choosing a penis over a vagina, used the word to mean cock "Sucky hachi cocky?"

hair (short for *hair people*) a longhair, hippy "Some hairs bought the mansion."

hairbender hairdresser; hair stylist; beautician "I'd love to help that hairbender open up his new shop . . . with a bomb!"
  Syn: **Bruce the hairdresser** (hetero sl); **hairburner** ("Some hairburner you are! You couldn't put a curl in a pig's ass."); **haircranker** (*kwn* Seattle, late '60s); **Mr. Beverly.**
  Related terms:
  bulletproofed said of a hair style stiff with spray.
  get the hair cranked to have the hair reshaped, curled, vitalized.
  spray queen hairdresser who uses too much hair spray and too little talent.

hair fairy (*kwn* SF, mid '60s, *dated* due to upsurge of popularity in long hair) man with a fixation that his long hair feminizes him "It's amazing what a hair fairy can do with a teaspoon of dye."
  Related term:
  hair bar his hangout; Chucker's was San Francisco's leading hair bar in the early '60s.

hairpie the vulva, see ***muff.**

hair shirt hirsute chest "I just washed your hair shirt, and I can't do a thing with it."
  Related terms:
  wear a hair shirt to beat the chest. Syn: **pull out[put on] the Steve Reeves suit.**

hairy 1. (*dated*) complex, involved, entangled. A subject best left unsaid is hairy "I like Chuck, but every time I go over, he starts gettin' too hairy; I wish he'd stop trying to make me." Syn: **heavy 2.** (*dated*, Ariz teen sl, late '50s) satisfying, great.

half-and-half 1. poorly executed circumcision **2.** (*fr* pros sl) sexual act of alternating cocksucking with fucking.

half-boy (*pej*, *?fr* colloq *half a man* = one who is crippled either in his body or mind) youth outwardly appearing straight but in actuality gay.

halfway around the world (*fr* pros sl) fellatio and ***rimming** performed without licking the rest of the body as in a complete ***trip around the world** "Call me later, sis; I'm only halfway around the world an' I want this to be a complete trip."

half world ('50s, *fr* Fr argot *demi monde* = half world = the world of nonrespectibility) the homosexual underground—a world where he doesn't have to hide his feelings.

hallucinate (*kwn* LV, '70) to talk through one's hat; to be seeing things "What makes you think that cute thing is after you? You're only hallucinating!"

handbag (*Brit gay sl*) generic for gifts, presents.

handmade said of a large penis which supposedly attained its size by having been continually stroked or used in fucking.
Syn: **hand-raised[-reared]**.

hang short for hang up the phone "I've got to hang; call me tomorrow at the crack of noon!"
Syn: **hang up on somebody's face**.

Happy Birthday (*exclam*) sarcastically applied to pests, such as roadhogs, who act as if they're privileged "She's all over the road—it must be her birthday."

happy valley the cleft separating the right buttock cheek from the left; vulgarly, the crack.
Related terms:
ski up and down Happy Valley (late '60s) to rub the cock in between and over the buttocks of the partner. Some place the penis into the crack, like a hot dog into a bun, and slide it up and down.
Syn: **cracking; crack-run; skinny rubbing**.

hard 1. firm, solid, muscular, not yet sagging "Over thirty, and my arse is *still* hard!" Syn: **tight 2.** (*adv, kwn* LV, mid '60s) quite a lot; often precedes *fat righteous* "I dug you hard fat righteous, man!"

hard daddy (*women's prison sl*) the lesbian *husband* who sets up housekeeping with another woman.

Hardly Davidson (*camp, kwn* SF, '71) small low-power scooter.

hard[-on] ((early '50s) state of erection in the excited cock (L = *penis erectus*) "All that dirty talk gave me a hard."
Syn: **bar-on** (*dated*); **bone-on** (*obs*); **boner** (considered adolescent: "This book was written by a boner"); **booboo** (*fr* baby talk: "He's perverted—the only thing that'd give him a booboo would be a knothole in a wooden duck"); **bowsprit** (*rare*); **cock-on** ("The only way I could work up a cock-on now, is if you were to slam a window down on it"); **hot-rod; jackhammer** (= black erection); **live wire; pinky; pulse** (*fr* the throbbing sensation found in erect penises); **putter; putting iron; rod[-on]** ("Does watching hot dogs defrost give you a rod-on?"); **upright grand[organ]**.
Related terms:
hardly (*camp*) inch-long erection.
hard-on failure (*camp*) the inability to get a hard-on because of old age.
raise a beam to develop an erect cock. Syn: **get it up; raise it; tune it up** ("He tunes it up just *passing* the panty counter.")
spring to suddenly and unexpectedly have an erection "Just show him a picture of a peter and watch his jewels spring."
talk it up to tell ribald stories to get it hard. Syn: **charm a snake**.
trip all over the dick to be tongue-tied and concerned with concealing the erection when talking with its cause.

Harlow 1. Jean Harlow **2.** gay nickname for one who is blond and daring **3.** (*camp*, black gay sl) nickname for a fellow black who fails to meet the dishwater blonde requirement "Don't give me such a strange look, Harlow, just cause Ma Nature gave you one."

hateful bitch (*camp*) unobtainable doll. Always used humorously, but made to sound spiteful.

hauncho virile, see *butch*.

have to experience carnal knowledge of somebody "I am *not* wanton—I haven't had anybody since I stepped free from the elevator."

have a bad day to be in such foul humor that it affects the appearance; to look terrible and feel the same way "They used to tell me I looked like the boy next door, but I've been having a bad day for the last ten years."

Ant: **have a good day** ("I'm not one to dish, but, when I'm around *her* I always have a good day"). Syn: **look good and naked.**

have a case of the vapors (*dated*) **1.** to go to a *baths, usually cancelling previous plans by claiming sudden illness "He told me he couldn't go because he was feelin' under the weather, but I bet an eyetooth it was more a case of the vapors" **2.** to feel dizzy, faint "Oh, Martha! Take away this glass of wine; I'm beginning to have a case of the vapors."

have a cup of tea to use a public toilet for having sex.

Syn: **have a tea engagement.**

have a face to wear a beard or mustache.

have a From Here to Eternity (*kwn SF, mid '60s*) to have a torrid love scene on the beach "You've never had a From Here to Eternity? My dear, it certainly beats brushing straw off the balls."

have a Roman Spring (*kwn SF, mid '60s, fr* Tennessee Williams' novel *The Roman Spring of Mrs. Stone*) a last fling before old age [*retirement] sets in "She'll probably have *her* Roman Spring in a dirty bookstore!"

have eyes for to want, desire "Do you have eyes for some *joto* chocolate?"

have fairies at the bottom of the garden (Aus, *fr* Bea Lillie song) to be homosexual "That bloke 'as fairies at the bottom of 'is garden."

have oneself to be excited; worked up into a frenzy "He has himself every time he sees that butch idol of his in the papers."

have people (les prison sl) occupied homosexually behind bars.

have the large news for somebody to let someone else in on a little secret; to pass on information "I have the large news for your ass, sweetie; you couldn't live on four bits a month!"

hawl out a personality (late '60s) to unzip the fly and remove the cock for sex "That man was so hung—it took me ten minutes to hawl out his personality."

hay 1. disheveled, matted hair "You really ought to have something done about that hay before they bundle you up into a bale and sell you for fodder." Syn: **pubes** (*camp*); **straw** ("Losin' yer straw, Sparkle Plenty?"); **wig** (*dated:* "Rake out your wig, dear—I don't want your cooties makin' pigs o'themselves until my guests clear out") **2.** (late '60s) any inferior, low-grade marijuana, see *weed.

hazel (Cape Town gay sl) sex.

he (*rare, camp*) inserted into conversation when speaking of a burly lesbian.

head 1. glans penis; the acorn-like bulb forming the uppermost end of the penis. Syn: **acorn** (translation of L *glans* = acorn); **almond rock candy** (= glans penis as a fellator's confection); **bulb; crown** (*cf* sl *crown* = head); **German helmet** ("His German helmet is a work of art"); **onion** (= the large, bulbous head); **red bonnet** (*camp*); **saucerhead; turnip 2.** (*fr* naut sl *bulkhead* = the latrines) the toilet; any bathroom "Is the head in that store cruisy?"

headache band (*camp, fr* woman's hair accessory = a band rainbowing the forehead down to the ears then being fastened under the hair) headband worn by a man.

head date performing fellatio in order to avoid anal bombardment; sucking to avoid fucking.

healed (*fr* pros sl) carrying a weapon for protection.

Related terms:

cheese-scraper (*kwn* San Diego, mid '60s) knife or razor carried for protection.

tex (*kwn* SF, '70) a gun "He pulled his tex, man, and blew that motherfucker clean away." Syn: **joint** (black sl)**; piece** (black sl).

wean a Texan (*kwn* SF, '70) to carry a gun.

healers (?*fr* rhyming sl = *feelers*) the hands, paws "Your body is so tense, Sergeant; let Mama take care of all that with her magic healers."

health movie (orig: film shown to high schoolers to teach them the evils of drugs, alcohol, reckless driving, *etc*) situation which apes such a preacher feature "I'm such a health movie—I'm everything my mother's against."

healthy having a toned, tapered body "How much is the healthy brunette."

hearts (*fr* narc sl *horse hearts*) pink, heart-shaped amphetamine tablets often serving as petrol for sex marathons.

heaven just too, too marvelous for words "Jello and wine is just *heaven* on a hot summer night."

Syn: **heavenly.**

—s (*exclam*) see ***gracious** "Heavens! There must be mule blood in *that* child."

heels 1. (*camp*) masculine footwear; men's shoes "I've got to get me a new pair of heels; these sissies are jus'bout done for" 2. (*camp*) one's common sense in general "Watch your heels, Mae!" = **a.** watch your step **b.** watch what you say.

Related terms:

break a heel (*camp*) 1. to trip 2. to twist the ankle 3. to slip.

on heels (*camp*) 1. high, tall. A car which has been channeled is said to be on heels, just as a man who towers over one is on heels.

put the cake on heels to bake a layer cake.

he-ing it (*dated, kwn* LV, mid '60s) 1. assuming the masculine role 2. acting big and tough "Tuck your dress in and stop he-ing it!"

Ant: **she-ing it.**

Helen [**Helena, Helene**] placed into compound nicknames playfully poking fun at others.

—Hairburner gay hairdresser.

—Moviestar someone who tries too hard; a future failure; a shlump "Of course it's Helen Moviestar—look at its teeth; they're all capped!"

—of Troy one whose beauty could have launched a thousand ships—a thousand years ago, see ***mess.**

—Roobenbitch one claiming the knowledge of how to apply cosmetics correctly. Syn: **Miss Avon Produce.**

—Twelvetoes a dancing maniac "Will the real Helen Twelvetoes please sit down?"

hemorrhoid baby (Haw gay sl) hemorrhoids generated by too much fucking too long.

hep hepatitis.

he-rags (*obs*) masculine clothing: lumberjack shirts, baggy pants, wornout shoes, *etc*.

hermaphrodite (*fr* L // Gk *Hermaphroditos* = son of Hermes and Aphrodite) 1. one born with the genitals of both sexes 2. (*pej*) the stereotype homosexual. (It is worth noting that slang words for ***castratos**, those without genitals, also double as slur words for gay men) *fr* Pliny's *Natural History:* "Individuals are occasionally born who belong to both sexes: such persons we call by the name of hermaphrodites. They were formerly called Androgyni and were looked upon as monsters, but at the present day they are employed for sexual purposes."

Syn: ***dyke; hermafrodita** (ār-mǎf-rō-dē'-tā, *fr* Sp); **hermaphy; moff; morph** ("Know how a morph pees? Out of a mud flap!"); **morphdite; muffie.**

hero candy football player, or some other sport's idol, who will allow a homosexual fan to blow him.

heron (black sl) heroin.

Syn: **smack** (narc sl: "He was so skinny that junkies would ask him where he scored the good smack"); **smizz** (*kwn* LV, mid '60s, carny rendition of *smack* = *smeeazack* = *smizz*).

Related term:

kiss on some smack to mainline heroin.

heyrube (*fr* carnival sl = cry for help when trouble breaks out between circus workers and local yokels) commotion, disturbance.

hickey 1. purplish bruise found mainly about he neck region and taken as evidence of intimate contact; mark caused by passionate kissing "Now the shoes come in hickey red." Syn: **monkey bite** ("Don't you ever tell me that you don't get planked—there's monkey bites all up and down your spine"); **rose tattoo** (= any bruise) **2.** (*kwn* Wis teen sl, early '50s) crumpled, used prophylactic.

Syn: **bubble gum.**

hidden treasure someone who winds up being sexier than first anticipated "He turned out to be hidden treasure—looks aren't everything you know."

Syn: **jackpot; tomato surprise** (late '60s).

high (*fr* black & narc sl) **1.** under drugs or liquor; bombed **2.** feeling good; carefree "Just lookin' into that man's hairline gets me high."

high acres pants which are too short for the wearer. Not conconsidered chic.

Syn: **pants featuring much flood[high-water].**

the high and hippy drug user who thinks he's got all the answers.

highballs (*camp*) eyelids of a drunk "Better take her home—her highballs are sinkin' under."

high colored (*kwn* SF, black gay sl, late '60s) black idiom thickly interspersed with archaic pronunciation and slang; blackese as spoken down home "Chile, whan dat man talkin' high culurd, you be lucky if you *evuh* know what he mean 'cuz all her wuds, dey all runned t'gedduh."

higher (*exclam*) answer to the casual greeting "hi!"

high fi mouth of one who lacks the intelligence of knowing when to keep it shut "Tone down the high fi, dear, I can't hear the brownies cooking."

high Russian (*kwn* Texas, '70) act where a homosexual is fucked and sucked simultaneously by his acrobatic partner. Syn: **big [super] J.**

high tea 1. (pun made upon the afternoon teas of high society + narc sl *tea* = marijuana) casual get-together where marijuana is smoked **2.** (*kwn* Southwest, mid '60s) gossip session outside of a park's public lavatory **3.** ('71) liquid concoction made by boiling marijuana stems and seeds in water; this brew is then drunk to obtain a high. Syn: **pot liquor; stone soup[tea]** ("Momsie just *adored* the airplane ride back home; she should have, I kept pumping her full of stone tea.")

hijack (prison sl) to rape another man. However compare with gay pun: "A hijacker is a boy who play with himself in airplane."

Hilda (Cape Town gay sl) ugly, ugly, u-g-l-y "There *ain't* no such thing as hilda hazel."

hill[billy] bourbon party punch mixed from cheap rot-gut wines "Don't doll up in your best spun glass, Mabel; they're just featuring hill bourbon, I'm afraid."

Hilltop Drive the upturned buttocks shaped visually like a rounded "m."
> Related term:
> **drive [it] up to Hilltop Drive** to practice *coitus in anus*.
> Also see *layer cake.

himmer (*dated,* hetero sl, late '50s) male homosexual. Based upon the joke of the parishioner who deposited a ten-spot into the Sunday church basket; urged by the pleased decon to select a hymn, the generous donator said, "I'll take him, and him, and . . ."

hincty (hink'-tē, *fr* black sl) paranoid, afraid of being arrested or beaten "Stop being so hincty; we haven't had Alice Blue clean up our act in weeks."

hinge on a barn door pants fly.

hint of mint ('50s) trace of homosexual tendencies.

hips, lips and armpits[fingertips, potato chips] (*exclam,* mid-late '60s) a *gay line paralleling "Anything goes!"

hip to it[the score] (*fr* black sl *hep* = in the swing of things, early '30s; or ?*fr* or related to narc sl *on the hip* = laying upon the hip and smoking opium; or ?*fr* black dial *hep* = to help + *hip him* = set him wise) **1.** to be aware, knowledgeable **2.** to know of a person's homosexuality.

hiss 1. to speak hatefully to somebody "He hisses on Henrietta hard—he never lets that queen up for air" **2.** to bring criminal charges against one **3.** (*interj*) recognition of bitterness and/or threatening nature "Hisss! There goes your best argument!"
> Syn: **meow!**

hit to go wenching; to go anyplace "I suppose you've already hit the park and drained every stag dry."

hitched gayly married.
> Syn: **tied up** (mainly prison sl).

hit it 1. to perform to the best of one's ability; to give it all you got **2.** to make tracks, run "I had to hit it for real, when I saw that bus aimin' for me!" "Hit it, we don't want your kind hangin' around our corner!"

Hit it, Shirley (*exclam*) **1.** cry of encouragement = enjoy! **2.** command to leave.

hit somebody in the cocksucker and knock him on his moneymaker to hit somebody in the face so hard that the blow knocks him on his ass.

hit the sack[rack, springs] to make love "Do you want to hit the sack with me or stay awake all night playing silly head games?"

hit the screen (*camp*) hit the scene; to arrive "When will togas hit the screen again?"

hobo-sexual sex partner whose performance was inadequate.
> Syn: **bum fuck; loose fit.**

hobo slang (*kwn* '30s & '40s)
> Some of these migratory men were not loathe to sharing their Mulligan stew and bedrolls with younger runaways fed up with farming and out for Jack London-type adventure on the open road. These homosexual hoboes developed a gay slang of their own, most of which is passed into oblivion, unknown by today's gays: the tramp who fucked his boy was known as a **bunker** and **eye-opener.** The adolescent who usually doubled as cook/lover to a honosexual hobo was called a **bindle-boy** (*bindle* = bedroll) and **bo** (short for hobo); **bohobo; fuzz face; gazooney** (with the variants **ginzel, gonsel, gunzl** all transliterated *fr* Yid *gonz'l* = gosling); **hymie** (*fr* hymen); **pos-**

sesh (*fr* contraction of possession); **preschen** and **prushun** (originally "Prussian," *fr* a propagandistic WW I vision of German troops as bayonet-brandishing barbarians raping young boys in front of their mothers); **ringtail** (one who is wet behind the ears and asshole); **road kid.** None of these words implied effeminacy, only freshness and naivete.

A boy who turned on a tramp was a **candy kid,** and more likely the boy was also **canned goods,** or virginal. Probably he would be **bunker-shy,** adverse to homosexual coitus. In mission halls and Salvation Army flop-houses, these inexperienced lads might meet a **church mouse** or **flinch bird** who proposition young vagrants. One can imagine him praying casually into his sleeve, "Hail Mary, full of grace, help me snare that pretty face!"

Searching for an accommodating asshole among the tramps in a hobo camp was known as going on a **whoozle hunt.** The actual fucking of another man was called **bunking up, jungling up** (?*fr* sl *jungle* = hobo camp) or **playing hide the sausage.** The ass itself became the **dirt run, old dirt road** and **old rip.** These words seem to indicate that pederasty was more important than fellation among the homosexual hoboes.

hock (*fr* Cockney rhyming sl = cock) the homosexual man.

hold a show 1. to be the center of attention in a public place, such as a supermarket **2.** to star in a sexual exhibition [*circus] given for paying customers. Syn: **give a circus**[exhibition].

hold court 1. to host, entertain socially; to reign **2.** to occupy the best cruising stall in a men's room.

hold each other's balls said of homosexuals who are lovers "There they go down the aisle of that tearoom holding each other's balls."

hold mud 1. to be poker-faced, cool as a cucumber, unperturbed "I was carryin' three trues when Velma stopped me, but I held my mud an' didn't get shaky" **2.** to have control over the bowels while being fucked anally; to refrain from defecating on the penis. "That motherin' punk oughta be taught some manners about holdin' his mud—he shit all over me when I shoved it in him."

hole it (late '60s) to clamp the anal sphincter muscle about the probing shaft; this produces anal tautness, a criterion of fucking.

holiday hair fancy hairdo.

Hollywood a small town in Southern California heralded as the Olympus of cosmologists; the fount of celluloid mythology. The town itself becomes **Tinsel Town** in the vernacular, while Hollywood is used to form compounds which convey the sin city element of the movie capital:

—**blue** cobalt glass.

—**canvas** the silver screen.

—**cocktail** potent combination of benzedrine tablets and gin.

—**glasses** pair of wrap-around sunglasses, especially when worn at night.

—**gold** easy pickings.

—**hill** YMCA chock full of homosexuals.

—**numbers** sex acts taking their slang from numbers, *eg* 69.

—**rejects** (*kwn* LV, late '60s) handsome men who wanted to make it big in the movies but wound up on the police payroll instead; cops whose biggest roles are when cast as decoys by the vice squad.

—**tablets** imaginary pills producing beauty. Extended to mean hormone pills or suntan capsules "You could drop Hollywood tablets from now until the cows stopped cruising—but you'll

never get rid of Miss Adam's apple."
—**Uterus 1.** anus, see *a-hole **2.** (*kwn* LA, late '60s) the Hollywood Tunnel.
—**weight problem** (*camp*) large bosom.

hollywop (*kwn* LV, mid '60s, ?*fr* hog-tied) to embarrass a friend by pulling his pants down, exposing him to passersby.
Syn: **hogglewap; hollywog** (All three words seemingly coined from pure fantasy); **pants somebody.**

holster the pants fly "Put your gun back into your holster . . . I'm not impressed with small caliber pieces."

Holy Week any period of time when one abstains from sex "I'm starting my Holy Week today—I found out that I contacted a dose."

home-cooked biscuits[cookies] one's lover; guardian of the home-front as opposed to the streetwalker "He might sample exotic foods, but he'll always come back to those home-cooked biscuits."

homi-polone (hō'-mē-pō-lō'-nē, Brit gay sl, *fr* Parlyaree // It *uomo* = man + polone = woman) man taking the passive role in anal investigations.

homo (*pej,* hetero sl, *fr* homosexual // Gr *homos-* = same; not *fr* L *homo* = man) male homosexual "You should have seen the little homo run" "Homo is where the hard is" "Rub-a-dub-dub three men in a tub—homos."
Syn: **four-letter man** (H-O-M-O).
—**lover** (*pej,* hetero sl) straight man who has homosexual friends.
—**milk 1** (teen sl) homogenized milk "Pour me a glass of homo milk, John!" **2.** semen, see *come.
—**scope** horoscope charted specifically for homoerotic readers. It presents the twelve constellations in a composition which is half serious and half comical.
—**sexy** handsome homosexual "Go tell that cute homosexy that I'm dying t'eat, er, meet her."

honest girl (*camp*) an admitted homosexual.

hon[ey] [hooney] 1. live-in lover "My honey is stone business—he knows how to get behind me and yet come out ahead" **2.** (*voc*) vocal announcement of the punchline "Taco Town is just like Oakland, honey—everybody's ugly!" "Spill it, hon, I'm all tea and sympathy!" "Hooney, the only person you're competition for is an overripe octogenarian hiding out in Macy's basement!"

honey in the hips fluidity of the pelvis when dancing or copulating "You'll have honey in the hips even when you're seventy—ain't *no*body walk as graceful as you."

honeypot the vagina.

honi-honi (hō'-nē-hō'-nē, *fr* Haw gay sl) to kiss "All that katoka like do is honi-honi; she no give puka to anekay."

horny seeing sex in everything; lusty, in heat "Take off your clothes—Lassie's horny."
Syn: **geared [up]; in season; jacked up; randy** (?*fr* obs *rand* = rant); **steamy** (?*fr* seamy); **wired[-up].**
Related terms:
got the horns to be horny "I can't walk around LA without gettin' the horns—there's so many pretties." Syn: **have fever** (*fr* song title *Fever* recorded by Peggy Lee); **wear [a pair of] horn-rimmed glasses.**
pull in the horns to bring an embarassing erection back into soft form again. Most often a command to one who is leering: "Pull in your horns!"

horrible movies (*camp*) TV horror movies.
horsecock (*camp*) bologna.

horsenuts (*camp*) round, fried potatoes.
hot 1. passionate, see *****horny** "He's as hot as a pregnant fox in a forest fire!" Syn: **hot to trot 2.** ('72) said of anything, person, *etc* which is noteworthy.
hot cha-cha ('70, *fr* '30s sl) to have fun, live it up, make whoopie "I'm fed up with being your scullery maid—I want to hot cha-cha."
hot milk (*fr* the milkish color of semen) see *****come** "I'm goin' t'shoot more hot milk into that hole than you've ever sucked."
hot tuna (*exclam, kwn* NYC, '71) superlative reserved for sexy men. Purred very nasally.
    Syn: **dynamite!**
house rearranging (*fr* pros sl, '30s) **1.** to enhance one's appearance with new clothes, a fresh hair style and the like **2.** to undergo a sex-change operation.
how's the [silly old] cunt[sweetness, tits] (*interj*) How are you?
how's tricks how's your love-life been? Wisecrack answer to this greeting is "Oh, the same old six(es) and nines!"
hug 'em (*exclam*) shouted to one who is poured into tight pants.
huggers (early '60s) hip-huggers, generally tight pants which ride low on the hips "My huggers just broke my hips!"
    Syn: **lo-boys** (early '60s).
hugo (*camp*) huge, enormous "Honey, ain't no sign hugo enough to stop *me!*"
humble gas braggart.
humble somebody (*kwn* LV,· late '60s) to humiliate somebody by pulling off his clothing and then shoving him outside.
humpy (late '60s-'71) tall and handsome; answer to a queen's prayer.
    Syn: **flawless** ('71-'72); **hunky** ('71, *fr* *****hunk**).
hunch to back oneself onto a man's merrymaker "Go look for a doorknob to hunch, queen; leave me alone!"
hung estimating cock size—especially used of long penises "How hung is he?"
    —like a doughnut having a vagina; being a woman.
    —like a [stud] field mouse to possess a small penis "It was dismal! He was hung like a field mouse and I wasn't in the mood for being tickled to death." Syn: **hung like hickory dickory's dock.**
    —like a horse[bull, old mule, showdog, stallion, stud] equipped with a large penis "When I get a man hung like an old mule, I have more than I can handle."
    Also see *****well hung.**
hung on somebody in love with a person "Poor baby. you're really hung on that bastard, aren't you?"
    Syn: **hung up behind one** ("You're only hung up behind him because he has tattoos on his tool.")
hungries (*kwn* LV, late '60s, used of SF) the have nots that swarm the city streets at night; the down-trodden "Want to walk around with the rest of the hungries and see if we can score?"
hungry 1. (euphemism for cock hungry) greedy, wanting ever more; sexually ungratified. **hungry girl** = promiscuous homosexual **2.** excessively capitalistic.
hunk (*kwn* SF, late '60s-'72) handsome, broad-shouldered man.
husband [hubby] partner in a stable gay relationship who assumes the more dominant, masculine role. Some homosexuals resent such unimaginative role-playing labels as husband and wife "Bug off, Louise; I'm looking for a husband."
    Syn: **big daddy** (*fr* pros sl = pimp: "Big daddy, my glass needs refilling"); **bossman** (black gay sl: "Your bossman must've cost a heap o' quarters"); **daddy; gallo** (gä'-yō, Mex *fr* Sp = rooster); **miss man** (*kwn* LV, black gay sl, mid '60s:

"I seem to have lost miss man in the vicinity of the bath-room"); **old man** ("You know how to cook and sew? Good for you, you'll someday make the perfect old man"); **papa.**

hustler (fr Du husselen = to shake: cf underworld sl shakedown = demand for money) a male prostitute. Hustlers fall into two categories: the street variety and ***models [call boys]**. Street hustlers, who often deny being gay, develop a tough but invit-ing approach selling their maleness. The words used to refer to hustlers by all nonhustlers—including ***johns** and rivals—attack the hustler's pursuit of virility combined with his busi-ness instincts.

Syn: **ass pro** (fr ass professional; however cf Judaeo-Spanish aspro = Turkish piaster // Gk: hustler who is known for get-ting fucked); **bird taker** (obs); **buff-boy; bunny; business boy; career boy** (youth who is striving to make a profession out of prostitution); **cocktail; coin-collector; commercial queer** (Brit Gay sl); **crack salesman; dick peddler; fag boy** (police parlance = dangerous hustler); **fanny-boy** (rare, who will allow anything to be done with his ass); **flesh** (fr sl flesh-peddler = streetwalker); **foot soldier** (kwn SF, '70: hustler who walks the streets at night); **gay dirt** (mid '60s: admits to being gay but is dishonest all the same); **gigolo** ("A name on the door rates a gigolo on the floor"); **he-whore** (kwn LV, mid '60s: also **he-haw boy;** cf dated **Jack's ass**); **Hollywood hustler** (kwn LA & LV, mid '60s: a too slick hustler); **husband for a weekend** (one obtained during the week-end rush for services); **iron [hoof]** (dated, Brit gay sl, fr Cockney rhyming sl pouf = queer); **joy boy** (rare); **mayate** (mā-yä'-tā, Mex // Aztec mayatl = colored beetle: interestingly enough = Negro in Pach Sp); **merchandise; outdoorsman; party boy** (paid escort to a ga[y]la function); **pimp** (teen sl, '50s; probably used because they didn't know any better); **poonce** (pej, Brit); **prick peddler; professional queer** (Brit gay sl); **puto** (poō'-tō, fr Sp puta = whore); **rent[-er, boy]** (Brit gay sl, but also found in US: standard joke among homosexuals has become the too-often heard hustler whine, "I've got to pay the rent, man, that's why I sell it"); **Rita** (Camp Town gay sl); **sport[-ing goods]; steer meat; street mechanics; swishblader** (camp, '70); **traba-jado** (trä-bä-khä'-thō, Arg-Sp = worked over); **trader [dick]; venereal boy** ('40s, fr venereal = of Venus the love goddess, not the disease); **whore; working girl** (camp).

Some high-schoolers, incorrectly labeled **pimps** by their class-mates, believe that **hustling** would make them rich overnight, so, instead of **waiting slop** (working as a grill man in a cheap diner) they **take the pay** by **trodding the turf** or **dogging it** (fr sl dogs = feet).

While starting **on the beat[game, turf, walk]** the inexperi-enced, up-and-coming **choirboys, cowboys** (fr sl = show-off), **raw jaws**—those new **in the racket**—wait to be approached by a ***john** or **dogger** (kwn LV hustler sl, mid '60s: fr sl dogface= a soldier + sl John Doe = an obviously fictitious name; note Yid proverb alle y'vonim hobn ein ponim = all soldiers look alike). Professionally he may observe and try to emulate those of his peers who have attained position: **champ[ion]**, a well-paid hustler who **stings** his well-heeled **marks** (fr under-world sl, '40s); **king hustler** or **pro**, making as much as **two bills** ($200) a night; **torpedo**, taking in **TE bread**, ie top elim-inator money, thousands of dollars.

When an **outlaw** (freelance hustler) or a **single-o** (fr carnival sl = an act good enough to stand by itself on the billing) has to **hit the streets** to make a **quick twenty**, he's probably on the make for **scoring an overnight** with a **hit** (rich man who takes a steady interest in him; cf criminal sl *hit* = murder victim with hobo sl *hit* = alms-giver).

Those who never really had the calling have to settle for what they can get: **coffee, hamburger, hershey queens,** and **s[ex-and-] b[reakfast] boys** denote the price of their favors. **Miss Nickelodeon** (*fr* narc sl *nickle* = five dollars), also a loser, goes to bed with somebody for five bucks or less. It is incredible how business-like hustler vocabulary becomes. **Punching it,** being anally passive with a client, was explained by one informant as being related to the hours recorded on a time card: one punches in and out. His sexual stomping ground is his **office** and even the most insignificant phone call becomes a **transaction.**

Besides the sexual market, a **wheeler** (*kwn* LV, hustler sl, late '60s) can moonlight as an independent drug salesman. **Vice-boy cigarettes** (marijuana) used to be sold in the mid '60s by the boys to their clients before getting down to brass beds. At regular **stations** (where drugs are bought) pubescent, loud-mouthed **racketeers** receive their supply of **ups** and **downs** as well as the hard stuff [**two-for-one**]. If he were on it as well as selling it, he'd be hiding his **bee bites, pricks, tattoos** or **tracks** as well as his practice of **working the fags** (robbing the clients through violence or blackmail). During the late '50s, house calls were made by the **delivery boy** or the **COD boy** (cock on delivery) with his prominently displayed packages. **He-madames, house mothers** (*camp*) and **misters** ran male-order houses—**hardward stores, jag [peg] -houses**—but only **poultry [shellfish] dealers** madamed **chicken houses.** Those who managed hustlers were referred to as **landladies** and **sweet ladies** if female while male counterparts were **pushers** or **steerers.** For more recent variations of this theme see *model.

Hustlers too have their sexual proclivities: a **goofer** ('40s) or a **baggage[box-]-boy** allows only his cock to be the currency of sexual sale, while a **two-way man** is obviously more flexible. Most hustlers claim they protect their manhood by **keeping the belt on** (not allowing themselves to get fucked). Others, however, **pack** or **punch it** which is complete acceptance of the customer's cock anally. Some will even **work with the cramps,** and suffer intestinal gas pains while getting it up the ass.

Hustler argot is heavily dependent on macho terms from black and chicano sources as well as some earthy Yiddish idioms: **dig it** and **shag ass** (*fr* black sl: "Man, dig it! I have to shag ass if I'm going to be on time"); **bato** (vä'-tō, *fr* Pach,? // Sp *gato* = cat), **mano** (mä'-nō, *fr* Pach // Sp *hermano* = brother) both indicating a good head; **tapado** (tä-pä'-thō, *fr* Pach: a square, a nonhustler); **schmuck** (*fr* Yid: a jerk). When arrested on the usual **vag** (vagrancy) charge, he may need to rapidly flip the pages of his **score card** (address book) to come up with the bail necessary to enable him to **walk** (be bail bonded), and return to dodging the police, fighting his rivals, and searching for the monetary value of love.

Also see *model.

hyper hypertensional, subject to hysteria "Stay away from coffee— you're hyper enough the way it is."

I bet I can flip you and dick you before you can throw me and blow me (prison sl) a threat made by a challenger who considers himself more manly than the attacked.

ice palace 1. a home lavishly decorated in crystal **2.** a store which sells crystal.

I could kill for that overdone cupidity.

the icks (fr Mart Crowley's The Boys in the Band // sl icky = childhood description of filth) intense guilt pangs about the night before.

im (kwn SF, '70) one's image "What can I do to improve my im?"

I'm in love (interj) a *gay line conjuring instant replay of one's first romance. A poke-fun-at-yourself way of saying that you're physically enamored of someone.

imitation pearls (camp) dandruff flakes.
Syn: **hayseeds.**

IMM (police sl) the criminal charge of impairing a minor's morals.

I'm sorry (interj) an immediate defense mechanism vouching for a spoken opinion = I disagree with you; I'm sticking to my guns "You're not stuck on him? I'm sorry, he could park his galoshes under my bed any day."

in-and-out (fr pros sl) normal copulation between a man and a woman.
Syn: **regular trick; straight lay; western lay.**

incendiary blonde (fr '40s Betty Hutton movie of same title) a flaming faggot who extracted his wavy blonde curls out of a bottle "Why don't you seat that incendiary blonde over there with the other perishables?"
Syn: **gold-digger** (pej); **product of Sweden** (kwn SF, '71).

incest carnal relations between two similar types. Moralistic homosexuals consider intercourse between two effeminates, two of the he-men type or an effeminate and a woman to be filed under the heading of incestuous. To violate your sister is a no-no "Make it with Tom? Don't make me laugh! He's my sis; anything including fringe benefits would be incest."
Syn: **sister act.**
Also see *ki-ki.

India (ĕn'-dē-ä, fr Mex gay sl // Sp = indian woman) a homely queen with heavy peasant features.
Syn: **Miss adobe face; squaw.**

inhale to eat voraciously, ravenously; to devour quantities of food pilfered from the refrigerator "Don't inhale all the nuts; we may have visitors dropping by."

in-laws (fr pros sl) prostitutes working for the same pimp.

in-sisters (pun made upon *incest) two effeminates in love with one another.

in skirts (obs, '20s) said of a man who wears the garments of a woman "You look too much like a gorilla ever to go in skirts, Regina."

in slacks (*obs.* '20s) said of a lesbian dressed as a man.

integrated 1. permitting both homosexuals and heterosexuals on the premises "The Sexual Freedom League is integrated, isn't it?" **2.** (*rare*) hermaphroditic "I never made it with anyone who was, er, integrated."

intermediate sex (herero sl) homosexuality.

in the closet afraid of admitting to being homosexual; covert "Ever since we've moved from Portland, we've been in the closet."

in the jewel box 1. in trouble; in hot water "Don't talk to me about that one; she's in the jewel box as far as I'm concerned" **2.** under control "Don't worry about losing your job at Macy's, hon; it's all in the jewel box."

in the life (*fr* pros sl) being a well adjusted homosexual "I've been in the life two years now, so don't try being foxy with me, girl."

in the making said of one who is going to be made "That grocery boy ain't my lover, but he is in the making."

ipo (ē'-pō, *fr* Haw) a sweetheart.

iron-head teenage girl with her hair done up in rollers [irons]; also called **iron maidens** except in Las Vegas where they went by the name of **be-bop-a-rollers** "Wool's Worth—the united nations of the iron-heads!"

Isadora ('70) **1.** nickname denoting the splendid grace and adventuresome zaniness of Isadora Duncan, celebrated dancer and teacher: and by extension, gay folk heroine "Let's go, Isadora, time for us to shake our beads" **2.** a long, long scarf, relating to the one that inadvertantly caused Isadora's death "How do I look in this Isadora, Chuck?"

—ish suffix used to create a new adjective (***cocksuckerish**) or to convey a rough approximation of the time, as in "It's threeish."

ish an issue of a magazine "Did you get the last ish of Gayzette?"

it (third person sing neuter *pron*) **1.** the penis "Here's the part where he shoves it into her coozey" **2.** the vagina "I pay them them a quarter if they pull up their dresses and let me touch it" **3.** (*fr* Elinor Glyn, popular novelist of the '20s: Clara Bow was the first to exemplify it on the screen) sex appeal, glamour "Betty Grable had it all tied up in her legs" **4.** Depersonalizing pronoun for any one of the following three: **a.** one who is stripped of rank by his fellow homosexuals "Remember Miss Ed? It's been coming around again" **b.** ***pick up** "Honey, I brought this trick home and fucked it in time to the Rose Bowl game on the tube" **c.** someone going through a sex change procedure "How does it look in drag, like a star or a retired business woman?"

It's been real (*interj*, mid '60s) a form of farewell which expresses genuine delight "It's been real, John-John; try to come back again before you go to Kansas."

ivy pie (early '60s) the clean-cut college student.
    Syn: **piece of ivy pie.**

jacked up 1. energetic through stimulants "That girl's jacked up behind coffee" **2.** see *horny.
jack off (*fr* L *iacere* = to throw, as in *alea iacta est* = the die is cast) to masturbate "His sex scene consists of jacking off while you walk around in lingerie."

Syn: **ball off** (*fr* black sl *ball* = to fuck, reinforced by *balls* = the testicles as makers of semen); **bang the banjo; beat off; beat the bishop[dummy, meat]** ("it's so neat to beat your meat in the Mississippi mud. . . ."); **crank the cream separator** (*fr sl cream* = semen); **diddle** ('30s, used of either sex: "Get her a dildo to diddle with"); **dollop the weener; fist it off** ("Hey, Legs! There's a five in it for you if you fist it off for me!"); **flip it [around, off]; flog the bishop[donkey, pork]** (*rare*); **flub the dub** ("One of those rubbish queens is a real doll . . . I wait for him t'come pick up the garbage on Tuesday, and then I flub my dub while checkin' him out through the Austrians"); **fuck the fist; grind it [the ice cream machine]; grip it; hot rod it** (*fr* black sl, late '60s); **jeff off** ('70s); **Jerk off** (early '50s); **jerk the gherkin** (*rare*); **knit** (*camp*, mid '60s: "He'd rather stay home and tend to his knitting"); **make a milk shake; night-club** (see *prison terminology); **paddle the pickle** ("He knew one hundred and twenty ways to paddle the pickle"); **play solitaire; pound off** ("They were so horny and bored on Midway, that they were poundin' off on their way to mess"); **pound the meat; pull [it] off** ("I'd rather have an old hen than pullet"); **pull the pud[ding, wire]** (*dated*); **pump off** (analogy made with pumping a handle: "What has that fancy school been teaching you—how to drive or pump off?") **rub it off; run off by hand** (mid '60s); **sew** ('40s, *fr* sowing seed: "Let mother teach you how to sew, child"); **smash the stake** ('70, seemingly a pun is made here on the militant slogan "Smash the state!"); **squeeze it off; strangle the stogie** ('70); **sweep off** (*rare*); **tapdance** ('40s); **TCB** (*kwn* SF, black gay sl, '70, *fr* black sl = to take care of business); **toss off; wank on it** (Brit); **wave the wand** (*camp, rare:* all fairies have wands); **whack it; whank** (Brit); **whip it; work it off** (late '50s); **wrench off** (connection with sl *plumbing* = genitals).

Related terms:
cherry in the hand (*fr* sl *cherry* = virginal) never having masturbated.
circle jerk (late '50s) formation of males, usually teens, who gather for group masturbation. Considered a "safe" outlet for teenagers during their homoerotic stage. Syn: **sewing circle** (*camp*).
color in the coloring book (*kwn* LV, mid '60s) to look at erotic pictures while masturbating.
dishonorable discharge coming home and jacking off after not scoring.

double jacking (early '60s) mutual masturbation by two men. Syn: **dealing** ('50s); **playing chopsticks** ('40s); **pole vaulting** (*kwn* LV, mid '60s); **swordfighting** ('70).

hair-job (*kwn* SF, late '60s) a fetishistic form of masturbation where one man rubs his long hair over the hard-on of his lover.

hand game [**gig, jig, jive**] male masturbation Syn: **big stroke time** (*kwn* LV, late '60s: "If some ugly sister ever asks you what time it is, just tell her, 'Big stroke time!'"); **manual exercises** ("Oops, it's two o'clock—time for my manual exercises if I want to stay in shape"); **manuela** (mä-nōō-ā'-lä, Mex pun made upon *manual*); **one-two** (the counts number the up-down stroke); **puneta** (pōōn-yā'-tä, Mex *fr* Sp *puño* = a fist); **solo played upon a private pump organ.**

hand job masturbation performed by one man upon another. Syn: **armswing; jerk-job; JO** (acronym formed *fr jack off:* "He pulled it between my legs an' gave me a JO while he pile-drived me with his tongue"); **local** (*kwn* SF, '72, *fr* massage parlor sl: "They come in for a local"); **manicure** ("He used to get a manicure every afternoon").

have a date with a handkerchief (*kwn* LV, mid '60s) to masturbate with a handkerchief nearby.

the housewife's hour (*kwn* SF, '71) midafternoon: a masturbation period enjoyed by housewives, shut-ins and stay-at-homes as an interruption to boredom.

in honor of someone thinking of a specific person while masturbating "Moose Bernardski, this is in honor of you!"

jerkin's hand lotion [**for boys**] (late '60s) mama's hand lotion substituted as a lubricant by adolescent sons experimenting with autoeroticism.

joyce off (*kwn* SF, late '60s) to practice female masturbation. Syn: **dunk the doughnut** (*rare*); **finger** ('40s-'50s); **lock in the mirror** ('40s).

mother and [**her**] **four children** (*kwn* NYC, black gay sl, late '60s) the masturbator's best girl friend—his hand: the thumb is the mother to the four fingers. Syn: **five-fingered Annie** (late '60s); **old lady five fingers.**

peel and chew a bamboo cane (*lit* translation of Chin phr) to masturbate and suck off.

whack-silly (late '50s) **1.** addicted to self abuse **2.** (*fr* the belief that consistent masturbation causes mental deterioration) crazy. odd.

—freak 1. a chronic masturbator, one who plays with himself more frequently than we can tolerate or do ourselves "The jack-off freak has a motto: 'I got it, but you can't have any'" **2.** homosexual who enjoys masturbating his partners **3.** (*pej*) an idiot, from the archaic superstition that overindulgence caused feeblemindedness.

Syn: **diddler** ('30s); **hand queen; Handy Andy** (mid '60s); **Jackie** (*kwn* NYC, late '60s); **jerky** (late '50s); **monk** (*kwn* Southwest, mid '60s, *fr* religious novice punned with sl *monkeying around* = playing around [with oneself]); **tapdancer** ('40s); **Wanda Wandwaver** (also = one who brags about his size); **Yankee** (*fr* sl *yank off* = masturbation).

—journals regularly published homoerotic magazines featuring seminude, nude, and semierect poses of attractive men and boys. Individual magazines usually cater to the appetites of the buyer, *ie* emphasis will be placed on particular regions—the crotch or the ass—or particular kinds of "types" will be featured. Other magazines feature situations that appeal to fetishists. Syn: **bod-comics; boylies; butt-books; cook-books; fag mags; flavor-comics; hand books;**

masturbation manuals (late '60s); **paper pussy** (*kwn* LV, mid '60s); **pornzine; pricktures** (= pictures of hard cocks); **smudge** (*fr* smut); **storeyettes** (Brit gay sl: photographic series of endless affairs—always different, but always the same).

—the jaws or **jack the jaws off** to talk without making a point; to beat the gums.

jack somebody up (prison sl) to stun a boy with a weapon before raping him.

Jacques Pennier (zhak'-pen'-yā, *kwn* LA & LV, mid '60s) a JC Penny's department store. The French pronunciation lends a little class to the popular, bourgeois store chain.

jaded faggot 1. (*pej*) one who is spent, burned out **2.** one who is blasé about his deviation.

jades (*camp, kwn* SF, late '60s, *fr* play made upon sl *shades* = sunglasses) gay sunglasses.

   Syn: **bad lamps** (*dated*); **boy watchers** (*dated*, late '60s); ***hollywood glasses; hoods; spy-smashers** (*dated*, sleek wraparounds); **tea timers** (*dated, fr* sl *tea* = marijuana); **tinted bo-peeps** (*rare*).

jailhouse turnout [JTO] one who went into prison predominately straight but who returned to the "outside" as an overt homosexual.

jaisy (hetero sl, early '50s, *fr* blending of Daisy and Jane) homosexual.

jam 1. (*fr* just a man) heterosexual, see ***straight 2.** a spontaneous party often ending in a spirited orgy or free-for-all with fighting, *etc* **3.** (*rare*) feces "Do you dig jam? Then jam it up your ass!"

jam fag (*obs*, '40s) **1.** the bona-fide homosexual **2.** an intelligent homosexual.

jam jacket (*kwn* SF, late '60s, *fr jam* = straight) **1.** a straightjacket. Syn: **health jacket 2.** (*rare*) a girdle "Shut your hole, Bess, or I'll put the stays back into your jam jacket."

jam sheet (*rare*) shit list, group of people out of favor "I don't think you better come; you're still on her jam sheet after your melting remarks on her cocoa-brown living room."

jam-up and jelly-tight (*kwn* LV, late '60s) excellent, just peachy "There is *one* thing that you could do to make this neighborhood jam-up and jelly-tight—move out!"

Jane 1. lesbian client of a streetwalker **2.** (*kwn* SF, '70) the woman in us all, but especially the feminine qualities in men "Faggot-beaters are repressed fairies who don't give in to their Jane." Syn: **Miss Pinky** (*kwn* Cleveland, mid '60s); **Miss Thing.** Ant: **Sam** (the masculine nature in us all, especially in lesbians).

Janet Jobless (*kwn* SF, '70) an unemployed hip chick.

janey (*kwn* LV, les sl, late '60s) the vagina.

jass (*interj*) variant of yes, used answering the telephone "Jass? House of Wax! This is Mrs. Wax speaking!"

jaw queen 1. doer, see ***cocksucker 2.** (*rare*) a gossip.

Jeanie boy (*obs*, hetero sl) effeminate lad "Some kind of jeanie boy you are—rubbing people the wrong way."

jeans at half mast (early '50s) pants lowered below the ass for sexual purposes "There I was, jeans at half mast, an' when I looked up there was a cop not ten feet away."

jelly-box the vagina.

Jenny (*camp*) gay nickname for Johnny "Jenny's ego is always hangin' out of her capris."

jerk off see ***jack off.**

jessie (Cape Town gay sl) jealous.

jet the juice to ejaculate "He'd always go to sleep after he jetted his juice into an old pillow."

Jewel Box Revue (mid '60s) theatrical group of transvestite entertainers who traveled about the Eastern US.

jewelry 1. male genitals "Take out your jewelry, lovebug, I want to inspect the carats—vein by vein" **2.** (*camp*) the studs on a leather jacket.

jewels (chōōlz) rings and things; the spangley female trappings "It's a small miracle the stage didn't collapse what with all those jewels these queens had on."

Jewish by hospitalization circumcised but not of Jewish background or tradition. Syn: **jewish by operation not by nation.**

Jewish compliment (*kwn* LV, mid '60s) a circumcised cock "Does he feature the Jewish compliment?"
Syn: **Jewish national** ("He plays with the Jewish national! He attends to tasting kosher cuts only.")

Jewish Renaissance overelaborate furniture in doubtful taste.

jilly (*kwn* Cleveland, mid '60s, ?*fr* Jill, diminutive of girl's name Jilly or mispronunciation of *jolly* = gay, or *jelly*, similar to but different from **jam*) obvious gay boy "Butch numbers won't have anything to do with you if you're a jilly."

Joan Crawford sling pumps 1. pumps, a type of woman's shoes which make "gunboats" appear tiny **2.** (*camp*) a pair of men's shoes.
Syn: **Joan Crawford ankle-strapped, open toed, fuck-me's.**

job (jōb, *kwn* LV, hustler sl, mid '60s, *fr* the boils which plagued Job) facial blemish; inflamed pimple.

jocker see **prison terminology.*

jock sniffer towel boy; attendant in a gym.

jock-strap 1. a masculine-looking, athletic person **2.** a slow witted person; a dumbbell **3.** (*camp*) a girls bikini.

jock-strap art (late '60s) erotic photos of men nude except for a posing brief or jock-strap.

jodido (khō-thē'-thō, Mex) a **fag.*

joey (Aus hetero sl, *fr* Aus *joey* = baby kangaroo) boy erotically fostered by an older guardian.
Syn: **mignon** (mēn-yōn', *fr* Fr = lamb: "One does not serve *mignon sans le* bone.")

john 1. (*fr* company name of John Douglas imprinted upon toilet seats) toilet "He just went into the john—fly after it, girl!" **2.** (pros sl, *fr* John Doe, an undeceiving alias) the client; the one who pays for it. Syn: **geezer** (Brit pros sl); **steamer** (Brit, *fr* rhyming sl *steamer tug* = mug = sap) **3.** (*obs,* les sl) straight man who digs lesbians. Syn: **dyke daddy.*

johnniecake (*obs,* early '50s) boy loved by an older man.

joint 1. the penis, see **cock* **2.** (*fr* narc sl) marijuana cigarette "Fire up a joint, Dog Nose, an' we'll see what comes." Syn: **jay.**

joint distribution sexual freedom.

jointess (*camp*) the clitoris.

join the Baptist revival (*kwn* SF, black gay sl, '71) to urinate "After this beer, it'll be *my* turn to go join the Baptist revival."

joog see **fuck.*

joosh (*fr* dial = Jewish) **1.** gaudy, showy, nouveau riche; startling but distasteful **2.** impressive even if out of place: wearing a genuine diamond tiara with last year's housedress.
Syn: **Miami-ish.**

Josephine (*camp*) gay nickname for Joe or Joseph "Why do they call you worldly, Josephine—is it because you're shaped like a globe?"

joy jelly fruit-flavored body salve; a lubricant jelly which turns out to be a taste treat.

joys 1. (*fr* pros sl, '30s) an athletic supporter; jock.

"Baby, I might be in another state, but I'm still snappin the elastic on your joys." Syn: **G-string** (*camp:* "His biggest thrill is fucking guys through the straps of their G-strings"); **holsters; joy-straps; lockerroom tux**[edo] (*camp,* late '60s); **maidenform bra** (*camp*); **male pouch; protecto** (*fr* protection); **queer's**[faggot's] **lunch box** ('40s-early '50s); **snackpack** ("I snuck it across the border in my snackpack") **2.** (*kwn* Wis, teen sl, late '50s) marijuana joints.

juice 1. semen, see *****come **2.** fluid emitted from the aroused vagina **3.** body sweat **4.** to sweat, especially when sexually stimulated; to become musky "And does he juice! Mmm, those thighs just *sizzle!*"
—**cy** delectable "What a juicy little body!"

juicy fruit homosexual with diarrhea "*Gas* what happened to our friend the juicy fruit!"

juke[y] (pros sl *fr* Gullah) bawdy, disorderly.

Julia (*kwn* SF, '70) jewelry.

jump (*rare, fr* jazz sl, '40s; *cf* the joint is jumpin') one's home, living quarters "You ought to christen your new jump with a rip-roarin' orgy!"
Syn: **joint** (black sl); **pad** (*obs,* late '50s-mid '60s).

jump on some beans to swallow pep pills.

jump on somebody's beads 1. to cause physical damage; to beat somebody. *Cf* sl *jumping all over somebody with both feet.* **2.** to belittle somebody "My mother used to jump all over my beads if I ever came home with my rubbers muddy."
Syn: **get on somebody's case; jump on somebody's chest** [tits]; **jump stink.**

jungle meat any black man "My stars! One more hour in the sun an' you'll look like jungle meat!"
Also see *****dinge queen** (*black*).

jungle up (late '60s) **1.** to sleep many people in one bed "Jungle up, Bossy! This ain't no prayer meetin'. . .we gotta fit two more people into this rack!" **2.** to cuddle up "Come to bed, Doug, and jungle up—I'm chilly!"

just for camp just for laughs, fun, something to do. In Britain one finds **just for cod**[crazy, giggles].

kaka (kä'-kä) **1.** feces, anything which turns the stomach "That's a lot of bull kaka!" **2.** back talk, guff, wisecracks "I don't take no kaka from Lily Law, honey!" **3.** an explicit negation = don't "Kaka! It's too expensive and it's not worth, it" **4.** (*exclam*) a curse "Oh, kaka! I burned my finger on his hot pans!" **5.** (*rare, kwn* LA, late '60s, *fr* resemblance of dis-colored bruise with fecal coloring) visible bruise caused by passionate suction when kissing, see ***hickey** "Is that a kaka on your neck, girl, or the Purple Heart?" Syn: **erotic mark of Cain** (*camp*).

—**queen** one who is sexually gratified by being shit upon or by eating excretion; a human toilet. Syn: **brown lipper; chocolate drop** (*kwn* SF, '72: "Don't tell a chocolate drop to 'cut the crap'—he will"); **PCQ** (=poundcake queen); **shit queen** ("A shit queen doesn't read palms; he smells them.")

Kansas City workout (*dated*) **1.** standing on the corner watching all the boys go by **2.** to inspect something closely.
Also see ***eye fuck.**

Karma Miranda (*camp*) gay nickname for a homoerotic hippy.

Kate 1. another homosexual "Stop holding in your stomach, Kate, it's just your sister" **2.** cute, beautiful "What a kate chandelier —it must weigh a ton!"

Katherine (*camp, fr* heroine of Shakespeare's *Taming of the Shrew*) **1.** gay nickname for male homosexual when he appears in the role of hostess **2.** one who presents himself with courtly style and grace "Then he said to the diplomat, 'Fancy meeting *you* here, Katherine!'"

KD'ed (acronym for **knocked up**) made pregnant "Try as he may, a working boy ain't never gonna get KD'ed."

keep the queen's peace (*interj*) goodby "In case I never see you again, which would add years to my life, keep the queen's peace!"

kept boy young lover who is kept, *ie* has all his bills paid for by an older homosexual. Pretense jobs for kept boys: gardeners, chauffeurs, house boys, valets, private secretaries, *etc.*
Syn: **keptive; mistress** (*camp*); **sugar babe** (mid-late '60s).
Related terms:
set-up flat or apartment where a ***sugar daddy** keeps his younger lover.
Syn: ***garçonnière.**

kicky (*fr* jazz sl *kicks* = amoral pleasure, '40s-late '50s) **1.** witty, lots of laughs. Syn: **campy 2.** provocative, spicy, naughty but nice "Shadrack, what you doin'—camouflagin' yourself in kicky rim-brown?" **3.** enjoyable, swell. Syn: **kinky** (*fr* Brit sl = queer).

the kids fellow homosexuals; that old gang of thine.
Syn: **the boys; kiddies** ("Kiddies! Something in the toilet just called me 'Mama!'")

kiki [kyky] lovemaking between two homosexuals, both of the same type, *ie* plug with plug and socket with socket.
Syn: **bitch with bitch** (Brit gay sl); **mother love** ('40s); **sixty-five** (dated); **tootsies** (Brit gay sl, *fr toots* = woman).

Kim 1. (*camp*) gay nickname for Ken[neth] "Everything's coming up roses—right over Kim's sweet grave" **2.** (*fr* Kim Novak) general nickname for any blonde queen "Wanna come over and see Kim's hair—she keeps it in a bottle."

Kim Konga (*camp*) one who browbeats those weaker than he; a bully.

kingdom (*kwn* SF, '70) superb, stupendous, great: used in praising excellent marijuana "If Floradora comes over with some more of that kingdom grass, send up a smoke signal!"

kintama (kēn-tä'-mä, *fr* Jap = golden balls) **1.** Japanese homosexual **2.** any Japanese male.
Syn: **Samurai Sue** (*camp, kwn* SF, '71: "It may be beautiful koto music to you, peaches, but to me its just Samurai Sue bangin' away on her rubber bands"); **Tokyo Rose** (*camp, fr* WWII Jap radio progagandist).

kip (Brit) bed.
Related term:
kip job an easy job.

kiple (*camp*) nonsense verb based upon the following joke: "Two gay boys were browsing in a bookstore; suddenly one turned to the other asking, 'Do you prefer Kipling to Browning?', to which the other blushingly replied, 'I don't know—how do you kiple?'"

kishkish 1. (?*fr* Polish Yid *kish* = kiss) a kiss **2.** (*fr* sl *kisser*) the mouth "Why's your kishkish open—expecting dinner to fly in?"

kiss 1. to practice oral copulation with either sex: **kiss it down** = sucking cunt, while **kiss it off** = suck cock **2.** to wear pants so tight that the material stretches across the anus. Syn: **kiss the ass** ("I wanted something in corduroy to kiss my ass") **3.** to fit tightly "Lookit the way that sweatshirt's kissin' that man's tits!" **4.** (*exclam*) crash; a toppling causing a great clatter "Oh, good, Joe's going to park—Kiss!" "He walked—kiss!—right into my statue of David."

kisses (*rare*) X's "How many kisses are there in 'Xerxes,' Elvira?"

kissing fish (*fr* novel by the same name by Monique Lange) lesbians.
Also see ***fish.**

kiss off ('40s, *fr* sl = to rudely get rid of someone) to embarrass strangers in public by blowing them kisses or by shouting in falsetto "There's my old PE coach—watch me kiss the bastard off!"

kissy (*fr* kissable) **1.** delightful, pleasing, grand (as in "Gee, I think you're grand") "You'll find me at the pool, judging all the kissy swimmers" **2.** swell, see ***kicky** "The new house we got is *heaven*—it has the kissiest closets . . ."

kit (Brit, ?*fr fit* in outfit) one's wearing attire.

kitchen queen 1. see ***rim queen 2.** (*dated, kwn* Oakland, mid '60s) one who stands while receiving a cock up the ass. This position is comfortable for the passive partner, since, while in an upright position, he is able to continue cubing vegetables for the salad.

klackers [kackers] benzedrine tablets.
Also see ***click and clack.**

kneesies 1. (*camp, fr* baby talk) the knees, legs **2.** fondling a person's leg beneath the table undetected by other guests. Other games of this ilk are handsies, nosies and toesies.

knick-knack 1. see ***small meat 2.** ('71) to get in as much cock as one can; to play musical beds; to sleep with many different people **3.** to fuck after being fucked, see *nooky push-push.

knishery (Am-Yid = hole-in-the-wall specializing in meat-filled turnovers called *knishes*) a brothel, cat house "A kibitzer is a gay boy working in a knishery."
> Syn: **knocking house** (Brit: "Didn't your mother run a knocking house?")

knitting circle (fr gay sl *knitting* = backbiting) group of gay boys who, much to the annoyance of cock-hungry homosexuals, stand around to loudly powwow and discuss the "whethers."

knocked-out (*adj*) **1.** blind drunk **2.** stoned on drugs **3.** punchy, sleepy **4.** awe-struck, impressed by beauty, deeply moved **5.** good in every sense of the word, see *groovy "Did you ever make it with that knocked-out hustler who lived next door?"

knock somebody out to please with cleverness or beauty "Jimmy West knocks me out—I never miss one of his reruns."

knock somebody's dick in the dirt to supply a friend with excellent marijuana; to share a joint with a buddy; to turn somebody on to some fine shit.

knock the dew off the lily to shake the last few drops of urine from the penis after relieving oneself "Oh, are you going to give a speech? Then it's time to go knock the dew off the lily again."

knot the corona of the penis.

know the facts of life to be sympathetically aware of a friend's homosexuality. Usually said of nongays.
> Also see *wise.

koo and kah (early-mid '60s) to chatter excitedly, especially said of one pepped up on amphetamine.

kosher [style] (fr Yid // Heb *kashar* = ritually fit to eat) circumcised.
> Syn: **cleaned; cut [out to be a gentleman]; nipped; skinned [back]; twenty-twenty.**
> Ant: **blind.**
> —**delicatessen** (*camp*) the land of Israel.
> —**dill [meat]** circumcised penis. Syn: **chopped cock, clipped dick; low neck and short sleeves** ("I'd like something in a low neck with short sleeves, if you don't mind—maybe you have a brother emigrating from Jew York?")
> Related terms:
> **briss** (fr Yid // Heb *b'rit* = convenant [with Abraham], *ie* circumcision) to circumcise "Streisand's probably the only broad who's ever been brissed!"
> **tailor** circumciser.

Kosher Nosher (*camp*, pun upon It *Cosa Nostra* = the mafiosi fraternity + Yid *kosher* & *nosher* = a nibbler) informal society of gays "Don't come over Thursday—that's the day I den mother the Kosher Nosher."

kumquat gob of ejaculated semen. One will say of clearing the throat: "I have a kumquat in my throat."
> Syn: **oyster** (*dated*); **pearl[drop]; sugar lump.**

KY lubricant circulated widely among physicians and other sodomists "His mother's knitting him a holder for his KY."
> —**club** the YMCA in your town. Syn: **KYMCA.**
> —**queen 1.** (*camp*) hospital orderly who massages prostate glands of male patients **2.** (*camp*) any doctor, medic "The KY queen told me I had TB, but that it could be cured with some expensive, *smart* shots." Syn: **Madam Curie** (*camp*) "Well, I'm a certified Madam Curie, and I say her makeup's been dead for years."

lace frilly men's fashions, see *clothing queen.
lace [curtains] dangling foreskin of uncircumcised penis "There's a sign above the urinals that reads 'Please keep your lace clean!'" Syn: **blinds; curtains; drapes** ("My dear! There was so much 'dust' on those drapes that I'd sneeze when I got near him"); **foreskin** (used in the joke: "After they clipped his foreskin he had three left"); **goatskin** ("Those dried apricots look more like retread goatskins"); **midnight lace** (= black man's prepuce); **onion skin; opera capes** ("Honey, he was dressed in his finest opera capes"); **peapod** ('71); **snapper** ('40s).
   Related terms:
draw the blinds to pull back the foreskin.
fry the onion skin to sunbathe in the nude.
ride a blind piece to fellate an uncircumcised man.
   Also see *blind, *kosher, *unsliced.
ladder (*camp*) lecherous old man cavorting after young boys.
   Related term:
step-ladder (*camp*) a step-brother.
lady 1. genteel, proper chap too *grand* to be manly; demure, fastidious fellow **2.** any homosexual man "Neither snow, rain nor sleet shall keep the ladies from their meat!"
   Related term:
act[be] like a lady to behave properly; to refrain from making coarse remarks at gatherings where the contenders are not all gay "Can't you be a lady—is cock all you can talk about?"
ladybug (*camp, fr* child's rhyme: "Ladybug . . . fly away home/ your house is on fire and your children will burn") gay nickname for a fireman "Eat some beans, Ladybug, then we'll gas!"
Lady Godiva (*camp*) gay nickname for one who parades nude about his home.
lady in waiting 1. (*dated*) one of a flock surrounding a *queen bee **2.** (*camp*) one who loiters in a men's room waiting to meet someone through a *glory hole. Syn: **heir to the throne** ("The heir in that throne room was so foul—I loved all nine inches of it.")
lampshade queen inferior decorator.
Lana Turner (*camp*) any fluffy sweater.
   —extract vanilla.
   —ice cream vanilla ice cream.
lapin (lä-pen', *fr* Fr = rabbit) schlock mink.
lardsack paunch, flabby belly "Haven't seen you in years, Lulu—hmm, preggy or just stocking up your lardsack?"
larking (Brit gay sl) dabbling in homosexuality under the guise of experimentation "Well, you know, the cruise lasted more than a week, so yeah, I did a little larking."
last man (black gay sl) the ultimate in masculinity: so good they broke the mold.

lather-up pornographic shots in the shower; sudsy snapshots.

latty (Brit gay sl, *fr* Parlyaree, // It *letto* = bed) room or apartment; pad, and therefore also the bed or the room it is in "What say we go up to me latty an' look at me 'itchings?"

laugh marks[lines] "crow's feet" on a lover or dear friend.

launching pad 1. the bed "They strolled ham in ham to the launching pad" **2.** convertible sofa. Syn: **portable fuck machine.**

Laura 1. gay nickname for Larry or Laurie "Never say 'dye,' Laura!" **2.** (Cape Town gay sl) love.

Laura LaPlant (*camp, fr* silent film actress) **1.** indoor horticulturist. Syn: **Georgana of the Jungle 2.** flower shop owner **3.** (*camp*) skunk (*genus:* Mephitis).

lavender color symbol for homosexuality "Have the neighbors burned a lavender cross on your lawn yet?"
     Related terms:
     —**boy[lad]** (*obs*) faggot.
     —**convention** group of homosexuals, especially if large.
     deep[er] tone of lavender homosexuality gauge "Well, your trip to Tijuana certainly brought out your deeper tones of lavender."
     have a dash of lavender said of somebody straight who has gay tendencies. Syn: **have a dash of lavender in the garden.**

lavish (la-vish') breathtaking, ravishing "Yes, it's true! I am *very lavish!*"

layer cake 1. the buttocks of the man on top as he fucks **2.** voyeur thrill from watching *all* the buttock movements in fucking.

lay law morality law affecting homosexuals or prostitutes—victimless violations.

lay with the moon (*fr* pros sl, '30s) to spend all night in bed fucking.

leading man masculinely reclining lover.

leading role having the floor, everybody's undivided attention "Pipe down, Borina! You haven't had the leading role since silent movies."

leather 1. subspecies of homosexuality, glorifying exaggerated manhood as an ideal for themselves and their partners. Some even do ride motorcycles **2.** leather fetishism; leather as a masculine symbol is worn next to the skin and even venerated "Yeah him—when he takes his leather off he also removes his masculinity."
     —**boy[jacket queer, queen]** appearing in leather a lot. Syn: **blouson noir** (bloo-sōn' nwä, *fr* Fr = black jacket).
     —**crowd** the subculture of the leather boys.
     —**merchant** one who deals in clothing and implements which appeal to leather fetishists.
     —**queen 1.** one who wears leather a lot **2.** a leather fetishist.
     —**s 1.** leather outfit "He creams his jeans when he goes shopping for leathers" **2.** motorcyclist's protective outergarments.
     Also see ***golden shower queen,** *SM.

leek water toilet water; cologne.

legitimate 1. being in a suspicious place or position for valid reasons "Your roomy claims that his visits to the cruisy library are legitimate. What's he doing—taking a Master's Degree in plumbing?" **2.** heterosexual "He's legitimate—probably waiting for his girl."

Legs name used to call slender, long-legged male prostitutes over to the car.

Leona 1. gay nickname tor Leo "Who puts the curl in your teeth, Leona?" **2.** the constellation of Leo, the mad lioness.

leprechaun homosexual from the old sod[omy].
     Syn: **Irish fairy.**

lesbian (*fr* Gk isle of Lesbos, home of the poetess Sappho, a famous admirer of women) **1.** female homosexual. Lesbian is a word not looked upon too kindly by gay women anymore. It now falls into the classification of a "dirty" word, calling to mind the stereotype *dyke "I would never have figured you for a lesbian"* **2.** (*camp*) frcm a queen's standpoint any woman or effeminate "You thought I balled that queen Big Billy? What do you take me for—a lesbian?"

Syn: (All of these pun on lesbian) **les; les-be-friends; lesbianka; lesbo; lesby; les girls** (*rare*, pun made upon Fr *les* = the + les- in lesbian); **Leslie** [-Anne]; **lessie; less-than-a-man's; lezbo; lezz; lezzy; lizzy;** and, lisped, **Thespian.**
—**converter** man who thinks he's got what a lesbian's been missing.
—**freak** heterosexual (of either sex) who takes a sexual interest in lesbians.
—**joint** straight slang for a bar or tavern where lesbians congregate.
—**queen** male homosexual who associates almost exclusively with gay women.
lesbos lesbian stomping grounds.
Syn: **lesbonia; lesboville** (*dated*).
let one's hair down 1. to admit to being gay "Why don't you let your hair down instead of keeping it in a closet?" **2.** to tell on someone else; to expose another's homosexuality.
let one's hair out (*fr* 1969 slogan of "let it all hang out" reinforced by gay invitation to "take off your hair and relax awhile!") **1.** to have a good time **2.** to let the hair grow longer.
liberated faggot (*kwn* SF, late '60s) **1.** male homosexual who is pleased to be what he is **2.** (*pej*) young, long-haired gay radical "Yeah, he's a liberated faggot; he's really achieved independence by belonging to a gay liberation group."
lick see *blow.*
lights eyes "I think she'd look better with a pair of black lights."
like Faust without holding back, excitedly "We carried on like Faust."
Also *cf* "He ran *like the devil!*"
Lilly [Law] (*camp*) the police, crime-fighters paid to protect us from each other (muggers, rapists, *etc*) and *not* from ourselves "Lily Law's gonna getcha if you don't watch out!"
Syn: **Alice Blue Gown; Alice blues; Belle Star** (*fr* star = policeman's badge: "That motorcycle Belle Star's kinda cute in her smart leathers"); **blue ballerina** (*kwn* LV, mid '60s: because they *dance* in, *ie* break down the door); **blue bellies; blue boys** (*cf* sl *boys in blue*); **the blue hand** (also **big blue hand:** "The big blue hand nabbed some of the kids at the clubhouse yesterday"); **chota** (cho'-ta, *fr* Pach = prick: "Chotas hay" = there are police or informers about); **cold wind from the North** (*kwn* SF, '71); **concert artists** (*kwn* Wash DC: because they *sing* on people, *ie* scold); **the furies** ("The furies are outside? Let's not walk out and get martyred"); **fuzz** (*dated, fr* hobo & carnival sl, ? // fuzz or lint which sticks to the clothes); **gay-stoppers** (pun on Gestapo); **gendarme** (zhan-darm', *fr* Fr); **Gertrude** (*kwn* NYC, black gay sl, late '60s: "Gertrude has no business poking her shnoz into my bedroom"); **jolly jumpers** (ardently antihomosexual cops); **Laura Lard** (*kwn* LA, late '60s, reinforced by black panther sl *pig* = cop); **Lillian** ("Know Lillian's motto? 'Let right be dumb!' "); **Lois Law; Mag[gie]** (*kwn* LV, black gay sl, mid-late '60s, *fr* rendition of ghetto term *the man* = white man in authority: "Mag gon cart you 'way, an' not to no chicken fry either"); **Miss Alice; Miss Lily; Miss Man** (black gay sl, also *fr* ghetto

rap *the man:* "That stringy wig ain't gon fool Mis Man"); **night-stick Annie** (= a door-shaker); **ossifer** (since WW I); **Pearl [Pureheart]** (*kwn* SF, '71); **Petunia Patrolman** (= the highway patrol); **Petunia Pig** (*rare*, '71); **pig** (*fr* black panther sl; especially used by militants to = armed policeman); **Priscilla** (Cape Town gay sl); **queen of clubs** (= police power: "If the queen of clubs doesn't want to kiss you, she hurts you"); **[Sam] Savage** (*dated*, early-mid '60s: rambunctious, kill-happy cop); **sharpy** (Brit gay sl, *fr* Parlyaree *sharpingomee* = constable, // It *cercare* = to search: "Sharpy's deekin', luv!" = the police have you staked out); **Tilly [Tight-twat]** (*camp*, mid-late '60s, because he runs a tight ship and keeps a tight asshole: "Tilly Tight-twat certainly turned off *his* night light!"); **tinman** (*rare*, *fr* sl *tin star* = policeman's badge: "Why so glum, chum—did the tinman drop a bucket of rain on you?"); **toys** (*dated, kwn* Ariz, teen sl, late '50s, *fr* wind-up toys or ?// pun sl **toy** = cock + *dick* = cop or detective = small town officials).

In their idle time, police are sometimes known to **vamp** (harass) ghetto homosexuals, especially one who is a *street **queen** or looks as though he might use drugs. With his **nails held up for drying,** the **sus** (suspect) is **tossed** (frisked) and busted if dope is found in possession. The prostitutes of the '30s would have said **slashed.**

If he is sent to the station house in a paddy wagon (see *wheels), he becomes a **girl being taken home** (*kwn* SF, '71). If he is driven by the arresting officers in a squad car, he travels in a **cock-car, dog wagon** (police station wagon often used for transporting police dogs), or a **whistler,** if the siren is sounding. The revolving red lights are the **bubble gum machines** or the **roaring crowns.**

In the pokey [**dungeonette; glasshouse** (LA municipal jail); **hall of injustice** (SF municipal jail); **hall of mirrors; mother's boarding house; shithouse; tower of London**], he is **fit in** (booked, mugged and sprayed with lice repellent) before thrown into a cell [**bird (monkey) cage**]. If he is also drunk, he rates the **Holiday Inn** [**plus bars**] (the drunk tank: "Hello, hon! I'm in the Holiday Inn—plus bars. When can you have me sprung?")

Two cops making their beat in a prowl car are the **Bobsey Twins** ("ever wonder what the Bobsey Twins do together on cold winter nights?"), **Dolly Sisters** or **the Gold Dust Twins,** and any legal police action on their part is their **sister act.** One of the duo is a **mother bull** ('50s), **tenderhearted pork** ('71); it is his job to be sympathetically engaged in friendly chatter with the apprehended. It is also his job to have a good memory and retain all told in confidence. If the pair patrol the park, they are called **sparrow supervisors** and the park itself is described as being **hairy** (= unsafe, well watched: *kwn* LV, black gay sl, late '60s). Some police enjoy doing this for a living—they are called vice and have an entry all of their own.

Related terms:

courtesan of the motors motorcycle cop, especially if he can be had. Syn: **Ranger Smith** (*kwn* Cleveland, mid '60s).

Dickless Tracy (*fr* prison sl = woman cop) policeman mocked for being less of a man than he pretends to be: a gutless-wonder.

fixer vice attorney.

fraternity house federal prison. **Wind up with the joint in your hand** = to be sent to prison, *joint* being a pun upon sl = prison + penis.

invite somebody to the ball to ticket a motorist "The California

Highway Patrol had to invite me to the policeman's ball—that's why I'm late."

meat tenderizer billyclub. Syn: mahogany dildo (*camp*).

pork chopper helicopter manned by police.

Miss Phoebe ('71) the FBI "Miss Phoebe always gets her man, honey!"

Praetorian guard security cop in a gay bar; by extension, the rent-a-fuzz. Syn: **Miss Mafia** (*camp:* = cop acting as bouncer); **royal guard.**

royal ballet (*camp*) police sent on a raid [**royal bust**].

royal opera a courtroom. Syn: **opera house.**

springer (*fr* pros sl) a bail-bondsman.

top tenor police sergeant.

watchhog (reinforced by sl *pig* = cop) hired detective, fink, spy.

Whistler's mother (*camp*) chief of police.

Also see *vice.

Linda Lovelyvoice ('71-72) female announcer, usually in an airline terminal, with a steady, monotonous purr.

line-up 1. gang rape; form of anal tag where only one person is "it" **2.** to participate in a line-up "Aw, go line-up on your mother!"

linguist anyone who is orally inclined "My friend, Harry the linguist, claims that relief is just a swallow away."

lip burning (*kwn* SF, '71, hip gay sl, *fr* sl **burning** = going in drag, // rejecting all of one's heterosexual past by burning clothes) wearing lipstick.

lip-flick running the tongue across the lips suggesting a delicious sampling. Used as a cruising signal.

lips puckered skin surrounding the anus "Hey, Mr. Pharmacist, do you have anything for chapped lips?"

lips licensed to thrill (*fr* play on words in movies where spies are licensed to kill) experienced cocksucker.

liquid eyes sexy eyes.
Syn: **movie star eyes.**

Lisa 1. (*camp*) the sugar side of Larry or Lawrence **2.** (*fr* Mona Lisa) male model, especially one who poses for pornography.

lisp [lithp] to speak, tell something "Shut your gashes, girls; Rex Reedless is going to lisp us something dirtray—she claims." **—er** to whisper "Oh, let me lisper in your ear."

literary hour bathroom time spent reading.

literature gallery dirty book store.
Syn: **fruit stand; gay supermarket; library** (*kwn* SF, late '60s).

little (*adj*) used conjunctively in praising a young, firm body "I did this hitchhiker I picked up—he sure was a cute, little, tight thing.

Little Abners 1. pair of thick heavy boots **2.** big feet.

littlefinger posh, elegant.
Syn: *piss elegant.

Little Sodom anyplace where homosexuality is.

little surprise[treat] a visual godsend "It's the little treats in the streets that make being a garbage collector worth while."

living doll[dream] (*dated*) a wower "What's that living doll see in you? Nobody else can even see around you."

LLM (*kwn* SF, SM sl, '72) long-haired leather man.

load liquid ejaculation; the wage homosexuals work for. My thesaurus—the Bible—calls it "spilt seed" and "pollution."
Syn: **wad** ("I got quite a wad in this," he said swinging his enormous tool, "Think you could take it, Blue Eyes?")
Also see *come.

local talent the *girls representing the immediate locality "If he's an example of local talent, I'm going back to Kenosha."

lockjaw 1. sore throat caused by sucking too many large penises **2.** salivating in anticipation of cocksucking.

lone queen homosexual loner.
> Related term:
> **lone wolf** antisocial lesbian.

long distance reading heckling, usually in the street or, better still, from a block away. **Closet queens* are the preferred victims.

long eye the vagina.

long-winded ('40s) taking a long time till ejaculation.
> Ant: **Easter bunny queen.**

long wine (black gay sl) strong, potent wine   "Now, Lu, ain't you shame for drinkin' all that long wine without your sistuhs?"

look good and naked to be beautiful.

lookie-freak 1. one who likes watching what he's doing sexually in a mirror. Syn: **face man** (= one who masturbates while looking in a mirror); **mirror queen 2.** see **watch queen.*

looking-glass people (*kwn* NYC, '70) haughty young men in love with themselves, see **flamingo.*

look up to stand straight, proud and tall   "You'd look up too if you had the size of his basket."

Lord of the Flies aristocrat of the cocksuckers   "I might as well go home, the Lord of the Flies is fifteen ahead of me."

lost at sea being driven to sex with one's own gender when confined in prison or forced to barrack living. When one is lost at sea, one is sexually confused.

love [**lovey, luv**] half-hearted endearment   "Don't leave me, love; who'll be here to push the bed away from the wall?"

lovie a love tap; romantic slapstick.

love it (*exclam*) approval   "You're saying Tom clipped Stan for five hundred bucks? Love it!"

love nuts (*voc*) endearment like **baby*   "Hello, love nuts; I live two blocks away, the coffee's on and the bed's warm—care to join me in a cup of sheets?"

lover 1. one's friend in all senses—social, sexual, *etc;* sweetheart   "Are you two lovers—even though you're not *preying* together?" Syn: **chain** (*fr* hobo sl *ball and chain* = boy taking female role); **chuff chum** (*dated*); **cooler** (*dated:* because he cools 'em down); **dolly pal** (*dated*) **2.** (*voc*) "Keep quiet, lover, you're better sex that way" **3.** (*rare, adj, fr* Cockney *loverly*) lovely.

lowered physiologically having a low ass making the torso appear long. Not to be confused with **buns to the ground** (*kwn* SF, '72) = a fat ass.

lube precoital fluid which sometimes occurs when the penis is stimulated; natural lubrication   "He lubed so much it looked like he pissed his pants."
> Syn: [**penis**]**butter.**
> Related terms:
> **Foaming Mignon** (*camp*) nickname for one who lubes a lot.
> **pearl** (late '60s) to lube   " 'You're pearling,' he said, as he gently nudged his newspaper up my ass."
> **—job** oiled bodies rolling and rubbing until the slick friction causes ejaculation.

lucky Pierre 1. the one in the middle of a threesome. Syn: **chicken* **on a spit; meat of the sandwich 2.** man at the end of a **daisy* **chain.**

Lucy (play of words upon *Lucy* + *loose hole*) abusive nickname for one accused of having a loose ass.

Luella Lipschits (*camp*) *yenta;* rumor-monger.

luke 1. leukorrhea **2.** female coital fluid.

lushious Lillian Roth ('72) **1.** gay alcoholic   "Where's lushious Lillian Roth—somewhere over the railing?" **2.** stinking sot; a wino, drunk.

Syn: **pickled pansy** (*camp*); **pink olive** (*dated*, '40s); **posie queen** ('71); **pot queen** (*dated*, '40s, before *pot* = marijuana); **stewed fruit** (*camp*).

lydia (*camp*) **1.** little **2.** "lid," *ie* one ounce of marijuana.

lyles (Brit gay sl, *fr* Anglo-Chinese *lai lo* = come here) legs "Cross your lyles, luv, your breath stinks."

ma title before the surname; in most cases, Ma indicates a fuddy-duddy spoil-sport "Shit, Ma McMillian is going to tell all the chicken to go home just because it's nine o'clock."

macaroni 1. (pros sl, *fr* black sl; *cf* Fr argot *mec* = pimp) a pimp. **Sweet mack** = gentle, nonviolent pimp **2.** (*pej*) an Italian "Stow it or you'll have the macaronies next door crossin' themselves a mile a minute!"
—**and cheese** unclean prepuce.
—**queen** (*camp*) the Pope. Syn: **queen of the Macaronies.**

machine gun kelly (*camp,* because it *machine guns* =dazzles onlookers) ostentatious necklace of paste emeralds.

macho (mä'-chō, *rare fr* Sp = virile) masculine ***hustler** "That macho is so into selling himself, he even sells his self."

mad (*cf* hipster sl *crazy* of the '50s) **1.** unrestrained, avant garde "Who *was* that mad masked thing who rode away with that Indian?" **2.** ostentatious "That diamond she had on her pinky was absolutely *mad*—I don't know how she managed to lift her hand" **3.** exciting, refreshing **4.** tickling the gay's funnybone; a corker, humdinger "This sun-tan lotion is *mad;* it really works—on my left armpit."

madam[e] 1. mature homosexual man "Listen to her counting her pennies—just like a Jewish madame on vacation" **2.** woman or homosexual man who plays the part of a prude; a prig "If you don't like the company, Madame Spook, you can leave—you're outclassed anyway" **3.** (*kwn* LV, mid-late '60s) one who leases his quarters to friends who pick up ***tricks** with no place to go. The madame is either paid with cash or as is more often the case, allowed to view or join the fun.

Madame l'Âge (mä'-dəm-läzh' *fr* Fr = Mrs. Age) old age, senility; Father Time "What mummification process do *you* use to keep Madame l'Âge from your door?"
Related term:
have Madame l'Âge as a hairdresser to have silver threads among the gold.

made up like Faust face smeared in several layers of pancake, rouge, lipstick, eyeshadow, *etc* "They had that corpse made up like Faust—it looked more like he was being readied for an audition than a funeral."

Madge (*camp*) gay nickname and vocative indicating an ill-dressed, dowdy homosexual "Better to have loved and lost, Madge, than to never have lost before!"

Syn: **Maude** (*fr* Mathilda: "Your neck isn't sunburned, Maude —those are bleach burns!")

madly broke very low on funds, possessing little or no cash.

Also see *money.

madness 1. festive, hysterically funny, see *mad "These socks are sheer madness!" **2.** something done for a thrill "I sucked him off just for madness."

Related term:

madness reigns (*interj*) said of anything which is pleasureable.

mandrota (mä-drō'-tä, *fr* Pach // Sp *madre* = mother) motherly bordello madame.

Mae 1. the one and only Mae West, her Confuciusness of the boys "Mae said, 'I used to be Snow White, but I drifted'" **2.** pet name adopted by one who reflects the attributes of Miss West, star and *all* woman.

Syn: **May.**

maggot hugger (*pej*) one who seeks the sexual company of derelicts.

magic marker (*camp*) lipstick.

magic time (*kwn* SF, late '60s) instant rapport; love at first sight.

magnolia queen homosexual reared in Dixie.

Syn: **southern belle.**

mahu (mä'-hoo, *fr* Haw = shaman who played the part of a woman) **1.** the simpering, prancing effeminate "This poem reads as if a love-sick mahu wrote it" **2.** title much like sir or Mr. "Why don't you call me on *your* nickel for a change, Mahu Jimmy?"

Related terms:

alano mahu (ä-lä'-nō-mä-hoo' = thou art a mahu) gay Hawaiian's version of "Come down to earth, you're just like the rest of us!" "What do you mean that I act like a real wahine when I get maka-haku? Alano mahu, and don't you ever forget it!" Syn: **anaka mahu** (ä-nä'-kä mä-hoo') *Note:* the stress of mahu is placed upon the last syllable when following alano or anaka.

mahu-lani (mä'-hoo lä'-nē, *fr* Haw gay sl = McFlower) any male homosexual but particularly if he is Hawaiian.

maka-haku (mä'-kä hä'-koo, *fr* Haw gay sl) drunk "Turn down the cigarette, please—I'm *très* maka-haku."

make see *fuck.

make mudpies ('70) to have sex in the bushes while it rains or drizzles.

make out to be successful in finding sex for the day/night/hour "How do you expect to make out, when that beak of yours gives you some pretty fancy competition."

Syn: **make the scene with somebody; score.**

—bar 1. gay bar where one is destined to find a partner **2.** gay bar with a going back area [**orgy room**].

—session period of time one spends making love.

make scissors of somebody to masturbate a woman with a pincers movement of a clitoris-rubbing thumb and an anus-tickling forefinger.

Syn: **do the bowling hold; hold a bowling ball.**

make the blind see to suck an uncircumcised penis (**blind meat**) "You're mad about Roman art? I didn't know that you made the blind see!"

make the plank (*fr* naut sl) to guide another's cock into the anus;

to be passive during anal intercourse "Where were you dur-
in reveille, Riley, making the plank again?"
> Syn: **ride the pole; sit on some dick.**

makeup (*camp, kwn* SF, black gay sl, late '60s-70s) varying shades
of skin pigment of black people "I won't have anybody else
around in a makeup darker than mine!"

malt somebody's balls (*kwn* SF, '70) to be overwhelmed, to have
the mind blown "His fourth helping malted my balls."

mama 1. person who assumes the wifely position in a gay marriage
2. (*pron*) oneself; the first person singular though used in
the third person "Mama got only *one* cavity—and that's where
the dentist fucked her" **3.** (*exclam*) oh, my; holy Hanna!
"Mama! That burger's green and talking!"

Mama Bear a hairy-chested queen.

manhole cover sanitary napkin.
> Syn: **rag; shmatta** (*fr* Yid = rag).

man's man (*dated*, hetero sl, '40s) homosexual male. Mocking
male servants attending to the needs of a bachelor.

mappy (*kwn* LV & SF, late '60s, *fr* Brit sl *map* = face) **1.** (*dated*)
descriptive of the brilliant psychedelic patterns of the young
moderns' shirts **2.** said of a face which is full of adventure,
character and expression; enchanting but not conventionally
beautiful.

margery (*dated*) affected, sweet, chitterish "You're letting *him*
run the projector—where will that margery thing ever get the
strength to flip the switch."
> Syn: ***nelly; *swish[y].**

Margo Polo (*camp*) any Italian man.
> **—'s** any Italian greasy spoon restaurant: any Luigi's Pizzaria
"Call Margo Polo's and have some nice Italian sausage—say,
about seventeen—sent over."

marijuanaful (*kwn* SF, '71) wonderful, said of *cannabis sativa*.

marion times (Cape Town gay sl) to wed, become married "She
wanted to marion times a wendy bag."

market meeting grounds for homosexuals interested in making
pick-ups.
> Related term:
> **on the market** in circulation.

married living together with another homosexual in a partnership of mutual consent "Barney got married last night—which
bar was it in *this* week?" "Oops! Something clever just
walked into the tearoom—pardon me while I go get married."

marshmallow pumps (*camp*) white sneakers, tennies "Don't you
go snickerin' at your mama's marshmallow pumps—they her
red shoes at a Saturday fry."
> Syn: **brothel sneakers** (Brit gay sl: "Just lemme slip into my
glorious brothel sneakers, dear—the ones I had dyed pink
for the funeral"); **marble sneakers** ("Hark—methinks I hear
the patter of little marble sneakers tripping through the
tulips"); **moonlight shoes** ('72); **powder puffs; runners** (such
shoes may be lifesavers when escaping rowdies); **running
shoes; sneaks; tenny pumps.**
> Related terms:
> **cocoa puffs** muddy tennis shoes.
> **on sneaks** on tiptoe; quietly "Come in on sneaks—my trick's
asleep!" "How'd you get the money—on sneaks?"

Mary 1. another homosexual; ***sis** "Don't push the panic button—it's just another mary safariing through David's Darkest
Baths" **2.** (*adj*) feminine acting "He's too mary to fuck me."
> Syn: **molly 3.** (*camp, fr* Mary—that grand old name) vocative
for all other homosexuals; personal, familiar "Turn off the
lights, Mary, we wanna screw!" **4.** (*exclam, ?fr* oath "Mary,

mother of God!") "Mary! That's a basket? Looks more like a mouse in a gunny sack."

Syn: **Alice May; Bess[ie]** (*fr* Good Queen Bess = Elizabeth I; "Listen, Bess, this honeymoon's about over"); **Betty** (*kwn* SF, '72); **Blanche** ("Love, Blanche, is *not* keeping score!"); **Brenda** ("Brenda, did the same dentist that did your teeth also manufacture your pearls?"); **Clarisse; Cora** ("That's not quite my bag of tea, Cora"); **Emma [Emmy]; Gussie** ("Gussie, did you hear about the two heads in the Stud pulling hair?"); **Maisie** ("Oh, Maisie, you shouldn't have bought it, but I'm glad you did"); **María** ("María, I've just kissed a boy named María!"); **Marjorine** ("Marjorine! This must be a cereal church; there's a surprise in every pew"); **Martha** ("Look at all the blood, Martha"); **Mintie** ("Vanity, vanity, thy name is Mintie"); *Ravonia; **Rose** (*kwn* Southwest, mid '60s: "Don't you think you should trim your thorns, Rose?"); **Sally** (mid '60s: "You're a riot, Sally—ruin in our time").

the Mary Ann[Ellen] (underworld sl) act where a pickpocket pretends to be homosexual in order to pat another man about the hips and thus lift the wallet "Some guys work the Mary Ellen in grope bars; it's an easy haul."

Mary Magdalene originally, a reformed whore; now, any homosexual leaving his wicked, libidinous past behind "You haven't attended any of the parties I've invited you to—you're not turning Mary Magdalene on us, are you?"

Mary Worthless (*camp*) very old queen one might encounter at the gay saunas; a meddlesome old fool.

maso-sissy (*camp*) masochistic homosexual man.

masquerade (les sl) said of a lesbian who dresses up as a man.
Syn: **mack it** (les sl, late '60s).

maternity blouse (*camp*) shirt worn by a man which is not tucked into his pants.

matinee sexual encounter taking place during the early afternoon. But do not confuse with **feature a matinee** = to have the anus licked.

maverick tracks splattered gobs of semen "Just look for maverick tracks and crumpled kleenex and that's where I'll be saying mass."

May Ling (*camp, fr* Chin name = beautiful one) **1.** any Chinese homosexual, see *rice queen **2.** (*kwn* SF, late '60s) one skilled in the culinary arts; a gay chef.

meals on wheels teenagers cruising in automobiles up and down the main thoroughfares of town on a weekend night.

meat 1. the *membrun virile,* see *cock "Don't let your tons of hot meat boil over" **2.** (*camp*) jewelry "How much meat was she still wearing after the lights went back on?"
Related terms:
[pound of] chopped liver artificial gems; junk jewelry. Syn: **chrome** (*kwn* SF, SM sl, late '60s); **rocks** (rare, *fr* sl *rocks* = *ice* = stolen jewels); **slum** (*fr* carnival sl = kewpie dolls, trinkets given as prizes in concession stands: "Put away the slum! Wear an Elgin!")
sirloin (*camp*) expensive jewelry.
—case 1. bulging crotch, see *basket **2.** jewelry store showcase.
—rack outdoor setting, such as a promenade in a public park, where homosexuals gather to parade their wares and meet new friends "They'll spoil the new mall by making it another meat rack, just wait and see." Syn: **marketplace; meat market.**

mechanized screw a nonaffectionate love partner—he goes through the movements out of habit "I want some fresh, lively thing

with lots of pazazz—not some mechanized screw from the tubs."
Syn: **dead doll** (mid '60s).

medicine (*kwn* SF, '70, short for colloq *medicine for sore eyes*) an aside calling attention to a handsome man.
Also see *****contact.**

melt somebody 1. to bawl somebody out **2.** to have halitosis "How can I keep looking into your deep blue eyes when with every whisper you melt me?"

member (*kwn* LV, mid-late '60s, *fr* sl *clubhouse* = toilet room) a fellow gay. "There ain't too many members in Alaska" "Have any new members signed the clubhouse register today?"

menocker (mə-nok'-ər, *fr* Yid = man whose occupation is to remove all religiously forbidden veins and sinews from meat) a junkie; heroin addict who has perforated and exhausted all his main veins.

menu 1. toilet wall lined with grafitti "Read anyone good on the menu?" Syn: **clubhouse register 2.** list of sexual talents with respective prices "He doesn't go for a straight twenty—he's on the menu: one thing is twenty but it's fifty for another."

meow (*interj*) uttered when one bystander overhears a catty remark; a sound of warning that the fur is about to fly.
Syn: **dirty pee; purr; step back** (= watch out); **whoa.**

merchandise the body as a sexual tool kit "You haven't got the right merchandise to sell, kid—g'wan back home and get weaned first!"

mercy (*exclam*) vocal outburst to cover curse words. Equal to "upon my word" "Mercy! I just spent my last dollar on beer—I guess kitty will have to go hungry another night."
Syn: **mercy me; merthy** ("Merthy! I thought I was going to wear that bus!")

merry-go-round game of musical beds; being the lover of one person one week and then the lover of his best friend the next. Small towns are prime areas for hosting merry-go-rounds.

mess 1. homely, repugnant, ugly man "Sure he gets a lot of tricks—but who counts messes?" Syn: **chocolate mess; dog['s dinner]; gargoyle; gravedigger** (= one who looks as though he had been hit in the face with a shovel); **gravy train** (= person with a face that only a dog could love: "What time do the rest of the gravy trains show—I wanna leave before they get a chance to turn the rest of my face to stone"); **grotesque[ry]** ('70: "How do I keep the grotesqueries away from my gates—hang up garlic?"); **gruesome[ugly] sister; Grungette La Tour** (*kwn* Seattle, late '60s-'70, also *adj:* "Where'd you get the grungette latour pumps, dear—you should have left them for proper burial"); **haunting [of hill house]** ("The haunting at the other end of the bar is pretty crocked; let's buy him another beer an' see if he falls off his stool"); **Hilda** (Cape Town gay sl); **last of the graces** (*kwn* Seattle, '70: "The keeper's been leaving the last of the graces out after ten"); **the late show** (= undesirable dragged home as a last resort of all-night rambling); **lonely woman** (= gay ugly duckling, old balding queen); **maid of the mist** (late '60s: "He was *the* maid of the mist—his starring role was playing the witch in Snow White"); **mishkeit** (mish'-kīt, *fr* Yid *mieskeit* = ugliness: "That poor thing's *such* a mishkeit! If he went to a costume party as a movie, he'd be 'Wait Until Dark'!"); **something to scare away flies; squaw** (see *****India); **turn-off; waffle-face; yesterday's wash** ('72) **2.** bungler, inept ninny "She's a real mess on that dance floor" **3.** (*voc*) "Listen, mess, how can you *make* something out of nothing?"

Related terms:

doggie diner night (*kwn* SF, '71) bad cruising night—too many messes.

frenched [kissed] by a mack truck (comparison with the looks of an accident victim) ugly, an eyesore. Syn: **ugly as home-made soap.**

parade of ugliness unattractive men. Syn: **the uglies** ("Mary! These cookies are hard enough to throw at the uglies!")

mew (*kwn* Southwest, late '60s) to complain in a low-register whine.

—**and snur** to whine and slur at the same time. Drug addicts mew and snur. Teenagers mew and snur to parents and teachers.

Mexican jumping beans amphetamines.

Syn: **beans** (narc sl: "Going *up* on beans is like coming *down* on acid.")

mickey mouse (*kwn* NYC, late '60s) crazy, goofy, screwy.

midnight-shot[-slot] all-night sexing with one who enjoys getting fucked.

Mighty Mouth (*camp*) gay nickname for one whose personality is orally centered, *eg* a cocksucker, rapid talker, blabber-mouth, chain-smoker.

milk route driving a *trick home in the wee hours of the morning "Milk routes around LA can be dangeous—the trick might live fifteen towns 'down the block'."

milk run[stop] bus or train depot's men's room when cruised by homosexuals in the late hours of the night "I met my hubby on the crapper next to mine at the milk stop in Dubuque."

Related term:

make a milk run to tour the all-night washrooms in an attempt to secure a partner "I'm not ready to make a milk run—some evil fairy slipped me an ugly pill after eleven."

milk the bar to order draft beer "I milk the bar until I get messed up enough to shake my beads like a mad Watoo."

milky way well-traveled path in a public park.

mince (Brit & Cape Town gay sl) to walk, stroll, arrive, run, etc. the precise definition all depends on the rest of the sentence's context: "You should have seen her mincing after that bus."

Syn: **minnie** (Brit gay sl); **swish** ("You just swish right up to him and tell him that he looks every day older than death.")

mince somebody up to confuse somebody "Don't mince me up, girl, I've got to remember which street we turn off on."

Minerva (*fr* Roman goddess of wisdom) the mind "that just bubbles my minerva" = that blows my mind.

minmin (*fr* baby talk) a minute "It'll take me a few minmins more to finish drinking my french fries."

Minny (?*fr* Minnie Mouse = the common-law wife of Mickey + sl *mickey mouse* = silly) **1.** a kind but simple-minded sort; one who is capricious, hapless, scatterbrained; a sad sack "Does skinny Minny have to write *all* her letters in crayon?" Syn: **Minny Haha; Minny Mouse** ("Wait a sec, kids, Minny Mouse has to put her word's worth in too!" **2.** (Brit gay sl) man who prefers the passive role in anal relations, see *passive partner.

miss 1. (*camp*) another homosexual "Isn't that the miss who traveled through New York on her looks? She almost made it two blocks" **2.** title preceding first or last name of a man ascribed as being gay "All that Miss Midas had to do was touch someone's thing, and he had ready spending money" **3.** also employed in numerous nicknames spoofing triumphant

contest winners (Miss Universe, Miss Idaho, etc) "When were you born, Miss Reno, in 1950 . . .'12?" **4.** (def art) the "Here, hon, put on miss shades so you can see."
—**Ann** (black gay sl) the white homosexual.
—**Claudette Crowbar** (camp) gay nickname.
—**dish 1.** one who talks back, a sasser **2.** nickname for a dog preferred by gays—poodles, chihuahuas, etc.
—**Fairgrounds** someone who has to wear tents to cover her fat.
—**Gooch** (fr Auntie Mame's secretary) **1.** any frowzy, dowdy wallflower **2.** nickname for close acquaintance "Why, Miss Gooch, wherever are you taking all those fag mags—to a weenie roast?"
Syn: **Miss Gunch.**
—**Gray** old queen trying vainly to look like a young princess.
Syn: **Elizabitch; forlorn faggot.**
—**Halloween 1.** ugly, grotesque, mask-like face "A good-night peck from Miss Halloween would be the kiss of death" **2.** a human vegetable downed by drugs; a dud between the sheets "Miss Halloween, the most unforgettable character I never met, sold her soul to Reader's Disgust." Syn: **Miss Vegetable.**
—**Niagara 1.** popularity winner **2.** someone who vomits profusely "Oh, look! Miss Niagara's falling into the sink again."
—**nickelodeon** juke box.
—**Peach** squealer, informer.
—**Peola** (fr Harlemese peola = light-skinned Negro, '40s) light black.
Syn: **Miss Tan Confessions.**
—**Photoplay** one who tells all he knows—and more besides.
—**Pickupsticks** gay lumberjack.
—**priss** (kwn Cleveland, mid-late '60s) girlish, limpwristed gestures "tone down your miss priss" = stop dropping your hands off their wrists.
—**Roma** a white wino "If I had a face like Miss Roma, I'd Spend the rest of my life apologizing."
—**Scarlet** (kwn SF, black gay sl, late '60s-'70, fr heroine of Gone with the Wind) **1.** black vocal dart aimed at the whites of their eyes. Blacklash against the good old days **2.** white racist homosexual "Miss Scarlet wouldn't be caught daid in this bar—too many spooks!"
—**Sears** (pej) woman unliberated—the American housewife "Put a $14.99 sale tag on a two dollar dress, and Miss Sears will grab it as a bargain."
—**Tarantula** hairy fairy.
—**thing 1.** affectionately effeminate "Why Miss Thing had to introduce me to Breath Valley, I'll never know" **2.** (pron) second person singular "Does Miss Thing want her smack now or after her eggs Benedict."
—**Thunderbird** a black wino.
missed (fr sl messed up = confused; however cf old adage of those who are missed by God as he hands out smarts) dumb, a mental jigsaw puzzle.
Syn: **missing.**
Related term:
Miss Points (fr colloq pointed head) one who has lost most of his marbles "Miss Points, I swan! You're as sharp as a rubber ball!"
Missed America female loser.
missiletoes attractive astronauts.
missionary work proselytizing others to the homosexual cause "What really turns me off missionary work is that so much time has to be spent for such little results."

Syn: **convert somebody.**

miss one's calling 1. to consciously deny homosexuality **2.** to be an effeminate heterosexual man.

mixed couple boy and his girl.

mixed marriage marriage between homosexual and a hetero- sexual "That's one mixed marriage I hope won't work out— the groom was kinda cute."

Also see *front marriage.

mocha chips freckles on a light skinned black "Honey, that girl's in the wrong shade of makeup—her mocha chips keep slidin' into each other."

Also see *makeup.

model (*fr* model = one hired to display clothing // MFr *modelle:* originally **male model**) **1.** male prostitute of the call boy variety who uses modeling as a front "Let's pool our money and get a model for the night—something tall, dark and lengthy" **2.** to be employed as a model "You should model; afterall, you're built like a Model T."

Models, unlike the average run-of-the-mill hustlers, admit to being gay. Like their co-hearts, however, they bank pro- fessionally on good looks and youth—advertised as nineteen translates as a very young-looking twenty-five. Youth is what establishes the price of admission—as well as almost always the additional requirement of appearing masculine and hav- ing a big piece of meat. Customers rarely request drag queens. It is advisable to make appointments with dependable model- ing agencies when paying for love by the hour. Not only are some independent models crooked [**creepers,** because they creep up to the pants pockets], but there are those who charge additional fees for "fringe benefits" after a timid customer's autistic approach ("I'd like you to pose while I sketch") has worn thin ("Oh, you wanted to fuck me? That'll be an extra ten spot, man!") Current price listings are: mod- el's place for one hour—$25; caller's place for one hour—$30; **taking on duos** [**doubles**] (having two in bed at once)—$50. Buyers generally like to **give quickies** (suck cock) and **work in a few rips** (ass-fuggle); if a gentleman caller inquires whether or not his model is **versatile,** it almost always means that he wants to fuck.

A meeting place where models pick up their phone messages without meeting their public is an **exchange** or the **union hall.** However, a **house** or an apartment lavishly decorated for the clientele, and run by a **guild boss,** is a **hustle finance** (*camp*) or a **show house** where a *john can select among all the boys for rent.

A few houses also cater to those homosexuals who pay well for their own fantasy to be recreated. When a model puts on a costume [**fantasy fit** or **trademan's uniform**], the customer is **digging fantasy.** The clothes chosen by the fetishists epitom- ize masculinity: cowboys, sailors, *etc.* A model acting out the cowboy theme is a **midnight cowboy** and he probably will wear a **flashlight shirt** (western shirt made of silk and decorated in fringe), while an ersatz sailor is a **sidewalk sailor** usually in **whites** (regulation summer dress—white and tight).

Related to the model is the masseur for men only [**massage queen** or **rub queen**]. He also admits to being gay and usually takes the insertor role in anal affairs, though he is quite adept at **blowing** his callers' troubles away. Many of his clients expect to be **vibrated** (anally masturbated with an electric vibrator).

Both models and masseurs share one asset: they are honest, dependable whores. And being gay, it is not uncommon

for them to pick up ***tricks** and have sex without monetary exchange [**freebies**].
   Also see ***hustler.**

moffie (Cape Town gay sl, *fr* sl *moff* = hermaphrodite) homosexual "Gail is the language of the moffie community."

moll 1. hard as nails queen **2.** to walk, skip or mince. "Can't you hear those young queens molling through the lobby?"
   Related term:
   moll about in the head loitering with intent to sex.

molly dyke (*fr* Brit sl *molly* = bosom, woman, effeminate + ***dyke**) the passive lesbian "Why does that molly dyke always have a smile for you? Did the bleach fry her brain?"
   Syn: **dress** (*dated, fr* pros sl, '30s); **fairy lady** (*rare*, hetero sl: "Then there was the fairy lady who said, 'Argyle it to me!'"); **filly; fine chick; fluff** ("Honey, I want this drag to look so for real that some big diesel'll think that I'm a piece of stray fluff"); **mama; Marge; midge; pinky; skirts** (*obs*).
   Related term:
   hit the sheets (les sl) to be passive to the overtures of another woman.

molly house (*dated*, Brit) a heterosexual whorehouse that would accommodate wealthy homosexuals.

mom lesbian who plays up her femininity.

money (usu treated with respect and longing since gay life doesn't encourage sublimation through hard work and steady pay) "I'll follow you anywhere money, er, I mean, honey!" "With inflation the way it is, it's cheaper to eat your money."
   Money in general: **bread** (*fr* black sl, '30s, kneaded from *dough*); **cakes** ('70: *in the cakes* = rolling in money; *low in the cakes* = without); **coin**[s] (orig black sl, now hustler sl: "He goes for coin"); **dust** (*fr* sl *golddust*); **get well** (*fr* pros sl) **l'argent** (lär-zhänt', *fr* Fr: "He's too anal . . . he'll never part with any of his l'argent"); **measures** (Brit gay sl, *fr* Parlyaree *medzer* = halfpenny // It *mezzo* = a half); **mona** (*kwn* SF, '70, *fr* Fr *mone* = capital: "I have just enough mona for one bottle and two straws"); **pennies** (mid '60s: "It takes many gay pennies to become Danish pastry"); **polly** (because money talks).
   Folding money: **bill** (*kwn* LV, hustler sl: $100); **cholly** (*kwn* LA, hustler sl, *fr* black sl = dollar bill).
   Coins: **confetti; half a rock** (*kwn* Wis, late '50s: $.50 piece); **jingle** (spare change scored by panhandlers: "He really tried to get some jingle off me"); **rocks** (*kwn* Midwest, '50s); **washers** (some prison usage).
   Pennies (not to be confused with *pennies* above): **boston beans; brown dollars**[noses] (*kwn* SF, late '60s); **bubble gum money** (*kwn* SF, late '60s).
   Related fiscal ter.ns:
   fuck money 1. cookie jar money saved to dial a model (dial-a-dokus) on a rainy day **2.** price of the baths. Syn: **hope chest fund.**
   in form rolling in dough; wealthy.
   monopoly money (*kwn* SF, '71) food stamps.
   purse (*camp*) wallet "It's Dutch treat, so bring your purse."
   skint (Brit, *fr* skinned) broke, without funds.
   street money (late '60s-'70) money earned from prostitution "My welfare check pays the rent, and my street money barely keeps me in food."
   tariff 1. sales tax "What's the tariff on the dildo with the feed-bag (*ie* vacuum cleaner)?" **2.** money chipped in for incidentals.
   unholy (*kwn* SF, late '60s) expensive. Syn: **too far; out-of-hand.**

wallpaper (*fr* underworld sl *paperhanger* = one who passes bad currency) counterfeit money.

would you care for a caramel[mint] (*camp, kwn* SF, '70s, ?*fr* '20s sl *sugar* = money) the offering of a bribe. Mint implies that the sum offer is considerable, while a caramel denotes penny candy   "Care for some mints, Judge?"

money trick ('71) occasional **john* picked up by a nonprofessional when the money gets low; a meal ticket.

Monica Movinghips (*camp*) star who reached the top on her hips.

monkey the vagina.

mono mononucleosis.
   Syn: **kissing disease; *third venereal disease.**

monsters pair of pumps.

moosh (Brit sl) mouth   "Tell 'er t'shut 'er moosh before I really give 'er somethin' t'cry aboot."

morgue case (*kwn* Southwest, mid '60s) **1.** typecasting as one of the living dead in a horror movie. Syn: **Miss Vampira   2.** fetishistic about death and moribund supernumeraries. Syn: ***coffin queen   3.** (*rare*) one who is as thin as a rail.

morner lovemaking in the morning   "A morner is wined and dined and then done to a turn in the morning."   "A morner is a nooner—only sooner."

morning dew (*kwn* SF, '70) early morning stragglers left over from last night's cruising.
   Syn: **morning dewdrop queen.**

moss chest hair.
   —y having hair on the chest.

motel time those last frantic minutes before closing time when the bar comes alive; the last call for alcohol   "Motel time, kids, everybody suck up and get out!"

mother 1. homosexual mentor; one who introduced another to homosexual activity. Syn: **gay mother; guide; guiding light; his protectiveness; mother hen   2.** (*pron*) first person singular   "Jass, your mother's been remade-up for the television crew."   "Don't worry, mother knows what she's doing."
   —gaga (*dated*, '40s) snooping gossip.
   —of pearl (*exclam*) used in place of "!Madre de Dios!"
   —Parker tough queen.
      Syn: **Hard-Hearted Hannah.**
   —superior 1. social "matriarch"   **2.** a blow-hard
      Syn: **mother hollyhock**

mouse 1. (*dated*, *fr* hetero sl *mouse* = flaccid penis + comparison of homosexuals with timid mice) cocksucker, he nibbles at another's crotch   **2.** (criminal sl) to blackmail a homosexual   **3.** ('71) to nickel and dime one to death; to panhandle.

mouth job 1. see **blow job   2.** (*camp*) severe scolding.

mouth of ages a big mouth.
   Syn: **mouth.**

move in ('71) to buy a pair of secondhand jeans   "And there they were in Goodwill, the jeans I would have dyed for—so I moved in."

movie life   "The last scene in the movie always seems to get out of control."
      Related term:
   reel ('71) a week   "We do it twice a reel"   "I'll be there for two more reels—pass it on!"

movie extra a nobody, straight man for the top banana   "He wasn't my husband—he was just a movie extra trapped in the wrong dressing room."

movie extras real life people; the plebians.

Mrs title for a gayly married effeminate.

Mr Stark Raving (*camp*) unknown today, Mr What's-his-name

"And it stars one of the most renowned and loved personalities —Mr Stark Raving."

Mr Steve Stunning handsome, musclebound would-be leading man.

M'sieu le (me'-ser le, *def art, fr* Fr = Mr the) the "I hope these weights will build up m'sieu le muscles."

much (*adv*) **1.** to a great extent; modifies adjectives: "That surfer's pubes was much teased!" **2.** greatly, many. Used with nouns: "The Caesar salad was a dismal flop—much fall of the Romaine Empire!" "He has much wallet" = he is a rich man. **—ly** (*camp*) exceedingly "I love you muchly."

mucho (moo'-cho, *exclam,* Mex gay sl *fr* Sp = a lot) spoken wolf whistle "¡Mucho! ¡Qué muñeco!" = what a doll!

mucho-much (*adv*) bilingual redundancy used like *much "He had mucho-much rust on his fly."
Syn: **mucho[-many]** "He was giving her mucho-many kisses below the belt."

Mucosa DeRosa (*camp*) **1.** nasal congestion, mucus phlegm **2.** by extension, the nose as the snot locker **3.** nickname for anyone who hacks and spits up phlegm
Syn: **Mucosa Della Rosa.**

mud 1. cool, reserve **2.** teces within the intestinal track.
—dy shitty.
—dy fuck one who excretes during anal intercourse.

muff 1. (*fr* muff = warm enclosure for the hands //MFr *moufle* = mitten) the vagina when erotically licked. Syn: **bush dinner; down; furburger; hairpie; knish-ka-bob** (*fr* Yid *knish* = dumpling = cunt); **muffet 2.** (*cf* muffle *fr* ME *muflen* = to envelop something to protect it) to tongue the clitoris and vulva. Syn: **dive [in the bushes]; fall in love; go South** (*dated*); **go under the house; kiss somebody's down** ("The picture showed Santa kissing Mrs. Claus' down"); **lap** (*pej*); **pearl dive; sixty-three[63]; sneeze in the cabbage; whistle in the dark; yodel [in the canyon of love].**
Related terms:
boating mutual cunnilingus. Syn: **falling head over heels [in love]; fifty-nining** (*camp:* half of *sixty-nining* because women lack penises).
bumper sticker tongue of a cunnilinctrice "Here! Get your bumperstickers working on some of these invitations—they have have to be out by noon."
give up the work (les sl) to refuse to cunnilingue (**eat pussy**). Ant: **give work.**
lawnmower the mouth of a cuntsucker.
—diver [duffer] cunnilinctrice, woman who orally gratifies her partner. Syn: **Connie; cunning linguist** (*fr* cunnilinguist); **cunt-lapper[sucker]** (*pej*); **diver; gash-eater** (*pej*); **growl-biter** (*pej, fr* sl *growl* = female pudend); **high-diver; lap-lover** (*pej*); **lapper** (*pej:* "That lapper's got a brain—yeah, somewhere between her cleavage"); **licker** (*pej,* hetero sl: *fr* vul sl *lickbox* = cunnilinctrice; "Her cunt's too small—it can't hold its licker"); **lover under the lap** ("Haven't you ever noticed that all lovers under the lap have shiny, bright teeth?"); **muffer; pussy bumper** (also any skirt-chasing playboy); **suckstress** ('40s); **top-diver** (Brit gay sl, *fr* sl *top* = head); **vacuum cleaner.**

mujerado (moo'-khar-ä'-tho, fr Sp = womanish) American Indian trained since childhood to be the sacred shamanistic vessel in various rites. He was dressed as a woman and scantified as a demigod.
Related term:
*mahu what the mujerado was called in Hawaii. Syn: **mahoi.**

munchies [munjies] food, but especially in-between meal treats.

Syn: **chuckies** (*dated*).
Related term: **have the munchies** to be hungry.

mung (*dated, interj*, '50s, *fr* teen sl = fantastically gory fantasy of hitting a pregnant woman in the stomach with a baseball bat) meaningless curse word "Mung! Somebody burned a hole in my new boyfriend!"

muscle-boy the young body-building Herculean "Where did muscle boy put the world down?" **2.** a muscle man: body builder.
Syn: **cushioned steel; iron angel** ("Hey, Regina, let's run down to Muscle Beach and watch the iron angels jerk the barbells off"); **muscle-gay[lady]** (*camp*); **piece of muscle** ("Isn't that piece of muscle in the chestcake mag?"); **topless lesbian** (*camp*).
Related terms:
put on one's birthday suit to exercise, to improve sagging body, a flabby waistline, *etc.*
steelies muscles.

mushroom a black's natural hairdo; an Afro "I used so much hair spray on his mushroom, it was bulletproof."

musical chairs cruising in a movie theater by moving from seat to seat until what is desired is found "Last time I went to see a flick I played musical chairs straight through the uncut Russian version of *War and Peace*."

music lessons sexual skills "Keep at your music lessons, Cherry, after all practice makes out."

mute (Brit gay sl) the vagina.

my chastity's grown over (*interj*) *gay line telling about the speaker's long abstention from getting fucked.

my dear [m'dear] (*exclam* & *voc*) "M'dear, why don't you give me your recipe for ptomaine pie?"

my pussy itches (*interj*) *gay line by one who wants to get fucked "My pussy itches, so keep your big-dicked husband locked up or I'll be on trial for incest."
Syn: **my pussy's twitching.**

Myra Breakfast (*camp*) a crab omelette.

nance (Brit) effeminate "Are you ready for that nance walk on that football player?"

nancies (Cape Town gay sl) nothing "Ever since Rita moved in with that client, she does nancies all day long."

nanti (Brit gay sl, *fr* Parlyaree, // It *nienti* = nothing) a negation "That chip-and-dale of his is nanti bonar, luv."

napkin ring (*kwn* SF, SM sl, '70) metal or leather hoop pulled over the penis and testicles; some are big enough to fit only around the base of the penis. Because the tightness of these rings traps blood in an erection, the loops literally add inches to a man's sex life.

Syn: **cock[laka] ring.**

nar-sissy (*camp*) narcissistic homosexual man.

natural homosexually motivated as far back as one can remember; born homoerotic "He's a natural—he came out the day he was born."
Syn: **pure** (early '60s).

neatarooney (*camp*) great, wonderful "Why I think it's simply neatarooney that you latched onto such a good-looking captain—bitch!"

neb (*fr* narc sl) nembutal.

need to appear compulsive urge to go out: cruising, barring, nightclubbing "I think I'll shave—I'm beginning to feel that I'll have the need to appear tonight at the prom."

nelly [nilly] outrageously effeminate; coy, silly "Nelly is a man with a school girl's esprit de corps."
Syn: **nellie-assed** ("Your nellie-assed mouth gets me in more trouble!")
Related term:
nell (*fr* colloq *nervous nelly*) overly effeminate male "Those hyenas sound like a gaggle of nells."

Neo-Gothic (*fr* the style of architecture) **1.** vacuous, ostentatious, empty, cold "Isn't that a worm-looking Neo-Gothic home—the one all in battleship gray?" **2.** said of one whose convictions are downright medieval, not up-to-date.

nervous 1. becoming tense while being fucked "Relax, kid, don't be so nervous—it all comes out okay in the end" **2.** to fart while being fucked.

nesh (*kwn* Texas, late '60s, *fr* Am-Yid pronunciation of national) to sell something legally which has been obtained illegally "Can you nesh me a ticket to Phoenix, cheap?"
—noo 1. stolen, acquired through the black market **2.** synonymous with *campy **"Where'd you find the nesh-noo shoes—at a blacksmith's?"
—noo airlines any airlines suffering from a rash of ticket rip-offs. Syn: **nesh-inal airlines** (*rare*).
—ticket illegally obtained ticket.

new ground (*rare*) heterosexual babe in a homosexual woods "Oh, oh! Lookit that one! Time for a new ground breaking ceremony!"

newspaper (late '60s) bathroom wall with much grafitti scrawled on it.

nice cheek delectable rump.

nicht (nēkht, *fr* Du = female cousin: for all those who wish to trip the *licht* fantastic in gay old Amsterdam) a gay boy's companion everywhere except in bed; *sister.

nicotine stains (*fr* Army sl) human dew found upon unclean underwear; shit stains.
Syn: **hash marks; sergeant stripes** ("A good rim queen could clean out those sergeant stripes better'n lye"); **service stripes.**

night club 1. a gay bar **2.** beer hall hidden in a warehouse district "They turn up the juke-box and then call it a night club." Syn: **Follies Bergère** (*camp*).

night-lighter queen who sleeps with another man's husband.

nimm (*fr* Yid *nemmen* = to take) to remove something dishonestly; to steal "Play it smart before some schmuck nimms your job."

nineteen-fifty said of gays who still believe in the ideals of the Eisenhower Administration (*eg* white sports coats and pink carnations); pertaining to the tavern-romanticist, the gay who still plays the same weary games.
Syn: **stepped out of a time machine.**

nipped in the bud circumcised as an infant.

nips breast nipples.
  Syn: **buttons; dinners; knobs; ninnies** (orig = breasts); **nums; piggies** ("He couldn't take his eyes off of Dallesandro's piggies all the way through the film"); **puppies; strawberries.**

nittery (*kwn* SF, late '60s) jittery and nervous, fidgety, speedy "I got so nittery when I took my driving test—the instructor was such a dream!"

no charge (*exclam*) snapped at one who can't keep his hands to himself.

noneck (*fr* Tennessee Williams' *Cat on a Hot Tin Roof*) an ignorant Southerner; redneck.

nonohe (nō-nō'-hā, *fr* Haw) lovely "What nonohe scarves—you look like the mummy of Zenda."

nooky push-push (*kwn* Southwest, mid '60s) one partner does push-ups over his buddy before the buddy does push-ups on him; the "you can fuck me if I can fuck you" routine.
  Syn: **knick-knacking; potting; putting on the pot.**

norma (*camp, fr* normal) 1. heterosexual, see *straight 2. homosexual claiming that he has seen the error of his ways and is returning to the straight world "Drop it, Norma, we all know your case!"

Norma Jean Marilyn Monroe.
  Syn: **MM.**

Norma Jean Nicotine 1. (*camp*) heavy smoker. Syn: **smoked meat; tar baby** 2. (*camp*) pack of cigarettes.

north or south (*adj phr*) circumcised or uncircumcised. Often posed as a question, but rarely, if ever, given as an answer.

nosh 1. (nŏsh, *fr* Brit teen sl, '50s) notion, idea "That's a fab nosh, Red Ryder!" 2. (*fr* Yid *noshen* = to nibble between meals) to suck cock.

nothing to stand up and clap hands [about] it's not worth mentioning; it's no big deal "He was nothing to stand up and clap hands—he didn't even like to kiss."

Nuella Nudeheels (*camp*) gay nickname for a barefoot boy with cheek—preferably two.

nuggets stools, shit.
  Related term:
  scatter [some] nuggets [among the poor] to defecate "I wonder whose beast keeps scattering nuggets in my flowerbed."

nui-nui (nŏŏ'-ē nŏŏ'-ē, *fr* Haw) 1. much "You flash nui-nui basket" 2. very "Anaka nui-nui nonohe" = you're very pretty.

number 1. designation for all one's tricks past and present; haphazard honeys registered like a click on a counter; casual *trick (once met thrice forgotten) "The way these queens cruise the street every night, they obviously don't know the adage: 'A number in hand is worth two in the phonebook'" 2. one's skit, act, *schtick;* contrived actions used to gain attention "Wait till I do my soft shoe number—all over her face!" 3. malediction, curse "He spilled vaseline all over your Supremes records? Are you going to put a number on him?" 4. routine, as in running a number on somebody "Strange that that particular publisher has to run numbers on everybody he deals with." Syn: **game.**

numbers game uninhibited sex session.

numero (Sp-Am gay sl) un trique; see *number.

num-num (?*fr nyamnyam* = to eat voraciously in many slave pidgin languages such as Gullah, Haitian French, Black Portugese, *etc*) 1. onomatopoeic for *yum-yum, sometimes heard when biting into a goodie 2. (*adj*) smashing, delightful 3. a beauty, treat to the thighs "Who's the num-num standing next to you in the picture?"

nylon milkpails bra.
nylons (*camp*) socks for men "Everytime the tenderfoot hic-coughed, his nylons fell down."

obesity chubby person "With all these little obesities running around what say we go into the sweat belt business, hon."
octopus disease the symptoms are fondling others in public places.
octo-pussy (*camp*) the octopus ride at carnivals.
off the wall crazy, insane, deranged.
of life (*kwn* SF, hip gay sl, '70) added for emphasis. Full of life, alive and kicking.
　　Related terms:
　　hotel of life run-down flophouse which rents out to interesting types. Cheap, "fun" hotel.
　　number of life one whose beauty is bewitching; someone you may not make it with, but who'll never be forgotten.
　　party of life a rip-roaring bacchanal.
　　shit of life extremely foul smelling excretion; animal dung "That kitty-cat's crap is the shit of life, honey! Only something living could have done that!"
　　toad of life old crone; busybody (female gender only).
　　　Ant & syn (typical gay irony): **—of death** "Honey, that's the law of death . . . it's so unrealistic" but "He has the body of death" = body worth dying for.
ogles (Brit gay sl ?*fr ogie* = to share or // ?goggles) eyes "Her ogles aren't brown . . . she's a quart low."
oh my goodneous (good'-nē-us, *exclam*) cry of praise.
oil pile (*dated*) teenager who still uses that greasy kid stuff—he probably goes in for roughneck sports like queer-baiting.
old fashioned enjoying the passive role sexually "I guess I'm just an old fashioned girl! Fuck me!"
　　Related term:
　　member of the old school anally passive romanticist.
old red goofy rotgut wine "If it doesn't taste like formaldehyde, then you know it's not old red goofy."
　　Related term:
　　tug on some old red goofy to drink wine from a bottle.
olohelohe (ō-lō'-hā-lō'-hā, *fr* Haw) nude.
oncer somebody who does it once, and never again with the same person; Mr. fuck 'em and forget 'em "Most people are leery of two-timers, but I'm leery of oncer's."
　　Syn: **one-timer.**
one hundred sex with no restrictions "After they got good and tanked, they began one-hundreding for dirt."
one night stand [**ONS**] having sex with somebody once, used of both the act and the participants; just one of those things, just

one of those glorious flings.

one upset sissy Mr. Nobody Knows the Troubles I've Seen, but he'll sure try to tell you about them   "I was one upset sissy when I saw them dragging Tommy away in nun drag to the paddy wagon, an' lemme tell you, I. . . ."

one-way baby[Charley, man, stud] **1.** *hustler **2.** one who insists upon doing *it* his way; everything's on his terms   "If eyes are windows to the soul, Jack Frost certainly got to those of the one-way baby's."

on one current strictly hetero or homosexual; never giving an inch to the other side   "Almost the entire West Coast is running on one current these days."

on stage 1. entertaining, performing   "Look Gertrude, two sailors— we're on stage!"   **2.** go to work   "I got to fly; I'm on stage at Bob's Burgers in ten more minutes!"   **3.** facing the day.

on the air full of hot air; getting on the soapbox.

on the gangplank in hot water, on someone's shit list, in disfavor.

on tour 1. experimenting with homosexuality   **2.** tourists rubber-necking gays in their haunts   "Saturday's a bad night at Dirty Dick's, too many straights on tour."

oops (*dated,* '40s, *exclam*) said when one recognized a fellow homosexual.

open house public washroom packed to the stalls; noon-hour whorehouse.

open one's health (*kwn* LV, late '60s) to blow off steam; to get angry and then act behind its force.

open the gate to bend over and spread 'em   "Sam Francisco, open your golden gates, I'm going to drive it on home . . ."

open the genitals (*kwn* SF, '71) to dress sexily, especially during warm weather.

Ophelia (*camp*) gay hippy; flower child.

order homosexual's hot date   "I'm in the mood for a pizza order."

orgy (*camp*) a group of people   "I'm having a small orgy over later."

orgy queen orgy enthusiast.
    Syn: **Roman historian.**

or what? isn't that so   "Is he gorgeous, or what?"

our Miss Brooks (*fr* the television series) **1.** male homosexual teacher   **2.** one who teaches, lectures   "Who are you to tell me how to wear my hair—our Miss Brooks?"

out for trade cruising for a quickie.

out of one's bag[gourd, squash] very drunk, high or mad.

out of this world (*dated,* teen sl, '50) fantastic, the most, the living end   "He had a tattoo of a cock on his ass that was just out of this world."

outrageous daring   "His levis were the most outrageous I'd ever tried to get into."

out to get even (prison sl) anally passing the buck by becoming the aggressor instead of the victim.

overact to make sloppy noises while sucking cock.

overripe fruit old faggot.
    Syn: **dried fruit** ("That dried fruits' been mummified for years—the other night the wrappings fell off.")

overs and unders overt and latent homosexuals respectively.

owl-taming (*fr* pros sl *owl* = girl working at night) **1.** answering customer calls after midnight   **2.** staying up at night and cruising.

owner (Brit gay sl) man who provides for a *kept boy.
    Also see *sugar daddy.

oyster (Brit gay sl, *fr* Brit cant *clam* = mouth as in the direct "Clam up!"; but *cf* Yid // Heb *oyster* = a treasure + sl *pearls* = teeth) the mouth.

packaged dressed   "I really dig the way sailors are packaged."

packaged goods well dressed beauty   "One great advantage of packaged goods is that you get to remove the wrappings."

pack it 1. to tuck the genitals into the right or left pantleg "Men in the armed forces are taught to pack it to the left, but you show more meat when you pack it to the right." Syn: **dress to the left[right]; pad[the ballots, basket]** ("Do things really grow big in Texas, or do the country boys pad the ballots?" **2.** stuffing some kind of cloth (usually socks) around the genitals to make them appear larger "Watch it, Lydia, your packing's slipping—we can see the heel of your nylon under your cuff." Syn: **prop the prick 3.** (hustler sl, mid '60s) to offer the ass for fucking.

> Related terms:
> **draped down the leg** working the penis to a semi-erect state to make it look tempting under pants "He had it draped so far down his leg he could hardly walk."
> **drape queen** one who packs with wadded up hankies or socks.
> **fake one out** (hustler sl // teen sl) to con someone into believing that the cock is large.

pagan delightfully wicked, hedonistic, living by the motto *"penitente non penitento"* = hard phallus, not penance "It's absolutely pagan the way that tee-shirt sweats up your pecks."

> Related term:
> **go pagan** to leave the "missionary" styles behind.

paint facial cosmetics "Gawd, but your nose is shiny; what do you use for paint—furniture polish?"

> Syn: **plaster; slap** (Brit gay sl); **war paint.**
> Related term:
> **paint up** to apply cosmetics. Syn: **put on a face** ("How will I ever be able to finish putting on my face when somebody stole my eraser?")

painted backdrop tattoos.

painted images 1. really famous celebrities, VIP's "I was sweet seventeen when I said 'bon sweat' to Hollywood's painted images—it was great fun, but it was just one of those stings" **2.** people who think themselves to be better than others "I'm fed up with the bar scene and its painted images!"

paint remover homosexual obstacles: ***faggot beaters,** hecklers, crusading politicians "Whatever happened to your eye—run into some paint remover with your heels on?"

paint the bucket 1. see ***fuck 2.**(*rare*) to use lipstick.

paint the daisies to park in a secluded place.

> Related terms:
> **pick strawberries** (*kwn* LV, mid-late '60s) to park in the desert.
> **watch submarine races** (*kwn* SF, early-mid '60s, teen sl) to park near the beach.

palace 1. one's living quarters, a dump　**2.** any establishment (cafe, bar) where homosexuals flourish "Operation! I'd like to know the number of Izzy's palace!"

Pandora (*fr* the Gk legend of Pandora's box) inquisitive and incautious "Someday, Pandora, you'll open the wrong box."

panic 1. political crackdown on gays. Syn: **purge** (pogrom against homosexuals)　**2.** closing time in a bar; person chosen during this time is called a desparation number. Syn: **crush hour; *desperate hour; *motel time.**

pansy 1. ('40s) male homosexual　**2.** (les sl) wishy-washy "What a pansy butch; she'd piss her pants if you said 'boo!'"
　—around to waste time. Syn: **fairy around.**
　—patch gay section of the park.
　　Syn: **piccolo park.**
　—up 1. spruce up, to wear the latest fashions　**2.** to lightly apply makeup.

panties 1. (*camp*) underbriefs　**2.** (*camp*) trousers.

pants race icebreaker for who can strip himself quicker.

panty queen fetishist for woman's panties; one who wears panties, sometimes even during sex.

papacito (pä-pä-sē′-tō, *exclam, fr* Mex = daddy) praise.

papa-daddy (*kwn* LV, late '60s) handsome father in the company of his young children; a good breeder put out to pasture as far as the envious are concerned "Pappa-daddy got a brand new sag!"

papal ban ridiculous, outdated moral codes.
　　Syn: **royal ban** ("They gave Ed Sullivan's trapeze show the royal ban.")

papaya the vagina.

pap-nibbler nipple sucker.
　　Syn: **tit queen.**

parade to show off one's stuff.

parade-rainer (*fr Don't Rain on My Parade* sung by Barbra Streisand in *Funny Girl*) wet blanket "I don't want to be a parade-rainer, boss, but your breath smells like number two."

Paris brothers (mid '60s, *fr* pun on pair of brothers with Paris [?where *Frenching* comes from]) homosexual brothers, particularly if twins.

park (Brit gay sl, *fr* Parlyaree *parker* = to hand over // It *partire* = to part with something) to give " 'Oo'll park me a fag, then?"

parliament (*camp, fr* FR *parlez vous* = do you speak) to talk "Parliament francais?"

party 1. orgy, sex session, see *****pig pile**　**2.** to copulate, see *****fuck**

passive partner the homosexual who prefers the passive role in ass-fucking; one whose main asset is behind (*med:* catamite, pedicant).
　　Syn: **anus queen** (*kwn* LA, mid '60s); **bang** ("That streetcar conductor turned out to be a damn good bang"); **bender; bottoms** ("At bottoms, he's tops"); **broad** (prison sl); **brownie queen [BQ]; browning queen [sister]; bucket boy; buff boy** ("That buff boy was to good to be blew"); **bum boy** (Brit); **cave queen** (*kwn* Midwest, late '60s: "Cave queens are in the habit of having their venereal ore mined"); **chuff[er]** (*dated, fr* ME *chuffe* = ill-mannered lout); **chut** ('20s, ?*fr* chuff + slut); **cuilón** (kōō-ē-lōn′, Mex *fr* Aztec *cuiloni* = sodomite; *cf* Sp *cul'on* = lard ass); **cunt** ("That cunt's got no ass—it's all in her cock"); **Daisy Duck; *effie; filly** (*rare*); *****fudy [futy]** (*dated*); **hoe** (black sl = whore; **hole; little lady** (*pej,* hetero sl); **mamacita; mula** (mōō′-lä, Mex *fr* Sp = female mule); **Nanette** ('70); **reary** (*obs,* '50s: = man shaped like a pear); **rumpy** (*obs,* 50s: homosexuals are sometimes considered a throwback to animal sexual behavior where

the upturned rump was the sex signal for males to mount the females. Female human bipeds developed exaggerated mammary glands to simulate the former physiological function of the rump); **turnover; twidget** (prison sl, *fr* twitcher); **veuve** (vŏv, *fr* Fr = widow); **whiskers** (*rare*); **works.**

patient unattractive, demented person "Where does that patient get her lines—from a gum wrapper?"

Patricia Boone dynasty [PBD] (*camp*) the flat fifties "How can you be nostalgic about the PBD when your pumps were in blue suede and you used to cry into your collection of forty-fives."

patsy (Cape Town gay sl) party.

payoff queen 1. hustler's client **2.** (*camp*) a buyer of anything.

pazassed (*camp, fr* possessed) blind rage in which someone bawls someone else out brilliantly "Whenever Peggy gets pazassed, she's as much fun as a black and white rerun."

Peaches (*voc*) gay nickname "Did I ever see your tummy, Peaches? Why, I can't see anything else."

pearl 1. a good egg, often used sarcastically "Yeah, he's a real pearl—you can string him on your necklace" **2.** drop of seminal fluid **3.** (black gay sl) nickname for a black queen.
Also see *drop a pearly; *give pearls.

pearl harbor to hit while someone's not looking.

pecker the penis, see *cock.
   —**tracks** semen stains on sheets or clothing "Dear Heloise, what do I do to remove pecker tracks from my park runners."

pecks pectoral muscles.

pee 1. to become excited, overemotional "Girl, I almost peed when he asked me to dance." Syn: **pee a river [for weeks]; pee in the streets 2.** to become indignant through fear "Miss Thing really peed when Velma called her over to the car" **3.** to excel "You really pee on the dance floor—I never saw anybody shake as good as you." Syn: **leave a puddle; piss** (superlative of pee: "You really pissed in those beans" = You cooked great beans) **4.** to be pleasing to the sense; exciting "That man of yours sure enough pees through the sweat glans" **5.** to scold "I'm gon pee in your face proper." Syn: **pee on somebody's fire and put it out 6.** to get the best of "That whore peed on you when she sucked your husband off in the closet."

pee'd stinking drunk "He was pee'd to the tits."

peepee (*fr* baby talk) **1.** urine **2.** to urinate "I'm neurotic, psychotic, and like to watch boys peepee." Syn: **piddle.**

peepers (*fr* '20s sl, kept alive through Mr. Peepers of '50s) **1.** eyes **2.** those who use their eyes professionally—detectives, spies, *etc.*

peg (*dated*) to size something up "Peg the cops in the ghost car trying to be nonchalant."

peg boy (*fr* naut sl, where kidnapped lads were made to sit on pegged benches to stretch them into shape) lad whose resources are tapped anally.

Penelope (*voc*) nickname for one who pines away needlessly "Poor Penelope! She's still waiting for that Les who went out ten years ago to buy some trojans."

penguin pelt tuxedo.

penis butter (*camp*) peanut butter.

pense (*fr* pensive) to think "Leave him alone, he's pensing—and that is the first time in three and a half years."

perform [royally] 1. see *blow **2.** to make a big production of everything; to call attention to oneself **3.** to flirt, extended to means coitus itself 'You should see Henry the Hawk perform when there's young stuff around" **4.** (*fr* pros sl) to participate in a *circus.

peter meter (*camp*) ruler measuring a man's extremity.

pets mostly small dogs and cats suitable for apartment living in the big city. Curled poodles dyed pansy pink belong to the **poodle people** (*kwn* SF, '70). Small, yippy pekes or hairless chihuahuas are **barbie dogs** (*kwn* SF, '70) and **earmuffs** (*kwn* SF, late '60s). Large longhaired dogs (the kind that take a minute to bark) are **polo ponies; rugs** (*rare*).

Two nasty vocatives have also been formed from the names of dogs, namely **Airdale** and **Rover** ("We'll take you to the cruisy park, Rover, only if you promise not to sniff all of the trees!").

phallus cum loudly (*camp, interj*) comment about an ejaculation.

phyllis (*camp*) philosophical, wordy; talking about abstractions when the object is sex "Don't get phyllis—the strain on your brain would sizzle your curlicues."

pickets the teeth "His ass was as white as my new pickets."

pick fruit to shakedown a frightened faggot.

pickup see *trick.

pick up one's heels to leave.

pick up pants and go home (*camp*) *gay line expressing sham modesty.

pick up the soap (*fr* naut sl) to be fucked "I picked up the soap for every Tom's hairy dick from Hong Kong to here."

picnic lunch a *trick whose cock is sucked—only.

piece sexual object; by extension any person "That medical piece glued her wing back on" = the doctor put his arm in a cast.

pig female competition "What makes you think Phil would look twice at another pig after the rotten marriage he had."

pigeon-titted indignant, irate "Now, don't get all pigeon-titted over what Joe said—all he wanted to know was how such a skinny neck could hold up so much damage."

pig pile homosexual orgy "Join the pig pile—you might luck out and be on the bottom."

Syn: **birthday party** (where all leave their clothes at the door); **cluster fuck**[party]; **flesh picnic; gang-fuck; GE** (= group expression); **group party**[therapy]; **love feast** ("How degrading—being caught at the love feast on Sunday with my Monday panties on"); **mass lay; pajama party; poke party** (late '50s); **sex marathon.**

Related terms:

mazola party an orgy where all participants grease up before sliding around on each other; a human salad. Syn: **Russian salad party.**

picnic orgy where the fellators take control of the doings. Syn: **jawfest; oyster stew; pricnic** ("There must be a pricnic over that hill—see the column of aunties?")

polaroid party orgy to which polaroid cameras are taken. The host furnishes the place, and the orgiasts replenish the host's pornography collection with fresh photos.

Roman night evening filled with orgiastic debauchery.

round-robin orgy designed for the trading off of partners; everybody rotates in a round-robin.

square dance orgy in which one half of the participants lie down in a circle while the other half does the fucking. Syn: **BQ party; wagon wheel.**

pig-suck (*pej*) homosexual man who has turned to women; hence any man who is interested in women.

piko (pē'-kō, *fr* Haw = navel) term of endearment.

pimp (*pej*) **1.** heterosexual woman's legally married spouse. Extended to mean common-law husband **2.** to sell anything "Why are you getting me drunk—wanna pimp me?"

—boots (*dated*) ankle boots "I get the shine on my pimp boots by kicking faggots' asses, man."

—cap (*dated*) porkpie hat worn cocked to the side.
—down to have expensive clothing.
—pants skintight pants, uncuffed and in wild colors.
pin (*dated*) to look.
pineapple queen [**princess**] Hawaiian homosexual "Why do you call them 'pineapple queens'—do they have green hair?"
pin it up to shut up, stop gabbing "Pin it up, queen; give the floor to something else."
pink homosexual "You can meet a straight on Polk Strasse, but that doesn't make him pink."
    —pig chattering high school girl; bobby-soxer.
    Syn: **pom-pom girl.**
    —puffed (Brit gay sl) winded, beat.
pinky ring (*fr sl* *pinky* = little finger) ring worn on the little finger, considered effeminate when worn by a man.
    Related term:
    wear a pinky ring to be established as a homosexual.
piss elegant [**PE, pissy**] fussy, respectable, proper, overly pre-occupied with one's conception of correctness.
    Syn: **chi-chi** (shē'-shē, *fr* Fr *chic* = fashionable).
    —faggot[**queen**] 1. one equating wealth and style with real achievement; one who lives in sham elegance 2. jealous reference to a rich homosexual. Syn: **cold cream queen** ('72 = one concerned with purchasing name products); ***eclair queen; grand bitch**[**lady, one, women**]; **Pam**[**ela**] ("Good morning, Pamela, and how are your sterling hemorrhoids today?"); **priss eminant faggot; Prunella** (= pompous fellow; "Prunella can't stand Oakland—she says the sky's unshaven.")
pisser the urinal trough "We stood at the pisser looking into each other's cocks."
piss pass 1. to *almost* get away with it 2. mediocre, unimpressive.
piss poor uneffective, inferior, trite "This piss poor version of 'The 1812 Overture' sounds more like kick the can amplified."
pissticide (*camp*) cheap wine which comes out of the body as quickly as it went in.
pit 1. armpit 2. any secluded place where sex goes on. Syn: **passion pit; snake pit.**
pittypoo 1. to tiptoe, to walk "I just now pittypooed into my ex—that little mistake cost me a smart five" 2. to be evasive "Stop pittypooing around and tell me what the bitch said."
pity (*interj*) sarcastic comment meaning "So what"; a voiced yawn "Did you hear about Ron's bust—pity!"
pixie 1. (hetero sl) homosexual with an elfin look 2. a pixie cut.
pixie dust 1. any powder-like substance, including dandruff 2. sex drive "That story just stirred up my pixie dust; I'm afraid it's off to the meat rack for me."
pixie sticks incense "Light some pixie sticks if you're going to smoke that shit in this house."
place card tombstone.
place names besides using already well known formations (LA, Vegas, Chi, *etc*), queens have christened towns, cities, regions and areas that have earned their censure or approval.
    Albaturkey (*kwn* N Calif, '71) Albuquerque.
    Allah (*fr pros sl*, '30s) Los Angeles. Syn: **Garden of Allah; Lost Angle Worms** (*rare*).
    Berserkeley (*kwn* SF, mid-late '60s) Berkeley.
    The Big Corner (*camp, fr* film of the same name) New York City.
    The Bottom of the Garden heavily populated suburban area south of San Francisco. Syn: **The Islands; The Penis-sula** (*kwn* SF, '70).
    Dairy Queen State (*camp*) Wisconsin.
    Dodge [**City**] (*kwn* SF, black sl, '70) Fillmore, one of San

Francisco's black ghettos.

East Jesus any small hole in the mud town; blink your eyes and you miss it.

The End (*kwn* SF, late '60s) Land's End, a cruisy San Francisco park near the ocean "You'll be queen of the maypole at The End if you rush out before the first tide."

Fag-shaft (*kwn* S Calif, mid '60s) Flagstaff, Ariz. "Having to spend Queen's Christmas in Fag-shaft? How rude!"

Finn's (*kwn* SF) Finocchio's, a night club which shows drag shows exclusively "What's a Mickey Finn? He's an ex-movie star mouse now working in drag."

The Garden San Francisco, since the soil seems conducive to pansies.

Gollywood (*camp*) Hollywood. Syn: **Tinsel Town.**
    Also see ***Hollywood.**

The Hat Shop (*kwn* LV, mid '60s, *fr* pros sl *white hat* = sailor) San Diego.

H of P (*camp, fr* house of prostitution) the A & P grocery chain.

Messico (mes'-ē-kō, *kwn* SF, '71 *fr* *mess + Mĕjico) Mexico.

Miracle Mile [MM] (*kwn* Calif, *fr* LA's Wilshire Blvd) **1.** (*kwn* LA) Ventura Blvd, stretch consisting of nothing but gay bars and motels **2.** (*kwn* SF) Folsom Street in San Francisco.

O-H-Ten (*kwn* SF, late '60s) Ohio and by extension a dull place, city.

The Old Folks' Home (*kwn* LV, early '60s) Las Vegas. Syn: **Plush Nothingness.**

Oregonon (ō-reg'-ə-non, *camp*) Oregon.

Place Pigalle (*kwn* SF) Polk Street, a gay cruising area, especially at night. Syn: **Boulevard of Broken Dreams [Queens]; Pig Alley** (*pej*); **[Polk] Strasse** (strä'-sə, *fr* Ger = street). **Turkey Run** (*pej*, '71); **Valley of Tears.**

Poison Palms Palm Springs.

The Puritan Wasteland anywhere in the Bible Belt; or any place between NYC and California for that matter "I don't *have* to know any Spanish, witch! I'm a puritan wasteland queen."

Queen City (*kwn* SF) San Francisco. Syn: **Emerald City [of Oz]** (*camp*); **Queen['s] Capital of the World.**

Rhinestone Heights (*kwn* SF) Lower Diamond Heights in San Francisco.

Santa Josefina (sän'-tä khō-sā-fē'-nä) San Jose. Syn: **Taco Town** (*pej*: "Oakland's just like Taco Town—everybody's ugly!") **Tamaleville** (*rare*).

The Smoke (Brit) London.

The Square In New York City, it's Times Square; in LA, it was Pershing Square; in San Francisco, it's Union Square: gay-hustler centers. What is it in your town?

TJ Tijuana "Oh, you're back from TJ? Did the star in your act die—didn't the vet get there in time?" Syn: **Tia's** ('60s, *fr* Sp *tia* + aunt + *Tijuana* = Auntie Joanna).

TL the Tenderloin District of San Francisco "There's always cop cars in the TL so you know it has to be a fun place."

The Turquoise Belt (late '60s) American Southwest.

under the big top (*kwn* SF, late '60s) located in New York city.

Vagina (*camp*) the state of Virginia.

The Vanilla Bottle (*rare, fr* sl *vanilla* = black) black ghetto.

plank 1. the counter in a bar. "Behind the plank" = working as a bartender or serving drinks **2.** see ***fuck.**

play 1. to proposition. Syn: **give one a play 2.** to be featured, to perform "I wonder what's playing at the bus station tonight?"

—**buses** to go home on a public conveyance after the bars close.

—**chipmunk** to fill the mouth with *nuts.*

—**ping-pong** (*kwn* Calif, '70) to debate an issue; to argue "Mary and Jimmy were playing their usual game of ping-pong, so I decided to split." **Ping for pong** tit for tat; nobody ahead in an argument.

—**solitaire on somebody** to ignore an old acquaintance.

—**squirrel** (*dated, fr* teen sl, '50s) to startle a buddy by quickly clutching for his crotch area. A first cousin of the grab ass game in the locker rooms.

—**the closet** to conceal one's own homosexuality for fear of being the butt of homophobic hostility.

—**the fruit market** (late '50s) to earn money by being a **hustler.*

—**the game** to stick to the rules of street cruising. A good way to learn patience. It is also a good way to wear out shoe leather.

—**the harmonicass** (*camp*) to act foolish, to "cut the fool" at a party.

—**the organ** see ***blow.**

—**the penny** (*kwn* LV, mid-late '60s) to blackmail a homosexual "you must've taken an hour with that chicken salad—was the poor dear playing the penny?"
   Syn: **put the penny on somebody.**

—**the river** to commit suicide by drowning.

—**windmill 1.** literally, to urinate with someone else criss-crossing **2.** figuratively, to stand at the urinal watching others as they relieve themselves "You try playin' windmill with that one, and he'll hang a sign on your eye sayin' 'closed for the season.'"

—**with a chick's meat** (*kwn* SF, late '60s) to flirt with a girl's boy friend or husband—particularly within her presence; to seduce him into a homosexual relationship.
   Syn: **play with her meat** ("Stop playing with her meat, or she'll break her fingernails on your face!")

played out   jaded; fucked to boredom, describing unexciting hustlers.
   Syn: **shopworn.**
   Also see: ***tired.**

player 1. (prison sl) inmate who plays ball with sex-hungry toughs **2.** (*fr* hip gay sl, '70) young man willing to try anything once "Your little player friend is as funny as the stations of the cross."

pluck 1. to plant one's seed into a boy's rump, see ***fuck 2.** to startle, unnerve, to cause eyebrows to rise "Mary, I was plucked when I found out you were older than my father."
   Syn: **pluck some eyebrows** (mid '60s: "That film's going to pluck some eyebrows in Omaha!")

pluck somebody off 1. to dismiss something demeaning with a snap of the fingers, see ***snap somebody off 2.** to give somebody the brush-off "Get away from the water fountain, Gunga Din, before mother plucks you off."

pluck some feathers 1. (*cf* Sp *pelando la pava* = plucking the turkey = courting, wooing) to get a piece of ass. Syn: **pull some petals 2.** to remove body hair—either tweezing the eyebrows or pulling some hair out by its roots "Mother's eyebrows are reaching her rosy reds again—time to pluck some feathers." "She better close her yap or there'll be a wet hen plucking some pretty fancy feathers around these parts."

pluck the fingers to snap the fingers in time to music or as a signal of condemnation.

Syn: **chop heads** (*kwn* SF, black gay sl, '72).
Also see *royal command, *snap somebody off.

plucky 1. young, under 21, but not children **2.** cute, robust and round-bottomed; fuckable.

plumbing the genitals "God had a girl in mind when he made you, until he got to the exterior plumbing."
Syn: *accoutrements; auxilliary; baggage; business ("Then there was the fable about the midget who kept getting kicked out of nudist camps because he kept sticking his nose in everybody's business"); equipment ("Did you wash behind your equipment?"); fixtures; gear ("He lost half of his gear in the first world war"); privates; secrets.
—**fixture** condom.

pocket pool ('50s) fondling the testicles (balls, as in billiards) while the hand is pocketed. A few men actually remove the pocket lining to better their game.
Syn: **handball; pocket polka[waltz].**
Related term:
pinch the cat to play pocket pool.

point 1. (prison sl) a lookout, see *prison terminology **2.** (Brit gay sl) any writing implement "Do you happen to have a point on you?"

poison ivy (*camp*) flowers sent by an unliked admirer "Tell the nurse to clear out some of this poison ivy or it'll soak up all my air."

Polish handball (*camp*, late '60s) small clump of dried mucus picked from the nostril; a "booger."

polluted drunk as a skunk.

polone (pō-lō'-nē, Brit gay sl, *fr* Parlyaree, // It *pollone* = sprout, ?*fr* Sp *pollo* = hen; *cf* sl *pullet* = young woman) any woman.

pom-poms 1. young girl's breasts **2.** *falsies; stuffing in bras used to build up an illusion of a large bosom.

ponies (*rare*) the feet.

poo nonsense syllable which serves as **a.** combination vocative ("Listen, Poo, we haven't got all day") **b.** a vocal exclamation point ("She talks as if she had a crash course in Eileen Feather's elocution dynamics, poo") **c.** diminutive ending added to artificial "-ie" (except for words already ending in an "ee" phoneme): "What a crate—I bet it gives milkie-poo!"
Syn: **poo-poo** ("Did you catch it from somebody in Hollywood, poo-poo?" "You bet your falsie-poo-poo eyelashes!")

pooper 1. anus, see *a-hole "Almost *all* Jewish men have piles in the pooper" **2.** an endearment especially used with dogs and cats "Does pooper wantum his dindins?" Syn: **poo-poo** ("My poo-poo bought this bathrobe for me last Christmas"); **pooter** (*lit* "farter", see *poot: "My pooter's no Mr. Gotrocks, but I love him all the same.")

poor baby (*interj*) conveys the same message as "I couldn't care less" "So that south-of-the-border tart turned into a pile of Aztec ruins—poor baby!"
Also see *pity.

poot 1. to break wind **2.** a toot on the car horn.

popper amyl nitrite ampule, see *amyl "If you ever get one of those faggots who bellyaches about gettin' fucked, just shove a popper halfway up his nose and watch those legs fly up." "What's 'amy intercourse'? That's two poppers up the ass."

popsickle (*fr* sl = the penis when fellated) to masturbate the lover pausing only to lick the semen when it begins to trickle out.

porcelain fountains urinals.

porchy (?*fr* portly) possessing a fleshy midriff.

pork 1. penis, see *cock **2.** cheapskate customers; nonbuyers.
Syn: **white-shoe trade** (mid '60s) **3.** ('70-71) to gormandize.

pork and beans (*kwn* SF, '71) a fat man.
    Syn: **Mr. Marty Robust.**
porny[**porno**] photography.
pose to stand in what seems to be a very seductive position "There's Miss Larry—the one posing with the tombstones."
    Syn: **strike a pose.**
    Related terms:
    pose queen narcissistic young men who stand for hours on end in ***gay bars** trying to look dramatic. Syn: **posies** (*rare*); **post queens** (*fr* simile made on the wooden stance of a post).
Post Toasties (*camp*) nickname for the mailman, especially if cute or gay.
pot pie (*kwn* SF, late '60s, *fr sl* pot = marijuana) young hippy.
    Syn: **paisley pussy; psychedelic sister** (= gay hippy: "The psychedelic sisters were over again—I've never *seen* so much *hip!*")
    Related term:
    mod squad[**-ers**] ('70) gay faddists who treat long hair and facial trimming as nothing more than a passing phase; those who are slaves to fashions and trends.
potty [**as a chamber**] (Brit) crazy, daffy, loco.
pound (*kwn* SF, late '60s-'72, *fr colloq* pound into shape) to work at getting that ruddy complexion; to groom oneself; shit, shower and shave before going out on the town "wonder who's been in the bathroom for two hours pounding for a mad date."
poundage 1. excessive weight "You'll need more exercise than sucking dick to work that poundage off" **2.** fat person "When that poundage does the rumba, it looks more like the 'Jersey Bounce.'" Syn: **piece of poundage; poundage queen** ("The motto of all poundage queens is, 'Pork is where it's fat!'")
pound somebody into putty to beat the living hell out of someone "Did he fuck you over? Want me to get Jew Lewis to pound him into putty?"
powdered and perfumed primped up, dressed to the nines, looking like an ad out of *Esquire*.
powder the nose (*camp*) to leave a group of friends to go urinate "He went to powder his nose, and as big as his nose is, it should take about two hours for him to return."
pratt for somebody to bend over for a sodomist.
precious (*voc*) title for just anybody "Precious! Balling with you was a box-office flop!"
    Syn: **presh** ("What took you so long, presh—signing autographs in the Strand balcony?")
precious (pres'-ē-us', *kwn* SF, '70) cute as a bug's ear.
preen oneself in ('71) **1.** to pat oneself upon the back; to congratulate oneself **2.** to try to impress others with feats of merit.
pregreased 1. see ***greased up 2.** sweaty about the anal area "One more pass at funkyin' that chicken, and I'll be pregreased."
press the button (*fr* hetero *sl* = to manipulate the clitoris) to massage the prostate gland of a passive homosexual. One whose prostate is rubbed by a lover's cock during anal intercourse is said to have **had his button pressed**[**pushed**].
press the dress to have business matters underway: to ready oneself for work or social festivities. But "Press the dress!" = shit or get off the pot!
prestige fuck[**piece**] (*fr* L *praestigiae* = conjuror's tricks // *praestringere* = to blindfold) **1.** a celebrity, expecially one who is kissed and then told on. After all, it isn't everyday that a lowly soda jerk gets to blow headline material "You would have slept with Dracula, just because he was a prestige piece." **2.** token piece of ass, slept with to prove

something "He's only thinking of you as a prestige fuck—I guess it's the only way a young American ever gets to meet any royalty these days."

Syn: **status fuck.**

Related terms:

for the prestige as in "I wouldn't bed down with anybody who wasn't a movie star; and then I would only do it for the prestige—*theirs.*"

prestige fucking 1. hobnobbing with Hollywood gods and goddesses in their bed chambers **2.** brown-nosing the boss.

pretender to the throne 1. vice squad officer, see *****vice** **2.** young man who tries to get out of being drafted by claiming homo-erotic tendencies.

pretty (*fr* ME *praty* // OE *praettig* = tricky) **1.** winsome lad, see *****chicken 2.** (*adj*) handsome "He's so pretty he looks like a baby-faced killer!" "He's beautiful, but he's sure not pretty" = he's got a wonderful mind but he doesn't have the face to go with it **3.** describing the source of one's hard-on "This truck driver we knew had the prettiest butt you've ever laid" "He was covered in wall-to-wall zits, but he sure had a pretty cock."

prick see *****cock.**

prick-lick 1. a fellator, see *****cocksucker 2.** ((*camp*) homosexual's tongue "He's wasting his talent wrapping his prick-lick around some Blue Chip Stamps."

prick parade (*fr* Army sl, '30s) medical inspection of the genitals, usually for venereal diseases.

Syn: **short-arm inspection.**

prima donna 1. one whose chief drive is being the center of everything "Just what we need—another prima donna to brighten up Oshkosh!" "Prima donnas do most of their boosting at Frederick's in Hollywood" **2.** stickler for convention; one who spends hours preening. "The definition of a prima donna is someone who'll drink beer out of a glass instead of a can in a leather bar."

prima tuna (*fr* the blending of *prima donna* + immature) impetuous, rash "Let's not be prima tuna about this—I never did say I would go home with you."

prime young, fresh, muscular.

Syn: **tender.**

prime it to help it along, *ie* masturbating while cocksucking "Prime it, sweetlips, I've got to catch the four o'clock express."

prince 1. well dressed male homosexual **2.** prince Charming Syn: **blue prince. 3.** attractive, together gay guy who finds beauty in everything.

princess of the bed skilled at lovemaking.

Princeton style (*fr* a "popular" recreation pursued in British boarding schools and American ivy league dorms) fucking the thighs.

Syn: **English method;** *****leggins** (see *****prison terminology**).

princepessa (prin'-chĕ-pes'-să, *fr* It = princess) **1.** nickname for a delicate man **2.** (*pron*) second person singular "Does prin-cipessa want a BJ before or after breakfast?"

Priscilla Tiebacks (*adj*) frilly, superfluous "See that hot, Priscilla Tieback's tiara—it must be a queen's pawn.

prison terminology

As far as the study of gay slang goes, prisons present us with an entirely unique phenomenon: homoerotic words, pri-marily about anal rape, were devised and are used by hetero-sexuals; these men, called **situation[institutional] homosexuals,** have temporarily turned to homoerotic outlets as an only resort.

This behavior has given rise to a distinct branch of gay slang.

The federal penitentiary is the **joint,** and a newly sentenced prisoner is a **fish[-face]** (?*fr* fresh, as for example in freshman; also *cf* underground sl *fish* = a dupe). **Mullet** (a type of eatable sealife) are **sized up** by the other cons, old timers, until each newcomer establishes his sexual position (**fore or aft**). He is the butt of homoerotic jokes: sometimes he is **chirped** (whistled at), or he might have his cheek tweaked (**blubber** or **wolf's handshake**) by a hopeful contact. The fish is assigned a cell, called a **house.** If his roomy (cellmate) is overtly aggressive, the boy is said to be **fruit for the monkey[s]** and probably will be **broken in,** be **made fag [girl, punk]** or **put** (pulled down), particularly if he is a **cutie** or **peach fuzz** (young). In most cases, the new arrival's penis [**johnson, jock, shovel, swipe**] isn't given a second look: it's sweet virgin ass that turns 'em on. In prison parlance, the asshole *faute de mieux* is generally **goose-hole, Hawaiian eye** (*fr* prison sl **Hawaiian disease,** also **lakanuki,** *ie* "Lack of nooky," no women aboard ship), **ring, roundeye.** If the lad is still a virgin—anally—he is called a **kewpie doll,** his anus being his **bullhead, cherry, prune** ("Use a lot of spit, man, this guy's still got his prune!"). After he has been **opened up** (fucked), his ass is referred to as **gash, nooky, pussy. Spread** (submit) once and he's a **marked woman** or ***punk** for the rest of his **semester** (time).

The sexually dominant prisoner uses an aggressively masculine vocabulary to prove that he has **kept his ass** (refused to be used as an anal buffet). Each word is muscular. He himself is called **anus bandit, bronc[o]-buster, daddy-o, duke** (*fr* carnival *sl* **duke it out** = to hand something over), **gut-butcher [reamer, stretcher, stuffer], hip-hitter, jocker** (very common), **short-arm bandit, tusk, wolf** (also very common). A group of rapists is a **wolf pack** while one working **single-o** is a **lone wolf.** The act of rape is a **gang-bang[splash], jump, short-arm heist.** If a stray lamb finds himself surrounded by a pack of **givers** (as opposed to **takers,** *ie* those who "take it up the ass"), he will be given a **gang-splash,** a kind of sinister surprise party, especially if he is a **first cop** (virgin), promising fresh anus. The first to gain anal entrance, a highly prized honor, is called the **welcome wagon.** The second in line is **sloppy seconds,** while the third fucker is **bloody thirds** (no other slang terms are used after thirds, probably because the prize is such a mess by then). **Wedding bells** are composed of the victim's comments mixed with the squeaks of the mattress.

When a wolf is hot to trot, he is **drove up, geared up, jacked up.** He is out to **get some ass [booty, flesh, hide, hump, hunk, knee, leg, nooky, pants, skin, tail, ussypay],** and his hunt for a punk to fuck is **climbing[running] the tier** (*kwn* Leavenworth prison). When he confronts his victim, he might **put the blade to him.** This usually works out to be holding a knife around the victim's throat while fucking him. The threat **blood on my blade or shit on my dick** suggests that the quarry either submit or be cut open. The rapist is not usually adverse to a **blanket party:** coercing another into a submissive position by covering his head and torso with a blanket to hinder escape (a case of a wolf pulling the wool over somebody's eyes.) Some of the wolves are **kid-simple,** *ie* they have an overwhelming desire to manhandle younger men [**kids**]. During the '40s, such a man was a **KF [kid fruit]** and his loverboy was a **kife** (kid + wife).

He was also called an **uncle** ("Bend over and tell your 'loving' uncle all about it") and the passive partner became the **cousin**· or the **nephew,** logically. The queens = **gear boxes** (*fr* Cockney rhyming sl *gear* = queer), running true to form, preferred to call the nephew **niece.**

Jocker is synonymous with wolf: his role in prison parodies the husband's relationship in a marriage: however, jocker is *not* synonymous with the outside gay expression ***husband.** Jocker is a white-slaver, a master of correction; his manmade wife is answerable only to him. If he needs money, he can sell his **jodie** (*fr* Army sl = man deferred from the draft, '40s; also *cf* black sl *jodie* = the back street lover who takes over while the former sweetheart is overseas) to the highest bidder. This auctioning is **putting a kid on the block,** and all proceeds from the sale go to the jocker.

There are ways of being forcefully **held down** (rolled over on the belly), **shagged, snared.** One is to procure a bodyguard called **protection** who is expected to watch out for his boy, or **protection punk,** who, in turn, is required to tender his anus to his **steady:** payment for services rendered. ("You think *you* have it rough paying through the nose—a protection punk has to pay through his asshole.") Another way of side-stepping gang-fuckings is open prostitution. This is resorted to by the **canteen[commissary] punk** who thinks of himself as a trader and so manages to stay alive while lost in the jungle. He offers to suck cock or proffers an upturned fanny in exchange for a **box** or **deck of weeds** (a carton of cigarettes), **cotton** (*fr* benzedrine soaked in cotton in nasal inhalers), **cross-tops** or **splits** ("bennies"), **hay** (*kwn* Calif prison sl, '71: cigarettes), or comestibles like **chicken feed** or **pogue bait** (*fr pogue* = young rooster who gets his tail feathers plucked in prison // Parlyaree *pogey* // It *poco* = little thing, bit: the terms include all digestible items used to entice, but also extended to cigarettes and money sometimes), **rubber** (gum: *snap some rubber* = to chew gum), **scoffins** (*fr* hobo sl = food in general), or **washers** (loose change).

Not all prison sex, however, is centered about the desecration of a forced a-hole. Some happily **get down** (participate in homoerotic acts) while shielded in a tight-squeeze cranny called a **deviation corner** ("We call the bean queen's deviation corner 'Hernando's Hideaway.'") A comrade, poised as a look-out, is expected to **give six** (*fr* Am-Yid *zex* = ixnay!, *lit* "six": to sound a warning if authority approaches). The spotter is called **jigger** (*fr* sl *jiggers* = the cops). **lookout queen** (*camp*), **point** (*fr* Army sl *on point* = on guard), **runner** (*fr* running back and telling if anybody is coming).

Other major sexual pastimes are **leggins** and **sucking peter:** leggins consists of reaching ejaculation by rubbing the cock between willing oiled or sweaty thighs; in a manner of speaking, it is getting someone right between the thighs. It is also known as **rubbins, slick leggins, thighs, thigh sandwich** ("Not enough buns to go around? Then try a thigh sandwich.") Prison fellation is **copping a bird[cock, crown, doodle, hot one, joint]; cuffing a carrot, playing the schweinte, polishing the knob, rooting.** The act of fellation is **short-arm practice** (not to be confused with a short-arm heist: "How did you get such color in your lips. . .short-arm practice?"). The sucker is styled a **fruiter, hot brains[head], mechanic, merchant, muzzler** (*pej:* "The only good thing about that fat-ass muzzler was his fat-ass wallet"), **penis machinist** ("That penis machinist was the biggest waste of time since Romeo balled

Julie"), **rooter** (*fr* Cockney rhyming sl = fruiter) **rootin'tooter.**
From the last two terms, we could surmise that the adolescent chant: **Rooty-toot-toot, rooty-toot-toot,/we are the boys
from the institute;/ we don't smoke, and we don't chew,/
and we don't go with the girls who do—whooo[psie]** (*or* **our
class won the Bible**) has its origins in penitentiary cocksucking. This rhyme, usually shortened to **"Rooty-toot-toot!"**
is also used to taunt known prison homosexuals. A fellator's
mouth is a **cocksucker** ("Hit him in the cocksucker!" or a
jockwarmer (*fr* sl *jock* = penis).

Two men who decide to make a go of it in prison want to
be **hitched, *married, spliced.** Their usually even-steven relationship .(turning the other cheek) is known as **flip-flop
[-ping], patty cakes, putting on the pot** (*fr* sl *pot[ty]* = toilet),
shot-for-shot (favor for favor, give and take), **stew-for-beans,
swapping cans, swapping out.** The men are referred to as
pancakes, pot-partners, a queer-couple, waffles.

Men who were homosexual before arrest and conviction are
usually called **queen[ie]s,** but they are also known as **gear
boxes, lavender boxes, lollifliers** (*pej*), **on the street queens,
pink-tea freaks, pure[true] homosexuals** (as opposed to
situation homosexuals). A prison with a large percentage of
homosexual inmates is a **fag factory[joint], peg house.**
Frequently homosexuals are segregated from the rest of the
men and housed in a galvanized ghetto called **Hollywood Hills**
(*camp*), **queen's row, the Quarter** (referring to New Orleans'
French Quarter). A cell full of queens is **a camp** ('50s) and
the men living there form the **players,** those who **play the
role [part]** by appearing as womanly as possible with plucked
eyebrows, shaven legs, powdered noses, fastidiously pressed
bonorues (prison uniforms, *fr* sl ***bonar**), *etc.* The more colorful
characters, **ace queens, boss queens, main queens,** are highly
in demand sexually. The queens, usually imprisoned on
charges of larceny, bring their own slang inside the walls
and add to the prisons' slinguistic melting pot. Camp terms,
however, are taboo to the jockers who will call a shirt
a shirt and not a **blouse.** The queens pay special attention
to their choice of words. They segregate the terms used outside
and inside: the ***alice blues** did the busting, but the **screws**
do the guarding. They also invent terms to fit the occasion
(**stringing pearls** = to serve time); but on the whole the
majority of the words in this book form the basis of their
contribution to prison rap.

When love is in bloom, contraband loveletters are passed
between inmates. The "sending" of such an epistle is **flying
a kite[pigeon],** and the note occasionally ends with **always**
or **7-11** (*fr* package stores always open) both meaning "I love
you[r sweet ass]" ("He won't find no 7-11 at the bottom of
his induction notice.")

One thing prison teaches is to keep cool, termed **holding mud.**
If a con breaks down or expresses emotion in any way
(such as **copping out** = admitting to loving someone in prison),
he is said to have **blown his class[soul].** An interesting idiom
for being enamoured is **having the nose wide open,** from a
fighter's being caught off guard ("That cookie with the out-
of-this-world shoulders has my nose wide open.")

Fond affection sometimes leads to jealousy, the chance of
being jilted, and even possibly, vengeance. Kicking an adversary in the face is **putting the boots[heels, kicks, spikes]** to him.
A hard blow on the face is **one last kiss** (*fr* song which ends
with the hero's being punched in the musical "Bye, Bye, Bird-

ie"): Homemade knives[**blades, hawks,** ?*fr* a hawk's sharp beak; **shanks,** because that part of the leg is usually the blade's point of entry] may also be resorted to. If the knife hits its mark, the blade has **drank** 696969's arm, leg, *etc*. If one has been killed, he has been **deep sixed, offed, snuffed** [**out like a candle**] **wasted** or **popped,** if he was shot to death. (All these words originate in black ghettos). If a fight is witnessed by the authorities, the participants are **tossed into the olive**[**black**] **pit** (solitary) or **slammed** (beaten by guards) or even given a taste of **black Annie** (a whip).

Those who abstain from homosexuality might **play with hank** (cock). A masturbator [**diddler, hand-artist**] will thumb through smuggled-in pornography [**battery chargers, hank books**] while **hanking** [**and yanking**]. Masturbation to erotic fantasies (such as envisioning a dream partner) is **cabareting, going cabareting, kicking the gong around** (*obs*, '20s, *fr* narc sl = to smoke the dream-drug opium in Chinatown), **night-clubbing.** If each night becomes **jack night** exclusively, the man is brushed off as being **jerk silly, married to Mary Fist** (enslaved to autoeroticism). Jacking off another guy is a **hand-o** or **handshake** ("They were givin' each other hand-o's during the best part of the movie"). Some prison terms have acquired ambivalent meanings through the love-hate, trust-fear relationships brought about by the abnormal prison conditions: **bluebird,** a kiss or a blow delivered by a fist (*cf* OE *buss* = a kiss with sl *bust in the mouth*); **go down** to suck a penis or to die, croak, kick off.

Among the related terms about or originating in prisons, the most common are:

bucket a portable toilet. By extension, the anus.

bug wing, the bedlam of a prison. Crazy people are **flip artists, wigs.**

hippo a politician, a smooth diplomat who brown-noses his way to an easy job or position.

horny-o hypersexual inmate.

jacked-up [**on cotton**] high (on benzedrine).

jug-up chow, mess call.

party pad cell devoted to homoerotic activity during riots.

rapo a convicted rapist (of women). This is a term of abuse on the level of cocksucker. Sheep lovers are also shunned.

screw baiter inmate who intimidates a young guard with homosexual propositions.

swap spits to kiss passionately.

telephone somebody up alleged to "cure" known homosexuals by fastening wires to their testicles through which high voltage electricity is shot; this procedure is to frighten queerness out of their system. Subjects undergoing this electric analysis can eventually learn to stimulate an erection when shown heterosexual pornography, if only to avoid further "treatment."

tin throne the metallic toilet in each cell.

Also see: *Lilly [-Law].

prissy 1. "veddy proper" **2.** prude "Why don't you wear cut-offs, prissy, afraid your correction socks will show?"

professional chicken (mid-late '60s) **1.** one who strives to stay young and beautiful forever. Syn: **Peter Pan; superboy 2.** young hustler who charges an arm and a leg for fucking **3.** winsome boy hired to act as *bait to entrap prominent homosexuals. Syn: **worm for the hook.**

professional guest 1. *kept boy who doesn't put out for his host **2.** guest who stays and stays and stays "A professional guest knows his place—everywhere else."

profile side view of a tight rump or a magnificent crotch "I like him already—look at his profile."

promote 1. to proposition somebody **2.** to butter up.

props 1. padding, see *falsies **2.** furniture, especially the functionless kind "Take my money, but don't leave a ding on any of my props" **3.** everyone else, to one who is suffering from delusions of grandeur "Another riot like that and we'll let the props eat cock!"

prospect likely candidate "It's funny, dear, but do you think something is wrong? My prospects never turn out to be tricks."

pros[s] (*fr* pros sl) **1.** a prostitute; female streetwalker **2.** (*camp*) a promiscuous gay boy.

    Syn: **bona roba** (Brit *fr* Parlyaree // It = good merchandise); **book-keeper; bunter** (*obs*, orig meant a female rag-picker); **fancy woman** (*dated*); **gay girl** (Brit hetero sl; also see *gay); **grisette** (gri-zet′, *fr* Fr = a working-class woman); **harlot** (*fr* OFr *herlot* = rogue); **hooker; kelsey** (carnival sl); **les girls** (lā girlz′, Brit gay sl); **les perles** (lā-per′-elz, *fr* Fr = pearls); **local camp bicycle** (Brit hetero sl: the neighborhood trollop); **messalina** (*fr* Valeria Messalina, wife of the Roman emperor Claudius); **mistkiefer** (mist′-kē-fər, *fr* Ger = shit-jaw: a slovenly whore); **prossy; prosti-cutie** (mid '60s); **prostituta** (prōs′ tē-tōō′-tä, *fr* Sp); **prostitutke** (prōs′-tē-tōō′-kä, *fr* Yid = young whore); **puta** (pōō′-tä, *fr* Sp); **putana** (pōō-tä′-nä, used by Greeks & Italians *cf* Putana, a Hindu demoness: "Well, *this* putana has a migratory headache!"); **Sadie** (*fr* Sadie Thompson in Somerset Maugham's "Rain"); **saleslady; scrubber** (*dated*); **sporting girl; talona** (tä-lō′-nä, *fr* Mex ? // Sp *talon* = heel, *cf* sl *pushover* & *soft-heel*); **tapin** (tä-pēn′, *fr* argot // Fr = drummer); **wanton woman; yes-girl** (*obs*).

—act 1. flattering, encouraging noises manufactured for the sex act **2.** soft-soaping. **The same old pross act** the same old bullshit.

    Related terms:

bucket broad (*fr* pros sl) woman of ill-repute who permits her clients to copulate her rear (med: *paedicatio mulierum*).

bully (Brit) a prostitute's pimp. Syn: **nooky bookie; sweet man.**

cadet (*fr* pros sl) a white-slaver.

caso (Brit, *fr* Parlyaree // It *casa* = house) a brothel. Syn: **carsey** (Brit gay sl); **crystal palace** (a fancy whore house); **house; the loving rooms** (*camp, kwn* SF, '71); **maison joie** (*fr* Fr = house of joy).

dog-lady(-woman) an ugly whore.

Elvira (*kwn* SF, '71) a high-class **call-girl.**

Ginger (*fr* pros sl) a dishonest prostitute "I would sit next to you, Ginger, but I'm allergic to penicillin." Syn: **creeper.**

Juanita (khwä-nē′-tä, *kwn* LV, late '60s, *fr* pros sl) female prostitute who is friendly with gay boys.

messer (*fr* pros sl) a girl who is new to prostitution; an unskilled whore. Syn: **amateur; choker[essa].**

old firm (*fr* pros sl) the prostitution business.

sit for [some] company to work as a prostitute in a bar.

sitter a whore who cadges drinks in a bar. Syn: **B-girl.**

string (*fr* pros sl) group of prostitutes all handing in their wages to one pimp. Syn: **stable.**

three-way girl (*pej, fr* pros sl) whore who will allow her customers to use her vagina, mouth or anus; also agreeable to female clients.

zook (*fr* pros sl) an old whore. Syn: **aunt** (*fr* pros sl)

proteins food in general "We gotta stock up on some proteins if we're goin' campin'."

proud 1. well built, shaped; sensory "He has a proud body, honey— all them detours in the right places" **2.** (*dated*, '40s) cutting all ties with a homosexual past.
Also see *****retire.**

Prunella Paranoid 1. the first to panic in a raid ("Eek! My heart stopped!"); a worry wart **2.** one whose frightened eyes dart everywhere.

PS (*fr* phonetic coincidence connected to "piss") to urinate "He's PS'ing out kidney stones as big as your cabbages, Mr. Schwartz."
Related term:
add a PS to take a pee.

psych barn insane asylum, psycho ward, the looney bin "He put the knife to five people before they cooped him up in the psych barn."

PT see *****cock tease.**

PT boat cute sailor who gets a big kick out of putting queers on.

puff up (Brit gay sl, *fr* Brit sl *pouf* = *****fag**) to groom oneself carefully, especially the face **2.** to paint the face "My dear, that chit was puffed up like a gargoyle in drag!"

pug nose "Sure you can rim me—is your pug clean?"

pull a Camille to overdramatize trivial incidents; to use the school of elocution to one's own best advantage "When it's time to pay the rent, that one just pulls a Camille—works every time!" **2.** affectionately = to be a mite hammy, melodramatic.
Syn: **pull a Marie Dressler** [Sarah Bernhardt].

pull a face 1. to grimace as when tasting something acrid **2.** to make a face at someone; to stick out the tongue "Why is that carload of assholes looking at us, Bernard—did you pull a face when we drove over?"

pull a Loretta (*fr* Loretta Young's '50s TV show introduced by the twirling hostess) to enter a room with fanfare, style and grace "He has to make such a big deal out of everything; you should have seen him pulling his Loretta at the blood bank."
Syn: **make a grand entrance.**

pull a Saint Augustine (*fr* St. Augustine, known rake and holy man) **1.** to leave a wicked, sinful past and become religious, philosophical or a priest **2.** to be a religious homosexual.

pull a wingding (either *fr* black sl *wingding* = loud party or *fr* narc sl *throw a wingding* = feign withdrawal symptoms) **1.** to simulate a spasm or mental relapse to draw sympathy from others **2.** to go berserk; to pull a scene, have a fit "Kong will be sure to pull a wingding in the Congo Room if you're late again" "Stop pulling a wingding, you'll soon have some ciggies."

pull some petals down (petals *fr* pedal pushers) to slide a man's trousers and briefs below his hips before proceeding to fellate.
Also see *****quickie.**

pull the covers to expose a fellow homosexual to his straight friends, boss, *etc;* to let others in on the secret "Watch out for him! He thinks it's funny to pull the covers on his sisters at work." Considered a tasteless thing to do despite gay liberation's policy of keeping nothing hidden.
Syn: **open the closet** ('72: "I sure opened *his* closet! He blushed so bad I think it burned his hair!")
Related term:
there goes the headboard (*kwn* LV, mid '60s) said after some-

body really did a bang-up job of pulling the covers: leaving nothing unsaid as to who was what.

pull the drapes to zip the pants fly back up after sexing "Pull the drapes, Hero, the audience went home."

pull the plug to go to bed, especially after heavy partying.

pumpkin do (*camp*, black gay sl) Afro hairstyle, particularly if streaked with red tint.

pumps (*camp*) man's shoes.
   Related terms:
   high-heel[ed] pumps man's knee boots.
   oxford pumps office shoes "It took me *hours* to master the Shimmy in my new oxford pumps."
   Also see *cuban pumps, *heels, *marble pumps.

pump winter (*fr* weatherman rap = cold front) **1.** to expect hard times ahead **2.** to be penniless "After this next glass of wine, I'm pumping winter."

punch out to pass out after excessive partying.

punishment 1. an uncomfortably large penis **2.** accepting such a cock into the mouth (biting off more than one can chew) or anus.
   Syn: **show-stopper** (= penis so large all one can do is gasp or giggle); **sore prize** (pun made on surprise).

punk (*pej*, prison sl, *fr punk* = decayed wood used only for tinder; however *cf* sl *punk* = prostitute + dated prison sl *punk* = bread [molded into a vagina and fucked while still fresh] // L *panis* = bread) **1.** sexually oppressed, constantly raped victim; usually straight Syn: **angel** ("Hey, angel, when are you gonna grab your ankles for me?"); **brat; candy pants; dancer; de los otros** (Mex = one of them); **flesh; fuck-boy; gal-boy; ginch** (*rare*); **girl boy; green boy** (*dated*); **gunch; hide; jailhouse pussy; kid; MP** (= Mexican punk); **nick-nack; piece of hot apple pie[hump, snatch]; pink pants; pleasure punk; pog** [poger, pogie, pogue]; **PP; pressure punk; pretty boy; prison pussy; public property; *pushover; pussy boy; quiff; quim** (*rare, fr* sl = vagina); **raw-ass; roundheels** ("Paging Ruby Roundheels to the rear!"); **sex boy[punk]; singer; slavey** (*dated*); **stick pussy; stuff; taker; youngster 2.** to be active in force-fucking; to emasculate another man figuratively.
   Related terms:
   bee wrap a flower rape another convict. Syn: **take somebody's buns** (*kwn* NYC, teen sl, '70); **turn somebody out.**
   reformed punk ex-punk turned active.
   Also see: *prison terminology.

punny 1. funny, said of a well delivered pun "You didn't think it was punny because you didn't say it" **2.** tolerated despite all the bad puns "Yep, you're pretty punny, Punjabber!"

pupil latent homosexual who associates with gays to learn and experience more than what books have to offer.
   Syn: **teacher's petted** (*camp*).
   Also see: *tourist.

puppy's dinner (late '60s) one whose good looks range between average and mediocre. Your trick is *never* a puppy's dinner; it's always another's who is. Even worse is a **dog's dinner** (see *mess).

purge 1. douching; brushing the teeth or washing the mouth out with a gargle is **purging out the hole[mouth] 2.** war waged by the city fathers against all forms of erotica, see *panic.
   —chocolates laxatives decorated up as bite-size chocolates "Gimme an E-X-L-A-X! What we got? Go, team, go!" "Who slipped the purge chocolates into the Kool-Aid?" Syn: **purge pills** ("Alice May! I'm out of purge pills! Now how

am I gonna face the welfare line?")

The Purple Hand symbol of the Gay Liberation in San Francisco. In 1969 a band of gays picketed the Examiner because of an anti-homosexual editorial, and were drenched from above with printers ink. One of the demonstrators angrily imprinted the side of the building with his ink-stained hand. Others repeated the gesture, stamping their disapproval on the Examiner. Purple hand seems to be a play of words on *lavender,** often associated with male homosexuals, and the "black hand" death notice of the mafioso during the '20s.

purple passion in the ovaries (*kwn* Cleveland, late '60s) **1.** elaborate way of saying "he's gay" **2.** an urge to be rutted; the call of the wild **3.** (*exclam*) oh my "Purple passion in my ovaries! Look where you are driving!"

purps (*fr* purple pills) some form of pill which when taken induces intense dizziness and drowsiness. Often used as an aphrodisiac.

Syn: **buddhas** (*rare*); **sexiseltzers** ('70).

purr somebody down (*kwn* Southwest, mid '60s) to have the last word—at any price; to be vocally agile and quick to comeback cleverly.

Syn: **lay one to earth.**

purse (*camp*) any container as carried by a man, *eg* briefcases, lunch buckets, manila envelopes, wallets, *etc* "Your purse looked like 'North to Alaska' *before* the rushes" "I had a mess of the pictures made up purse size."

purse somebody [**out**] (*fr* archaic joke that all sissies hit with their purses) **1.** to fight back **2.** to knock somebody out in a boxing match "She sure as shit pursed that jam mother clean out of his *head*!"

purse stuffings do-dads, worthless knick-knacks; geegaw.

Related term:

to be just purse stuffings to be almost nothing—both literally and figuratively "His dee-dee was just purse stuffings, puss—nothing to take a bus across town for."

push-button resident homosexual who takes gay strangers on tours of all the local hot spots; conversation is the essential means of meeting a push-button.

Syn: **lamplighter.**

Also see *flashlight.**

pushing out (*adj*) said of a man who has the right bumps in the right places at the right times. A muscle-builder is pushing out when he wears clothing, because you can still use those muscles.

pushover one easily persuaded to join in sexual activity; an eager beaver "Before we leave, dear, say 'good evening' to Linda and her pushover."

Syn: **roundheel; softheel.**

push winter to age, get old, get security "Most of his jokes push winter after five o'clock."

puss (*voc*) form of address "Puss, if Christ had been born today, we'd all be wearing teeny electric chairs around our necks."

pussy 1. woman's sex organ, by extension any female "Me Tarzan—you pussy!" **2.** (*camp*) mouth or anus of a homosexual "Here, hon, work your pussy over this hamburger—it's great therapy!" **3.** (*camp*) man's crotch. Usually accompanied by clutching one's own genitals with the right hand "That's a real pussy down south—the clit overacts during the warm seasons" **4.** affected "You sure look pussy in Wedgwood blue shades" **5.** (pōō-sā′, *kwn* SF, ?*fr* sl puss = face // Ir *pus* = mouth) male homosexual.

—good (*camp*) pretty good; well. Answer to the inquiring of health.

—out 1. to take the coward's way out. Syn: **punk out 2.** to change one's mind "So, she's not going to Messico to ward off bandidos with her yoyo after all—I *knew* she'd pussy out" **3.** to break a date.

—tightener 1. alum **2.** pedopholin, medicinal liquid used in checking anal warts. It looks and is applied like a corn ointment, left on for a half an hour, and washed off. It is reputed to put "snap" back into the anal tissue.

—up 1. to gussy something up. Syn: **bitch it up 2.** to dress, decorate—especially precisely "Who pussied up the roast? It looks divine!"

Related terms:

eat pussy 1. to perform cunnilingus **2.** (*camp*) to be heterosexual (said of men) "Not *all* men eat pussy, you know."

one's pussy oneself "My pussy's *glad* there's a crack in the window—gives this dump some personality."

put a hurtin' on someone['s ass] (*kwn* NYC, black gay sl, late '60s) **1.** to copulate brutally, see ***fuck one rotten 2.** to whip the tar out of somebody **3.** to give somebody the blues.

put a hurtin' on something (*kwn* NYC, black gay sl, late '60s) to affix total attention to one item, *eg* put a hurtin' on the ice cream = digesting a great amount of ice cream "Mary! You sure put a hurtin' on this cigarette—it's more than half gone" "Honey, I typed up them orders rushingly—I really put a hurtin' on miss typewriter."

put a story on somebody to lie; make excuses; have an alibi.

put blush on the nose to dress stylishly.

put it into a different gear 1. to switch roles **2.** to change the mind; see an idea in another light "He must have put it into a hundred different gears before he finally decided to grope me."

put on a few hesitation marks "hesitation marks" = scars on wrists of attempted suicides. Gaining weight is enough to make some queens suicidal, so, instead of saying "putting on a few pounds, dear?" one may subtly dig the knife deeper with a "putting on a few hesitation marks, precious?"

put on a show to overbearingly flaunt one's homosexuality; a "give-'em-what-they-want" attitude "Oh, so he thinks fags are sick, does he? Well, let's give him a show he'll never forget."

put one's case out in front to admit to being homosexual.

put on pink [purple] pants to dress up for a gala event "Put on your purple pants, Sid, the Calendar Queen's been turning off lights and hanging up balloons."

put the boots on somebody (prison sl, *fr* practice of sheepfuckers lacing heavy boots to sheep to hinder their escape) to rape a man anally.

put the seeds [back] into the apple pie to be politically subversive; to mock bourgeois standards.

put the whip to somebody (Brit gay sl) to needle, nag.

put us back a few thousand years to give homosexuality a bad reputation by doing something degrading in public; to drag all other gay boys down into the gutter.

python (*camp*, ?*fr* misrepresentation of boa constrictor) long, feather boa.

Q (*dated.* hetero sl, *fr* initial letter of ***queer**) male homosexual.
Syn: **Q-boy; Q'er.**
Related term:
Q'ey queer, strange "Americans think that anything foreign is Q'ey.

Q-cards calling cards left and exchanged by gay men. Such cards, having the appearance of professional business cards, contain one's name and address along with a risque saying or picture beneath the name, *eg* a gay pilot's Q-cards might contain his name and a picture of two bees blissfully locked together over the caption "fly United."

quaint sweet, charming but not meaty enough, Walt Disneyish "How quaint! His table is set with Astro Turf placemats!"

quake somebody to have the interest kindled "He quakes me" = he sends me.

quean up (Brit gay sl, *fr* sl *quean* = ***queen**) **1.** to fall into homosexual company **2.** to assume girlish mannerisms, such as coating the face with cosmetics and fussing with the hair.

queen (*fr* Brit **quean** [spelled differently, but pronounced the same] = woman of low morals // Gk *gyne* = woman) **1.** designation among male homosexuals for one another. Generally, a queen is thought of as the fellow who plucks his eyebrows, splashes on Chanel No. 5, *etc* "A queen is a man who goes to blue-blooded movies" "My land! It's reigning kings and queens!" Syn: **radish** (translation *fr* It) **2.** (*pej, camp*) heterosexual man. Just as any woman is called a lesbian. A getting back for the epithet ***queer** combined with dragging pompous straights down to the queens' level **3.** (*voc*) title "Queen Cecil didn't give up cigarettes—he gave up quitting" "Don't look now, queen, but your secret recipe is leaking out" **4.** as a suffix naming one's locality (much like the *-er* and *-ite* in Berliner and Wisconsinite: "The Berlin queen had you check-mated") **5.** one's sexual preference and/or idiosyncrasy, *eg* "jelly queen" = one who likes jelly on his toast or lovers.
—**Anne** (*camp*) gay nickname for Andrew, Andy "The only sweet prince that'll guide queen Anne to her rest will be the 55 Sacramento (a bus line in San Francisco)."
—**bee** wealthy dowager who surrounds herself with a worshipping entourage of young, handsome, but homosexual men; motherly hag who pays for all her boys' drinks. Syn: **queers' woman** (Brit gay sl).
Related term:
swarm the young men who drink at the lady's expense.
—**for a day** man who whoops it up on his red-letter day—birthday, *etc* "Santa Claus is, at Christmas Eve, a queen for a day."
—**ie** gay nickname, often for a pet poodle "Here, Queenie,

Mama's got a nice big bone for baby" "Sticking to your gums, queenie, does *not* mean blowing your brains out."

—Mary a fat homosexual; one who is immense as the ship.

—mother 1. (*camp*) homosexual's actual father "Didn't the queen mother ever slip you any Mother-Goose-me rhymes?" **2.** adult who gives a latent homosexual his first glimpse of what it's all about.

Also see: ***mother.**

—of diamonds 1. one managing a jewelry store **2.** one dripping in costume jewelry.

—of hearts gay heartbreaker; has many lovers on the string.

—of Scotch homosexual alcoholic.

—of Sheba black homosexual "Before I knew what was happening, the Queen of Sheba let the cock out of the bag and was corning me as if ass was going out of style."

Syn: **queen of spades.**

Also see: ***dinge queen** [*black*].

—of tarts a prostitute's pimp.

—of the load man who ejaculates copiously (he comes buckets).

—of the range a chef; cook.

—on a broomstick 1. one who sweeps like a mad witch **2.** janitor.

—sheepshit (*kwn* SF, black gay sl, '70) one who has been jilted, cheated, hurt; one who has the blues.

Related term:

feel like queen sheepshit in shinola to feel really lousy; run-down, depressed and alone.

—Tsetse Fly ('70) black homosexual. Not derisive, except when addressing a heterosexual blackman.

queer (*fr* Brit sl *quare* = unusual) **1.** (*pej*, hetero sl) epithet for that which is homosexual "Ya meet a lot of them fuckin' queers when yer in the Navy, man!" "Hear about the queer parakeet who would sneak into the coop and blow a cockatoo?"

Syn: (queer as a noun): **brunser** (*obs*); **cat** (*pej*, Aus sl, *fr* catamite = boy kept for homosexual purposes, // Etruscan *Catmite* // Gk *Ganymēdēs* = Ganymede); **deviate** (*pej*, *fr* L *de-* = from, off + *via* = path, way "There she was, telling me about deviates and I wasn't twenty minutes away from my last cock"); **fly ball; fun son** (*fr* funny = peculiar); **gear** (Brit sl *fr* Cockney rhyming sl = queer); **hash** [hesh] (*obs*, '30s-'40s, he + she); **hormone** (teen sl pun made upon ***homo,** late '50s); **kwink** (*kwn* Ariz teen sl, late '50s: "Did you ever let a kwink make love to your pecker, man?"); **loop** (Brit sl); **misfit** (short for sexual misfit); **one of them**[those]; **Oscar** (Brit sl, *fr* Oscar Wilde); **pathic** (*obs*, ?*fr* pathetic); **perv** (Brit sl) **pink-o** ('40s: also identifies any person subscribing to a subversive idea); **pirujo** (pē-rōō´-khō, Mex); **prevert** (redneckese *fr* pervert; often preceded by *one of dem goddamn*); **ponce** [punce] (Aus & Brit sl); **Poncy Ponce** (Aus sl); **quay** (*rare:* blending of queer + gay); **queebie** (*kwn* Ariz, teen sl, late '50s: "Don't try any of your queebie tricks on me!"); **queerie** ("That little 'queerie' is the only one I know who shoots Sal Hepatica"); **silly** (*fr* the theory that stock homosexuals behave as if silly, giggling schoolgirls: "Who's the big silly in the lavender outfit— Mobina Grapenuts?"); **silly savage**[thing, sod] (*sod* being Brit *fr* sodomite); **sodsucker** ("That sodsucker was born and bleached a Presbyterian"); **tante** [tata] (*fr* Fr = aunt[ie]); **tutti-frutti** ('50s, *fr* It = all fruits, used because of the similarity of frutti with ***fruit** + reinforced by Little Richard's song "Tutti-Frutti"); **twank** (*dated*, Brit sl, '30s); **violet** (*dated*); **woman-hater; wonk** (Aus sl); **zanie** (*fr* zany = ludicrous // It *zanni* = masked buffoon; *cf* Mattachine, gay organization named after a court jester).

Syn: (queer as adjective): **funny [acting]** ("He's funny that way" = he's queer); **funny money** (*fr* sl = counterfeit bills; "Which Caesar *wasn't* funny money, teach?"); **kinky** (Brit sl); **kwinky; like that; off-color; PDQ** (= pretty damn queer); **poufy** (Brit sl); **scammered** (*fr* criminal sl ?// Ir tinker sl *glammy* = something bad, jinxed); **so** (Brit sl); **that way.**

2. (*pej*) as a word of self-mockery, homosexuals sometimes use the word much in the same way blacks use "nigger," though one rarely refers to himself as queer—it is always someone else ("I'm gay, but you're queer"). "A queer electrician, dear, is somebody who blows the fuses" "Queers never yellow!" **3.** (kǎ-wē'-ä, *camp*) heterosexual, from the reverse reasoning that "we're not the queer ones; they are!" "What are you doing with that *queer* book (*ie* girlie magazine)—swatting flies?" **4.** (*pej*) being truly perverted. Child-molesters, kill-happy rapists, dog-humpers and the like are all classified as being queer to the average gay "Some of the kids are just gay, but then there are a percentage who are stone *queer!*"

—as a three-dollar bill [**-football bat, -nine-dollar bill, -square egg**] unredeemably homosexual.

—baiting (Brit teen sl) luring, beating and then robbing a homosexual.

—bashing (Brit teen sl) beating up homosexuals simply because they are homosexuals.

—corner (hustler sl, late '60s) city block where hustlers line up waiting to be propositioned by homosexuals.

—for desirous of; fond of. Syn: **fruit for** ("Kid gloves? He'll buy them! He's fruit for anything genital"); **mad about** ("I'm simply mad about the goys!")

—somebody (*pej*) to seduce somebody into a homosexual act—the implication is that some trickery is involved "I want you to tell me the truth, son; did your biology teacher ever queer you?"

quelle (kel, *adv, fr* Fr = what[such] a ———!) **1.** what a "Quelle boche!" (*lit* what a mouth) = what a blabbermouth! "Drop it honey—quelle breath!" **2.** how "Quelle rank of you!"

qu'est-ce que c'est (kes' kə-sā', *phr fr* Fr = what is it? whatever does it [this, that] mean?) handy reply when playing dumb, fresh off the farm, unworldly. Akin to maiden's "Why, Sire, whatever are you talking about?" "He wants me to suck him off—qu'est-ce que c'est *suck?*"

quickie 1. rushed act of copulation; a briefing in an alleyway or bushes; a flash in the pan "Tone down—you sound like the soundtrack musical score of a quickie!" **2.** person one has sex with once; a transparent romance "How should I know who he was—it was only a quickie."

Syn: ***bang-bang-bang; five-minute shack up** (*kwn* LV, mid '60s); ***one night stand; quick one** ("let's stop in at the local glory hole, boys, and have a quick one"); **quick piece** ("Tell me, quick piece, is my hair on straight?"); **short one; tête-à-tête** (*fr* Fr = head-to-head).

—station public washroom where homosexuals suck off their pickups; public john where frustrated men retreat for impersonal blow jobs.

quick queer homosexual picked up off the streets after the bars close "I bounced his ass out of here by three—he was just a quick queer. I'll forget the cocksucker's face by my five o'clock shadow."

quiet wink (*camp, dated, kwn* LV, mid '60s) said of anything lacking subtlety (a queen can't make a quiet wink—her false eye-lashes are too weighty). When something comes crashing to the floor, one may say: "Like a quiet wink—*bam!*"

quiff (*fr* naut sl, mid '60s, // vul sl = vagina) generic for gay men who oblige thrill-seekers out for a blow job. Looking for pussy is searching for a girl, but looking for quiff is hunting out a fellator who will probably pay money to suck cock "Shit, man, that quiff's as European as the George Washington Bridge."

rabbit a fellator, see *cocksucker "The noises from the bushes are certainly loud—are the rabbits trying to bring back Holly-wood?"
    Related term:
  down the rabbit hole into the mouth and down the gullet.

rabbit-scraper (late '50s) black market abortionist "They busted the rabbit-scraper on a six-nine-two: holding a fork with intent to fondue Sue."

rack (*fr* naut sl) the bed.
    Related term:
  hit the rack 1. to go to sleep "I've got to hit the rack; I have a busy schedule to follow tomorrow" **2.** to take somebody to bed.

radio (*exclam,* prison sl) be still; shut up. Also used as a verb: "Did you tell Brando to radio?"

rag 1. sanitary napkin "Such finesse! A rag floatin' aroun' in the fuckin' john!" **2.** (*pej*) any woman representing a threat to a gay boy "What's that rag's hobby—giving torturous mani-cures to fluff-dried poodles?" "The way that rag sings! Even a fool could tell that Carnegie Hall isn't in her cards." Syn: **piece of rag** ("Don't bring your piece of rag here—the candle goes out at nine sharp") **3.** (*fr* colloq *chew the rag*) to gossip, criticize, speak badly of one absent. Syn: **rag on someone** ("I'm not raggin' on your trip, Bruce, but . . .")
    Related term:
  have the [mean]rag on 1. to be menstruating **2.** to be ornary, crotchety.

Raggedy Android (*camp*) gay nickname for a poor *hustler.

railed banished; sent out of town; tarred and feathered.

railroad (*fr* narc sl *tracks* = hypodermic needle marks) the arm of a hardcore drug addict. If the needle pricks have scabbed over, the arm is compared with the Santa Fe railroad.
  —er a mainliner.
    Related term:
  run a railroad to be addicted to heroin.

railroad queen (*dated,* '40s) homosexual who haunted "hobo jungles" and rail yards in hopes of stumbling across a stray tramp to love.

rainbow (*fr* narc sl) tuinal capsule. Tuinals are blue on one side and red on the other; they are depressants.

rainbow queen 1. one who practices interracial love-making; one who doesn't object to another's race, creed or color **2.** white woman with a brood of mulatto babies.

raincoat condom; rubber sheath rolled onto the penis before coitus to prevent impregnation or catching VD.

    Syn: **overcoat; rubber; topcoat.**
    Related term:
    ride bareback to fuck without a raincoat.
    Also see *come-drum.

raise a queen (mid-late '60s) to trick someone into confessing his homosexuality to others; to bring somebody else out of the closet.

raisin ('71) scab or some other temporary blemish.

raisin-hunting looking for a black partner in the black sections of town.

    Related term:
    raisin queen white who turns to black lovers. "If the wings fit, you raisin queen—fly, fly away!" "Johnny McBrown the raisin queen!"

rake 1. fingernail "Wait till she puts her rakes to your back" **2.** to scratch "I'll rake those cat eyes clean out of her nelly head!" **3.** to comb the hair "If Goldielocks hadn't been so busy rakin' out her curls, she wouldn't have gotten ate up by the three bares."

rally 'roun' the flagpole said of a group who take turns sucking a pickup's penis.

Ralph (hetero sl) used to ridicule effeminate, timid, mousey men. Other sissy names are Cecil, George, and *Cy "Ralph here doesn't mind if we take his money, do you, Ralphy?"

Ramona Rottencrotch (*camp*) unsanitary man in need of drastic hygienic measures before the garbage men haul him off; one who smells terrible "Put on a little soul music, Ramona Rotten-crotch—like a requiem mass."

    Syn: **crust queen.**

randy 1. (*adj, fr* Scotch = having a coarse approach // *obs rand* = rant) lecherous, see *horny **2.** (*dated, kwn* Chi, early '60s, ?*fr* Scotch *randy* = a scolding woman) gay nickname for a dissatisfying lover "I'll always love you, Randy—till breath do us part" **3.** (*dated, kwn* Chi, early '60s) to throw up, puke, upchuck "He randied after he did me—another miscarriage!"

rank (*fr* OE *ranc* = overbearing, strong kin to OE *riht* = right // L *regere* = rule) coarse, foul, vile "How rank! His earrings and bracelet don't match!"

    Syn: **crusty** (= cruddy: "Why not bathe your crusty bod—afraid of losing your priority on the bubonic plague?");
    raunchy (*fr* teen sl, '50s, // WW II sl: "Don't use my bed for any more of your raunchy numbers—I'm getting tired of burning the sheets after you're through.")

    —somebody 1. to insult someone with a cleverly offensive remark "I'm not ranking you, Edgar! You *do* have some good lines—but they're all in your face" **2.** (prison sl) to degrade a heterosexual man by buggering him and then blabbing to his friends that he loved it.

rapid (*fr* rampent + connection of bus depot overflow with transients) busy, crowded; *cruisy "Was it rapid?" = was it very cruisy?

rat somebody's mind (*fr* ratting hair) to play psychological chess; to disturb another's mental orderliness; to bewilder.

    Syn: **mind fuck; rattle somebody's mind** (used both negatively and positively: "I won an all expense paid three-day excursion to Fire Island? That truly rattles my mind" "Don't talk French! It rattles Miss Animation's mind so.")

rattle on to talk at great lengths about absolutely nothing worthwhile; to rant and rave; ramble.

rave (*dated, fr* Brit teen sl, late '60s) subject of crucial admiration, such as a singing idol; a strong personality.
　　Syn: **superstar.**

ravish (ra-vish' *kwn* SF, late '60s-'70) ravishing, stunning, indescribably beautiful "Oh, a ravish new coat—been to Goodwill's again?" "How ravish—everything but the spurs!"

Ravonia (răv-ōn'-yə, *kwn* LV, mid '60s, *fr* sl *rave on* = to ramble) **1.** used as a silly prefix attached to a given name "Ravonia Chris, you've cut my hair *much* too short!" **2.** (*exclam*) attention-getting device such as "hey!" "Ravonia, Ravonia! I'd *pay* for *that!*" **3.** (*adj, ?fr* revolting) gauche; in questionable taste. The quip, "how charmingly quaint" is redressed as "how ravonia!" "Italian Provincial painted white and gold: how ravonia!"
　　—Sue 1. a twerp "What did Ravonia Sue do, dunk the tombstone into his Bank of America credit card?" **2.** (*exclam*) = My stars! "Ravonia Sue! Orgies can be some *kind* of superfine—ask the man who owns one" "Ravonia Sue! If football players grab ass, why can't we?"
　　Related term:
　　set up Ravonia Sue to dupe somebody "Let's draw straws to see which one of us sets up Ravonia Sue!"

read 1. to tell somebody off—but good "I hope you read that priest for callin' you a 'queer!'" **2.** to recognize other homosexuals; to have nonsexual eye-to-eye contact with a fellow homosexual. Readers, in this sense, choose to keep the information learned as secret **3.** to recognize anything "I don't know her car well enough yet to be able to read it."
　　Related term:
　　given the grand reading recipient of a severe scolding.

read the classics ('71) to read a newspaper's classified ad section; to job-hunt "If you lived with me, doll, you'd never have to read the classics. All you'd have to do is flex your muscles in my pool."

read the music ('40s) to know the ropes—gaywise.

ready whip (late '60s) nocturnal emission "I had some ready whip in my 'jammies' this morning, honeybunch, so I'll just have some coffee for breakfast."

real authentic, the real McCoy. Since a basket to a gay boy will call up only the image of a crotch, one must speak of a *real* basket in terms meaningful for the Easter pageant.

real fine thing on somebody shapely, curvaceous body "That little number has a real fine thing on her."

really (*interj*) **1.** affirmation said by one who is in total agreement with a statement "He must have married that sow thirty-five pounds ago!" Ans: "Really!" (= how right you are!) **2.** when the tone is shifted to sound like a question ("really?"), the speaker is being snide. He is, in essence, saying: "You're just finding that out—where have you been hiding?" **3.** (*exclam*) expresses resigned boredom: "I could go for you in a big way, baby!" Ans: "Really? How nice for you!"
　　Syn: **for God's true; rally** (affected pronunciation).

real people generic for agreeable, easy-to-like/live-with persons.
　　Syn: **good people** (*dated*, mid-late '60s).

real thing 1. the vagina as opposed to the anus **2.** a heterosexual woman **3.** coitus between a man and a woman.

ream see *rim.

rear the posterior. Sometimes used in puns dealing with anal intercourse: "Ever hear about the little Greek boy who ran away from home? He didn't like the way his father was rearing him."
Also see *ass.

recruiting center any public washroom where a cocksucker is apt to encounter fresh material for his research "Been tripping over a new brand of kisses at the recruiting center, Corky?"
Related terms:
chicken-recruiter a *toilet queen who has nothing to do with you unless you're young.
recruit young heterosexual who goes to the local toilet to get blown.

rectum fry (*camp*) to rectify.

red carpet tongue.
—treatment 1. to lick out the ass, see *rim **2.** to give a tongue lashing.

redemption center 1. a church **2,** mission hall for transients "I mean, Miss Clean raced through this parlour with so much elbow grease that she had the place dolled up like a Catholic redemption center."
Related term:
[sister] Sally's redemption center a Salvation Army kitchen.

red-hot momma (*camp*) young homosexual who thinks of himself as a sex symbol ("hot shit").

red light warning (*dated*, mid-late '60s) in some *baths or bars, a red light is flashed on giving the patrons a chance to leave before an impending raid.

rednik (*fr sl* *redneck* = rural WASP + Yid suffix *-nik* as in *beatnik*) communist-type as opposed to flag-wavers.

red top (les sl, early '50s) female homosexual who is attracted to blondes.

reformed retired from the field, *ie* homosexuality. Often said of one who sets homosexuality aside for a heterosexual future "So Jerry's a reformed piccolo player, huh? That'll go rough on him with our musicians' union."

refrigeration service (*kwn* LV, mid '60s) sexual relations enacted between any repairman making a house call and the customer "Maybe you could set up a little refrigeration service with your gas and electric man the next time he comes over to check your meter."
Related term:
Culligan (*exclam*) remark of approval made of a handsome repairman.

regulate [it] to lead a nonhomophilic life, especially said of one raising a family in suburbia. "He regulates it" = he's straight.

reign to live a full, happy life of a demanding, pushy queen.

reject 1. an erotically loathsome ogre; the unmarriagable "Rejects keep their crisco in the pantry—swingers keep theirs under the bed" **2.** to shoo somebody away; to decline a proposition.

relaced having rejoined gay society after giving heterosexuality a play; coming back to one's gay senses "He *was* out to rinse his miss priss away—but he's been relaced since *that* act."

repeat performance second, third and even fourth meeting with a *trick whose first encounter was memorable enough to warrant encores.

repertoire 1. homosexual's little black book, *ie* list of partners "He has VD! Mother of pearl! I was last on his repertoire!"
Syn: **trick sheet 2.** various sex positions one will allow "Hi there, stranger, is browning on your repertoire?"

rernt (*adj, fr* Texan dial = ruined) **1.** untidy, sloppy **2.** too old to tangle, past the heyday, over the hill.

rest stop the navel as offering focus to an oral copulator.

retire 1. to go out of circulation; to settle down **2.** extended to mean death.

> Syn: **go into cold storage; leave the stage** ("You better leave the stage before the flab settles around your ankles"); **take the veil; turn in the crown** ("What do you do after you turn in the crown—take in laundry?")

return of the swallows vomiting.

reversible 1. bisexual **2.** able to lay or be laid.

reverse western (*fr* pros sl) heterosexual position with the woman straddling the man.

review the case to do a little soul searching "You better review your case, Larry, you don't see any nineteen year olds chasing you, do you?"

rhinestone bracelet (*camp*) The Bayshore Freeway in San Francisco, but extended to mean any well-traveled freeway or highway.

> Related term:
> **hit the rhinestone bracelet** to leave, hit the road.

rhinestones (*fr* Rhine river in Germany) **1.** key word in calling attention to another's homosexuality "He was dressed from head to pumps in rhinestones" = he's gay **2.** any jewelry worn by a man "Pawn your rhinestones—I want to go rape the furniture stores."

rhinestud (*camp*) strong man who turns out to be a cream puff.

rhinestudded 1. (*camp*) fucked by a German **2.** covered in rhinestones; sequined "When I die I want to be buried face down so that the whole world can kiss my rhinestudded arse."

Rhonda (*camp*) gay nickname for Ronald, Ron[ny] "What you doing, Rhonda? Praying to San Andreas de Fault?"

> Related term:
> **Rhonda Flaming** (*camp*) Ronald Reagan "Dear Rhonda Flaming, welcome to Bay Ghettos—racist tract!"

ribbon clerk homosexual with a desk job.

rice paddy (*fr* Haw gay sl, late '60s) belong to the Mongoloid race (Chinese, Japanese, Korean, Vietnamese, *etc*)

> Chinese gays are called **ornamentals, soy-sauce pies, Suzie Wongs.** Any reasonably priced Chinese restaurant is **Shuffle's** (*kwn* SF, late '60s, *fr* loose house slippers Chinese waitresses are fond of wearing). A man with **yellow fever** (a sexual fondness for orientals) is a **rice paddy hattie** or **rice queen** (*kwn* SF, '71).
> Also see ***kintama.**

ride queer (*dated*, teen sl, '50s) the "third wheel" in the back seat of a car.

ride the train (*dated*, '40s, *fr* the train of a formal gown) to appear in ***drag.**

rien de tout (ron-də-to͞o', *n* & *adj*, *fr* Fr = nothing at all) **1.** something not worth the effort "I need that rein de tout like the desert needs another spoonful of sand" **2.** talentless, useless "His performance was rien de tout."

riffed intoxicated.

> Syn: **ripped** ("He was too ripped to ball.")

rig 1. (Brit) the penis, see ***cock 2.** (*v*) to stand at the urinal with an erection. Syn: **troll.**

righteous (*fr* black sl) **1.** meriting praise, good, snazzy "A Pepsi sure would taste righteous after a roll-around" **2.** genuine, authentic, factual; *eg* **righteous shades** = prescription sunglasses as opposed to the drugstore variety.

> Related term:
> **righteously** (*adv*) really "I'm righteously tellin' ya, Queenie, I saw him scorin' reds from Ted."

riha (Brit gay sl, a garbling) head hair.

rim (*vt, fr* a circular or round border; variant *ream* is *fr* Brit sl = to diddle a woman in the ass // ME dial *remen* = to widen the opening of a hole, to open up) **1.** to lick or suck anus **2.** to lubricate the anus with saliva, usually as a prelude to fucking "Tense? Try getting rimmed!" **3.** (jocular) to lick with great gusto "Rim that stamp, Mabel!"

There are synonyms literally up the ass for anilingus, the medical euphemism for sucking ass (not to be confused, however, with brown-nosing for personal advantage.) Some of the popular heterosexual terms for vulva-tonguing are also used by homosexuals to describe rimming: **eat somebody out; tongue somebody out.**

Syn: **ass-blow; blow some ass; clean up the kitchen; eat jam** ('40s); **eat poundcake** ('40s); **KS** (= kiss shit); **lickety-split; play the piano** (seemingly a pun on rim and Rimski-Korsakov, Russian composer); **ream [somebody out]; shove the tongue; sit on a face** ("I'd like to sit on your face, but the bright light might crack your makeup"); **smear somebody's tuna** (*kwn* SF, '71); **snarf** (orig = to smell bike seats); **suck [asshole]** (as in the curse: "Well, suck my scruffy Italian ass"); **take a trip to the moon** (the moon = buttocks); **thirty-nine** (3 = buttocks + 9 = face buried within the fleshy burrow); **tell a French joke; tongue-fuck; toss a salad; white-wash [the back forty]**.

Related terms:

feature a matinee (*kwn* LA, mid '60s) to be/get rimmed.

good soup (*kwn* SF, '71) ass to be tested and tasted by a rimmer.

mustache key word discussing mouth-to-anus activity; *eg* "He has an ocre mustache" "He sprouts a brown mustache every time he leaves the androgyny's place."

pickle the rosey to be the first to come in oral contact with another's formerly secluded anus.

trade rings to rim while being rimmed.

—job act of rimming. Syn: **rim shot; ring job; tongue sandwich.**

—queen an ass-licker in all meanings and shades of the word; also affectionately **Rimski** ("And what does Rimski crave for breaky this morning—a nice bowl of upturned assholes?"). Syn: **asshole bandit** (early '50s); **birdcage cleaner; bottom-sucker** (*kwn* SF, '71); **kitchen cleaner [queen]** (because he "cleans it out"); **rimmer; soup-sipper** (*kwn* SF, '71).

ripe for tomato season = ripe for pickin'; *ie* ready to be paired off with another man in unholy matrimony.

ripe fruit latent homosexual who is easing into gay life.

road game using prostitution to travel, particularly by hitchhiking. Also used of homosexuals who cruise in such a fashion.

Related terms:

hitchpussy (*camp*) traveler asking rides from motorists.

road queen 1. homosexual hitchhiker. Syn: ***express queen; highway queen; road kit** (*fr* hobo sl) **2.** (*camp*) a truck driver "It must be a great scum pit—all the road queens get fueled up there."

traveling salesman (hustler sl) the vagrant ***hustler**—he cruises by exposing his thumb.

Roberta (*camp*) gay nickname for Robert, Bob[by] "What a busy place you have here—I feel like I've been stranded on a Roberta Hope 'Road' set."

rock (*fr* pros sl, '30s) **1.** one whose sexual performance is under par; a real lemon **2.** a jerk; one who exhausts his audience with dated disc jockey jokes ("he's got a million of 'em").

    Syn: **bad lay; punk dunk** (= loose fitting vagina or anus); **reezock** (carny rendition of rock); **slibe** (slīb, ?*fr* slime: "For a slibe, your ass looks pretty good.")

rocking chair anal erotic position in which the insertee faces the active partner and sits down into his lap and the two rock back and forth.

rock out ('71) to enjoy oneself to the fullest "We could go to the Louvre's tearoom and rock out on some of its art collections."

roll (*fr* narc sl) a roll of ten wrapped benzedrine tablets.

roll-around an instance of coitus; a roll in the hay.

rolling nut[peanut] factory man with large testicles.

Roman candle (mid '60s) **1.** penis of an Italo-American "You got what it takes to make Roman candles sparkle" **2.** any Italian man.

rosary chain of events; a progression or series of any sort. Rosary is the key word in expressing length and time, especially wasted time: "My God! It's a rosary of keys—how'll you ever find the right one in time?" "He was big enough to make a bead on my rosary of life."

    Related terms:

    do a rosary 1. to waste time, stand in line, wait "I can't do this rosary tonight, Al—let's come back tomorrow" = looking at a block-long queue **2.** to serve time **3.** to make a career out of the military.

    read a rosary (*camp*) to talk to oneself; mumble; move the lips.

    the same old rosary the same old thing "Can the same old rosary, Maude; just tell me why my records sound as though they've been played with a dinner knife!"

rose piddle ('71) rose oil or perfume.

rose tattoo bruise, especially one caused by excessive sucking.

rouge (*fr* FR = red // L *rubeus* = reddish & cognate of *ruby*) **1.** outdated make up for highlighting the blush on the cheek and nose. As a key word, rouge reveals homoerotic topics "What did Slasher think we had in our veins—blue rouge?" "I hope they took his rouge away for a month" **2.** (*rare*, prison sl) catsup "I like rouge on my horsemeat, cooky!"

    —the lips 1. to apply lipstick **2.** (*camp*) to belt somebody in the mouth.

rough trade ruffian element which sometimes crosses a homosexual's path. Almost always, rough trade is fellated first after which he turns sour "'Rough trade' is a liberal who was unprejudiced until he had his cock sucked."

    Syn: **piece of rough trade** ("What's with the blackeye—run into a piece of rough trade?")

    Also see ***trade.**

route one's sexual preference "Eat out girls? No chance! I don't go that route."

    Related term:

    homo route (hetero sl) homosexual activity "Most guys go the homo route when they're still kids."

royal 1. dignified, quality, commanding **2.** massive, of impressive size or amount "She had a *royal* case of mono" "Honey, he has the *royal* scepter" **3.** hospitable, right "My slogan—'treat 'em royal!'"

    Syn: **regal** (mainly Brit gay sl: "Then there was the regal Jewish queen who had stocks in Ben Gay.")

    Related terms:

    come on royal to assume a haughty attitude. A queen who comes on royal with the police answers their questions curtly.

    royally completely, whole hog "They royally blew him off the face of miss map" "I'll fix her ass—royally."

—ban 1. city ordinance; a blue law **2.** (*camp*) a boycott.

—bar a *gay bar.

—buns attractive posterior.

—command sharp fingersnap delivered like an irate customer signaling a lax waiter. The meaning of the snap depends on the position of the arm and facial expression. If the arm is held higher than the head (titled back majestically), and the snap is a small thunderclap, we may understand the meaning to be: **a.** agreement (smile); **b.** commanding a handsome stranger over (coy smile); **c.** condemnation = off with his head (frown or glare). If the snap is delivered at chin level, the clicker is but marking an emphatic beat to a witty statement, usually his own. If the fingers are snapped loudly in an adversary's face, the ultimate insult has been leveled.

Also see *pluck somebody off, *snap somebody off.

—coronation severe beating about the head and shoulders.

—crown head; noggin "She lost all the diamonds out of her royal crown" = he lost his marbles.

—gown 1. floor-length evening gown **2.** (*camp*) tuxedo.

—ist heterosexual man who is sympathetic with homosexuals; some of his best friends are. *Note:* royalists do not sleep with their gay chums. Syn: **camp followers; camper** (*fr* setting up camp(; **homo-lover** (*pej*, hetero sl). Related term: **sympies** (*dated*, late '50s, *fr* sympathetic & not to be confused with sl *simp* = dull witted) straights who claim to "understand"; they think they're hip because they happen to know one fag ("There, there, I understand, just don't touch me!")

—neck long, slender neck; a swan's neck.

—pumps 1. high heels **2.** (*camp*) dress shoes; Sunday-go-to-meetin' shoes "Shine up the royal pumps, dear. Truman Capote's having a garage sale."

—room 1. the bedroom **2.** (*fr* sl *throne* = toilet) the bathroom "And this is the royal room where dwelled the lips that launched a thousand hips into orbit."

—ty group of queens.

visiting royalty gay out-of-towners.

rub-belly (*fr* sl *rub* = to commit frottage) one who rubs his cock against another's stomach until the friction causes an ejaculation.

Also see *belly-fucker.

rubber dish 1. insult that flops **2.** faux pas.

Related term:

hardless bitch one who is poor at being evily clever.

rubber palace [rooms] insane asylum.

rubber queen rubber fetishist; one who wears rubber, fucks on rubber sheets, *etc.*

rubber walls (Brit) to go totally mad; flip out "I will go rubber walls if you tell me I owe you money one more time."

rubdown wrestling match with evident homosexual overtones.

Syn: **rub-off.**

rubies (*camp*) lips.

Syn: **ruby red lips; ruby reds.**

Ruby 1. (*camp*) gay nickname for Rudolph, Rudy "Tell me, Ruby, is your face premeditated?" **2.** (*camp*) man whose lips are a prominent feature.

rug 1. man's toupee **2.** poor-quality wig for a woman **3.** pubic hairs.

Related terms:

Indian rug cheap dime-store wig done in braids.

rug cleaner oral copulator.

shampoo the rug to dribble saliva onto the pubes while sucking cock.

ruin somebody's Easter to sabotage plans (disrupt parties, cancel invitations, place negative thoughts into someone's head, *etc*) "Henry the VIII ruined Anne Boleyn's Easter—forever."
Related terms:
Happy Easter, Sugar (*exclam, kwn* SF, '71-'72) a wish for the very worst. If a friend gets to make it with a handsome devil the speaker had eyed earlier, he is greeted with a "Happy Easter!" between clenched teeth.
pull the newspaper out of somebody's Easter basket to expose a person for the rascally knave he truly is; to deflate an ego.

run a game[number] to do a routine.

run a line 1. (prison sl) to act as a sex receptacle for a squad of men awaiting their turn in line **2.** used of fellators doing a good business in theater toilets **3.** (*camp*) to sell tickets; a girls who runs lines may also be a bank teller.

run a tour 1. to barhop **2.** to be a rubbernecking tourist in a *gay bar** "Take a donation at the door of all those running a tour after ten."

run for somebody (*kwn* Ill, les prison sl) to faithfully reunite with a former lover on the outside after having finished doing penal time. The girl waiting on the outside is said to **run for her lover.**

run in the nylons clue that one's homosexuality is showing.

run off (short for colloq *run off at the mouth*) to say too much, to be loquacious.

run, rabbit, run (*exclam*) warning slipped to a fellow homosexual when the police have been sighted within the vicinity.

runway high forehead.
Related terms:
oil on the runway shiny forehead of a bald(ing) man; a chrome dome.
runway hairline receding hairline.

rush (*fr narc sl rush* = overwhelming surge of good will brought about by a drug injection) found in the expression **catch a rush** = **1.** to be taken by surprise "And don't think the Pope didn't catch a rush after Luther finished tacking up those circus posters on the church door" **2.** when spoken of a dead person = turning over in the grave.

rushingly (*kwn* NYC, black gay sl, late '60s) quickly, fast.
Syn: **flashing[ly]** "Get this carriage into motion, girl—flashing.")

-s (*camp*) past participle suffix = *-ed*. Used in the following words: **excites** = excited; **stones** = stoned, *ie* under the influence of a drug; **whips** = whipped, *ie* weary.

safari (*dated*, '50s) a younger entourage surrounding an older person.

safo (sä′-fō, *fr* Sp = Sappho who "lesbiated" during the seventh century) lesbian.
  Syn: **sapphite; sappho** ("Your sappho friend really made an impression here—she broke the chair she sat on.")

saggers old mens' flabby breasts.

Sally (Cape Town gay sl) a suck.

salon (*kwn* SF, late '60s-'71) cave-like hideaway formed by shrubs and overhanging foliage. Some salons are big enough to hold twenty men, but most are small—just right for two.
  Syn: **shrub club.**
  Related term:
  Coco Chanel's salon (*kwn* SF, '70) one of the largest groves located at San Francisco's Land's End (see **The End** under ***place names**).

salt and pepper queens integrated gay couple; a white in love with a black "There were so many salt and pepper queens, I thought it was a cop car convention."

Sam (*kwn* SF, '70) the masculine counterpart of ***Jane**. From a gay standpoint, Sam is an insensitive negative aspect of life unless balanced with Jane.

Samantha (*camp*) gay nickname for Samuel, Sam[my]. Do not confuse with ***Sam** above.

Samoa-Samoa 1. man who saunters about his home nude or with a towel tied around his hips **2.** a colored domestic "Samoa bring massa him rim-onion aid."

sandpaper (*rare*, *fr* sl *sandpaper* = toilet paper) to wash and clean something "Go sandpaper your hands!"

sandwich 1. *menage à trois*, see ***three way 2.** specific ***three-way** where two men simultaneously fuck the ass of the third partner—the **meat** between the **two slices of bread.** Syn: **double-entry.**

San Francisco faggot (*pej*, *kwn* San Diego, early '60s) **1.** any man who talks tough but winds up spreading his cheeks for other men. ***Hustler** types and ***leather queens** fall into this category **2.** self-acclaimed heterosexual who really likes boys.

San Fran suntan (*kwn* SF, '70) a pallor.

sapphite ring (*camp*) sapphire ring.

satchels large bags underneath the eyes "They haven't invented the cream yet that'll cover up *these* satchels."

Saturday night at the movies (*kwn* S Calif, *fr* pros sl, '40s) cocksucking session (***line-up**) in the men's washroom of a movie theater.

say a mouthful (*rare*, '40s) to severely rebuke.
say high mass (*euphemism*) to kneel and fellate "He had to get up before nine and go say high mass—it was an early sunrise service, y'know."
Syn: **receive holy communion.**
say it (*exclam*) said when agreeing with a statement = you're right!
scandal soup (*camp*) tea as a gossip's refreshment.
scarper (Brit sl, *fr* Parlyaree // It *scappare* = to escape) to leave, run off; equivalent with American sl *bugging out.*
scenery general word for anything admired lustfully "I didn't care for the steam room though—fogged up the scenery.
Related term:
have a lot of scenery to be cruisy, *ie* packed to the roof with eligible men.
scenic 1. said of a place which affords fine cruising **2.** beautiful, well worth seizing "If she's not too scenic, just throw a flag over her face and go for old glory."
score 1. to locate a paying customer **2.** the purchaser of a **hustler* **3.** (*dated*, late '50s- mid '60s) IQ rating "He has a score" = he's a brain.
scour out the pussy to gargle; use a mouthwash.
scramble on somebody's head (*kwn* SF, '70, *fr* Hell's Angel sl *scramble* = motorcycle race) to beat up on somebody.
scrape job illegal abortion.
Syn: **coathanger operation; rabbit job.**
Also see **rabbit scraper.*
scream 1. to be obviously homosexual "Who writes your screamplay, darling?" **2.** to speak in an excited falsetto; by extension, to blabber hysterically "What were you screaming about just then?"
—basket [box] to have large genitals.
—er 1. the obvious queen **2.** (*dated*, mid-late '60s) radio DJ.
—ing flagrantly homosexual.
—ing chorus group forming a singer's background.
—on 1. to pick a fight, usually by dragging a reputation through the dirt **2.** to criticize "Miss Nader certainly screamed on the poorly made carriages" **3.** to enthusiastically like an item "I scream on statues of naked goddesses."
scuffle 1. a job "My scuffle cleans some pretty good coin" = I make good money from my job **2.** to work.
Syn: **gig; grind** ("I just don't have it in me to grind—I need more freak time")
scum bag (*fr* sl = prophylactic) a disreputable rascal; a knave.
scum pit small, lunchcounter restaurant; a greasy spoon.
Syn: **ptomaine palace.**
see how you are (*interj*) reflecting the speaker's insight about the listener's moral frailties (stinginess, envy, *etc*); roughly equivalent to "shame!" "See how you are? Wishing evil things on your lover like that!"
see the big dot[s] (*rare*, '70) to go to a movie "Lemme take a two article shit, then we'll see the big dots."
see you in bed (*interj*) see you later; bye-bye.
segregated used of a bar with an exclusively gay clientele.
sell somebody the medicine [show] to convince someone of a friend's outstanding qualities; to middleman for somebody "He don't have to sell me the medicine show, man, let me find out for myself."
sell wolf tickets to badger, yell at someone.
send somebody up (Brit gay sl) to ridicule, tease, make fun of another's standards.
sentral (*rare, camp, fr* central) sensual.
serial serious; devoted to one steady partner, steadfast and true-blue.

serve [some] tea to group together outside a restroom or bar to gossip; to gab everyone else's tricks out the door.

serve up some buns to bend over and spread the cheeks "I'll never forget the day I served up some toasted buns to some black guy at the tubs."

service to supply the means with which a regrettably nonreciprocal male finds orgasm; vulgarly, to be the hole for a piece of trade. Usually being serviced = same as being fellated, but anal intercourse may enter in at times.

—**station** any place, but generally a park restroom, where high school boys stop off on their way to school to be serviced.

set 1. group of friends, see *circle **2.** female breasts "He leaned over to get a better look at her set" **3.** (dated, fr musician sl) party.

set the table to change the bed linen; make the bed "Hazel Nagila always keeps her table set—she never knows when dinner is going to stay overnight."

sewer line[s] the telephone as the instrument of relaying fresh, juicy gossip. On a much broader level, the homosexual grapevine "Give me a buzz on the sewer line, Miss Montessa, after you've *orged* yourself."

sex incorporated for humorous effect into many words that normally begin with the syllables "ex-" or "six-"; eg sexciting, sexercise, sexpedition, sextile, sexty, etc.

sex anyone? direct line used to get a laugh when introduced to a shy crowd.

sexobatics out-of-the-ordinary sex positions.

sexteenager young man who tries out homosexuality, see *chicken.

Seymour (hetero sl) appellation given to weak or defenseless men "Seymour has a voice bell-like enough to sing vapid things like 'Honeycomb.'"

SFRB (kwn LV, '70) campy invitation to choose one of the following: oral intercourse (s-uck); normal coitus (f-uck); oral-anal copulation (r-im); or anal intercourse (b-rown). This presentation of a multiple choice is for jocular context and not posed as an actual question. Much more an in-joke than *sex anyone?

shake Norma (fr sl Norma = heterosexual) to abandon heterosexuality for homosexuality; to squelch a heterosexual past in favor of homoerotic ambitions.

shaker 1. homosexual loitering in front of a urinal shaking his penis pretending to knock the few remaining drops of urine from his organ. To say "it's a shakers' convention" = every urinal is occupied by a homosexual (no matter how you twist and shake, the last few drops go down your lake) **2.** (rare) hand, especially the right one.

shake the bushes to meet and fellate men in the densely wooded thickets of public parks.

shank woman without virtue; loose, immoral shrew.

shape up to to go to a place "Let's shape up to Finn's and throw matches at the flames."

share the rag (kwn SF, '70) to be hostile; to shift the guilt to another's shoulders, to pass the buck. Usually said of irate women who attack queens without provocation "Lady, don't share your rag with *me!*"

shatsy (shot'-sē, fr Ger Schatz = treasure) an endearment "We didn't know what it was, shatsy, but it was the world's largest, so we had to go see it."

Shattered Shane (camp) gay nickname for a heroin addict "You had your television mopped by some Shattered Shane—sweet Jesus, that sounds like some nineteen-fifty melodrama."

she (pron) he, used by effeminate homosexuals for themselves and friends. Eventually, however, most men end up being called she, which presents something of an identity crisis to those unaccustomed to the gay vernacular "Someday she'll come along—the man I love!" "She's black with ten inches—and I'm green with envy."

the shelf the balcony of a movie theater.

Related term:

on the shelf 1. sitting in the balcony **2.** (*dated*, '40s) still canned goods, *ie* virginal.

shell peas (*fr* pun made upon *pee* = urine) to unzip a partner's pants fly "Been shelling peas? Your kneepads are filthy!"

shells (*rare* if not *obs* altogether) clothing. Replaced by **rags, threads, vines,** and ***weeds.**

shine somebody on (70, *fr* black & motorcycle sl) to give someone the cold shoulder "Last time I saw Ron, he shined me on."

shit queen one with an abnormal interest in human feces, see ***kaka queen.**

shit, Sheila[Shirley] (*exclam*) expresses surprise, or, as is more often the case, utter exasperation and disgust. The names Sheila and Shirley give the otherwise blunt curse a harmonious, euphonious vitality "Shit, Shirley! This is the seventh time I've missed that Paul Newman flick on the tube."

shit through the eye of a needle to have diarrhea.

shlonger (*fr* Yid = a serpent) a lengthy penis "Did you ever swing on that shlonger of his?"

shmatta (shmät'-tä, *fr* Yid *schmatte* = rag) **1.** sanitary napkin, see ***rag** "Teething on a shmatta?" = cat got your tongue? **2.** woman with the morals of a blowfly **3.** a housedress; broadly any expensive garment casually dismissed as a hand-me-down "Oh, you mean this old cashmere shmatta?"

shnockered feeling the full effect of a narcotic "I'm too shnockered to talk to you about love right now."

shoot a mouse to urinate.

shoot eyes 1. to flirt **2.** to stare "I'm not one to say you're hefty, babycakes, but some man bearing a striking resemblance to a Captain Ahab has been shooting eyes at you all evening" **3.** to glower.

shop by phone 1. to make a date with a ***model 2.** to make homosexual contact by phone.

shop door the fly of a man's trousers "He came so much that he had to hang a 'be back at five' on his shop door."

shop name contrived nickname; one's invented stage name; alias. *eg* Dementia, Gina Lottabridge, The Mantrap, The Toothsome Fairy = "Bucky", *etc.*

shopworn having the worn look and feel of an old whore.

Also see ***tired.**

short circuited (*kwn* Calif, *fr* hip sl, late '60s) forgetful, absent minded due to overdosing drugs, usually LSD or downers; trailing off in the middle of sentences.

short roses (*fr* concept that long-stemmed American beauty roses = romantic feelings and courtship) **1.** romance nipped in the bud **2.** (*adj*) brief, to the point "He saw to it that my thing with Ted was short roses" "You wanted to talk with me? Okay, but make it short roses."

shot (?*fr* single shot multivibrator where one input will give one predetermined output) single orgasm.

Related term:

shot in the dark not knowing who was copulated, usually said of a faceless fuck at an orgy.

show biz 1. one's homosexual surroundings, *ie* gay society **2.** life.

Related term:

that's show biz that's the breaks of the game; that's the way the cookie crumbles (titty flops, artichoke hearts, meat balls *etc*) "He was found in a zipper factory—dead—with tongue lacerations? Well, that's show biz!"

showdog 1. any large dog trained to ravish female performers on stage "She's too young to take on a showdog—turn her loose with a Mexican hairless instead" **2.** any slick, fast-talking salesman, particularly one who steers servicemen into jewelry shops.

showgirl 1. homosexual showoff; one who hogs the limelight, not as common as *star **2.** cocksucker who gives a great performance **3.** (*kwn* LV, mid-late '60s) any Las Vegan homosexual; gay citizen of Show Town **4.** female impersonator "That showgirl died of lead poisoning—*Time* gave her a bad review." **5.** go-go boy; male dancer who kicks up his heels for leering clientele.

show kids homosexuals making a livelihood from the theater (actors, dancers, musicians, *etc*) "The Barn is where all the show kids go after four."

show tunes copulative grunts and groans; sex noises.
Related term:
hum a show tune groan with erotic pleasure.

shrimp 1. a small penis, see *small meat **2.** a toe **3.** to suck the toes of a partner, see *toe queen "His bag is shrimping drunk sailors."

shrimp job 1. act where man is sucked and fucked by his lover simultaneously, see *big J **2.** eroticism centered about another's tootsies.

shrine (*camp*) word used with tongue-in-cheek drollness to describe a place considered a dump.

shrink shocker (*kwn* SF, hip gay sl, '70-'71, *fr* sl *shrink* = psychiatrist) liberated, outspoken, unapologetic homosexual (from the gay militant's point of view); a bizarre homosexual in need of shock therapy (from a headshrinker's point of view). What yellow journalism calls an "acid head" ("Acid Head Rapes Mom!") "I guess it's all that health food that makes the shrink shocker turn so *green*."

shuck with somebody (*kwn* Southwest, late '60s, *fr* sl *shuck* = to lie) to put on an act of passionate interest during foreplay; to pretend to be erotically excited to keep from stifling a yawn. *Hustlers, looking at homosexuality as a sickness to be fleeced, call their insincere fooling around **shucking with it** ("I'm not queer, man, I just shuck around with it!")
Syn: **pulling a whore act.**

shug (diminutive of *sugar) an endearment "How was my has-been husband, shug—better'n nothing?"

shyckle (Brit gay sl) a wig "Get your shyckle on straight, luv, sharpy's out to ask you a few questions."

sick (*adj*) demented, mentally deranged; sickening by another's ethical code; anything conducive to nausea. To *hustlers and many *straights, the homosexual is sick. To the homosexual, however, it is the hustler who is sick, since he keeps denying his own sexuality; many straights are considered sick because they keep a closed mind about almost anything unknown. "A shit queen is sick except to another shit queen."
Syn: **ill** ("That's one ill woman ahead of us—she'd fall to her knees anywhere if someone'd yell 'mess call!'")

Sidney-Marie (*exclam*) outcry of joy, surprise, or indignation "Sidney-Marie! I like 'em built for speed not comfort!"

signal sit (*dated, kwn* LA, early '60s) usually found in the verbal phrase "to do the signal sit" = to sit at the bar buying expensive drinks. This practice of flashing bills signals that the sitter is willing to pay for his fun.

sign the register to make an appearance at the park's public toilet "I haven't time for a hearty breakfast, I have to go sign the register before that giddy queen hogs up the only throne in the house."

sil (short for silly) **1.** a looney character, see ***dizzy queen** **2.** (*dated*, les sl) female infatuated with another woman.

simp (*fr* simpleton) half-wit, numbskull.
   —y foolish, absurd "May you grow new teeth and skin, you simpy sumbitch!"

singang pack of rowdy, rambunctious homosexuals.

singer 1. prison sex slave, see ***punk 2.** perpetual pessimist; a chronic critic **3.** jalopy, see ***wheels.**

singe somebody's face to shove the cock all the way down the throat.

singe the finger[tips] to run the hand over a marvelously developed body. Often accompanied by a sssst sound, in imitation of being burned.

sing it out to complain, condemn at length; to express an opinion, especially if true. Feelings are often hurt when one sings [it out].
   Related terms:
   singing long verbal assault; stinging lecture.
   sing out, Marie (*exclam*) encouragement voiced to a fellow homosexual who is telling the truth. Syn: **tell it!**

single-barreled misogynistically homosexual. The single barrel refers to the anus.
   Also see ***double-barreled.**

SIR (*kwn* SF, *fr* Society for Individual Rights) homophilic organization. Pamphlets describing the positive aspects of homosexuality are printed and distributed by SIR as well as the monthly magazine *Vector*. Dances, picnics and other political forms of get-togethers are sponsored by SIR.

sis (*voc*) an endearment "Sis, the only things your pussy draws are things with wings."

sissy (Brit spelling: **cissy**) **1.** (hetero sl, *fr* sister) the effeminate homosexuality-bound son; a word with which alarmist fathers mock their own four-eyed, anemic offspring "If my kid ever became a sissy I'd break his fuckin' neck!" **2.** passive homosexual male "Honey, a *real* man—right in the middle of this nest o' sissies!"
   Related terms:
   the sissy (late '60s) dance step satirizing the elastic-wristed homosexual. Syn: **sissy stomp** (*kwn* LA); **sissy strut** (black gay sl).
   the sophisticated sissy (late '60s) slower, more hootchy-kootchy rendition of the dance.

sissy-suck 1. timid, poorly executed performance of fellation **2.** inadequate, deficient "Remember those sissy-suck medallions your real mother used to wear—they were big enough to hang on a wall."

sister one homosexual who is a close confidant to another—he will share anything but his bed with friends. A sister is sexually neutral with his comrades; he is a chum, not a lover. Sisters are in the same business, but only as competition **2.** (les sl) male homosexual befriended by lesbians.
   Related term:
   moya sestra (mō'-yä ses'-trä, *fr* film The Cat People, lit // Russ = my sister) blurted out by one homosexual when he sees another.
   your sister (*pron*) oneself "Your sister's fantastic voyage was behind 500 mics of 'baby jesus' acid!"
   —act 1. any skit acted out between two gays **2.** coitus between a gay boy and a straight woman.
   —in distress homosexual marked for trouble with either police

or young toughs "Mary! summer's really here! I can set my watch by the shriekings of our sisters in distress."

—in-law (*fr* pros sl = whore working for the same pimp) another homofilly living under the same stable. One borrows sugar from a sister-in-law, but never sex.

sitch (*fr* situation) predicament "I wouldn't find myself in a sitch like that faggot."
   Syn: **picklement** (*fr* baseball sl *pickle* = caught between bases.)

sit on a gold mine (*fr* pros sl, '40s) not sharing the riches, *ie* body. Used of beauteous heterosexuals ("It's all right for others, but I'll stick to girls, if you don't mind") and financially unused gays "Man, oh, man! What buns Joey's got—that kid's just sittin' on a gold mine."
   Syn: **he's fine but he's not mine!**

sixteener 16-paged comic book depicting the sex lives of cartoon greats such as Steve Canyon, *etc.*

sixty-eight 1. mutual fellatio wherein only one participant reaches climax "Sixty-eight, honey! And you haven't seen the *half* of it!" **2.** an IOU "He got it on a sixty-eight" = he got it on trust.

sixty-nine (*fr* numeral 69 showing two curled bodies) to practice orogenitalism "Know what the square root of sixty-nine is? 'Eight something'." Syn: **double header; head over heels [in love]; loop-de-loop** (late '60s); **play hoop snake [with somebody]** (*fr* mythological hoop snake who bit its own tail to form a ring for rolling down hills); **p's and q's.**
   Related terms:
   catch a sixty-nine to participate in mutual orogenitalism "I caught this marvelous sixty-nine in the garage attic."
   dinner beneath the bridge sixty-nining attempted by two partners who keep their knees bent throughout the entire performance "We'll have to fake it dinner beneath the bridge style; the rooms they give ya here have such small cots."
   route sixty-nine practice of sixty-nining. Syn: **linguistic exercise; six à neuf** (*fr* Fr); **soixante-neuf** (swä-sänt′-nöf *fr* Fr); **vice versa** ("Gay kids are just like straights; it's just that the gay ones dig their vice—versa.")
   sixty-niner a devotee of 69-ing "Wasn't it the gay sixty-niner who said 'two heads are better than buns!'" Extended to mean any male homosexual. Syn: **sixty-nine queen** ("he headed him off at the ass.")
   thirty-eight one half of sixty-nine, *ie* mutual fellatio with only one ejaculation. Syn: **34½; 37½.**

size abstract importance associated with the length of the penis "He doesn't go out for size—he says."
   Related term:
   thumb queen homosexual claiming an ability of correctly guessing the length of another's penis by the size and shape of the owner's thumb.
   —queen homosexual attracted solely by the length of his subject "Sure I'm a size queen—any size!" "Two things I detest—size queens and small cocks!" Syn: **big dick queen; whaler.**

skeet shooting (*kwn* SF, hip gay sl, '70) masturbating a partner and orally catching the ejaculated semen as it shoots through the air.

skin diver one who performs oral genitalism.

skinners 1. hands that can't stay to themselves. Syn: **Claws; hooks; paws 2.** sadists, whipcrackers.

skinny (*kwn* LV, late '60s, ?*fr* teen sl *do the skinnies* = to copulate) the scooped hollow located at the sides of each flexed gluteus maximus   "Pat Arno on the skinnies for me, will ya, Vern?"

skinny rub to rub the stiff cock between the buttock cheeks until climax; there is no intromission.
  Syn: **cracking; skiing down Happy Valley.**

skin queen ('71) one who regards his sex partners as objects rather than people; a gay sexist   "You're such a skin queen—all you think of is how tight the asshole gotta be."

skirt (*camp*) man's trousers.
  Related term:
  hitch [pull] up the skirt to pull at the pant cuff, usually while balanced on one foot.

slack [slag] (*kwn* SF, hip gay sl, '70, *fr pej* Brit sl *slag* = white woman dating a black man) going into an elegant ***gay bar** to hustle drinks. A game which develops into cat-and-mouse: the bolder the man who is treating becomes, the bigger the brush-off he receives.

slam somebody 1. (prison sl) to beat, see ***prison terminology 2.** (*dated*) to lock somebody in jail [the slam]   "What did Lillian slam her for—expired pushcart licenses?" **3.** to criticize   "We're not slamming you, Burt; there's nothing to slam."

slap (Brit gay sl, *fr* dated cant) face makeup   "Are you forty under all that slap?"

slay hearts to be breathtakingly beautiful; to have what it takes to be a femme fatale   "It's the muscles your muscles have that slay hearts."

slay somebody to betray another into the hands of his enemies.

sleepers sedatives, barbiturates, tranquilizers; also rotten movies, waltzes at rock concerts and boring neighbors.

sleep on each other to neck in a public park, used of teenagers.

slickered (*cf* Aus *shicker* // Yid-Heb *shikor* = drunk) intoxicated.

slick it down to coat the penis with a lubricant.

the slide (*dated*) establishment where men dressed as women solicit a male clientele.

slide into jelly (late '60s) to become fat[ter].

slip to age; lose muscle tone; to sag   "Slipping? That's rolling down the hill with the brakes off!"
  —page flab and facial wrinkles; signs of physical decay.

slip into a pile of shit to reach a peak in depression.

sloff it in (*fr* onomatopoetic *sloff* = a gagged gurgle) to shove the cock into someone's mouth.

slut hut 1. a whorehouse **2.** one's domicile, home   "Let's get out of this slut hut, Isabella, and air our clothes out."

SM sadism (*fr* Marquis de Sade, 19th cent Fr author) and masochism (*fr* Leopold von Sacher-Masoch, 19th cent Ger novelist); sexual pleasure derived from fetishes, pain, torture, domination, *etc*. The forms of SM range from very mild fantasies (wearing of uniforms, for example) all the way to heavy extremes.
  Syn: **sadie-maisie[mazzy]; S and M.**
  Related terms:
  B and D bondage and domination; sexual excitement related to binding and/or being bound in various positions with different types of binders (rope, handcuffs, leather thongs, *etc*). Forcing to perform and/or performing a variety of demeaning and contemptable actions for sexual satisfaction.
  bedroom leather shiny, fastidiously kept leather used primarily as a sexual front.
  blue velvets (*camp*) entire leather outfit.
  bondage queen one receiving erotic/masochistic gratification through the practice of being tied up, humiliated and then raped.
  brown leather newcomer to the leather crowd because he

doesn't know what color to wear (black leather is "in").
Syn: **white leather.**

chapel torture room equipped with implements of fun and games; a chamber of 'horrors" filled with toys. Syn: **game room; playhouse.**

concubine new recruit to SM practices who is bottoms.

cowboy overassertion of masculinity, usually in SM bars. Cowboys are desired by SM'ers, but the reverse may not necessarily hold pee-water.

fladge fiend[freak, queen] one who enjoys whipping or being whipped "That crippling sound you hear is some fladge fiend singing."

fladge party sadomasochistic romance with the passive partner being sweet-talked with whiplashes. Syn: **flag party[session].**

fluff all other gays as contemptuously viewed by SM'ers. Syn: **fluffy sweater set; twinkle toes.**

fucking buddies two who are not lovers cruising together for threesomes, *etc.*

garage queen (*camp*) a *closet case leather queen.

glass booties[slippers] (*camp*) leather boots. Syn: **naugahide slippers** (*camp*).

GSQ = a *golden shower queen; one who digs being pissed on, *etc.* Syn: **PF** (= piss freak); **PF flyer.**

***leather** the fetishistic wearing of leather is a subbranch of SM.

love bunny someone who cuddles with an SM'er; an SM'er's *trick who does not play rough.

M 1. masochist **2.** master.

Mary Motorcycle (*camp*) male homosexual whose sacred calf is a leather-upholstered motorcycle. Syn: **Motorcycle Mary.**

master partner who assumes psychological and physical dominance in the sex fantasy. Syn: **slaver; top man.**

milk to pinch the nipples severely and fasten pinching devices, such as clothespins, to them.

motor motorcycle. Syn: **murdercycle** (*camp*); **range.**

motorcycle drag[lace] (*camp*) leather outfit as worn by a motorcyclist.

Nora Naugahide (*camp*) one dressed in leather.

OD's (*fr* Army *sl*) olive drab, *ie* fatigues.

overlay motorcycle insignia; usually worn over leathers.

people on the other side gay non SM'ers.

play games to recreate fantasies as a sexual expression, *eg* being confined in a simulated jail and cruelly treated by a personal guard.

play god (*rare*) to carry out an SM fantasy to death, literally.

rivets (*camp*) studs on a leather jacket. Syn: **chrome.**

S 1. sadist **2.** slave.

sad-ass (*camp*) sadist "Know what Santa the Sad-ass sings at Yuletime: 'Sleigh bells sting.' "

slave[queen] masochistic partner in an SM passion play. Syn: **bottoms; S.**

slavist (*rare*) one who is equally excited with either the sadistic or masochistic role. His theme song: "The Object of my Aggression."

sleeper plain gold ear hoop.

toys sexual instruments of fun and pain (cock rings, cat-o-nines, handcuffs, leather gags, prick stretchers, whips, *etc.*)

vanilla bar a *gay bar that is not SM. Syn: **fluff parlor.**

wear[show] keys to display keys as a sex symbol. Traditionally keys worn on the left = sadist; right = masochist; in the middle of the back = open to suggestion. This code key varies everywhere, however.

whipper snapper (*camp*) sadistic whip wielder. Syn: **Wanda Welt** (*camp*).

smacky cute, attractive "A cop showed me his smacky badge and ruined love's greatest moment."

small meat a little penis (usually under six inches), symbolized by holding the little finger erect. To a *size queen, anything under ten inches is small meat: "Only nine inches? Sorry to hear about your deformity."

Syn: **biteful; dink[y]** ('40s, *fr sl dinkey* = insignificant // Scotch *dink* = neat); **IBM** (*kwn* LV, mid '60s = itty bitty meat); **frigid digit; jelly bean** (late '60s; Ant: **jawbreaker**); **knick-knack** ('70); **little meat** ("I love the little things about you—like your meat"); **minnow** ("Imagine my jow when his minnow grew into Moby's dick!"); **parlor peter[size]; peepee meat** (= child's penis); **pencil** (not to be confused with sl **pencil dick** = long, skinny cock: "What do you think this is—a pencil sharpener?"); **pinkie** ("Don't put a rubber over your pinkie, girl, or you'll smother it"); **short circuit** ("He spent all night trying to plug in his short circuit"); **shrimp[meat]** (*fr sl shrimp* = man of short stature); **tad** (*fr* dial *tad* = boy // ME *tode* = toad; also *cf tadpole* = wiggling gelatin-like stage of froghood); **tassel** (*rare*); **wagette** (*fr* sl *wag* = little boy's penis + feminine diminutive; also note sl *little red wagon* = cock).

Related term:

drip-dry lover (mid '60s) man with a small penis "He's a drip-dry. . .his joint is too short to shake." Syn: **Miss Rhode Island** (*fr* Rhode Island, the smallest state: "Don't let Miss Rhode Island push you around—he's no big meal!") Ant: **Texas longhorn.**

smart ('30s) smartly styled, elegant, fashionable **2.** sarcastically used of disasters, mismanagements and items of unimportance from the speaker's viewpoint "I think I'll go water the smart weeds" "Those teenies are stealin' a smart Rambler? They'll be s-o-r-r-y!" **3.** free-form adjective used much like the seafarer's "fuckin'" (as in "What's the fuckin' time" = what's the smart time?) "Show us where we are on the smart map, Captain!" "There's no smart cheese on *that* bagel, Gussie."

smegma (*camp*) because smegma's slang equivalent is *cheese, smegma is sometimes used jokingly to mean cheese as a dairy product "Still on your cottage smegma diet, Lardo?"

—roni (*camp*) **1.** macaroni and cheese **2.** any unclean dockworker.

smooth trade impeccably groomed male prostitutes catering to the needs of the rich. These youths are nurtured at being socially adept (and adaptable) with prominent figures.
Also see: *model, *trade.

smorgasbord on wheels (*kwn* Southwest, mid-late '60s) crowd of attractive beaux as seen by a homosexual driving past in his automobile.

smut 1. dirty, no-holds-barred sex "I'm in the mood for smut—not a tearoom social!" Syn: **orgy-room sex 2.** man radiating tawdry sex. Syn: **piece of smoot** (*camp*).

—ty (*adj*) lusciously lewd, raw.

—ty piece man oozing sex from every pore: highly complimentary.

snack bar homosexual key club offering its men-only membership a large orgy room "There was a great snack bar off of Miracle Mile, but it lost business when the gay fascists barred guys over thirty from joining."

snackpack 1. jockstraps, see *joys **2.** pocket-size box of tissues carried by park queens for last minute cleanups.

snake 1. see *cock **2.** two-faced woman.
snake pit 1. den of iniquity **2.** dingy, dim-lit *gay bar where the brazen clientele frighten straight gawkers. Syn: **snake den.**
snap [*it*] **1.** to tighten and loosen the anal sphincter muscle during ass-fucking, a feeling most savory to the active sodomist **2.** to rotate the buttocks while being fucked anally.
    Syn: *bite; **chuff; clamp** [**it silly**]; **cooch** (*fr* the hootchy-kootchy dance popularized in carnival midways); **fluff** [**it**] ("A pork-packer doesn't want you to fluff it when he socks it t'ya; he wants you to roll over and stay dead"); **grind** (*fr* the stripteaser's bumps and grinds).
snap shit (*fr* naut sl) to get the lead out, buckle down and get to work "Tell Conchita to snap shit, or she'll miss all the orders coming in."
snap somebody off 1. to convey displeasure by directing a loud fingersnap towards the offending party. The closer the snap is made to the offender's face, the larger the contempt. "Snap that, toad!" = take *that!* **2.** not to give somebody a chance to redeem himself; shut somebody off "The Chronicle sure snapped the mayor off."
snap somebody's bra straps (*camp*) to break someone's back; to throw one down and render him helpless.
snarf 1. to sniff bicycle seats, see *rim **2.** (*camp*) to smell anything "Did you snarf the flowers? They sure didn't smell sweaty."
snatch somebody's wig-hat off to pull somebody's hair out of their head; to throttle an opponent.
    Syn: **snatch somebody baldheaded.**
sneak queen homosexual's unfaithful lover "Get this, you sneak queen, this gown isn't big enough for the two of us!"
snow 1. (black gay sl) white people in general "Too much snow in that town, girl, gets *way* too *cold* for my blood" **2.** sobriquet for an albino Negro **3.** (*fr* narc sl) cocaine, see *stardust.
    —**banks** (black gay sl) porcelain white butt of a Caucasian homosexual.
    —**blindness** (*kwn* SF, '70) being dazzled by a friend's newly dyed blond hair "Cliff must have been here—it looks as if everyone is undergoing treatment for snow blindness."
    —**flake queen** ('40s) homosexual who has his partner masturbate onto his body.
    —**flurries** (black gay sl) trouble with the whites.
    —**plow** black man who rapes a white boy.
so (*adv*) very much like —, in the same vein as —, —**esque** "His bathroom is so Esther Williams—it's like a friggin' underwater ballet just to douche."
so a (*adv*) to such a degree "He's so a Yasha!" = He's such a fool.
soap job homosexual coitus utilizing soap lather as the lubricant.
social commentator a blabbermouth.
socialize to spoil what could have been a beautiful relationship with too much chatter; to talk oneself right out of bed.
social worker 1. homosexual who cruises the welfare lines **2.** (*kwn* LV, mid '60s) homosexual who is the first to introduce himself to cute out-of-towners—the biggest hot spot they'll be shown will be his bedroom **3.** (*kwn* SF, black gay sl, late '60-'71) homosexual who dates members of another race, *eg* black man who has a white lover is **doing social work.**
Sodom (*fr* Heb *S'dom* = biblical town destroyed by God) any place, such as a town or penal institution, with a large percentage of male homosexuals.

—**partner** pickup for a *****three way** "The sodom partner has *got* to go—his swish alps are avalanching."

—**roulette** society's gamble that a young man sent up with hardened criminals will not suffer anal indignities but will someday return to his friends and relatives a better man.

—**y factory** jail as a training base for homosexuals.

Sod O My U (*camp*) boys' school where homosexuality runs rampant "Was the graduation get-up from Sod O My U leathers or black lace?"

sofa case (late '60s) an unconfident homosexual; he stays at home pining away "That's as bad as a sofa case madly in love with a closet queen."

soft as puppy shit 1. delicate, breakable **2.** generous, giving, trusting.

softie lax, unaroused penis.
Related term:
petrified softie cock that can't become erect—they say—because of large liquor intake.

soiree (swä-rä´, *fr* Fr) social affair given by and for homosexuals. Not to be confused with *****party** which hints at an orgy later on in the evening.

some several[s] 1. (*adj*) several "How many cooks went out on strike? Oh, some several!" **2.** (*adv*) at times, sometimes "There's been some severals when I stayed up with him when he was puking his fool head off."

something to settle the dust (*camp*, '40s) drink of old red-eye.

so music musical

soonest soon "See you soonest, ducklips!"

SOS (anal invitation coined by foolhardy sailors) = stoop over, sport!

so sweet he comes honey attractive, handsome.
Syn: **so sweet he drives a Coke truck; so sweet he humps Bambi.**

souffled ('71) drunk "Know how to sleep when you're souffled? With one foot on the floor."
Syn: **snot-flinging drunk.**

soul sauce 1. (black gay sl) soul music "Put on some soul sauce; the wake is over!" Syn: **sounds** (late '50s-mid '60s: "Turn on some sounds" = turn on the radio) **2.** black man's semen, see *****come.**

soundproof bra padded bra.

soundtrack bestial noises made during sexing.
Related term:
donkey serenade slobbering noises made by fellator as he sucks cock.

soup 1. sweat **2.** anal oil **3.** broadly, fecal matter "You got soup all over your dick, man!"

—**y** muggy; sticky and sweaty.

sour 1. unpleasant **2.** poor, faulty "That's a sour excuse!"

sour come 1. foul-tasting semen **2.** (*camp*) sour grapes "Sounds like sour come to me; I think you'd *love* getting into his drawers."

south of the border ('40s) the vagina.

souvenir (*fr* pros sl, '40s) husband of an ex-whore.

sow 1. any fat homosexual **2.** (*pej*) obtrusive homosexual "What's in that sow's head—cold kasha?"

sparks imitation jewels.

spatula case (*kwn* SF, '70) boy who is so filthy that the encrusted grime must be scraped off before fucking commences.

specialize (pros sl) to be tops at making love in some specific way.

speckies (*dated*) treckles brought out by repeated sun exposure.

spikey (Brit) nasty tempered.

spinach queen (*kwn* SF, '71) man who sucks a cock just after it has fucked his ass.

spin-the-bottle mentality said of a die-hard romanticist still living in the past.
    Also see: *nineteen-fifty.

spit baby (*fr* gay maxim "you can't make babies out of spit") the ejaculation caught within a cocksucker's mouth "So she's having an affair with a fruit! Whatcha worried about—spit babies?"

spit [somebody] out the window (*dated*, '40s) to refuse swallowing semen after performing fellatio. Often considered insulting.

split 1. the vagina **2.** (*fr* black sl, '60s) to leave "The love-birds split after they saw the Austrian shades in the toy-toy room."

split belly any woman "You *know* split bellies can't drive."
    Syn: **split stuff** ("So the split stuff above us moved, eh? Another successful hearth transplant."); **split tail.**

split egg (*fr* pros sl, '40s) heterosexual coitus in which the man and woman both lay sideways.

split party party with male and female homosexuals as guests.

spook somebody's joint to frighten away someone else's trick by excessive camping "I just can't take you to supermarkets anymore, Mess, you spook my joints."

spooney (Brit) effeminate acting heterosexual.

spooning (*dated*, Brit) adolescent explorations of homosexual behavior, usually in boys' schools.

spoon position where two tribades rock each other into orgasm.
    Syn: **lying spoons; spoons.**

sporty willing to give homosexuality a try.

spot (*kwn* NYC, short for hot spot) any place besides a bar where homosexuals meet.

spot somebody out to stalk a *trick "When I found out that piece of shit was spotting me out, I put spot remover on my shopping list."

spray somebody's tonsils to come in his mouth.

spray starch the psychic substance keeping heterosexual wrists straight.

spread jam to lie "You spreadin' jam, or is that on the level?"

the Spreckles don't live here[there] (*interj*) **1.** said of one who keeps a sour disposition **2.** there's no sugar left.
    Ant: **that don't need no sugar!**

spud queen fat person, see *obesity.

square somebody to have heterosexual coitus "Square your wife before you square your mistress: remember the priorities."

squash (*fr* black sl) head, by extension brains "Mind-fucking gives me a limp squash."

squat to pee (*camp*) to be so effeminate that it really is difficult to detect gender "Wow, when that Miss Humperdink gets into drag, she really squats to pee."

squaw valley (*camp*) kitchen "Wish I had me a nigger in Squaw Valley—white or black, I don't care, I'm not prejudiced."

squeal 1. young, anal tightness **2.** to make sounds of pleasure and/or protest while being fucked "Harry's such a sadist—he can only get his rocks off when I squeal like a stuck pig."
    Syn: **squawk** (especially used of *chicken).

squeeze beads to be religious.

squinky dashing.
    Syn: **squeaky.**

squirm to wiggle the ass while being fucked "I'll have that big cowboy squirming in five minutes."

stage 1. another theatrical term for life "That's the stage, girl—

unfeeling and unreal" **2.** one's place of employment.
Related terms:
clear the stage to get rid of people "Clear the stage, I've got a splitting headache."
on stage 1. being a public spectacle **2.** at work.
set the stage to make the bed before sex.
—crew outdoor workers—ditch diggers, garbagemen, *etc.*
—hand nine-to-fiver.
—manager 1. boss **2.** a pimp.
—name 1. female impersonator's professional title—Hirta Mingle, Tara Sunder, Seth Pool **2.** an alias, *nom de plume.*
—struck in love.
stallion hung like one.
standard equipment ordinary sized cock.
Standick (*camp*) gay surname = Stanwyck.
stand-in married homosexual's back street lover.
Syn: **summer replacement** ("My summer replacement *should* be toll free—after charging all those years.")
stand up and cheer[shout] female orgasm.
star 1. a strong personality; magnetic "A star is bored!" **2.** a showoff, egotistical "It's really hard being a star! 'How would you know?'" **3.** any male homosexual "Who's the new star at Kelly's garage? Ty Hardon?"
Related term:
starlette young homosexual, especially if a real character.
stardust cocaine "The nightingale sings its fairy tale/ And I am once again with you—stardust!"
Related terms:
hoping reflexively sniffing long after having had cocaine nasally.
shovel snow to "snort" cocaine.
velvet mallet the effect of "coke" with a marijuana chaser.
winter wonderland euphoria produced by cocaine.
star-struck heterosexual fascination with homosexual life.
stash 1. (*dated*) moustache **2.** (*fr* black sl) drug cache **3.** (*fr* black sl) to hide something of value.
stash back (mid '60s) to pose seductively for passersby.
Related term:
stash back the ass to tense so that the buttocks are clearly outlined.
station 1. cruisy bus or train depot **2.** park bench.
Related term:
stationed sitting on a park bench.
stations (*fr* Lenten stations of the cross) trials, tribulations, hassles "I don't know if I can be my old gay self with all the stations lately."
Related terms:
do the stations of the cross at Saint Trinian's (*kwn* SF, '72, *fr* series of English satirical movies of the '50s) to cruise all eight floors at the Embarcadero YMCA in San Francisco.
read somebody the stations 1. to gripe "Don't read me the stations, dear, I already told you—twice—that the red-headed punk would keep you broke" **2.** to scold.
statue queen beautiful, young gay in love with himself.
Syn: **narcissistic fairy.**
stay cream rubbed on an erection, it is claimed this will prevent premature ejaculation.
steak house a *gay bar or key club where sex goes on.
steam a beer (*kwn* NYC) to nurse a drink "There's no need to steam your beer, Alan, they're only twenty cents a throw."
steamer trunks (*camp*) said of someone whose *basket is so full that it looks inorganic ("stuffed").

Stella (Cape Town gay sl) **1.** a thief   **2.** (v) to steal.
Stella Dallas 1. soap opera theatrics   **2.** a loser, especially if
    melodramatic "Stella Dallas here is addicted to life—know
    where she can go through withdrawals?"
step blisters to walk great distances.
step out to meet Jesus 1. to step in front of a moving vehicle
    2. to jaywalk.
stepper someone who gets something done.
stewed fruit 1. drunk homosexual   **2.** one overcome by heat
    (natural or steamroom variety).
stir some shit (kwn San Diego, late '60s) to gossip.
stone queer a thorough homosexual.
        Syn: **stomp-down queen.**
stop some more (camp) *gay line knitted from a Freudian slip.
store queen one who likes and is good at shopping.
story hang-up, modus vivendi "What's his story—is he majoring
    in comic books?"
straight 1. (n) heterosexual; following the straight and narrow
    "Why do you hang around straights—hope some of it might rub
    off?" Syn: **BM** (Cape Town gay sl, fr baby maker or bloody
    man); **buga** (boo'-ga, Mex gal sl, cf boogieman); **citizen; civilian;
    cleavage queen** (camp); **commoner; het[ero]** ("Hetero is hor-
    rible! Gay is gruesome!"); **homie** (ho'-mē, Brit gay sl, fr Parly-
    aree // It uomo = man); *jam; **Norma; norm[al]; normal bag**
    (Cape Town gay sl); **outsider; peasant; punt** ("Punts think that
    marriage is a wonderful institution—I personally don't care to
    spend the rest of my life in an institution"); **pussy pusher; reg-
    ular guy** (teen sl); **square** (dated: "Oh, fudge, they're squares,
    that means I'll have to be nice"); **straight-arrow; straightnick**
    (dated)   **2.** (adj) heterosexual "Chuck can't even talk to
    a cute straight man without breaking into tears and begging."
    Syn: **cow-simple** (= sexually allured by women); **VF** (= very
    formal). Ant: **crooked.**
    —arrow queer conventional-appearing gay boy. Syn: **straight
    gay.**
    —for the nearest dressmaker (camp) one whose heterosexuality
    is not convincing.
    —somebody code for indicating someone's heterosexuality
    "That's the one you're after, the rest aren't for you" = he's
    the only straight one in the group.
    —trick normal heterosexual position.
strap some of that good pussy on me invitation to fuck.
strawberry kool-aid (camp) Jungle Gardenia perfume.
strawberry patch 1. naturally red pubes   **2.** dyed red pubes.
street clothes ordinary wearing apparel.
        Syn: **civvies.**
street queen homeless, penniless, usually long-haired gay.
street trick sidewalk pickup.
Stretch (camp) pet name for a big cock and/or its owner "I can't
    have you drive me into the salon, Stretch, even though I
    do love making an entrance."
strides (fr black sl, '40s) pants.
string[bean] queen tall, thin gay boy "Well, the stringbean queen
    certainly outdid herself this time around."
strung out on someone (fr narc sl strung out = addicted) to be
    hopelessly in love.
stud epitome of manhood   "Hiya, stud, can I run my fingers through
    your DA?"
    —busting beating homosexuals.
    —house 1. men's dormitory   **2.** male brothel.
    —ly masculine "How many studly members did you let in
    under the gate?"

—**service** hiring a man, usually for bedtime companionship.
stuff **1.** sex appeal "Baby, I got the stuff to turn you on like a sun lamp" **2.** erogenous zones of the body "Wear some tighter duds to show off your stuff, and you'll stop your circulation" **3.** sexy man **4.** see *punk.
stuffed right and pressed tight dressed in tight pants.
stuffed turkey middle-aged *obesity.
stuffins said of a cock too large and thick to comfortably handle.
    Syn: **meat leftovers; stuffins for the turkey.**
stumble all over the dick tongue-tied when talking to an attractive person.
stunned (*camp*) stoned "One toke and you're stunned on your ash."
stun[ners] (influenced by sl *stones* = jewelry) paste jewelry; rhinestones.
sublimation (*kwn* SF, late '60s) cigarettes.
suck **1.** to practice orogenitalism, see *blow "I suck-a de motion!" **2.** to lack polish; anything of the poorest quality "The earth doesn't have gravity—it just sucks" "Vacuum cleaners suck!"
    —**and waffle** (Brit) dimwitted, wishy-washy.
    —**er** **1.** (hetero sl) male homosexual **2.** any task draining the doer of his energies; a catastrophe, bummer "The rent is the biggest sucker out of it all."
    —**ers** lips "All I want for Christmas is a divorce from those suckers."
    —**fuck, tickle balls and rim** to be an expert lovemaker.
    —**hole** **1.** mouth "Shut your suck-hole, the draft is blowing your mustache away" **2.** see *glory hole.
    —**onal** = seconal; a sedative children call "reds."
    —**shoppe** (suk sho'-pē) gay afterhours coffe-shop.
    —**sy** attractive to a cocksucker's taste.
suck up **1.** to drink alcoholic beverages "Keeping sucking up that ale and by tomorrow morning your breath will smell like a cacophony of asshole." **2.** to really put the food away. Syn: **suck down** ("Never heard of cyclones? Wait till you see my baby brother suck down the food after a hard day's.")
sucky blah, nowhere, yesterday's news "What a sucky deal we gave the Indians!"
suction cocksucker's standard of excellence "How's his suction?" = how good does he suck?
suds (*fr* black & teen sl) beer.
sudsing to fuck in the shower.
suffer (*exclam*) = eat your heart out!
sugar **1.** one's current heartthrob "One thing! I really like some spice in *my* sugars" **2.** kiss, as in "give me some sugar" = give me a kiss **3.** (*voc*) = hey, mac "Listen, sugar, there's something shitty around here besides this rolling pin!"
sugar daddy (*fr* '20s sl *sugar* = money) older man who supports a younger lover ("My heart belongs to daddy, because my daddy treats me so well")
    Syn: **angel** (*rare*); **papa gateau** (pä'-pä gä-tō', *fr* Fr = daddy cake); **Santa Claus** ("There must be a Santa Claus—I saw a want ad for one"); **sponsor.**
sugar finger **1.** middle finger **2.** to insert the finger into a partner's ass, see *finger fuck.
sugar loaf a *kept boy.
    Syn: **sugar babe.**
sugar mama effeminate homosexual who keeps her lover.
sugar pants tight slacks (because they draw flies).
sugar shaker clenched fist.
sugar trick (*kwn* SF, '70) one left with the bar bill.

Related term:

sugar trip cadging someone into buying drinks before leaving with someone else.

summer stock used in the expression "it's the same old summer stock" = it's the same old thing.

sunflower seeds amphetamine tablets.

sunken treasure 1. latent homosexual **2.** man's *basket.

super (fr superlative) **1.** exhilarating, refreshing, wonderful **2.** an affirmative "Super, we're all going to Greece" **3.** (adv) very, absolutely "Impersonation isn't a crime—it's super good eaves-dropping" "Superchicken is when you don't dig chicken, but you see that and you do!"

sure, shug (interj) sarcasm directed at pie-sky promises "'I'll make a million with these hips'" Ans: "'Sure, shug!'"

Susan Saliva slobbering cocksucker; homosexual living by his spits.

swan song leaving the audience to fare for itself, bowing out.

swarm bar packed to the gills *gay bar.

sweater girl[queen] one who wears expensive, fluffy sweaters; hence a dead giveaway.

sweathog squat, fat female "Has he rolled his sweathog bride across the threshhold yet?"

sweet 1. young, tender, mouth-watering **2.** (kwn LA, '70) short for sweet talk "I'll sweet to Greg about it."

—cakes (voc) an endearment "Your two o'clock is still here, sweetcakes, on your collar." Syn: **sweethips.**

—heart (voc) ironic endearment "Reenlisting, sweetheart, is like cutting off your cock so you don't have to piss anymore."

—ie (voc) "Let me run my fingers through your hair, sweetie, the towels àre all filthy" "Gimmie another drink, sweetie, I can still hear you." Syn: **sweetie-pie** ("Turn over, sweetie-pie, I wanna slip into something comfortable"); **sweetness** ("Sweetness, the old masturbate's home"); **sweets** ("Friends are people you look for, sweets, and look out for"); **sweetums** ("Twenty-years old, sweetums? That means twenty years of shit passing through.")

sweet leech (dated, les sl) lesbian who sponges off her lover.

sweetlips 1. man with sensual, full lips **2.** good kisser **3.** term of affection **4.** (fr naut sl) a farter "Speak again, sweetlips, I'll find you yet!"

sweet people (dated, hetero sl) male couple; not meant derog-atorily "The sweet people have done wonders to their yard."

swift 1. ahead of one's time, avant-garde **2.** clever "Was that swift? You almost killed us all trying to light your cigarette while driving." **3.** good-looking.

Syn: **swift-looking.**

swill (camp) a tepid swell "Gee, it's just swill that you dropped in from Europe—where are you going to stay?"

swing to be open, free "He swings" = he's okay.

Related terms:

swing butch to be virile, manly. Ant: **swing femme.**

swinger one who enjoys pluralism.

Syn: **jalador** (khä-lä-thōr'; Mex = hauler of ashes).

swing wide 1. to roll with the punches **2.** (n) satyr; whoremonger.

swingy 1. bisexual **2.** fun; predecessor of groovy and kicky "One more earthquake and this swingy metropolis will be renamed Pancake Village."

swish 1. passive homosexual "Remember the swish who traded his menstrual cycle in for a Yamaha?" Syn: **swisher 2.** to overplay homosexual gestures, by extension to walk "Gone swishing!" Syn: **butterfly** ("Queens butterfly through Cost Plus because they can't afford Europe"); *mince; sashay; switch; walk with a lisp** (kwn SF, late '60s).

—y effeminate, tinged with homosexuality; attuned to playing the passive role. Syn: **swish** ("It was caught in a fire—now it's swish charred.")

syrup (*cf* Fr *sirupeux* = syrupy = "corn," "schmaltz") mushy music.

taco tunes (*camp*) Mexican music.

tacky general word for describing anything of poor quality or uncouth; dowdy; inferior; in shabby taste "His bone was so tacky I had to bury it."
Syn: **tangy** (*kwn* SF, late '60s); **tatty** (Brit gay sl).
Related term:
tacks tacky people.

tadpole found in the expression **going to the tadpole ball** = **1.** to keep company with sailors; to be in the swim of things **2.** to tour a docked ship.

take a bow to leave, usually by suicide, because of the feeling of not being wanted.
Syn: **let someone else on stage.**

take a hair to follow a whim "One day he took a hair and started ticklin' the ovaries" = he discovered girls after being gay.

take a legal piss to use a men's room legitimately.

take a trip around the world [**in eighty ways**] to lick a lover's body—everywhere.
Syn: **go around the world; go all over town with somebody.**
Related terms:
grand tour the licking itself ("We'll make the grand tour at my place, baby, just let me stop at the next Safeway and score some butter.") Syn: **spit bath; tongue bath.**
fellow traveler companion in trips around the world.
Ich bin von Kopf bis Fuss auf Liebe eingestehlt (*fr* Ger song in *The Blue Angel* = I'm from head to feet in love) also refers to a trip around the world.

take a turn in the barrel (*fr* naut sl) to be fucked after being the fucker so many times before.

take it anyway open to all varieties of sex aggression.
Ant: **specialize; take it one way.**

take it easy (*interj*) farewell; answered sometimes with "I'll take it anyway I can get it!"

take one on a trip (*dated*) to lie.

take one's bed (*kwn* SF, late '60s) to sleep with another man's husband.
Syn: **get one's bed** ("Honey, Ralph and I are offering you board, so don't get my bed.")

take out insurance (pros sl) **1.** to travel with another for safety **2.** two people cruising in order to attract a three- or even a four-way.

Syn: **double-dating.**

take the vapors (*dated*) **1.** to let off steam in a *baths **2.** (*camp*) to wash dishes professionally.

take your trip (*imp*) do what you want, just don't bother me.

talent young, attractive boys "Personally, I don't like my talent looking hired."

Related term:

talent scout person engaged in recruiting what he considers promising young boys.

talk dirt[y] 1. to use obscenities to bring on climax **2.** to make a come-on to a passing lovely.

talk in blues and greens (late '60s) to speak stoned on acid; sometimes, to babble, be inarticulate.

talk in [deep] hues of magnolia to speak with a southern accent.

talking (les prison sl) engaged in homosexual activity.

talk shop to talk about gay subjects.

Related term:

talk slop talk about sex, usually in glowing terms. Syn: **give a blow-by-blow.**

talk to management (*camp*) pray to God.

talons fingernails.

Syn: **shithooks.**

tam (*fr* tam o'shanter) any cap or hat.

tampered with having experienced homosexuality (especially anal intercourse) at an early age "He was tampered with at the age of thirteen; an uncle, I think he told me."

tangerine (?*fr* rhyming sl) methedrine.

tant (?*fr* t'ain't = t'ain't one or the other) area between the genitals and the anus.

tarantula eyes outrageously made-up eyes "I have a rumor in the top drawer that Alice Cooper's tarantula eyes are for real."

tar baby chain smoker.

Syn: **smoked meat** ('71).

taster tongue "He just worked the old taster right up there."

tasty tantalizing, inviting.

—cover tightly fitting pants "Who's the cattle stampede in the tasty cover? He sure shows a lot of beef."

—upholstery righteous threads.

tat (Brit gay sl) a white elephant, an eyesore.

tat queen (Brit gay sl) antique dealer or collector.

tat up (Brit gay sl) to piece something together; to create something new out of leftovers.

tattoo boy one who flashes assorted tattoos.

—queen homosexual who has a sexual interest in tattoos.

tavern maid (*camp*) guy who collects the empty bottles in a *gay bar.**

TBH (Cape Town gay sl) can be made.

tea 1. (Brit gay sl) urine **2.** (*dated, fr* narc sl) marijuana.

Related terms:

have some tea engage in small talk.

read the tea leaves to smoke grass.

tea engagement an appointment kept with someone in a public john.

teagarden what usually surrounds popular men's rooms: a park.

teahouse [of the August moon] public toilet.

Syn: **bif** ("I left the window open in the bif in a desparate attempt to save mankind"); **clubhouse; cornhole palace; cottage** (Brit gay sl); **crapper; greenhouse; lonelyhearts' club; loo** (Brit, ?*fr* Waterloo punning water closet); **luncheonette; marble palace** ("Such a big word—did you learn that from reading the walls at the marble palace?"); **palace** (*rare*); **penile colony; shithouse; shitter; tearoom; throne room; toy-toy**

("How were the toy-toys in Albaturkey?"); **trading post** (*kwn* LV, black gay sl, mid '60s).

Related terms:

cottage (Brit gay sl) to loiter in washrooms "The dear was nicked for cottaging."

tearoom trade men who dig getting blown in public lavatories.

toilet queen homosexual haunting the porcelain halls of a men's room for chance meetings with other men. Toilet queens have toilet cruising down to a fine art. They are skilled scribes who send small messages of love (ballpointed onto flimsy toilet paper, no easy feat) underneath the toilet partition. They also are clever with their hands, and are accustomed to masturbating interested men from beneath the partition. "If Tilly doesn't carry that toilet queen away the crabs and cooties will." Syn: **closet queen** (*rare, fr* water closet); **johnny queen; privy queen; stool pigeon; tearoom queen; throne queen; Toilet Tessie** (*camp* nickname: "That's as sad as Toilet Tessie standing in front of a stall without a dime"); **washroom faggot** (*pej*).

teddy bear anybody who is cuddly "I'm afraid 'Teddy Bear' had all his money tied up in bonds—*bail* bonds."

tee'd [to the tits] [very] drunk.

teenie-weenie collectively, teenagers willing to unzip for cocksuckers; they love having their suckers pecked.

telephone hustlers those who leave their phone numbers on the walls of public toilets.

Related term:

telephoner the one who answers the ad.

telephone trade former trick who keeps calling for more. Enough of them and a phoned-in telephone trade has been built up.

tell me (*interj*) = I know all about it.

Syn: **I'm hip; *really.**

telly (Brit) television set "He's got his telly on a five-finger discount."

Syn: **bozo box; ghost box** (especially used of early-in-the-morning TV).

temperamental homosexual "You know how these stars are—temperamental."

tender chick (les sl) homosexually inexperienced teen-aged girl "I sure could dig a tender chick—I'm fed up to here with tough old birds."

tenderfoot latent homosexual, who, with a slight push, could become gay.

tender talent young, bored boys who seek out cocksuckers when nothing else is happening.

ten-inch somebody (*kwn* SF, late '60s) **1.** to lie, tell a fish story **2.** to tantalize, arouse "Stop ten-inching me, man, Mexico can't be as great as all that."

tent (*camp*) homosexual's room.

Syn: **star's dressing chamber [room].**

tenting same as *camping.

terrible actress mommy. Syn: **the war department.**

terrif terrific, first rate.

thanks a house sarcastic thanks a lot "You ate the last brownie? Thanks a house, doll!"

thank you remark = I agree "The joke's in his mouth, honey? Thank you, I couldn't have said it better m'self."

Syn: **good night!** (*kwn* SF, '72).

that hole (*pej*) third person pronoun "That hole's house ain't bad—if you dig compost heaps."

Syn: **that one** (not necessarily pejorative: "Ebry time dat one flush dis crapper, it fuck up the telebizhun.")

the 1. often prefixed to imply individuality, *eg* **The Animal** = one who eats **2.** prefixed to place or locale to indicate familiarity, hipness and acceptance, *eg* **The Beach** = San Francisco's North Beach area **3.** used before specific words to make common nouns sl, *eg* **the fear** = paranoia.

them as found in **one of them** = heterosexual "One of them was so scared, he was eighteen inches higher sitting down."

theme party masquerade party with a theme "The theme party is 'gods and goddesses,' so I'm going as Norma Jean."

the party's over (*interj*) an irritated good night.

thick ('71) enjoyable, splendid.
    Syn: **heavy.**

third sex homosexuality "The third sex is here to stay; only the addresses change—Greece, Rome, Berlin . . ."

third venereal disease (*kwn* NYC, late '60s) hepatitis or mononucleosis.

thirty-forty-dead (ther'-for-ded') remark showing how some homosexuals view their longevity.

this one first person singular, at times, interchangeable with ***that one** "This one doesn't look like a cow—his eyes aren't brown enough."

those (*pej*) women.

three B's 1. the limits of the gay ghetto: bars, baths and beaches **2.** (hustler sl) blow job, bed and breakfast.

three bags full (late '60s) that's a lie; bullshit!

three decker (pros-hustler sl) one man fucking another man who is fucking a woman.

three-letter man (*pej*, hetero sl, *fr* F-A-G) male homosexual.

three-sheeting (carnival sl = hanging posters over old posters) to continue wearing makeup after the performance "In *The Damned*, Helmut Berger shows an example of three-sheeting by keeping his Marlene Dietrich makeup on at a formal dinner."

three-way group sex between three participants "Ain't no three ways about it—he's packing."
    Syn: **chance sandwich; design for living; flesh sandwich; menage a trois** (mā-näzh'-ə-twä', *fr* Fr = houskeeping set up by three people); **seance a trois** (sē-äns'-ə-twä', *fr* Fr = meeting of three people "He's so dumb, he thinks a seance a trois is when some queen calls a few twats back from the dead."); **three high; threesies; three-way split[swing]; triple shag.**
    Related terms:
    couple freak (late '60s) husband who digs seeing his wife in bed with another man as well has having sex with him.
    couple friend one who goes to bed with a straight or homosexual couple.
    sharpen the pencil to instigate a three way.
    three-layer cake anal intercourse simultaneously performed by two men in a three-way.
    —marriage living arrangement in which three people try to maintain a mutual sex life.

thrill orgasm "How d'ya get yer thrills, kid—by pissin' up ropes?"

throat caesarean (*camp*) throat slit from ear to ear.

throne (*camp*) toilet seat "C'mon down off of that throne with your hands up!"
    Syn: **high chair.**

throw it up [in one's face] to never let somebody live something down.

throw lines to retort more brilliantly than attacked.

throw some piss to browbeat, intimidate.

tiara (*camp*) **1.** any headcovering worn by a homosexual "Will

the Motorcycle Mary in the front row please remove her tiara!"
2. homosexuality.
Related term:
to doff[pawn] the tiara to settle down to the porch rocker; tucked away in the closet.

ticklers fingers.

tight pin somebody (*dated, fr* black sl *tight* = friendly) to stare.

Tijuana Bible really putrid pornography "I'm wallpapering my den in Tijuana Bible."

Tijuana racetrack the diarrhea run from bed to bucket.

tiki to urinate "I have to go tiki so bad my back teeth are whistlin' 'Swanee.'"

Timesqueer (*dated,* hetero sl) homosexual cruising NYC's Times Square.

Tink[er Bell] (*camp*) **1.** pleasingly plump gay boy "You've got a lot of excess weight, Tink—all from the mouth up" **2.** anybody who wears bells.

tinkle to piss.
Syn: **twinkle.**

tinsel 1. glittering facade covering cheapness and vulgarity **2.** gray streaks starting to appear in the hair.
Syn: **tinfoil.**
Related terms:
cut away the tinsel to present a true picture of life.
tinseled hair hair dyed or streaked with gray.

tip originally, to take mincing steps; now, any arriving, departing or walking is handled by the word (*cf* Brit gay sl *mince* wed precisely in the same manner) "Tip on out and tell me if it's raining."

tired decrepit, overworked, threadbare, tiring, on its last legs.
—lines stale jokes; last year's wisecracks.
—old thing[queen, woman] 1. homosexual who has spent all of his youth and vigor **2.** one who has been had by everybody **3.** someone with the same tiresome routine in bed.
—rabbit penis incapable of erection.

tish (*fr* dial *tetch* = a touch) small amount, pinch, wee bit "His foreskin was a tish green—so we had to amputate!"

tisket a-tasket (*exclam, dated,* kwn LV, mid '60s) calls friend's attention to outstanding *basket* somewhere around. If the whole nursery rhyme verse is chanted, the first color describes the shirt worn while the second color symbolizes the pants, *eg.* "Tisket a-tasket, a green and chartreuse basket!"

tissue-paper titties wads of kleenix stuffed under sweaters; used by both teen-aged girls and their imitators.

tit (*fr* colloq *as necessary as tits on a bull*[*nun*]) useless, good-for-nothing; butterfingers.

tit king (les sl) lesbian attracted to large-breasted women.

title a name somebody builds up for himself "What happened to your title—trade it in for a sandwich?"

tit-o'-whirl (*camp*) the tilt-o-whirl ride at carnivals, fairs, *etc.*

tits 1. the breasts, including the nipples. Syn: *boob[ie]s; titties* **2.** courage; unmeditated gall (*cf* syn *balls*).
Related terms:
do the tits to slave over the hot stove "I always down one highball before I do the tits—helps me to get into the creative swing of things." Syn: **sling the tits over a hot stove.**
hang up the tits to retire.
nit tits microsopic breasts. Syn: **two beebees on a bread board.**
oh, my tits (*exclam*) I'm so stoned.
one's tits pronoun "Fuck your tits, you overgrown butterfly."
show the tits (*imp*) feel free. A command to stop worrying

and have fun.

stoned to the tit[s] very intoxicated from drugs, booze, you name it (you take it).

take off the tits to disrobe. Syn: **get out of these tits** ("I can't wait to get out of these hot tits!")

tangle tits to do battle "Were you around when Japan tangled tits with Russia?"

the tits excellent "That tapestry is the tits!"

tilted tits wrinkled or uncomfortable clothing.

tit-trimming anxiety reactions brought about by an overdose of narcotics.

to the tits (*fr* sl *to the t's* = do it up right) a lot, utmost "He was pilled to the tits."

trim some tits 1. to lose weight **2.** to forget about cares by smoking grass.

unload these tits 1. to disrobe **2.** to get something off one's chest; to confess.

titty sexual intercourse with a female "Wanna get some titty, sailor? We'll tell you how to get to the maternity hospital."
—**freak[queen]** homosexual who really gets off on men's nipples "I must be a titty queen—I feel so well breasted."

toad (*pej*) **1.** hag **2.** homely girl; "dog."
    Related terms:
supreme toad any withered, spiteful granny.
toad hollow office pool.

today's trade is tomorrow's competition a *gay line belittling *trade.

toe[-jam] queen homosexual foot fetishist "Toe queen's slogan, 'If the shoe fits, share it!' "
    Related term:
socksy possessing sexy feet and toes as appreciated by a toe queen.
    Also see *zories.

together (pros sl *fr* black *get it together* = to work things out) physically and psychically beautiful.

toilet 1. a dump "The most lavish restaurant translates as toilet when *you* get bored" **2.** the anus, see *a-hole.

toilet water (*camp*) draft beer.

Tomasina (*camp*) gay nickname for Thomas or Tom "Oh, the marks on the ceiling—Tomasina was just filing her toenails."

tomato (tō-mä'-tō, *camp*) tomorrow "See you tomato!"

tomato sauce blood.

tomboy 1. lesbian **2.** (*camp*) effeminate trying to appear masculine and menacing.

Tom Mix bonnet (*camp*) cowboy hat "Did you ever see a more vulgar display of Tom Mix bonnets in your whole?"

Tondalayo (*camp*) gay nickname for the easily recognized homosexual "Don't worry about looking bad, Tondalayo—nobody looks at you when you look good."
    Syn: **Tondalayo Brown [Lipshitz]; Tondolea.**

tongue-on (*camp*) joke transferring the erectile physiology of the cock to the tongue.

tonnage weight problem.

tonsil swabbing kissing.

Tonsila (*camp*) singer "Of course I'd love to hear you sing 'Oh Holy Night,' Tonsila, how about next Christmas?"

Tonya (*camp*) gay nickname for Tony "One more crack like that, Tonya, and I'll tear your eyes out with my teeth."

toodles 1. goodbye **2.** (*voc*) "Toodles, there's a broken heart for every light on Broadway."

too funny (*kwn* SF, '70) weird, unreal, bizarre.

tool see *cock.

too much [TM] (*fr* colloq *too much for words*) **1.** mind blowing, far out, something else **2.** overbearing "She wasn't even alive in Europe; she wasn't enough for New York, but she's too much for Indianapolis."

Syn: **too[-too]** ("This coffee cake is simply *too*, Chet—you simply must give me the recipe!")

too real of a man looking authentically female.

toosh (les sl, *fr* Yid = fanny) **1.** sex organ of a woman **2.** (*voc*) dearest "Say there, toosh, what could you show me in bright lights?"

too special exceptional.

tooth somebody to death to continue sucking after ejaculation when the cock is especially sensitive.

toots 1. (hetero sl) male homosexual **2.** (*voc*) "You're *too* mellow, toots, maybe you should be investigated."

tootsie roll 1. turd, dung **2.** brown-papered joint, *ie* marijuana ciggie.

—**casserole** nonnutritious nosh.

top drawer (*dated*) the best, cream of the crop.

topped (*fr* Brit cant *topping* = hanging) literally, hanged, then extended to death by any means; also fired or asked to leave "I was topped from Fred's Pub for walkin' on me 'an's."

torso job fondling of a woman's breasts.

to say the least about the most a *gay line used as an introduction to a long drawn-out tale.

toss a pigeon (*fr* carnival sl *hock* or *toss a pigeon* = to throw a bag of shit on the sides of a competitor's tent) to have a bowel movement.

toss beanbags to masturbate allowing the ejaculation to hit the partner.

toss cups to read tea leaves "I don't toss cups, but I can prophesy what will happen to you if you keep messin' with my Billy Joe."

toss freaks homosexual lovers who take turns being sexually passive and active.

toss the salad (*rare*) to comb the hair; to dry the hair. Do not confuse with *toss a salad* = *rim.

to the pits excessively, a tremendous amount "He had stocks and bonds to the pits."

touch the toes bend over and spread the legs before being fucked.

touch up 1. groping **2.** cosmetic surgery "You look like a week older than death—I think you need a touch up."

touche pipi (tōōsh-pē-pē', *fr* Fr = touch cock) to think the homosexual experience consists of simply touching a penis "They just came out, they're thirty-three, and all they want is touche pipi."

tough teddy (Brit) British juvenile delinquent; a teddy boy.

tourist heterosexual gawking in a gay environment.

Syn: **checker** (because he "checks it out").

Related term:

tour time a *gay bar packed with heterosexuals.

townie (*fr* carnival sl = local resident) troublesome heterosexual.

TP toilet paper "He wants to know why his housewarming gift hasn't been exhibited—tell him we had to use up all the TP."

trade passive activist; nonreciprocal sex partner, usually straight "Trade only fools himself, since he doesn't consider himself—as yet—gay."

Syn: **dead doll** ("I'm not working out on him—he's a dead doll just sitting back while the queen spends her Halloween early by bobbing for apples.")

Related terms:

carriage trade frustrated heterosexual who contacts homosexuals for occasional *blow jobs.

commercial trade oné who participates in homosexual sex for money; *hustler.

gay trade nonreciprocating homosexual.

kissing trade he hugs and cuddles but that's as far as he goes.

—name nickname or alias, such as Christine Cornhole, Kitty Litter or Wanda Bett.

—secret homosexual information not freely given to those not friends.

traffic the flow of available partners.

trailer girl (camp, fr pros sl) homosexual living in a trailer park.

tra-la-la (trä-lä-lä', dated) dainty, frilly.

Syn: **flossy; goo-goo** [stuff] (hetero sl: "He likes his shirts plain—none of that goo-goo stuff for him"); **la[-la]; tishy.**

transvestite (camp) the television set   "What's on the transvestite at ten?"

Also see *TV[er].

transvestor (camp) put down of big burly men: accusation of looking like a *bull dyke in *drag.

trash go out and be dirty; have sex with as many people as possible. Syn: **go trashin'** 2. one who trashes   "Honey, even trash has to go out once a week."

—y wonderfully vulgar   "Those white levis make you look so trashy!"

—rack magazine rack with girlie pictorials.

traveler's aid homosexual who's charity work consists of offering accomodations for weary young traveling men.

trenches deep face wrinkles.

très (trä or trez, fr Fr) very, so.

tribute for Judy taps.

trick 1. short-term sex partner   "May all your tricks be treats!"

Syn: **floater** (because he floats in and out of one's life); **live one** (especially used of one who pays); **personal party; pichon** (pē-chõn', fr Sp = pigeon); **pickup** ("Let's play $52 pickup!"); **Trixie** 2. a turn   "I missed a trick on that."

—cyclist (Brit gay sl) a psychiatrist   "The trick cyclist looked so funny trying to fight off temptation."

—out to be unfaithful to a regular lover.

—room decorated for sex.

—sheet any piece of paper, but usually a matchbook cover, with room for a phone number.

—suit easy to remove clothing. Syn: **drive-in levis.**

—towel used for quick post-coital cleanups   "The chicken doesn't look all that greasy, but I'll take a dishrag and a trick towel anyway." Syn: **Veronica's veil** (camp).

tried no longer virgin anally.

triple hip drug-using bisexual.

triple threat queen one who'll fuck a mouth, anus or armpit.

trip somebody (dated) to entice another into sexual relations.

trip to the baths risk, gamble   "Putting down three to see that movie is like a trip to the baths."

trisexual (camp) he'll try anything once.

triss 1. a catamite, see *effie 2. (camp) electricity   "Let me turn down the triss first, lover!"

—y effeminate.

trod the boards[planks] (fr striptease dancing) 1. to work 2. to be a bartender in a *gay bar.

trojan horse manly facade.

troll 1. to walk about with the fly undone 2. young *toad.

—ing ground (Brit gay sl) gay cruising area in a park.

—the toilet cruise the toilet.

tropical describing a room with wall-to-wall potted palms.

—fish Polynesian princess.

trout rich, vulgar old woman in mink.

   —fishing describing a *hustler's hunt for a rich old woman to keep him.

truck driver 1. homosexual, male or female, with masculine characteristics **2.** benzedrine **3.** (*obs*, pros sl) braggart who compensates for his latent homosexuality.

truckers (*fr* sl *truck* = to travel) shoes.

the trucks (*kwn* NYC) area along Hudson River docks where many trucks and truck vans are parked overnight. Homosexuals use this area in warm weather for nighttime orgies.

true confession admitting one's homosexuality to a straight friend.

trues tuinals: powerful barbituates.

TS transsexual.

   Syn: **Christine Jorgensen; Copenhagen capon; Danish pastry; sex-change** ("I didn't marry the sex-change for what he was, but rather for what he *had*"); **transsectional; turnabout.**

   Related terms:

   go Copenhagen to have one's original sex changed by means of the surgical knife. Syn: **go to Denmark.**

   something's rotten in Denmark (*camp*) said of a sex-change.

tube queen (*dated*) one who watches television a lot; broadly, a stick-in-the-mud.

tubs the *baths "I can't go to the tubs, I look too much like one myself."

tuck describing middle-aged girdle wearers; extended to any man who sucks his tummy in.

tulip sauce a kiss.

tumble a fruit 1. heterosexual having sex with a homosexual, either on a dare or as a kick **2.** to rob a homosexual **3.** to fleece homosexuals "These ghetto bars have been tumbling fruits for years."

turkey (*kwn* SF, '70) anyone over twenty-one as seen by a *chicken freak "Turkey meat isn't bad—and it's filling besides."

   —run any cruisy street in the wee hours of the morning.

   —trotter middle-age jogger.

turnabout night night when regular bartenders and performing artists switch roles to the amusement of the clientele.

turn a trick to make contact for a sexual interlude "Turning tricks to Ted is like opening a pack of gum—seven sticks a day."

   Syn: **pull a trick** ("I traveled over Europe twice just by pulling tricks out of Singapore bars"); **socar** (sō-kär', Mex, ?*fr* Sp *sacar* = to take something out); **voltear un trique** (vōl-tā-är' ōōn trē'-kā, Mex: "El volteó un trique ayer" = he tricked yesterday.)

turn communist ('71) to pop seconals (reds) habitually.

turn handstands to really catch attention "Your bleached levis really turned out to be come-fuck-me's: you had the whole block turning handstands."

turn on the sprinkler to urinate.

turn somebody out (pros sl) to beat sadistically.

turn the teacup over to die "Why the garage sale? Did your lover finally turn his teacup over?"

turn-on anything inspiring a positive reaction "Such a turn-on, going to bed with a brewery."

   Syn: **put-on** (Brit).

turnout one who comes out of an all-male institution gay. A **Navy turnout** is one who went in heterosexual but came out dreaming of pecker.

TV[er] 1. transvestite; man who receives satisfaction from dressing in women's clothing "Right on, Soul Brother, out the door with my colored TV." Syn: *drag queen; paint queen; rapid

transit (*dated*); **turnabout** ("A turnabout is fair pay.") **2.** (*kwn* Southwest, mid '60s) a gossip.
TV-guide scientific study of transvestites.
TV-special annual drag contest, usually held on Halloween.
TV style (pros sl, late '50s) anal intercourse positioned so that television could be viewed—if so desired.
twat 1. (*pej*) the vagina **2.** (*camp*) any fur piece or poorly made wig **3.** (*camp, rare*) man's crotch "You small-twat punk!"
TWAT (*camp*) TWA airlines.
twatch (*camp*) wrist watch "What time does your twatch say?"
twat say (*camp*, '50s) What did you say? The entire routine went: "Twat say? Cunt hear you; bare ass me again. I cunt finger you out; jazz forgot."
tweek somebody to embarrass.
twenty-twenty see *kosher.
twilight (*dated*, '20s-'30s, *fr* that hermaphroditic time of day when it is neither night nor day and all the sky is swathed in purple) denotes that which is homosexual.
—**crowd** homoerotic population. Syn: **twilight world.**
—**girls** gay women.
—**men** male homosexuals. Syn: **twilight boys; twilighters; twilight lads.**
twinkle toes (SM sl) the opposing team dressed in bulky knit sweaters, tight bright pants and tennis shoes and so considered effeminate.
twins homosexual lovers who wear identical clothing.
twirls (Brit sl = keys) set of house keys.
twirl the pearls to dance.
Syn: **carry on like a mad Watoo** (late '60s); **do fancy footwork on the daffodils** ('72); **massage the maple** (*fr* '40s sl: "Gangway! Mama's gon t'massage the maple so good that they gon have t'fire all they janitorial he'p"); **roll the rolls** (= to bump and grind); **shake the beads** (= shake, rattle and roll); **spread some good [Sunday] leather** (*rare*); **turn on the sizzlers.**
Related terms:
bun-boogie shaking the ass while dancing.
go-go boy young man who dances, often nude, in gay bars or clubs.
red shoes (*fr* '40s film *The Red Shoes*) **1.** dancing or fancy shoes "I can't stop dancing, it must be these red shoes" **2.** (*fr* Judy Garland's red glass slippers in *The Wizard of Oz*) musical genius "Yeah, most queens feel that Barbra Streisand fills Judy's red shoes."
Salome (*camp*) dancing queen. Syn: *shaker (*rare*).
Zulu bingo dancing in a bar on Saturday or Sunday night "Wanna play Zulu bingo?" = want to go dancing this weekend?
Twiss (*camp*) Christopher, Chris "The biggest bummer to a casket freak, Twiss, is resurrection."
twist 1. crackpot (friendly) **2.** sex pervert (unfriendly).
—**ed** warped, demented "Listen, that twisted thing is old enough to be your son!"
two dots and a dash male genitalia.
twosies a couple having sex, as opposed to group sex.
two-toned funnies ('71) the double standard, *ie* men can have mistresses but wives can't have lovers.
type anybody who physically stimulates; a dream image come to life "I'm just not my type, if you get what I mean."

udders 1. flabby breasts of an old man **2.** (*camp*) large pectoral muscles of a bodybuilder.

ugly walk strut of a troublemaker; rabble-rouser swagger "Drag out your ugly walk, here comes dirt."

unchic not cool; smoking during sex is unchic. Also see *chic.

Uncle Samantha Uncle Sam; the federal government "Uncle Samantha's rounding up more meat this spring to keep torch singing in style."

underwear (*camp*) a *drag queen's five o'clock shadow "Your underwear's showing!" = you need a shave.

unfuckables very young boys.

unfurnished apartment nude body.
   Related term:
   dress an unfurnished apartment to get dressed.

uniform 1. unmistakably gay clothing, from leather to lace **2.** someone in the military, see *armed forces.

unpack a case to tell all, especially to a qualified psychiatrist.

uns (short for sl *undies*) man's underwear "They come from miles away just to touch that gash attendant's uns."
   Syn: **binders** (*fr* pros sl, '20s); **bum bags** (Brit, '30s); **dainties** (*camp*); **holsters; panties** (*camp*); **slips** (*camp,* usually refers to long johns); **traps** ("Don't leave any lipstick on my traps—it worries my wife.")
   Related terms:
   braces too-tight jockey shorts. Syn: **uplifts.**
   scants (*fr* scantie) bikini style undershorts. Syn: **sling for an arrow** (*kwn* LA, mid '60s); **V-dipper[s]** (*kwn* LA, mid '60s).
   SIS ('20s) step in suits, *ie* silk undies.

unsliced uncircumcised.
   Syn: *blind; **blind as a boiled turnip** (with a foreskin which draws back when cock is hard); **Canadian; nearsighted; tref** (*fr* Yid // Heb *t'refa* = unfit for human consumption, according to Judaic law).
   Ant: **skinned.**
   Related terms:
   skinning sucking an uncircumcised cock. Syn: **cure the blind; draw the drapes; make the blind see; ride a blind piece; sponge off the dust.**
   wear a turtle-neck sweater to be uncircumcised; still have a foreskin attached. Syn: **wear it up in [pin-] curl[er]s.**
   —bologna uncircumcised penis. Syn: **blind meat[piece]; Canadian bacon; goy toy** (*fr* Yid // Heb *goy* = gentile); **Roman roll** (coined by *Queens' Quarterly* magazine = prepuced penis as object of beauty).

untogether confused, homely, disarrayed.

untried relatively fresh to homosexuality.

up fucking "Hippies say far out, but gay hippies say far up!"

Related terms:
up it (*exclam*) fuck you!

uphammer (late '60s) to interrupt another's train of thought; to break into a conversation with a *non sequitor*.

upholstery clothing "Get yourself some new upholstery! Remember what Mae said: 'Look your best—who said love is blind!'"

upset somebody to unnerve, to disorganize "The way he wore those levis was so upsetting, I still can't think straight, and, come to think of it, I never could."

upside-down cake (*kwn* Southwest, mid-late '60s) lesbian who makes it with a gay boy.
Also see *butcher boy.

upstage someone to step on another's lines; to outrazzle another's dazzle.

up the apple maker in the rectum "They look everywhere but up the apple maker, and they never find it."

uptight (*fr* black sl orig = getting it all the way in + boots being laced all the way to the top = good) under pressure; jittery; unable to flow "I'm not uptight about dying an unnatural death—I just want to die in an unnatural act."
—ing causing other to be uptight.
Related term:
freeze out to clam up because of paranoia.

urinal yellow muddy shade of yellow "What brand of cigarette got your teeth such a bright urinal yellow?"

utter (*adj*) quaint, gauche.
Related term:
the utter award booby prize "They'll probably give Poland away as the utter award."

vache (väsh, *fr* Fr = cow) another homosexual "Somebody retire that vache before she color-keys the entire house in rim brown."
Related terms:
LaVache (*camp*) surname some homosexuals toy with.
Quelle vache (kel'-väsh, *fr* Fr = what a cow) said of clumsy person.

vacuumed up 1. died **2.** occasionally, killed, murdered.

Vagina (*camp*) Virginia.
Related term:
Vagina Littlefinger (*camp*) a snob—even his gallstones are mother of pearl.

valley of [in]decision the small of the back; tickled by one testing to see whether or not his partner will permit further liberties in buttocktry.

valley of tears popular cruising area.

vamp 1. old homosexual who thinks he's Theda Bara **2.** to annoy, tease relentlessly, torment "When's the IRS gonna vamp the

Disney Church?" **3.** said of professional female impersonators who harass heterosexual tourists by flirting "Some of the customers really eat up the vamping routine."

vampire 1. drooling old man who swoops down on young stuff as they parade to and fro "Twilight! The vampires are out!" **2.** another homosexual who gets the trick you followed; an usurper "Some of those vampires give it a mercy killing—they spit it out."

—**run** (*kwn* NYC, '72) desperate attempt to locate sex in wee hours of the morning.

van dyke 1. lesbian with traces of a moustache on her upper lip and, though rarely, her chin **2.** (*kwn* SF, '70) lesbian truck-driver.

Vanessa Redgrave tresses red hair.

vanilla 1. (*camp*) a black man; often found in the vocative "Did you just see that, Vanilla? Some queen just walked into the john with a drill press" **2.** rigid, conforming, goody-goody "This neighborhood is too vanilla for the licks of us."

Related terms:

Miss Vanilla Moviestar a toothy, squeaky-voiced blonde.

Vanilla ice-cream 1. (*camp*) Lana Turner **2.** a bottled blonde.

vanity belt weighted sweatbelt worn around the waist which allegedly melts pounds off.

Syn: **weight lifter.**

vaseline (*camp*) butter.

vaseline lips (*camp*) one wearing lip gloss.

Vaseline Villa a gay YMCA.

Vasser girl (*camp*) homoerotic alumnus "Hope they put the Vassar girl on television, so we can turn her off."

VB (*camp*, '71) vegetable brain; an inability to deal with reality "He has a case of VB" = he's nuts.

VD (*fr* Army sl, WWII) venereal disease "You think you contacted VD? Then you better go to the clinic an' have your gun cleaned!"

Syn: **Cupid's itch** (*dated*, '40s); **dirty barrel** (*fr* Army sl *gun* = penis, '40s); **occupational hazard** ('70s); **rusty rifle** (*fr* Army sl, '40s); **souvenir** (originally, case contacted from a prostitute).

Related terms:

bend a pipe on the pisser to have a stinging sensation when urinating.

burn to infect someone with a venereal disease. Syn: **give someone a burn** (*fr* the burning sensation experienced as one of the first symptoms of gonorrhea.)

clap case of gonnorhea "Free love, my ass—you *still* pay with the clap." Syn: **dose** ("What's wrong, dear—uno *dose*, cha-cha-cha?"); **gonny; gonorita; head cold** ("He can't go out with you tonight on account of his *head* cold he contacted last week"); **morning drop** (*fr* discharge of pus); **[the] rash** ("I'll be back in a flash with the rash!")

clean untouched; uninfected with VD ("He did have the clap, but now he's clean!")

forbidden fruit homosexual infected with VD.

NSU = nonspecific urethritis; looks like clap (the penis drips), but isn't.

peter machinist VD doctor "The peter machinist made an appointment for me later on this month—his place."

pipe-cleaner (*fr* sl *pipe* = cock) **1.** used hypodermic **2.** one of the VD clinics.

the plumber's the free VD clinic.

red-light receipt case of gonorrhea contracted from a prostitute.

Syn: **receipt.**

shanker running syphlitic sore; extended to mean, any kind of scabby sore "You can tell the one who works Forty-second Street—he's the one popping shankers—all night long."

siff syphilis "He claims he caught siff b;' sitting on a flashlight." Syn: **siffy; siftless; syph** ("Talks as if he had syph of the mouth.")

siff lips (*pej*) queen handicapped by oral cavity coldsores "Drink your burger, Siff Lips, before it coagulates."

syph-o a syphilitic "I'm afraid I had to sit with the rest of the syph-o's waiting to get in."

vegetarian man who does not suck cock, often said of *trade.

veil never used alone but the key word of the following expressions:

leave a few veils 1. to tear up the town, have an uproarious good time 2. to be the life of the party, the talk of the talkies "How many veils did you leave in Alaska?" = How much fun did you have in Alaska?

take the veil to step out of circulation by either "marrying" (becoming a bride) or by living as a recluse (becoming a nun).

wear a crystal [cut-glass] veil to ineffectively conceal homoerotic identity.

wear a mourning veil to deny oneself homosexual pleasure; to filter out homoerotic temptation.

venetian blinds (*camp*) a prepuce "I have nothing against venetian blinds, as long as they aren't *on* or in me."

Venus in blue jeans (*dated, fr* late '50s rock song) congenial high-school student.

Venus flytrap (*camp*) homosexual born either under the sign of Libra or Taurus—both ruled/protected by Venus.

Venus with a penis (*fr* Jay Little's *Maybe Tomorrow*, '50s) beautiful, baby-faced boy.

Vera [Lynn] (*fr* Cockney rhyming sl) gin; by extension, one whose gin intake is tremendous "Go sit on your *own* face, Vera!"

verda [warda] (Brit gay sl, *fr* Brit carnival sl; *cf* Anthony Burgess' *viddy fr* Russ *vidyet* in *A Clockwork Orange*) to look at something.

Veronica [Lake] (*camp*) gay nickname for one who acts sultry "Oh, is Veronica's china from back East—Korea?"

very gay ('70) ironically spoken with the last word rising to the pitch of an "I-told-you-so!" = alarming, solemn; not funny, McGee "Then he called me from the emergency ward—oh, it was all very gay!"

vibrations ('40s) wordless communication (not to be confused with sl *bad vibes, good vibes, etc*).

Related terms:

pick up the vibrations ('40s) to reach erotic gratification by watching others have sex.

send out the vibrations ('40s) to make "bedroom eyes" at someone.

vice (*fr* L *vidium* = wickedness, immorality; but *cf vice* = buffoon, *fr* Vice, a character in medieval morality plays) 1. the vice squad 2. a vice cop.

Syn: **orgy[pussy, whore] patrol** (mid-late '60s: "Throw away that joint! There's a matinee of the orgy patrol"); **Velma** (*camp*: "What's your story? Why won't you get out of your car? Are you Velma or the Zodiac Killer?"); **vice bulls** ("The vice bulls closed the tubs because they couldn't stand the competition."); **Vicky [Vice]** ("The only recession I've ever seen is Vicky Vice bending over"); **Victoria** ("Victoria's not wearing a tie-dyed shirt—she's just a sloppy eater"); **Vivian [Vice]** ("See all those cars in front, I think Vivian's getting ready to ring down the curtain on this john.")

Related terms:

duck blinds two way mirror. Syn: **trojan horse.**
fruit run mass arrests in parks and washrooms.
ghost car unmarked vice squad car "The only visitation I've ever received has been from a ghost car."
peep-hole squad vice squad specializing in washrooms "Looks like the peep-hole squad raided his wedding—he's been in the clink for over a month now." Syn: **agents provocateurs; crapper dicks** (*dated,* early '50s: "A crapper dick has got to have good eyes to be able to see everything from behind a ventilator"); **decoys** ("Decoys don't carry billy clubs—they carry dildos"); **shakers** (those who entice homosexuals *fr* shaking the penis after urination); **urinal sniffers** ('72: cops who entice: "Maybe I am prejudiced after all—I can accept golden shower queens but urinal sniffers make me sick.")
Victoria 1. (*camp*) gay nickname for Victor "It's almost as funny as Victoria Hugo's stuff" **2.** the vice squad, see ***vice** "Where does Victoria dine—at Circe's hot-dog den?" **3.** victorious "Alexander was great because he was victoria in field and bed."
view from the bridge (*dated,* early '60s. *fr* Arthur Miller's play) the latest count of available men milling about a cruisy park "How's the view from the bridge today—fabulous, I hope."
view master one who isn't very secretive about eyeing others. Syn: ***basket-watcher; crotch-peeper** (*kwn* SF, late '60s).
Viking queen 1. blonde **2.** man whose hair has been tinted Scandinavian blonde ("My dear, your hair looks as if you've dyed.")
village sing (*dated,* '50s, *fr sl The Village* = NYC's Greenwich Village, haven for the avant garde) lesbian cocktail/introduction party.
Virginia ('70, *fr* Virginia Slims, cigarettes supposedly made for feminine hands only—"you've come a long way, baby!") a cock-long cigarette "And he stubbed his Virginia out in my egg yolk."
Also see ***Vogues.**
Virginia Maylips (*camp, fr* Virginia Mayo's celluloid lips) **1.** lips painted with a luscious, ruby red lipstick **2.** any person with full red lips.
vision of loveliness = a walking dream, a living doll "It was just too gorgeous for words—he was a vision of absolute loveliness!"
visit mother to heed Mother Nature's call; to relieve oneself at the toilet.
Vogues (Brit gay sl, *fr* Vogues, pastel-colored cigarettes) cigarettes: "coffin nails" "In the bars you're more apt to hear 'Pass me my Vogues!' rather than 'pass me my Camels!' "
vultures old queens posing the threat of competition to other homosexuals.

wack-o (*fr* colloq *wacky* = erratic) irrational human being "What sign is that wack-o—Studgitarius or Caprihorny?"
Syn: **weird-o.**

waffle iron hair curler "Here's a waffle iron for those blonde hairs you keep sprouting from your teeth."

waiteress (wā-tər-rēs′) [homosexual] waiter or busboy "Wait-er*ess*! May I *please* have a fork—I never seem to have shaken this terrible habit."

walker (*kwn* SF, late '60s-'72) cruiser whose pace is so speedy that it renders any probable introduction impossible.

walkin' in the night very black. Used of "soul" music and coffee.

walk queer street to be homosexual "I guess I was just cut out to walk queer street all my natural born days!"
Syn: **tour fag alley.**

walk tight walk proud; walk on through the storm.

walk with somebody to be somebody's sweetheart "I walk with Spike—he's my ol' man!"

the wall (*kwn* SF) sea wall along the San Franciscan beach "It must've been someone I ate at the wall last night" = excuse me for belching.

wall queen 1. homosexual who supports himself against a wall (in an elevator or alleyway) while he has sex "That wall queen was as warm as a nap" 2. (*kwn* SF, '70) homosexual who reads bathroom walls; by extension, one who locks himself in a toilet stall for hours.

walls (*dated*, on a par with sl *pad*, late '60s) place of living; an apartment; home; one's digs "I have eyes for some new walls, Jack!"

Wanda Wandwaver (*camp*, *fr* '60s sl *wave the wand* = brag about size) gay nickname for a penile braggart.

warbler (*rare*, *kwn* LV, mid-late '60s, *fr* hip sl *finger-warble* = soft tapping at the forehead to open the "third eye") sudden psychic realization accompanied with euphoric states of mind and giddiness; occidental "satori."
Syn: **flash** (*fr* narc sl).

warm-up (pros sl) washing a man's penis before coitus affording detection of any veneral dripping.
Syn: **precheck.**

warpaint facial cosmetics "Know how she takes her warpaint off? She calls a construction company and they send a big black ball over to knock it off."

warpath lips lips coated in lipstick.

warpath water cologne.

washer condom "Your plumbing needs a new washer if you want to keep tinkering around *this* sink."

wash the egg out to clean out the rectum; take an enema.

wasted load anybody who is a waste of time—a dingbat, turnoff, *etc* "Tell that wasted load to roll over and play dead—

for about ten years."

watch queen 1. the homosexual voyeur; one who would rather view than screw "Don't let a watch queen be chairman—he'll let the 'eyes' have it" **2.** (*rare*) homosexual who watches his and his partner's copulation through a mirror, see *lookie freak.

Syn: **benrus queen** (camp, *fr* Benrus = watch brand); **Bo-Peep** (*camp*); **doodle gazer** (mid-late '60s); **eyeball queen; keek** (*rare*: = peeping Tom); **Lady Elgin** (*camp*); **peek[peep] freak; spy queen** (late '60s).

Related term:

go to the opera (*fr* opera glasses = small binoculars) to spy on the neighbors with a pair of binoculars "Almost time to go to the opera—that humpy number next door is taking his shower."

watch the buns drop 1. to be around long enough to see an ex-friend become old, fat and unwanted **2.** to revel in an enemy's misfortune.

watch the heels (*imp*) = be careful; watch your step "Watch the heels, Mae! Remember he who excuses himself, accuses himself."

watchtower (*camp*) a *gay bar, where, for some reason, the only thing that gets done is a lot of looking "No contact, please!"

Syn: **bowl of wax fruit; look bar; touch-me-not garden; wax museum[palace, works].**

watering hole[spot] (Brit gay sl) neighborhood cruising locale, usually a park grounds or a bar "Think of all the buffalo meat that goes to the watering hole to relax."

water wings (*rare*) padded bra "Here, princess, let me fix your water wings before you swim back to Polynesia."

wawa (*fr* naut sl, // baby talk = water) drunk "Small wonder you're wawa—hair dye has ether in it."

Syn: **wavy** ("You're too wavy to drive—you couldn't see three inches in front of your wang.")

wax fruit expensive, stuffy young men who stand about in *watchtowers looking somehow very cheap.

wax job insertion of wax into a man's pectorals to enlarge them and give off the appearance of a bosom.

waylaid distracted because of intoxication "Boy, did we get waylaid, or what?"

wear a red[green] tie[sweater] to be obviously gay "He wore that red sweater to the grave, man—that's one sweater you can't take off."

wear invisible lipstick ('71) said of someone ready to explode into a vicious tirade; to be irritable, "on the rag" "He's not an ogre—you just don't know when he's wearing invisible lipstick."

wear permanent mascara (*kwn* LV, mid '60s) to have black eyes; a couple of "shiners" "Why the sunglasses tonight—wearing permanent mascara?"

wear some hair to wear the hair long, down to the shoulders.

wear the badge (*dated*, '40s) to wear a great deal of red so as to attract attention.

wear the bars to have a beer belly.

wear the kilt[s] (Brit) to take the female role when coupling with another man.

weed (*fr* narc sl, '20s) marijuana; used by some gays for its alleged aphrodisiac powers "Puff or two on some weed, man, really cuts your strings" = loosens one up.

Syn: **bush** (*fr* narc sl, late '60s); **funny paper** (*dated, kwn* San Diego, early '60s, *fr* newspaper used to wrap transported marijuana); **grass** (*fr* narc sl: "People who smoke grass shouldn't live in glass houses"); **grief** (*kwn* LV, mid '60s, *fr* Mex *grifa* = marijuana); **leaf** (*rare, cf* Moroccan Arabic *kif* = cannabis // Arabic = tranquility); **marigold** (*camp*, pun made upon *mari-* of *mari*juana + Acapulco *gold* = type of marijuana); **mota** (mō'-tä, Mex, *?fr* Mex sl *motor de chorro* = marijuana); **our aunt Mary** (*camp*, mid '60s, *fr* pun upon gay sl *aunt*[*ie*] + *dated* narc sl *Mary Warner* = marijuana: "Would you know if our aunt Mary arrived from Frisco yet?"); **pizza** (*kwn* LV, mid '60s, *fr* carny *pee-zot*= *pot*); **pot** (*fr* narc sl, '50s, // *obs* sl *pod* // Mex *potaguaya* = marijuana; "Pot works better than candy with these young kids nowadays"); **reefer** (*kwn* Texas narc sl, *fr* Mex *grifa* = marijuana: "Know where I can score a whole lot of reefer?); **yerba buena** (yär'-vă-wä'-nă, Mex = good grass).

Related terms:

burn some bush to smoke marijuana, particularly at an impromptu party.

Syn: **do a dooby** ('70); **fly Mexican Airlines; get some smoke; live in grass huts** ('70); **scrape some scum; suck up** [**some dope**]; **turn a few hits** (= take two to three puffs).

freeze on a joint to take several hits from a joint everybody else is waiting to taste. Syn: **rip off a joint** (*fr* sl *rip-off* = theft).

giggle weed marijuana which brings on uncontrollable laughter.

grasshopper (*dated,* late '50s-mid '60s) one who smokes; one who turns on" Syn: **hemp-humper; marigold queen; Miss Marigold; motorista** (*fr motor*); **pothead; Sylvania** (*camp*); **teasipper** (*camp, fr* obs sl *tea* = marijuana).

joint [**J, joy**] (*fr* narc sl, '40s, *?fr* joint = connection between this world and the next] a marijuana cigarette. Syn: **breezer** (brē'-zä, *kwn* NYC, '70); **brown one** (*dated, kwn* LA, late '50s); **dope cigarette; ladyfinger** (*camp* or *?fr* heroin addicts who downgrade "killer weed" for being sissified: "Care to nibble on a ladyfinger before we go into the theater?"); **sazeech** (sa'-zēch, *kwn* Lv, mid '60s. *?fr* carny rendition of of satchel of grass).

Miss Freeze (*camp*) one who clings to a joint for longer than his allotted toke. Syn: **Humphrey** (*tr* hip sl *Bogart a joint* = hogging a joint).

monster weed superb marijuana; "gold" Syn: ***kingdom weed; paralyzin' grass; petrifying stuff; powerful shit; stoney bush; stupifyin' grass.**

pizza maker (*kwn* LV, mid '60s) seller. Syn: **baker** (*kwn* LV, mid '60s).

pizzaria (*kwn* LV, mid '60s) dope den; home of a marijuana smoker "Your clothes are really rank! Either you visit Don's Pizzaria too often, or your washing machine's been repossessed."

potholder device such as an alligator clip to hold a marijuana butt (roach) when it is too small to handle comfortably. Syn: **clip** (short for sl *roach clip*); **crush; crutch; miser** (*kwn* LV, mid '60s: because it holds onto high-producing tars).

ragweed poor grade of marijuana. Syn: ***hay; lawn.**

sip take a toke.

tamale a poorly rolled joint. Syn: **Mexican cigarette.**

torch up (*fr* hip sl) to light a cigarette, but especially when it contains marijuana "It's torch-up time, handsome, so why don't you slip out of those nasty, dry clothes." Syn: **fire [flame] up; light up.**

weeds (*camp, kwn* SF, '70, *fr* widow's weeds = black vestments) clothing "All of his weeds are equipped with zippers and

snaps—which, of course, explains his magnetic personality."
Related term:

wear the weeds (*lit*, to be widowed) to bemoan a loss; to be said, glum "Why are you wearin' the weeds?" = Why so sad?

wee-wee (*kwn* les prison sl) a male.

well caped (*camp*, pun on *well kept*) looking young thanks to artifice: dyes, cosmetics, *etc*.
Syn: **tucked to filth.**

well hung having more than seven inches of cock "No wonder the ape man keep his jungle reservation—those monks were well-hung!" "She wants to buy a well-hung ivy." Syn: **big** ("I likes 'em *big!*"); **cocky; donkey-rigged; draped** (*kwn* NYC, hustler sl, '70); **long; stacked; tall; texan; well endowed [equipped].**
Related terms:

big hunk of meat *penis immensus;* large cock. Syn: **choker** ("What a tall 'un; I bet he has a choker on him"); **dangler; donkey; gallons; honker; horsemeat; jawbreaker** ("I thought Miss Mabel would feature a jawbreaker, but all she was carryin' was a blackhead in drag"); **long pole[pork]; lumber** ("There I was with an ice-cream cone melting in one hand and this big brute's in the other. It was the first time I ever had lumber à la mode"); **meat for the butcher** (implying "biting off more than you can chew"); **meat for the poor, the needy, the famished and the starving** (*kwn* NYC, black gay sl, late '60s); **swanska** (*rare, fr* Ger *Schwanz* = tail & penis); **tallywhacker** (*dated:* "By the time I got through kissin' that tallywhacker, he was so hot you could have fried eggs on his ass"); **Texas longhorn** ("He roped and hogtied a Texas longhorn on Forty-second Street"); **whalebone; whopper; yards of personality.**

busy line stripling who arranges most of his dates by phone. The implication is that his popularity is due to a long anatomical extension cord. He may or may not keep appointments for monetary gain "I'd *love* to drop in at your wake, but I have *such* a busy line!"

carry a big stick to show off by wearing tight pants.

longfellow (*camp*, often inserted into play pidgin: "Him longfellow") well-endowed man. Syn: **doctor** (*dated*, '40s); **Goliath** (*camp, fr* Old Testament Philistine giant: "The glory hole in that head is the size of a watermelon—Goliath must do his shopping there"; also a comical name for lapdogs or canaries: "C'mon, Goliath, do a tinky!"); **longhorn; long trade** (*kwn* LV, black gay sl, mid '60s); **man mountain; real piece; Taurus** (*fr* second zodiac sign symbolized by a bull: "Are Tauruses really all that hung? It all depends on how much bull is connected.")

Wendy (Cape Town gay sl) white "None of us come out without egg, Wendy; especially around the pink collar!"
Related term:

wendy bag a white man.

wet-and-warm (*pej, kwn* SF, late '60s) straight boy's girlfriend "Wet-and-warm's going to sulk over a Doctor Pepper."

wet dream (*camp*) any lathering substance squirted from a can nozzle, *eg* Gillette Foamy, whipped cream for desert topping, *etc* "What's that all over your face—did your wet dream come out of the wrong hole?"

wet lashes morbid details of a "sob story" "Spare me the wet lashes, I know *exactly* where you slept!"

wet lips lips made shiny from lip gloss applications.

what a beauty (*exclam*) praises the size of a man's vitals "Then he opened his coat and flashed! What a beauty, I mean, the police almost had to arrest me *too*!"

what do you [like to] do gay Freudian slip for "howdy do?"

whatever happened to Baby Jane? (*interj*) snazzy way of asking the old question, "whatever became of So-and-So?" Offered as a riddle, the answer might be: "Peter Fonda!"

what's your freak-show[story] = what's your problem. Snapped icily at someone staring or overtly critical.

wheel [it] out (*kwn* Southwest, teen sl, mid '60s) to remove the penis from the trousers "I wheeled out and let him touch it for a fiver."

wheels (*fr* black sl, mid '60s) any means of transportation, but usually referring to automobiles or bicycles "Caught clap again? Where you been parking your wheels—at the Shanky Town Y?"

Many of the motoring words pertain to elegant travel almost on the scale of a royal personage. Any vehicle driven by or transporting a homosexual is a **carriage, fairy boat, pageant wagon, royal coach** ("Just park the royal coach by the hydrant, Jackson, we shan't be a minute.") Even police paddy wagons acquire refined plumage by being the **golden retrievers** (*kwn* SF, '71), **queens' buses** and **salad bowls** (direct translation *fr* Fr argot *panier à salad*).

A status-conscious gay whose life centers around owning prestige automobiles is a **car queen. Rolly-Pollies** (Rolls Royces) and **baby buggies** (convertible sports cars) are indications of making it with a European flavor. A **Carolac** (*camp:* = Cadillac) or any other block-long car measuring the driver's wealth, is a **hog** (*kwn* Cleveland, mid '60s), **pimp-mobile [-wagon], queens' carriage, showboat** (*fr* pros sl). If this large car is difficult to handle in traffic, it is cursed out as a **Cleopatra's barge** or simply a **barge** (*camp*) "This car drives like a barge . . . *sinking!*"

A small car, particularly one which gives the driver trouble, is affectionately designated **Singer** since it behaves as if its engine were the gutless insides of a sewing machine; any car, big or small, which swerves to the left side of the road is called **Mothra** (*fr* Jap *Mothra* = benevolent giant moth in '60s Jap horror movies) because it too seems attracted to light. A production-line car chopped and chipped or otherwise customized to look "sharp" is a **[fastback] Volare** (vo-la'-ra, *kwn* SF, '70, *fr* It *volare* = to fly; *cf* song popularized by Bobby Rydell in late '50s) since so many Latin types seem to do it. A really with it **rodder** (car-buff) will work as **Wanda Windshield** (*kwn* SF, '70, gas jockey) to help support his habit and develop his hobby by becoming a professional mechanic.

In Southwestern desert areas, station wagons **buff[dog, fairy, milk] -wagons** are extremely fashionable because they are practical. Queens love them because they can seat so many *sisters for an evening's drive to the hot spots.

When walking, a gay takes the **Jewish [Italian, Polish,** *etc* depending on personal bias] **airlines** (*kwn* SF, late '60s) and complains about having to have done so when he arrives.

To protect his coiffure he more than likely will call or flag down a **banana car** (*kwn* SF, late '50s) driven by **Miss Milly** (short for **Milly Motorist**). If he hasn't enough money for a cab, the San Francisco queen can resort to the **African Railroad** (late '60s), the municipal bus line whose drivers are primarily black. A bus line taking a direct route to a well-known camping ground is the **Fruit Stripe Run** (*kwn* SF, '70). **Gray queens** and **honest-working girls** (*kwn* SF, '70, nine-to fivers) travel **crush hours** (rush hours) on the **freak express-**

es and the crowded and smelly **slave ships.** The longer distancing Greyhound is the **grey bitch** (*camp:* "Take the grey bitch to the bus station and I'll have somebody pick you up—legitimately.")

Queens elaborate heavily on pumpkin imagery (*fr* Cinderella) in their transportation talk; a rattletrap car is a **broken[-down] pumpkin,** and a car involved in a hit-and-run is a **runaway pumpkin** ("Did Cinderella's glass slippers get splintered by the runaway pumpkin?") and **your pumpkin just turned** = it's time to leave. **Cinderella's cadillac[carriage]** also refers back to the "gourdy" heroine as in "This queen of hearts just baked some tarts out of Cinderella's Cadillac."

whipped exhausted, fatigued, pooped.

Related term:

one whipped sissy tired *or* defeated homosexual; usually used of oneself "Honey, I'm one whipped sissy after that foxtrot—slip me a diet cola."

whipped cream nocturnal emission; the stuff wet dreams are made of.

whip somebody's head around (*fr* black sl) to turn somebody's head—negatively or positively.

white privileged; civilized; free, white and 21. Often used sarcastically of cafe society.

Related terms:

carry on as if white 1. to act immaculate, untinged **2.** to act like poor white trash; to frolic. Syn: **tramp it up.**

white woman (*fr* Christian women conducting themselves properly in front of natives) uninhibited homosexual "How can I tell the white woman? I just taste the Ac'cent on her hip boots."

whizz to urinate.

Syn: **take a whizz.**

whomp (*interj*) onomatopoetic sound to emphasize force, speed or excessive pressure and length. When spoken, the word is drawn out and made guttural—W-h-o-o-o-m-p! "He had eyes on—whomp!—way back to there!"

—it up 1. to suck cock with a frenzied passion **2.** to eat with a hardy appetite.

—on somebody's head (*cf* black *whop somebody upside the head*) to cause someone mischief; to beat someone.

whoops (*dated, interj*) said when one recognized another homosexual.

Syn: **coo** (*dated*, '30s).

who [which daddy] paid for the taps on her teeth said aside of one who's teeth clatter.

whore (ME *hore* // Norse *hora* // L *carus* = dear, akin to Skt *kama* = love) **1.** (*n*) man-hungry man. Usually opprobrius: "Stop rustlin' all my meat into your bedroom, whore!" but between friends = title or utmost affection: "Oh, you're such a whore, no wonder I love you so."

Syn: **Barbarella** (*kwn* SF, '70); **calendar kid; cheap thing; chippy; chuspanel** (chōōs-pä-nel', *kwn* Ariz, *fr* Papago = whore's vagina); **club date** (has many engagements in one day); **Delilah** ("Just flew in, Delilah? Your wings must be plumb fagged out"); **dirty lay** (*kwn* SF, mid '60s: abusive but admired); **dirty thing; fallen woman; floozy** ("A floozy is the sister who gets the man *you* were after"); **garbage woman; ginny woman** (?*fr* sl *gin-mill* [woman] = black harlot); **ground woman** (= has a mind lower than a basement); **gutter limits** (gay nickname); **hoor** (*fr* Ger-Yid *hur* = harlot; "Good hoors go by the motto: 'Handsome is as handsome does!'"); **hussy** (*fr* housewife:

"What did you expect from a hussy like her—flowers?"); **Jezebel; lay of the land; man trap; privates investigator; scandal girl** ("Twenty men later, this scandal girl found her way out"); **scarlet woman** (*fr* red being associated with whores); **scrubwoman** (usually in the expression *carry on like an old scrubwoman* = to whoop it up); **slut** (*fr* ME *slutte:* "Was that slut dead? Ever see a doornail?"); **swamp woman** (*kwn* Texas, '40s: "I'm sure the swamp woman's going straight—right after church"); **tart** (Brit sl = whore); **thirty-day boy** (= requires sex every day of the week); **working girl** ("More work and less pay makes Jack a working girl")   **2.** to walk the streets searching for a partner, see *cruise. Syn: **wear a change belt.**

—do beehive hairdo of suburban damsels; all the hair is teased and piled on top—then it is sprayed to hold its shape for the duration of the week[month].

—ella 1. trashy homosexual   **2.** (*adj*) whorish, lacking subtlety   "What a whorella neighborhood—lampposts on every corner!" Syn: **tart** ("Don't get tart with him—he runs a strictly non-profit museum.")

—'s color red; scarlet.

—'s diamond 1. rhinestone   **2.** glass.

—'s match the last match. To ignite the last match, according to superstition, means dying in a bordello.

—'s ovaries (*camp*) hors d'oeuvres.

—'s pneumonia sore throat caused by sucking too many penises.

—woman (black gay sl) brash, roof-raising effeminate. Syn: **chore woman** (*euphemism*). Ant: **dog[ish [mother]fucker.**

—you (*camp*) = who are you?   "Who am I? More important—whore you?"

—ing days one's youth.

who's she? (*interj*) a *gay line said of one who is outrageously arrayed or unbelievable.

widowed aunt well-to-do homosexual who survives his late lover(s)   "The widow looks very extinguished, I mean, distinguished this evening."

Wichita Yenta (*camp*) gay nickname for Glen Campbell.

wife submissive homosexual who assumes the "feminine" responsibilities in a homophilic partnership   "Would you lay off those European liberties with my wife, Bud?"
     Syn: **gallina** (gǎ-yē'-nǎ, Mex *fr* Sp = hen); **mama; old lady** ("He's my old lady, man!")

—tapping (*rare*) eavesdropping.
     Also see *husband.

wig shop (*dated*, late '60s, *fr* sl *wig* = crazy man) institution for care of the mentally ill.

wig stand the head   "Did he dent your wig stand any?"
     Syn: **wig box.**

wild exceptional; unusual, uncontrolled, uninhibited, daring, dynamic.
     Syn: *campy; *kinky; *mad.

—thing unruly, unrestrained homosexual, see *whore   "I'm inviting that wild thing to my party—I've run out of noise-makers."

Wilma (*camp*) gay nickname for William   "That dope went right to your mouth, Wilma; you haven't stopped talking since I got here."

wimp (*kwn* Seattle, late '60s, *fr* Wimpy, cartoon character in *Popeye*) twerp, fool.

—y silly.

windmill (v) to talk with the hands; flutter while speaking.
  —s queen's hands.
    Also see ***play windmill.**
window lady snob who tells others how to conduct themselves properly.
window queen (kwn SF, late '60s) homosexual who has a passion for collecting material possessions.
window shop to browse, just look over the material.
  Syn: **do light cruising.**
wings 1. hands; by extension, the arms "We wash our wings in this house!" **2.** one's homosexuality, connected to body just as wings are connected to fairies: "How old was she when she first got her wings?" = when he became gay; "my wings are all wet" = I'm soaked to the bone; "they pulled her wings off" = they beat him up.
wink to be uncircumcised "Does it wink?" = is it gentile?
winkers eyelashes "The winkers are real . . . it's her eyes that aren't."
wink somebody down (kwn Southwest, mid '60s) to wiggle the buttocks to gain attention "He winked some truck driver down—now he's booked for a road tour."
wise heterosexual well informed about homosexuality; tolerant, very sympathetic. Beautiful people are wise; jet setters are wise: they know at least one gay hairdresser. Some gays condescendingly call wise people **token-fag queers** and **closet cases.**
  —to somebody knowing that someone is gay "Do you think Florence is wise to us yet?"
witching hour late, after bar cruising when you don't care which is which.
with it (mid '60s, fr jazz sl = aware, in the groove) unquestionably gay.
without the potatoes spineless, limp; incomplete "This weed is like hash—without the potatoes, baby!"
woman (camp) mature, adult homosexual man "Only thing I read in that SM bar was a chapter of 'Little Women!' "
    Related terms:
    that woman (pron) third person singular "That woman's counting her biceps to see if they're all there—one . . . yep, they're all there."
    the[this] [old] woman (pron) oneself; first person singular "The old woman just got fucked with a Touch of Sweden."
Wonder (camp, short for "Wonder Woman") gay nickname "This must be the dark room, Wonder; things are getting developed."
wong 1. the penis, see ***cock 2.** (kwn Wis, teen sl, late '50s) cord used to signal stops on a public conveyance: "pull the wong" = pull the cord; but "ring the wong" = push the doorbell.
woolies pubic hairs "Keep your lovely hula hands off his steel woolies—I saw it first!"
  Syn: **wools.**
Wool's Worth (camp) Woolworth's five-and-ten.
words ('70) trivia with which talkers put their friends to sleep; a lot to say "That piece has many words" = he talks a great deal about nothing.
work to make a full-time occupation out of cruising; to work hard at scoring cock. One may work bars, corners, parks, toilets, etc.
    Related term:
    do the work to be a full-pledged homosexual.
  —bench (fr sl work = to fuck) bed; fold-out couch.

Related term:

table cloth bedcover.

—on someone to devote total attention to the person being cruised; to cruise by making "him" feel as if he were the only man on earth "Call back a week from now—I'm busy workin' on some hunk installing my pink princess."

—out on it to intensively suck cock for an extensive period of time—say, half an hour.

—room bedroom as nucleus of comfortable seduction "That cigarette stand would look nice sinking into my workroom rug."

—the siren to catterwaul; make noise by either breaking out into uncontrollable laughter (guffawing) or by crying.

wrap off originally = masturbation; however also came to mean getting done (because the sucker wraps his lips about his subject).

wrapping[s] clothing "*Some* creatures look better *in* their wrapping than *out* of it."

wreck one who is rundown; a living ruin.

Syn: **Charles Atlas** (*camp*); ***mess; piece of wreckage.**

—ed exasperated, shattered, left with the mouth open "Did you take note that everything was in matching Marilyn Monroe champagne color? I was wrecked!"

—ing company group of loud, obnoxious homosexuals out to startle heterosexuals "There's a wrecking company backing a duel at Hollywood and Vine."

—the beads[head, mind] 1. to impress tremendously "Those yummy rugby players wreck me" 2. to be iconoclastic, a toppler of order 3. to unnerve "Spiders wreck my beads—the only cobwebs in my place are made out of chiffon."

wringers lips "Until I lose some pounds, you'll never see another slab of chocolate pass these wringers."

wrinkle (*dated*) vagina "Kiss her in the wrinkle with your dick, man."

wrist-slapper homosexual do-gooder.

writing a book[novel] sarcastically descriptive of someone who claims he is not gay, even though he associates exclusively with homosexuals "Oh, maybe you're writing a novel? What better way to get material than on your knees."

X rather generally accepted euphemism for *sex*.
—'ey sexy.

xerox queen ('71) one whose sex life is so narrow that he treats all lovers alike—as if they were all copies of each other.
Also see *jaded faggot.

X-rated provocative, sexy "X-rated undies are very brief."
Related term:
think x-rated fill the head with lascivious thoughts.

xylophone as in **Miss Xylophone** = one so thin that his ribcage sticks out—like an undernourished chicken.

YA (= young action) boys easily persuaded to join homoerotic activity.

yakenals (*fr* sl *yak* = jabbering) nembutals: a tongue-loosening barbiturate.
Syn: **yukenals.**
Also see *suckonals.

yaloo (ya-loo', *kwn* LV, mid '60s) the head, one's "melon" "He wanted to turn his hubby's yaloo into some hard cash!"
Related term:
give yaloo to fellate. "The mayor's wife gives yaloo! Why, that's *just* awful—what's her number?"

yang (?*fr* sl *yank* = cock or ?*fr* Chin *yin-yang* principle of natural forces: *yin* = female, *yang* = male) the penis.

yankee's yawn open fish mouth of climaxing man.

yanner (*kwn* LV, black gay sl, late '60s) shabby; sadly dressed; raffish.
Syn: **ratty; roguey.**

yard (*fr* black sl, // *backyard woman* = mistress) to be unfaithful, commit adultery "Take down the fences—yarding can be great fun."

yardage big dick "Did you sew up the deal to get this yardage on discount?"
Related term:

measure somebody with a yardstick pin the tail into the dunkee.

yasha (yā'-shä, *fr* Russ = peasant nickname) dolt.

yawn bummer; dull, lifeless "Too many yawn's don't make an orgy."

yikyo (*fr* sl *icky* + *yoyo*) dimwit "You can't even drive a nail in straight, yikyo, what makes you think you could drive a car?"

you asking me or everybody else (*kwn* SF, '71) squelch directed against a loud personal question in a public place.

you got my nose open admission of love = I love you "You got my nose open, you knew *just* the right can opener to use."

you just had a chance not to say that (*exclam*) said after catching a faux pas or hearing something stupid.

young enough to get under the gate just under the legal age.

you pour yourself very well (*interj*) = you look good in tight pants.
Syn: **you look like you grew those pants.**

you're running up a bill (*exclam*) a kind way of keeping off a pest.

you're talking too loud reprimanding a gropey nuisance.

your hole (*interj*) you lie like a rug.

your mother (*pron*) first person singular "He wasn't as easy going up your mother's popo as a Johnson and Johnson Q-tip."

you said that to say what said to try to get clarification.

youthos (*fr* youth + pathos) said of those forced to grow up quickly and therefore missed out on their childhood/youth.

yoyo 1. tiny penis, see ***small meat 2.** child molester's delight **3.** stupid person "I'm twice the man that yoyo is and three times the woman he'll ever get."

yuke (yūk, mid '60s, *fr* sl *juke* = bawdy raucousness // Gullah) to be excited "I really yuked on that coffee."
Syn: **get one to yuking.**
—**and yah** to chatter excitedly.
—**up on somebody's bod 1.** to make love expertly **2.** to savour sex.
—**y 1.** exciting "Fag mags are yukey! I don't read them— I just skin through 'em" **2.** (*kwn* Midwest, mid '60s) the opposite: anything ugly, disturbing.

yummies 1. physically dynamic men **2.** genitals **3.** nipples.
Related terms:
get some yummies to fuck.
little yummies teenagers "I was just telling these little yummies here about when knighthood was in unplucked flower."

yummy cute, handsome "He's got the yummiest legs."

yuntif (yun'-tif, *fr* Yid // Heb *yom tov* = good day, *ie* holiday) any day you feel like celebrating "Must be yuntif, everybody's smiling."

zap (*fr* hip sl // onomatapoetic comic bookese) to embarrass publicly; defeat; cause a disturbance, such as by boycotting.

Zelda (Cape Town gay sl) pure-blooded Zulu.
Related terms:
Betty light-skinned Bantu.
colora (*fr* colored person) one of mixed blood; mulatto, quadroon, *etc*.

Zelda Gooch 1. (*adj*) unfashionable, passe **2.** (*voc*) klutz "Well, Zelda Gooch, I hate to watch and run . . ."

zero-sixty-nine (*fr* naut sl *0-69* = code for an airplane's flameout + '50s sl *Z's* = sleep) to pass out; crash.
Syn: **flame out.**

zip in on swoop down upon.

zipper club after hours establishment "The curtain goes up at twelve, but a zipper club doesn't start packing 'em in until after two."

zipper dinner hurried fellation, see ***quickie.**

zipper on down the freeway to career while driving, usually under an influence.

zipper sex cocksucking without bothering to lower the pants.

zip up the fly to quiet somebody "Zip up your fly" = shut-up!

zombie palace (*kwn* NYC) stand-up bar where nobody relaxes.

zoo number 1. overt passion for an animal "Did you dig the zoo number that Miss Tiajuana Tokus did with her Mexican coral snake?" **2.** (*n*) clumsy, animal-like "Move the T'ang vase—it's too close to the zoo number's landing patterns."
Related term:
do a zoo number to turn to animals for sexual expression.

zoo queen animal lover—sexually "You keep getting bigger and bigger dogs, Freda, turning into a zoo queen?"

zories (*fr* Jap) rubber thongs, shower shoes. Favored by ***toe queens.**
Syn: **galilee stompers** (*fr* teen sl, late '60s); **go-aheads; open-toed tennis shoes; rubber mules; slips** (*fr* colloq *slip-slop*); **toe billies** ("Ugh! There's something living all over the bottom of my toe billies.")

Index

buff, 87
buff boy, 111, 146
buffle, 38
buff-light, 38
buff talk, 94
buff-wagon, 212
buga, 190
bugger, 17, 38, 87
buggerantoes, 17
buggery, 38
bugskin, 38
bug wing, 158
bulb, 38, 104
bull, 38
bull bitch, 38
bull dicker, 38
bull dyke, 38
bullet-proofed, 102
bullets, 38
bullhead, 155
bull-in-boots, 55
bull pen, 38
bull ring, 19
bull-ring camp, 38
bully, 159
bum, 23, 38
bum bags, 203
bum boy, 146
bum fuck, 99, 107
bum-fugger, 17
bummer, 17
bump, 87
bumper sticker, 139
bumper-to-bumper, 38
bumping pussies, 38
bump with somebody, 38
bun, 23
bun-boogie, 202
bun-bun, 23
bunderful, 25
bung, 19
bunger, 17
bunghole, 19
bunker, 107
bunker-shy, 108
bunking up, 108
bung-hole, 19
bunny, 111
bun-pressers, 53
buns, 23, 38
buns to the ground, 128
bunt, 23
bunter, 72, 159
burglar, 33
burn, 205
burners, 38
burnies, 38
burnies, 38
burning, 127
burn some buns, 89
burn some bush, 210
bush, 209
bush dinner, 139
bushie moll, 38
business, 152

business boy, 111
bust, 39
bust a cap in an ass, 89
bust some suds, 39
bust the beads, 29
busy, 39
busy line, 211
butch. 39
butch as Kong, 39
butcher, 39
butcher boy, 39
butchered chicken, 45
butcher knife, 48
butcher shop, 39
butch fluff, 39
butch it up, 39, 41
butch number, 39
butch queen, 39
butch school, 39
butch-stone, 39
butt, 23, 39
butt-bang, 87
butt-books, 116
butter, 128
buttercup, 72
butterfly, 72, 192
butterfly boy, 73
butterfly ring, 72
butt-fuck, 87
button, 47
buttons, 141
butz, 39
buy queen, 39
buzzed, 39

C

cabareting, 158
caboose, 24
cackle, 40
cacky, 40
cadet, 159
cage, 40
cakes, 24, 137
calendar kid, 213
call boy, 111
call it, 40
call Ripley, 40
call Wardrobe, 40
Camille, 40
camp, 40, 56, 157
camp as a row of tents, 41
camp bitch, 72
camper, 26, 174
campfire girls, 22
camp follower, 174
camp it off, 41
camp it up, 41
camp names, 41
camp truck, 26
camp up a storn, 41
camp voice, 41
camp walk, 42

campy, 41, 42, 121, 215
can, 24, 42
Canadian, 203
Canadian bacon, 203
canasta, 27
cancel the act, 42
candy, 44
candy cane, 49
candy kid, 108
candy maker, 42
candy pants, 161
canetta, 24
canister set, 24
canned fruit, 48
canned goods, 21, 108
cannibal, 51
canteen punk, 156
capello, 42
capon, 43
capris, 53
card-reader, 42
career boy, 111
car-hop, 42
Carlotta, 42
Carmen(cita), 29
Carolac, 212
car queen, 212
carriage, 212
carriage trade, 199
carry a big stick, 211
carry on, 42
carry on as if white, 213
carry on like a mad
   Watoo, 202
carry on with, 42
carry somebody, 100
carry the groceries, 100
carsey, 159
cartso, 49
carve them out, 42
carwash, 42
case, 42
cash-ass, 42
Cash Flagg, 42
cash rack, 42
casket freak, 52
caso, 159
casting couch, 43
castratos, 43
casual drag, 68
cat, 56, 70, 165
catalogue queen, 43
catchable, 25
catch a rush, 175
catch a sixty-nine, 182
catch it, 33
catch one's lunch, 95
catty, 32, 43
caught between the
   pointers and setters, 32
cedarchest cissy, 48
CFD, 43
cha-cha palace, 43
chain, 128

champ, 111
champagne fountain, 97
champion, 111
chance sandwich, 196
change-machine, 24
change one's luck, 43
change over, 43
Chanukah snow, 43
Chanukah snow, 43
chapel, 184
charity case, 43
charity goods, 43
charity stuff, 43
Charlene, 43
Charles Atlas, 216
charm a snake, 103
charm bracelet, 43
charming, 43
charva, 87
chastise one, 43
chastity case, 43
cheap thing, 213
check, 43
checker, 199
check out, 43
cheeks, 24
cheeky, 27
cheese, 43, 186
cheesecake, 30
cheese scraper, 44, 105
cheesy, 44
cherry, 21, 44, 155
cherry flip, 44
cherry in the hand, 115
cherry picker, 21
cherry splitter, 44
chesty, 39
chew, 33, 44
chewess, 76
chew fish, 81
chew foreskin, 44
chew it, 33
chibby-chase, 44
chic, 44
chi-chi, 150
chick business, 65
chicken, 44
chickencoop, 45
chicken dinner, 45
chicken feed, 45, 156
chicken freak, 45
chicken hawk, 45
chicken house, 45, 112
chicken hunter, 45
chicken-little, 44
chicken-looking, 44
chicken on a spit, 45, 129
chicken plucker, 45
chicken pox, 45
chicken queen, 45
chicken-recruiter, 170
chicken rustler, 45
chickens-of-the-sea, 45
chicken-with-a-basket, 45

chillette, 46
chingus, 49
chin-strap and wheel-
    chair set, 25
chippy, 213
chippy bread, 46
chips, 24
chip the lips, 46
chirped, 155
chirujo, 72
chit, 46
chiva, 46
chocolate bunny, 62
chocolate drop, 120
chocolate lover, 63
chocolate mess, 133
choirboys, 111
choker, 159, 211
chokeressa, 159
cholly, 137
chop heads, 152
chopped cock, 122
chopper, 49
chora, 49
chore woman, 214
chota, 49, 125
Christ and two apostles,
    51
Christina, 46
Christine, 46
Christine Jorgensen,
    201
Christmas caroling, 97
chrome, 46, 132, 184
chrome-plated, 46
chuck a slob, 47
chuckies, 140
chuck-lover, 63
chuck slobs, 76
chudini, 24
chuff, 146, 186
chuff chums, 66, 128
chuffer, 146
chunk, 46
church, 28
church mouse, 108
chuspanel, 213
chut, 146
ciao, 46
Cinderella, 46
Cinderella's cadillac,
    Cinderella's carriage,
    213
Cindy, 46
cinnamon stick, 51
cinny, 46
circle, 46, 115
circle jerk, 47, 115
the circuit, 31
circus, 47
the circus, 62
circy, 47
cissy, 47, 72, 181
citizen, 190
civilian, 190
civvies, 47, 190

Clairabell, 47
clamp it silly, 186
clap, 205
Clarabella, 47
Clarabella Camp, 47
Clarabella Clown, 47
Clarabella Cow, 47
Clarabella Starr, 47
Clarabelle, 47
Clareen Coon, 62
Clarisse, 132
class, 47
classic(al), 47
claws, 182
clean, 205
cleaned, 122
clean (it) up, 39
clean queen, 47
clean up the kitchen,
    172
clean up the furs, 91
clear the stage, 189
cleavage, 47
cleavage queen, 190
Cleopatra's barge, 212
cleaver, 47
click, 47
click and clack, 47
climbing the tier, 155
clip, 36, 210
clip one's wings, 47
clipped dick, 122
clipping days, 36
clique bar, 47
clit, 47
clit closet, 47
clock, 47
close Polk Street, 97
closet case, 48, 215
closet dyke, 48
closeted, 48
closet name, 48
closet queen, 48, 195
closet queer, 48, 195
closet queer, 48
clothing queen, 48
club date, 213
club(bed) foot, 51
clubhouse, 195
clubhouse register, 133
cluck, 40, 44
cluster fuck, 148
cluster party, 148
clyde, 49
CO, 48
coal burner, 63
coat, 87
coathanger operation,
    177
cobra lady, 32
cochar, 87
cock, 48
cock and balls, 51
cock bath, 51
cock-car, 126
cock cheese, 44

cruisy, 56
crumpet, 21
crunch queen, 51
crunt, 57
crush, 57, 210
crushed fruit, 48, 57
crush hour, 146, 212
crushies, 57
crushvilles, 57
crust queen, 168
crusty, 168
crutch, 210
crystal lady, 57
crystal palace, 159
CS, 52
CT, 52
Cuban pumps, 57
Cubans, 57
cucumber queen, 57
cuff a carrot, 33, 156
cuilon, 146
culiar, 87
Culligan, 170
culo, 19, 57
cum, 52, 57
cum-cum, 52
cunker, 57
cunning linguist, 139
cunt, 18, 57, 146
cuntie, 57
cunt-lapper, 139
cunt-sucker, 139
cunty, 32, 57
Cup-and-a-half, 57
cupcake, 57
cupcakes, 24
Cupid's itch, 205
cups, 30
cup to feed you with, 57
curb service, 58
curbstone cupcakes, 58
cure, 58
cure the blind, 203
curlies, 58
curls, 58
curl the tail, 89
curtain calls, 58
curtains, 123
cushion, 24
cushioned steel, 140
cushion one's jewels, 58
cut, 19, 122
cut away the tinsel, 197
cute, 58
cuteness, 58
cute thing, 58
cutie, 44, 155
cut out to be a gentle-man, 122
cuts, 58
Cy, 58, 95
Cynthia, 58

D

dabbler, 32
daddle, 59
daddy, 59, 110
daddy-o, 59, 155
daffodil(ly), 46, 73
dagger, 49, 70
Dahlia dyke, 59
dainties, 59, 73, 203
dainty daddy, 59
dairy queen, 59
Dairy Queen State, 149
daisy, 59
daisy chain, 59
Daisy Duck, 146
daisy ring, 59
Dale, 37
dally, 59
dalmation queen, 59
damaged goods, 59
dance, 60
dancer, 161
dancer's belt, 60
dancey, 60
dandy, 73
dandysette, 70
dang, 49
dangle, 49
dangle queen, 60
dangler, 60, 211
dangles, 60
Danish pastry, 201
Danny Debonaire, 60
dark meat, 49, 62
darling, 60, 73
darling Daisy Dumpling, 60
dash, 60
daughter, 60
days, 60
DAZ, 60
dazzle dust, 60
dazzle the audience, 60
DBT, 66
dead doll, 133, 199
deadeye dick, 17
dead rabbit, 51
dead stick, 51
dealing, 116
dear, 60
dearest, 60
dearie, 60
debut, 60
debut, 54, 61
debutante, 60, 68
deckers, 60
deck of weeds, 156
decorated by Cost Plus, 23
decorations, 54
decoy, 62, 207
decoy(er), 27

de dulce, 60
deegy, 61
deep, 60
deep(er) tone of lavender, 124
deep sixed, 158
degenerate, 60
degenerate bar, 61
delicate-assen, 48
delicious, 61
Delilah, 213
delish, 61
deliver a baby, 61
delivery boy, 112
de los otros, 161
Denise, 61
den (of sin), 28
depress-o, 61
derrick, 70
derriere, 24
design for living, 196
desperate hours, 61, 147
desperation number, 61
destroy (somebody), 61
dethroned, 61
develop one's talent, 61
deviate, 165
deviation corner, 156
dew, 61
DG, 61
diamonds, 27, 61
dick, 49, 51
dick drink, 51
Dickless Tracy, 126
dick peddler, 111
dick somebody, 87
dicky, 49
dicky bird, 61
dicky broad, 71
dick(y)-licker, 51
dick(y)-taster, 51
diddle, 61, 88, 115
diddler, 116, 158
diesel (dyke), 70
dig, 61
dig a ditch, 88
dig boy ass, 88
dig fantasy, 147
digging fantasy, 136
dig it, 112
dig somebody fat righteously, 61
dike, 61, 70
Dilbert Dildo, 61
dildo, 61
dill doll, 61
dillpickle, 62
dilly, 62
dilly boys, 62
dime-a-dance, 62
dindin, 62
dindins, 62
dine in, 62
dine out, 62
diner's card, 69

drag darling, 68
drag eyes, 67
drag face, 67
drag fag, 68
drag gown, 78
drag hair, 67
drag hustler, 68
drag king, 67
drag lips, 68
drag mags, 68
drag mustache, 68
dragon, 71
dragon lady, 33
drag picture, 68
drag queen, 68
drag race, 68
drags, 67
drag show, 68
dragster, 67
drag store, 68
drag the fur, 91
drag the mink, 91
drag up, 68
drain the lizard, 68
drank, 158
draped, 68, 211
draped down the leg, 145
draped shape, 68
drape queen, 145
draperies, 22
drapes, 123
draw drapes, 68
draw the blinds, 123
draw the drapes, 203
dreamboat, 69
dreamboy, 69
dream whip, 69
Dresden china, 69
dress, 137
dress an unfurnished apartment, 203
dressed up like a spade hooker, 63
dress to the left, 145
dress to the right, 145
dress up, 68
dried fish, 69
dries fruit, 144
drill, 49, 88
drink, 59
drip-dry lover, 185
drip queen, 69
drive-in levis, 200
drive it to home base, 90
drive (it) up to Hilltop Drive, 107
drop, 24
drop a dime on some-one, 69
drop a pearl, 69
drop a whole string of pearls, 69
drop beads, 69
drop five (four, etc.) at

the tubs, 69
drop hairpins, 69
drop one's petals, 69
drop on it, 33
drop pearls, 69
drop the beads, 29
drop the cookies, 29
drop the load, 29
drop the plate, 29
drop the soap, 22
drop your camera, 69
drosophila, 86
drove up, 69, 155
drown one, 69
drown the ass in baby oil, 90
dry charge, 69
dry clean a rear, 88
dry date, 69
dry fuck, 59
dry hump, 69, 88
dry meat, 72
dry queen, 48
dry rub, 69
dry run, 69
duchess, 69, 73
duck, 69, 73
duck blinds, 207
duck-butter, 44
duck levis, 34
ducky, 69
dude, 69
duff, 24
dugout, 69
duke, 155
Dumbo-o (The Flying Asshole), 65
dummy, 49
dump, 69
dumper, 70
dump truck, 71
dungeonette, 126
dung palace, 70
dunk, 70
dunk the doughnut, 116
dust, 137
duster, 24
dusters, 27
dust somebody off, 88
dutch dumplings, 24
Dutch girl, 70
dyke, 38, 70
dyke city, 71
dyke daddy, 71, 119
dyke queen, 71
dyke queer, 71
dyker, 71
dykes a lot, 71
dykesville, 71
dyking, 71
dyking 't, 71
dynamite, 110

E

ear-baubles, 28
early bird, 72
Earl Stanley Gardner, 39, 72
earmuffs, 148
Easter bunny queen, 128
Easter queen, 72
East Jesus, 150
easy make, 72
easy mark, 72
easy meat, 72
eat, 33, 72
eat dick in the ear, 72
eat fish, 82
eat it all out, 72
eat it, lady, 72
eat it all up, 33
eat jam, 172
eat pound cake, 172
eat pussy, 139, 163
eat somebody out, 172
eat with the hands, 101
ecaf, 72
eclair queen, 72, 149
Edna, 72
eerquay, 72
effeminative, 72
effie, 72, 148
egg, 74
eggs (in the basket), 27
egg-sucker, 74
Egyptian queen, 74
eh-eh, 74
eight pagers, 74
eighty-six, 74
—ele, 74
electric queen, 75
elegant, 75
Elizabitch, 135
Ella, 75
Elvira, 159
Emerald City (of Oz), 150
Emma, 132
Emmy, 132
empress, 75
empress affair, 75
empress bench, 75
Empress Josephine piece, 75
empress towel, 75
encore queen, 75
The End, 75, 150
endowed, 75
enforcer, 75
English martini, 75
English method, 75, 154
English muffins, 24
entertain, 75
entertain royalty, 75

French photographer, 86
French postcard, 86
French prints, 86
French revolution, 86
French stuff, 86
French tickler, 86
French way, 34
Frenchwoman, 85
fresh fruit, 86
freshly butchered, 86
freshly killed, 86
fresh meat, 86
fresh one, 86
fresh piece, 86
fried chicken, 45
frigid digit, 185
frilly-dilly, 86
frog queen, 86
front marriage, 86
front page, 86
front porch, 49
front step, 86
frosting, 67
frozen fruit, 86
fru fru, 86
fruit, 73, 86
fruit bin, 93
fruit boots, 86
fruit bowl queen, 87
fruitcake, 73
fruiter, 156
fruit fly, 87
fruit for, 166
fruit for the monkey(s), 155
fruit jars, 87
fruit juice, 52
fruit market, 93
fruit picker, 87
fruit run, 207
fruit salad, 87
fruit's machine, 87
fruit stand, 127
Fruit Stripe Run, 212
fruitsy, 86
fruity (as a fruitcake), 86
frumpy, 92
fry the onion skin, 123
fu, 73, 87
fuchsia queen, 87
fuck, 87
fuckable, 25, 89
fuck-a-buck, 89
fuck boy, 161
fuck-flat, 93
fuck handles, 27
fucking, 89
fucking and sucking, 89
fucking buddies, 184
fuck in the ass, 88
fuck in the face, 89
fuck in the head, 89
fuck in the mouth, 89
fuck-me, 189

fuck money, 137
fuck movies, 89
fuck one rotten, 89
fuck pole, 49
fuck the fist, 115
fuck the teeth, 89
fuck up the ass, 88
fudge baby, 90
fudy, 90, 148
fuff, 73
fufu funnel, 90
fugitive from a chain gang, 59
full-drag, 68
full face, 91
full focus, 91
full house, 91
full up, 91
fumigate, 91
fun, 91
fun bone, 49
funch, 91
fundillo, 24
funky, 91
funny, 166
funny acting, 166
funny money, 166
funny paper, 209
funny-paper trick, 91
fun son, 165
fur, 92
furburger, 139
the furies, 125
fur-lined foxhole, 91
furnished apartment, 91
furniture, 91
furpiece, 91
furs, 91
fuse together, 88
futch, 91
future-ex-old-man, 91
futy, 90, 146
fuzz, 90, 125
fuzzies, 91
fuzz face, 44, 108

G

GAA, 92
gadget, 49
gadgets, 27
gaff, 60, 92
gaggy, 92
Gail, 92
gal-boy, 161
galilee stompers, 219
gallant, 92
gallina, 214
gallo, 110
gallons, 211
gal-officer, 70
gal pal, 92
gam, 33
game, 92, 142

game-player, 92
gamer, 92, 185
game room, 184
gamey, 64, 92
gander, 17
gang-bang, 92, 155
gang-banging the gums, 92
gang fairy, 93
gang-fuck, 148
gangrene contest, 93
gang-shack, 92
gang-shag, 92
gang-shay, 92
gang-splash, 92, 155
Ganymede, 93
gape, 93
garage door, 93
garage queen, 184
garbage-can gray, 93
garbage-mouth somebody, 93
garbage woman, 213
garconniere, 93, 121
The Garden, 150
Garden of Allah, 149
gargoyle, 133
garter party, 93
gash, 57, 155
gash-eater, 139
gates, 24
gate-swinger, 32
gay, 21, 93
gay as a goose, 93
gay as a rose, 93
gay bar, 93
gay boy, 94
gay cat, 94
gay chick, 94
gay chicken, 46
gay deceiver, 62, 94
gay dirt, 64, 94, 111
gaydom, 94
gay dude, 94
gayer, 94
gay girl, 73, 159
gay guy, 94
gay lad, 94
Gay Liberation, 94
gay lines, 94
gay life, 94
gay lingo, 94
gay man, 94
gay marriage, 94
gay milk bar, 45
gay mother, 138
gay-stoppers, 125
gay supermarket, 127
gay talk, 94
gay trade, 200
gay uniform(s), 56
gay wedding, 95
gay woman, 94, 95
gay world, 94
gazeet, 24
gazooney, 108

go groupie on some-
body, 97
go Hollywood, 97
go home with the
garbage-man, 97
go home with the
milkman, 97
go home with the
trucks, 97
go in drag, 68
going cabareting, 158
going the flash, 82
going to the tadpole
ball, 193
go into cold storage,
171
go it alone, 97
gold-digger, 21, 113
the Gold Dust Twins,
126
golden boy, 97
golden champagne, 97
golden queen, 97
golden retrievers, 212
golden screw, 98
golden shower, 97
golden shower queen,
97, 185
gold fish, 76, 98
Goldie Chanukah, 76
Goliath, 211
Gollywood, 150
go mad, 98
gone, 98
gone on somebody, 98
gone through the Civil
War, 86
gong, 49
gonif, 17
gonny, 205
gonorita, 205
gonsel, 107
goo, 52
gooboos, 98
good buddy, 38
good fuck, 98
good head, 98
goodness, 98
good night, 195
good people, 169
goodrich queen, 98
good soup, 172
goodyear, 27
goofer, 112
goo goo stuff, 98, 200
goop-gobbler, 51
goose, 88, 98
goose-eggs, 99
goose-hole, 155
gooser, 17, 18
goosey, 90
go over, 98
go pagan, 145
gopher tits, 98
gorgeous, 98
gorjesus, 98

go rest, 98
gorilla it down, 98
go South, 139
go *that* route, 98
got the horns, 109
go to buggery, 38
go to cathedral, 98
go to Denmark, 201
go to press, 88
go to the opera, 209
go to the river, 43
go to the veins, 98
go trashin', 200
goudou, 70
gougnotte, 70
go under the house, 139
go up the stairs, 98
government-inspected
meat, 22
go Wilde, 98
goy toy, 203
grab a hot one, 33
grab at the pearls, 98
grab for pearls, 99
Grace, 99
gracious, 99
graham cracker, 63
grand, 99
grand bag, 26
grand bail, 67
grand bitch, 149
Grand Canyon, 99
Grand Canyon Suite, 99
Grand Central Station, 99
grand entrance, 99
grand exit, 99
grand finale, 43, 99
grand lady, 149
grandma, 25
grand one, 149
grandpa, 71
grand tour, 193
grand woman, 149
grass, 209
grasshopper, 210
grassy-ass, 99
grapes, 99
gratis, 99
gravedigger, 133
gravy, 99
gravy for the meat, 99
gravy train, 133
gray boy, 94
gray cat, 32
gray lady, 25
gray queen, 99, 212
gray world, 94
grease, 99
greased up, 99
great beauty, 100
Great Lakes, 100
Greek, 88, 100
Greek love, 100
Greek side, 100
Greek way, 100
green, 100

green boy, 161
green discharge, 23
greenhouse, 194
green queen, 39
greta, 101
Greta (Garbo), 100
grey bitch, 212
grief, 64, 210
grief merchant, 100
grief up on, 100
grime material, 100
grimm's fairy, 25
grind, 177, 186
grinders, 100
grind off, 115
grind off the ice cream
machine, 115
grind some meat, 100
grip it, 115
grisette, 159
groceries, 100
grooby, 100
groove, 88
groove on, 100
groovy, 100
grope, 100
grope bar, 101
gropey, 101
gross, 101
gross somebody out, 101
grotesque, 133
grotesquery, 133
ground round, 101
ground woman, 213
the group, 46
group party, 148
group therapy, 148
grouse, 70
grovey, 100
growl-biter, 139
grow some wings, 101
grow tits, 101
gruesome sister, 133
Grungette LaTour, 133
GSQ, 184
G-string, 101, 119
guest star, 101
gugusse, 83
guide, 138
guiding light, 138
guild boss, 136
gum it to death, 101
gum job, 101
gummy, 101
gun, 49
gunch, 33, 161
gunpowder, 102
gunzl, 107
Gussie, 132
gut-butcher, 155
gut-reamer, 18, 102,
155
gut-stretcher, 18, 155
gut-stuffer, 18, 155
gutter limits, 213
guy-fucking, 89

H

hachi, 102
hagmouth, 32
hair, 67, 102
hair bar, 102
hairbender, 102
hairburner, 102
haircranker, 102
hair fairy, 102
hair-job, 116
hairpie, 102, 139
hair shirt, 102
hairy, 103, 126
hairy Mary, 39
half-and-half, 32, 102
half a rock, 137
half bent, 32
half-boy, 102
half-husband, 32
halfway around the
  world, 102
half world, 102
hall of injustice, 126
hall of mirrors, 126
halloween, 68
hallucinate, 102
ham, 24
hamburger queen, 112
hamilton wick, 49
hammer, 49
hand-artist, 158
handbag, 103
handball, 152
hand books, 116
hand game, 116
hand gig, 116
hand jig, 116
hand jive, 116
hand job, 116
handle, 49
handmade, 103
hand-o, 158
hand queen, 116
hand-raised, 103
hand-reared, 103
handshake, 158
Handy Andy, 116
hang, 103
hangar, 93
hang-down, 49
hang up on some-
  body's face, 103
hang up the tits, 197
hank, 49
hank books, 158
hanking, 158
hanking and yanking,
  158
happen, 53
happy, 93
Happy Birthday, 103
Happy Easter, Sugar,
  115

happy valley, 103
hard, 103
hard daddy, 103
hard-hatted Hanna, 75
hard-hearted Hannah,
  138
hardless bitch, 74
hardly, 103
Hardly Davidson, 103
hard-on, 103
hard-on failure, 103
hardware stores, 112
harlot, 159
Harlow, 103
hash, 165
hash marks, 141
hasta lumbago, 46
hatchi, 102
hateful bitch, 103
The Hat Shop, 150
hauncho, 103
haunting, 133
haunting of hill house,
  133
have, 103
have a bad day, 104
haveable, 25
have a car wash, 42
have a case of the
  vapors, 104
have a cup of tea, 104
have a dash of lavender,
  124
have a dash of lavender
  in the garden, 124
have a date with a
  handkerchief, 114
have a face, 104
have a From Here to
  Eternity, 104
have a good day, 104
have a lot of scenery,
  177
have a Roman Spring,
  104
have a tea engagement,
  104
have eyes for, 104
have fairies at the
  bottom of the garden,
  104
have fever, 104
have Madame l'Age as
  a hairdresser, 129
have one by the curlies,
  58
have oneself, 104
have people, 104
have some cream sauce,
  34
have some tea, 194
have the big beast
  going for one, 31
have the feathers fall,
  79
have the large news

for somebody, 104
have the mean rag on,
  167
have the munchies, 140
have the nose wide
  open, 157
having European
  accentuation, 25
Hawaiian disease, 155
Hawaiian eye, 19, 155
hawk, 45, 71, 158
hawl out a personality,
  104
hay, 104, 156, 210
hayseeds, 113
hazel, 104
he, 104
head, 104
headache band, 104
head and heels, 46
head artist, 51
head case, 42
head cheese, 44
head cold, 205
head date, 104
headhunter, 52
head job, 34
head over heels (in
  love), 182
head queen, 51
head worker, 51
healed, 104
healers, 105
health jacket, 117
health movie, 105
healthy, 105
hearts, 105
heaven, 105
heavenly, 105
heavens, 105
heavy, 102, 196
heavy cruising, 56
heavy-drag, 68
heavyweight, 51
he-blew, 76
hee-haw boy, 111
heels, 105
heifer, 32
he-ing it, 105
heir to the throne, 123
held down, 156
Helen, 105
Helena, 105
Helene, 105
Helen Hairburner, 105
Helen Moviestar, 105
Helen of Troy, 105
Helen Roobenbitch, 105
Helen Twelvetoes, 105
helirum legs, 89
he-madames, 112
hem it, 68
hems, 67
hemorrhoid baby, 105
hemorrhoids, 99
hemp-humper, 210

J

K

knock off a little, 88
knock somebody off, 33
knock somebody out, 122
knock somebody's dick in the dirt, 122
knock the dew off the lily, 122
knot, 122
know the facts of life, 122
know the words and the music, 95
know the words to the music, 95
koo and kah, 122
kootch, 19
kosher, 122
kosher boy, 76
kosher delicatessen, 122
kosher dill, 122
kosher meat, 122
kosher nosher, 122
kosher style, 122
kowtow chow, 34
KS, 172
kumquat, 122
kunker, 57
kwazakoo, 19
kwink, 165
kwinky, 166
KY, 122
KY club, 122
kyky, 121
KYMCA, 122
KY queen, 122

L

la, 200
labonza, 24
lace, 48, 123
lace curtains, 123
lacy lad, 73
ladder, 123
laddie, 73
lady, 123
ladybug, 123
Lady Elgin, 209
ladyfinger, 210
Lady Godiva, 123
lady in waiting, 123
lady-lover, 70
laka, 49
lakanuki, 155
laka ring, 141
la-la, 200
lamma hutching, 59
lamplighter, 163
lampshade queen, 123
Lana Turner, 123
Lana Turner extract, 123

Lana Turner ice cream, 123
lace, 49
lance it in, 89
landlady, 112
lanoola, 49
lap, 139
lapin, 123
lap-lover, 139
lapper, 139
lardsack, 123
l'argent, 137
larking, 123
lasser, 70
last call, 43
last man, 123
last of the graces, 133
later, 46
the late show, 133
lather-up, 124
latori, 46
latty, 124
laugh lines, 124
launching pad, 124
laundry, 27
laugh marks, 124
Laura, 124
Laura LaPlant, 124
Laura Lard, 125
LaVache, 204
lavender, 124
lavender boxes, 157
lavender convention, 124
lavender lad, 124
lavish, 124
lawnmower, 139
lay, 88
layer cake, 124
lay law, 124
lay of the land, 214
lay one to earth, 162
lay some pipe, 88
lay the leg, 88
lay the lip, 33
lay with the moon, 124
lazy-drag, 68
LBJ, 34
leading man, 124
leading role, 124
leaf, 210
leather, 19, 124, 184
leather boy, 124
leather crowd, 124
leather jacket queen, 124
leather merchant, 124
leather queen, 124
leathers, 124
leave a few veils, 206
leave a puddle, 147
leave the stage, 171
leek water, 24
leg, 49
legal drag, 68
leg-crushers, 53

leggin(g)s, 156, 157
legitimate, 124
Legs, 124
Lena, 62
Leona, 124
leprachaun, 124
Leroy, 63
les, 125
les-be-friends, 125
lesbian, 125
lesbian coverter, 125
lesbian freak, 125
lesbian joint, 125
lesbianka, 125
lesbian queen, 125
lesbo, 70, 125
lesbonia, 125
lesbos, 125
lesboville, 125
lesby, 125
les girls, 125, 160
Leslie, 125
Leslie-Anne, 125
les perles, 159
lessie, 125
less-than-a-man's, 125
let one's hair down, 125
let one's hair out, 125
let someone else on stage, 193
levis lady, 35
the levis lady of shady Spain, 37
levis queen, 35
lezbo, 125
lezz, 125
lezzy, 125
liberate, 36
liberated faggot, 125
library, 127
lick, 33, 125
licker, 52, 139
lickety-split, 172
licorice stick, 49
lifesaver, 44
lighten the load, 34
light meat, 49
lights, 125
light up, 211
like Faust, 42, 125
like that, 166
lilies of the valley, 100
Lillian, 125
lily, 73
Lily Law, 125
lily of the valley, 55
lily white, 73
limpwrist, 73
Lincoln Tunnel, 99
Linda Lovelyvoice, 127
line-up, 27
linguist, 127
linguistic exercise, 182
link-sausage (queen), 59
lip burning, 127

Miss Gunch, 135
Miss Halloween, 135
missiletoes, 135
missing, 135
missionary work, 135
Miss Lily, 125
Miss Mabel, 62
Miss Mafia, 127
miss man, 110
Miss Man, 125
Miss Marigold, 210
Miss Milly, 212
Miss Morales, 29
Miss National Park, 99
Miss Niagara, 135
Miss Nickelodeon, 112, 135
miss one's calling, 136
Miss Peach, 135
Miss Peola, 135
Miss Phoebe, 127
Miss Photoplay, 135
Miss Pickupsticks, 135
Miss Pinky, 117
Miss Points, 135
miss priss, 135
Miss Rhode Island, 185
Miss Roma, 135
Miss Sally's, 48
Miss Scarlet, 135
Miss Sears, 135
Miss Tan Confessions, 135
Miss Tarantula, 135
Miss Thing, 117, 135
Miss Thunderbird, 135
Miss Tijuana, 29
Miss USO, 22
Miss Vampira, 138
Miss Vanilla Moviestar, 205
Miss Vegetable, 135
Miss Xylophone, 217
missy, 44
misters, 112
Mistkiefer, 159
mistress, 120
mixed couple, 136
mixed marriage, 136
MM, 150
mocha chips, 136
model, 136
mod squad, 153
mod squaders, 153
moff, 106
moffie, 137
moll, 137
moll about in the head, 137
mollies, 35
molly, 131
mollycoddle, 73
molly dyke, 137
molly house, 137
mom, 137
mona, 138

money, 137
money-maker, 24
money trick, 138
Monica Movinghips, 138
monk, 116
monkey, 138
monkey bite, 106
monkey cage, 126
mono, 138
monopoly money, 137
monsters, 138
monster weed, 211
moon, 24
moonlight shoes, 131
Moor, 62
moosh, 138
mop, 36
morgue case, 138
morner, 139
morning dew, 138
morning dewdrop queen, 138
morning drop, 205
morph, 106
morphdite, 106
Morticia, 52
moss, 138
mossy, 138
mota, 210
motel time, 138
mother, 138
mother and (her) four children, 116
mother bull, 126
mother gaga, 138
mother hollyhock, 138
mother love, 121
mother of pearl, 138
Mother Parker, 138
mother's boarding house, 126
mother superior, 138
Mothra, 212
motor, 24, 185
motorcycle drag, 184
motorcycle lace, 184
Motorcycle Mary, 184
motorista, 211
mouse, 138
mouth, 139
mouth falsies, 79
mouth job, 34, 138
mouth of ages, 138
mouth queen, 52
mouthwash, 77
mouth worker, 52
mouth wrestling, 86
move furniture, 91
move in, 138
movie, 138
movie extra, 138
movie extras, 138
movie queen, 82
movie star eyes, 127

moya sestra, 181
MP, 161
MQ, 30
Mr. Beverly, 102
Mr. Marty Robust, 153
Mrs., 138
Mr. Stark Raving, 138
Mr. Steve Stunning, 138
Mr. Wong, 49
M'sieu le, 139
much, 139
muchly, 139
mucho, 139
mucho-many, 139
mucho-much, 139
Mucosa Della Rosa, 139
Mucosa DeRosa, 139
mud, 139
muddy, 139
muddy fuck, 139
muff, 139
muff-diver, 139
muff-duffer, 139
muffer, 139
muffet, 139
muffie, 73, 106
muffin, 21
muff tickler, 54
mujerado, 139
mula, 146
mulegian, 63
mullet, 155
munchies, 139
muneco, 65
mung, 140
munjies, 139
murdercycle, 184
murdering butches, 22
murines, 22
muscle, 49
muscle boy, 140
muscle-gay, 140
muscle-lady, 140
mushroom, 140
musical chairs, 140
music lessons, 140
mussy, 60
mustache, 172
mustache bar, 25
mustard pot, 19
mute, 140
muzzler, 156
my chastity's grown over, 140
my dear, 140
my friend Irma, 75
my pussy itches, 140
my pussy's twitching, 140
Myrna, 65
Myra Breakfast, 140

N

P

pee'd, 147
pee-hole, 51
peek freak, 209
peel and chew a
 bamboo cane, 116
peeny, 50
pee on somebody's fire
 (and put it out), 147
peep, 50
peepee, 50, 147
peepee lover, 74
peepee meat, 74, 185
peepee-puller, 52
peeper, 44, 50
peepers, 147
peep freak, 209
peep-hole squad, 207
pee willy, 73
peg, 147
peg boy, 147
peg-house, 112, 157
pegs, 53
pellin, 24
pelos, 82
peltz, 91
pencil, 185
pencil dick, 185
Penelope, 147
penguin pelt, 147
penile colony, 194
penis, 50
penis butter, 128, 147
penis-envy queen, 70
penis machinist, 166
The Penis-sula, 149
pennies, 137
pense, 147
people on the other
 side, 184
peppermint stick, 100
Percy, 73
perform, 33, 147
perform royally, 147
personal party, 200
Perthy, 73
perv, 165
perve, 88
petal, 73
peter, 50
peter-eater, 52
peter machinist, 205
peter meter, 148
Peter Pan, 158
petrified softie, 187
petrifying stuff, 210
pets, 148
Petunia Patrolman, 126
Petunia Pig, 126
PF, 184
PF flyer, 184
phallus cum loudly, 148
Phallus-Phantom, 62
Phyllis, 148
piccolo, 50
piccolo park, 146
piccolo-player, 52

pichon, 200
pick a rosebud, 21
pickets, 148
pick fruit, 148
pickled pansy, 129
picklement, 182
pickle the rosey, 172
pick strawberries, 145
pickup, 148, 200
pick up one's heels, 148
pick up pants and go
 home, 148
pick up pennies, 55
pick up the soap, 148
pick-up truck, 71
pick up the vibrations,
 206
picnic lunch, 148
picnic up on it, 33
piddle, 147
piece, 68, 88, 105, 148
piece of action, 17
piece of ass, 23, 87
piece of beef, 30
piece of hot apple pie,
 161
piece of hot pumpkin
 pie, 45
piece of hump, 161
piece of ivy pie, 114
piece of luggage, 24
piece of meat, 50
piece of muscle, 140
piece of Navy cake, 22
piece of poundage, 153
piece of pumpkin pie
 a la mode, 45
piece of rag, 167
piece of rough trade, 173
piece of smoot, 185
piece of snatch, 161
piece of wreckage, 216
pier angelies, 23
pig, 126, 148
Pig Alley, 150
pigeon-titted, 148
piggie, 64
piggies, 35, 142
pig meat, 44
pig pile, 148
pig room, 28
pig sticking, 100
pig-suck, 148
piko, 148
pile driver, 90
piles, 99
pilgrim, 18
pimp, 111, 148
pimp boots, 148
pimp cap, 148
pimp pants, 149
pimple joint, 45
pimple palace, 45
pimp-mobile, 212
pimps, 99
pimp pants, 150

pimp-wagon, 213
pin, 149
pinch palace, 102
pinch the cat, 152
pineapple queen, 149
pineapple princess, 149
pinga, 50
ping for pong, 151
pin it up, 149
pink, 149
pink-o, 165
pink olive, 129
pink panther, 94
pink pants, 161
pink-pig, 149
pink tea, 48
pink-tea freak, 157
pinky, 103, 137, 185
pinky ring, 149
pio-pio, 44
pipe, 50
pipe-cleaner, 205
pipes, 53
pipi, 50
pirujo, 165
piss, 147
piss elegant, 149
piss elegant faggot, 149
piss elegant queen, 149
pisser, 50, 149
piss pass, 149
piss poor, 149
piss queen, 97
pissticide, 149
pissy, 149
piston rod, 50
pit, 149
pit bull, 18
pitch, 88
pitch a bitch, 32
pit job, 26
pit queen, 26
pitty poo, 149
pity, 149
pix, 73
pixie, 149
pixie dust, 84, 149
pixie stick, 79
pixie sticks, 149
pizza, 210
pizza maker, 210
pizzaria, 210
pizzle(r), 50
place card, 149
place names, 149
Place Pigalle, 150
plank, 150
plank somebody, 88
plaster, 145
plate somebody, 33
play, 150
play a tune, 33
play both sides of the
 fence, 32
play bugle boy, 33
play buses, 151

play canasta, 28
play checkers, 82
play chess, 82
play chipmunk, 151
play dump truck, 88
played out, 151
player, 151, 157
play games, 184
play god, 184
play hoop snake with
  somebody, 182
play house, 184
playing chopsticks, 116
playing hide the
  sausage, 108
play leap frog, 88
play musical arrange-
  ments (on the flute),
  33
play ping-pong, 151
play solitaire, 115
play solitaire on some-
  body, 151
play squirrel, 151
play the closet, 151
play the flute, 33
play the fruit market,
  151
play the game, 151
play the harmonicass,
  151
play the horn, 33
play the organ, 33, 151
play the part, 157
play the penny, 151
play the piano, 172
play the river, 151
play the role, 157
play the schweinte, 156
play windmill, 151
play with a chick's
  meat, 151
play with hank, 158
play with her meat, 151
pleasure punk, 161
plow, 88
pluck, 151
pluck some eyebrows,
  151
pluck somebody off,
  151
pluck some feathers,
  46, 151
pluck the fingers, 151
plucky, 152
plug, 88
plug in the neon, 20
the plumber's, 205
plumbing, 152
plumbing fixture, 152
plunger, 90
Plush Nothingness,
  150
pocket polka, 152
pocket pool, 152
pocket waltz, 152

pog, 161
poger, 161
pogie, 161
pogo stick, 50
pogue, 161
pogue bait, 156
point, 152, 156
poison ivy, 152
Poison Palms, 150
poke, 37
poke pants, 34
poke party 148
poker, 50
pokes, 34
polaroid party, 148
pole, 50
pole vaulting, 116
Polish handball, 152
polish the knob, 33, 156
Polk Strasse, 150
polluted, 152
polly, 137
polone, 152
polone-homi, 70
polo ponies, 148
pom-pom girl, 149
pom-poms, 152
ponce, 112, 166
Poncy Ponce, 166
ponies, 152
poo, 152
pood, 73
poodle people, 148
poof, 74
poofter, 74
poon, 19
poonce, 111
poop-chute, 19
pooper, 152
poopoo nasty, 84
poopy, 84
poor baby, 152
poot, 152
pooter, 152
pop a cherry, 21
pop it in (to the
  toaster), 88
popo, 24
poppa, 70
popped, 158
popper, 152
poppers, 20
popsickle, 152
pop somebody open, 21
pop the cork, 21
porcelain fountain, 152
porchy, 152
pork, 50, 152
pork-and-beans, 153
pork chopper, 127
pork enema, 50
pork packer, 52
porny, 153
pornzine, 117
portable fuck machine,
  124

porthole, 20
pose, 153
pose queen, 82, 153
posie queen, 129
posies, 153
possesh, 107
post flyers, 84
post queen, 153
Post Toasties, 153
pot, 70, 210
potato finger, 62
pothead, 210
potholder, 210
pot liquor, 106
pot-partners, 157
pot pie, 153
pot queen, 129
potting, 142
potty, 153
potty as a chamber,
  153
pouf, 73
poufy, 166
poultry dealer, 46, 112
pound, 153
poundage, 153
poundage queen, 153
poundcake, 24
poundcake queen, 120
pound of chopped
  liver, 132
pound off, 115
pound one's popo, 88
pound somebody into
  putty, 153
pound the pud, 50
pound the meat, 115
powdered and per-
  fumed, 153
powder puff, 73
powder puffs, 131
powder someone's
  cheeks, 88
powder the nose, 153
powerful shit, 210
PP, 161
Praetorian guard, 127
pratt, 24
prattable, 89
pratt for somebody, 153
pratt-hunter, 18
pratt-man, 18
precheck, 208
precious, 45, 153
preen oneself in, 153
pregreased, 99, 153
present a debutante to
  the court, 37
presh, 153
preschen, 108
press the button, 153
press the dress, 153
pressure punk, 161
prestige fuck, 153
prestige fucking, 154
prestige piece, 153

put a hurtin' on something, 163
putana, 159
put a story on somebody, 163
put blush on the nose, 163
put it into a different gear, 163
put it to somebody, 89
puto, 111
put-on, 201
put on a face, 145
put on a few hesitation marks, 163
put on a show, 163
put one's case out in front, 163
put on best birthday suit, 140
put on pink (purple) pants, 163
put on the Steve Reeves suit, 102
putter, 103
put the blade to him, 155
put the boots on somebody, 163
put the cake on heels, 105
put the penny on somebody, 151
put the seeds (back) into the apple pie, 163
put the whip to somebody, 163
putting a kid on the block, 156
putting iron, 103
putting on the pot, 142, 157
putting the boots to him, 157
putting the heels to him, 157
putting the kicks to him, 157
putting the spikes to him, 157
put us back a few thousand years, 163
python, 163

Q

Q, 164
Q-boy, 164
Q-cards, 164
Q'er, 164
Q-ey, 164
quail, 46
quaint, 164

quaint bar, 93
quake somebody, 164
The Quarter, 157
quay, 165
quean up, 164
queebie, 165
queen, 157, 164
Queen Anne, 164
queen bee, 164
Queen Capital of the World, 150
Queen City, 150
queen for a day, 164
queenie, 73, 157, 164
Queen Mary, 165
queen mother, 165
queen of clubs, 126
queen of diamonds, 165
queen of hearts, 165
queen of Scotch, 165
queen of Sheba, 165
queen of spades, 165
queen of tarts, 165
queen of the gown, 68
queen of the load, 165
queen of the Macaronies, 129
queen of the range, 165
queen on a broomstick, 165
queens' buses, 212
queens' carriage, 212
queens' Christmas, 32
queens' church, 93
queen's gilded cage, 40
queen sheepshit, 165
queens' row, 157
Queen Tsetse Fly, 165
queer, 165
queer a person, 89
queer as a football bat, 166
queer as a nine-dollar bill, 166
queer as a square egg, 166
queer as a three-dollar bill, 166
queer baiting, 166
queer bashing, 166
queer bird, 70
queer corner, 166
queer couple, 157
queer for, 166
queerie, 165
queer pup, 46
queer queen, 70
queer's lunch box, 119
queer somebody, 166
queers' woman, 164
quelle, 166
Quelle vache, 204
qu'est-ce que c'est, 166
quickie, 34, 166
quickie station, 166

quick one, 166
quick piece, 166
quick queer, 166
quick twenty, 111
quiet wink, 167
quiff, 57, 161, 167
quim, 19, 161
quin, 73
quince, 74

R

rabbit, 52, 167
rabbit job, 177
rabbit-scraper, 167
Rachel, 76
rack, 167
racketeers, 112
radio, 167
radish, 164
rag, 131, 167
rag-cheese, 44
Raggedy Android, 167
rag on someone, 167
rag paper, 80
rags, 179
ragweed, 210
railed, 167
railroad, 167
railroader, 167
railroad queen, 167
rainbow, 168
rainbow queen, 167
raincoat, 53, 168
raise a beam, 103
raise a queen, 168
raisin, 168
raisin-hunting, 168
raisin queen, 168
raise it, 103
rake, 168
rally, 169
rally 'roun' the flagpole, 168
Ralph, 168
ram, 88
rammer, 50, 90
Ramona Rottencrotch, 168
ram-rod, 50
ranchera, 37
ranch queen, 37
rancid flower, 25
randy, 109, 168
range, 184
Ranger Smith, 126
rank, 168
rank somebody, 168
rapid, 168
rapid transit, 68, 201
rapo, 158
rasgar, 90
the rash, 205
rat someone's mind, 168

rosebud, 19
rose piddle, 173
rose tattoo, 106, 173
rose window, 25
rosey, 24
rosquear, 88
rouge, 173
rouge the lips, 173
rough trade, 173
round brown, 19
rounders, 24
roundeye, 19, 155
roundheels, 161, 162
rounding up the meat, 22
roundmouth, 52
round-robin, 148
round-up, 92
route, 173
route sixty-nine, 182
Rover, 148
royal, 173
royal ballet, 127
royal ban, 146, 174
royal bar, 174
royal buns, 25, 174
royal bust, 127
royal coach, 212
royal command, 174
royal coronation, 174
royal crown, 174
royal gown, 78, 174
royal guard, 127
royalist, 174
royal jelly, 53
royally, 173
royal neck, 174
royal opera, 127
royal pumps, 174
royal room, 174
royalty, 174
rub-belly, 174
rubber, 30, 53, 156, 168
rubber dish, 174
rubber goods, 53
rubber mules, 219
rubber palace, 174
rubber queen, 30, 174
rubber rooms, 174
rubber walls, 174
rubbins, 156
rubdown, 174
rub freak, 30
rubies, 174
rub it off, 115
rub-off, 174
rub queen, 136
Ruby, 174
ruby red lips, 174
ruby reds, 174
rug, 174
rug cleaner, 174
ruggies, 35
rughead, 63
rugs, 148

ruin somebody's Easter, 175
rump, 24
rump the cula, 88
rumpus delecti, 25
rumpy, 146
run a game, 175
run a line, 175
run a number, 175
run a railroad, 167
run a tour, 175
runaway pumpkin, 213
run for somebody, 175
run in the nylons, 175
runner, 156
runners, 131
running shoes, 131
running the tier, 155
run off, 175
run off by hand, 115
run, rabbit, run, 175
runway, 175
runway hairline, 175
rupert, 50
rush, 175
rushingly, 175
Russian salad party, 148
rusty rifle, 205

S

S, 184
—s, 176
sack, 26
sad-ass, 184
saddle it, 88
Sadie, 159
sadie-maisie, 183
sadie-mazzy, 183
safari, 176
safo, 176
safety, 53
saggers, 176
sailor queen, 22, 23
sailor's cup of tea, 23
salad bowl, 25, 212
salami, 50
saleslady, 159
Sally, 132, 176
Salome, 202
salon, 176
salt and pepper queens, 176
salt in the diet, 22
salt-seller, 23
salt-water taffy, 22
Sam, 117, 176
Samantha, 176
Sam Savage, 126
Samurai Sue, 121
S and M, 183
sandpaper, 80, 176

sandwich, 176
San Francisco faggot, 176
San Fran suntan, 176
Santa Claus, 191
Santa Josefina, 150
Sapphist, 70
Sapphite, 176
sapphite ring, 176
Sappho, 176
sarong, 28
sashay, 192
satchel ass, 25
satchel butt, 25
satchels, 176
Saturday night at the movies, 176
sauce, 53
saucerhead, 104
sausage, 50
savage, 126
say a mouthful, 177
say high mass, 177
say it, 177
sazeech, 210
S-B boy, 113
scalloped potatoes, 27
scalp hunter, 21
scammered, 166
scandal clothes, 56
scandal girl, 214
scandal coup, 177
scants, 203
scarf (scorf) up on a bod, 33
scarlet woman, 214
scarper, 177
scatter some nuggets (among the poor), 142
scenery, 177
scenic, 178
scepter, 50
scepter and jewels, 50
schlock Mexican, 23
schlong, 50
schmuck, 50, 112
schnitzel, 50
schwantz, 50
Schwarzesser, 52
schwartze, 63, 64
scoffins, 156
score, 130, 177
score an overnight, 111
score card, 112
scour out the pussy, 177
scramble on some- body's head, 177
scrape job, 177
scrape some scum, 210
scratch, 19, 57
scream, 177
scream basket, 177
scream box, 177

sugar pants, 191
sugar shaker, 191
sugar stick, 50
sugar sweet, 74
sugar trick, 191
sugar trip, 192
summer replacement, 189
summer stock, 192
sunflower, 29
sunflower seeds, 192
sunken treasure, 192
sunkist, 64
sunkist queen, 63
sunnyside up, 90
super, 192
superboy, 158
super J, 106
superstar, 169
supreme toad, 198
surf, 89
surprise package, 51
sus, 126
Susan Saliva, 192
Suzie Wongs, 171
swallow a sword, 33
swamp woman, 214
swanska, 211
swan song, 192
swapping cans, 157
swapping out, 157
swap spits, 158
swarm, 164
swarm bar, 192
sweater girl, 192
sweathog, 192
sweat-room fairy, 28
sweep off, 115
sweet, 192
sweet boy, 74
sweetcakes, 192
sweetheart, 74, 192
sweet hips, 192
sweetie, 74, 192
sweetie-pie, 192
sweet lady, 112
sweetlips, 192
sweet mack, 129
sweet man, 159
sweet meat, 50
sweetness, 192
sweet people, 192
sweets, 192
sweet thing, 45
sweetums, 193
sweet William, 74
swift, 192
swill, 192
swing, 192
swing butch, 192
swinger, 192
swing femme, 192
swing on it, 33
swing on some flivver, 34
swing wide, 192

swingy, 192
swipe, 50, 155
swish, 132, 134, 192, 193
swishblader, 111
swisher, 192
swish joint, 94
swishy, 131, 193
switch, 63, 192
switch-hitter, 32
sword, 50
swordfighting, 116
Sy, 58
Sylvania, 210
sympies, 174
syph, 206
syph-o, 206
syrup, 193

T

table cloth, 216
taco queen, 29
Taco Town, 150
taco tunes, 193
tacks, 193
tacky, 193
tad, 185
tadpole, 193
tail, 24
tailgator, 29
tailor, 123
take a bow, 193
take a Drano cocktail, 43
take a hair, 193
take a legal piss, 193
take a trip around the world (in eighty ways), 193
take a trip to the moon, 172
take a turn in the barrel, 193
take a whizz, 213
take it anyway, 193
take it easy, 193
take it in the mouth, 34
take it one way, 193
take off the tits, 198
take one on a trip, 193
take one's bed, 193
take out insurance, 193
taker, 155, 161
take somebody on, 34
take somebody on a ride, 96
take somebody's buns, 161
take somebody's pulse, 101
take the meat out (of the basket), 61

take the pay, 111
take the vapors, 194
take the veil, 171, 206
take your trip, 194
taking on doubles, 136
taking on duos, 136
talent, 194
talent scout, 194
talk dirt(y), 194
talk in blues and greens, 194
talk in deep hues of magnolia, 194
talking, 194
talk it up, 103
talk shop, 194
talk slop, 194
talk to management, 194
tall, 211
tallywhacker, 211
talona, 159
talons, 194
tam, 194
tamale, 210
tamale-pie eater, 29
Tamaleville, 150
tampered with, 194
tangerine, 194
tangle tits, 198
tangy, 193
tankers, 25
tansie, 29
tansie's formal, 29
tant, 194
tante, 165
tan track, 19
tan trouser(ed) snake, 50
tapado, 112
tapdance, 115
tapdancer, 115
tapette, 74
tapin, 159
tapioca pudding, 53
taquitos, 24
tarantula eyes, 194
tar baby, 142, 194
tar brush, 51
tariff, 137
tart, 214
tassel, 185
taster, 194
tasty, 194
tasty cover, 194
tasty upholstery, 194
tat, 194
tata, 165
tat queen, 194
tattoo boy, 194
tattoo queen, 194
tattoos, 112
tatty, 193
tat up, 194
tauatane, 74
tavern maid, 194

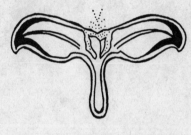

Z

Bibliography

Aldrich, Ann. *Carol in a Thousand Cities,* N.Y: Gold Medal Books, 1960.

Apollinaire, Guillaume. *The Debauched Hospodar.* Covina, California: 1st. Am. printing, by Collectors Publications, June 1967.

Baker, Sidney J. *The Australian Language.* Sydney, Australia: Angus and Robertson, Ltd, 1945.

Bates, Aaron. "As Free As Birds In a Preserve" *Gay,* vol. 3, no. 71 (March 6, '72) p 19.

Blake, Roger. *The American Dictionary of Sexual Terms.* Hollywood, California: Century Publishing Co, 1964.

Bowie, Joe D. *Half World.* Manhasset, N.Y: Kozy Books Inc, 1962.

Bulliet, C.J. *Venus Castina.* N.Y: Bonanza Books, 1928 and 1956.

Burk, Tom. "The New Homosexuality." *Esquire,* (Dec. 1969), 316-318.

Burks, John, Geoffrey Link. "The Gay Mecca." *San Francisco Magazine,* vol. 12, no. 4, (April 1970), 30-45.

Burroughs, William S. *Naked Lunch.* N.Y: Grove Press.

Collary, Rex. "Camp Beach, Boys, Pubs—In Australia." *Vector,* vol. 7, no. 5, (May 1971), 39.

Cory, Donald Webster. *The Homosexual in America.* N.Y: Paperback Library, 1st printing, 1963.
—John P. LeRoy. *The Homosexual and His Society.* N.Y.; Citadel Press, 1963.

Crowley, Mart. *The Boys in the Band.* N.Y: Dell Publishing Co, Inc, 1968.

D'Arcangelo, Angelo. *The Homosexual Handbook.* N.Y: The Olympia Press, 1968.

Dennis, Patrick. *Little Me.* N.Y: Crest Books, reprinted by arrangement with E.P. Dutton and Co, 1961.

Dorian, Lee. *The Young Homosexual.* N.Y: L.S. Publications, 1965.

Dyer, Charles. *Staircase.* N.Y: Avon Books, reprinted by arrangement with Doubleday, 1969.

Elli, Frank. *The Riot.* N.Y: Avon Books, 1966.

Giallombardo, Rose. *Society of Women: a study of a women's prison.* N.Y: John Wiley, 1966.

Grant, Otto. *Making The Team.* North Hollywood, California: Barclay House, 1969.

Goldin, Hyman E, Frank O'Leary, Morris Lipsius, eds. *Dictionary of American Underworld Lingo.* N.Y: Twayne, 1950.

Griswold, Jack H, Mike Misenheimer, Art Powers, Ed Tromanhauser. *An Eye For An Eye.* N.Y: Holt, Rinehart and Winston, 1970.

Hansen, Rev. Edward, Mark Forrester, Rev. Fred Bird. *The Tenderloin Ghetto.* San Francisco, California: Glide Urban Center, 1969.

Hauser, Richard. *The Homosexual Society.* London, England: The Bodley Head Ltd, 1962.

Henry, George William. *Sex Variants,* Vol. II. N.Y: Paul B. Hoeber, Inc, 1941.

Hopper, Columbus B. *Sex in Prison.* Baton Rouge, La: Louisiana State University Press, 1969.

Hotten, John Camden, pub. *The Slang Dictionary.* Piccadilly, London, 1864.

Hyde, H. Montgomery. *The Love That Dared Not Speak Its Name.* Boston: Little, Brown & Co, 1971.

Kany, Charles Emil. *American-Spanish Euphemisms.* Berkeley: University of California Press, 1960.

Karlen, Arno. *Sexuality and Homosexuality.* N.Y: W.W. Norton and Co, 1971.

Krich, Aron M. *The Homosexuals, as seen by themselves and thirty authorities.* N.Y: Citadel

Press, 1954.

Lester, Lance. *Lights Out Little Hustler.* San Diego California: Late-Hour Library, Phenix Pub, Ltd, 1968

Little, Jay. *Maybe Tomorrow.* N.Y: Paperback Library, Feb. 1965.

—*Somewhere Between the Two.* N.Y: Paperback Library, Aug. 1965.

Marshall, George. *The Beginner's Guide to Cruising.* Washington D.C: Guild Book Service, 1964.

Mencken, H.L. *The American Language.* 4th ed. N.Y: Alfred A. Knopf, 1955.

Mercer, J.D. *They Walk in Shadow.* N.Y: Comet Press, 1959.

Moody, Alexander. *The Gay World.* N.Y: Lancer Books, 1968.

Morse, Dr. Benjamin. *The Homosexual.* Derby, Connecticut: Monarch Books, 1962.

—*The Lesbian.* Derby, Conn: Monarch Books, 1961.

Neal, K.O. "A Good Year for Frabjous Fuchsias." *One*, vol. 12, no. 2, (Feb. 1964), 12-16.

Niemoeller, A.F. "A Glossary of Homosexual Slang." *Fact*, vol. 2, issue 1, (Jan.-Feb. 1965), 25-27.

Partridge, Eric. *A Dictionary of Slang and Unconventional English.* N.Y: Macmillan, 1937.

—*Here, There and Everywhere.* London: Hamish Hamilton Ltd, 1950.

Prewitt, Frank E, Francis K. Schaeffer. *Prewitt-Schaeffer Vacaville Vocabulary.* Unfinished ms, Vacaville State Prison, 1967.

Ragen, Joseph E, Charles Finston. *Inside The World's Toughest Prison.* Springfield, Ill: Charles C. Thomas, 1962.

Rand, Lou. *Rough Trade.* N.Y: Paperback Library, 1965.

Raul, K.B. *Naked to the Night.* N.Y: Paperback Library, 1964.

Rechy, John. *City of Night.* N.Y: Grove Press, 1964.

—*Numbers.* N.Y: Grove Press, 1967.

Rothenberg, Julius C. "Peanuts! The Pickle Dealers!" *American Speech*, vol. 16, no. 3, (Oct. 1941), 187-191.

Sagan, Edward. *Odd Man In.* Chicago: Quadrangle Books, 1969.

Salas, Floyd. *Tattoo The Wicked Cross.* N.Y: Grove Press, 1967.

Selber, Michael. "Get Your Rocks Off; Pull Your Pants Up." *Los Angeles Advocate*, vol. 3, no. 4, (April 1969), 3.

Severin, Reed. "'Faggot' Has Colorful History." *Los Angeles Advocate*, vol. 4, no. 6, (May 13-26 1970), 9.

—"Those Gay Words Had Start in Society's Contempt." *Los Angeles Advocate*, vol. 4, no. 3, (March 1970), 13.

Sontag, Susan. "Notes on Camp." *Against Interpretation.* N.Y: Dell Publishing Co, 1966. 275-292.

Stearn, Jess. *The Sixth Man.* N.Y: MacFadden Books, 1962.

"Talk Mavis." reprinted from the Cape Town Hearald by *The San Francisco Gay Free Press*, vol. 2, no. 11, (1971), 2.

The Guild Dictionary of Homosexual Terms. Washington D.C: Guild Press Ltd, 1965.

"The Homosexual: Newly Visible, Newly Understood." *Time*, (Oct. 31, 1969), 56-57.

Townsend, Larry. *The Leatherman's Handbook.* N.Y: The Olympia Press, 1972.

Turner, Lorenzo Dow. *Africanisms in the Gullah Dialect.* University of Chicago Press, 1949.

Vedder, Clyde, Patricia G. King. *Problems of Homosexuality in Corrections.* Springfield, Ill: C.C. Thomas, 1967.

Van Den Bark, Melvin, and Lester V. Berrey, eds. *The American Thesaurus of Slang.* N.Y: T.Y. Crowell, 1942; rev. 1953.

Vidal, Gore. *Myra Breckinridge.* N.Y: Little, Brown & Co, 1968.

Wade III, Tom. *Homo Sweet Homo.* Texas: Gaylord Publishing Co, 1968.

Weintraub, Joseph, ed. *The Wit and Wisdom of Mae West.* N.Y: Avon Books, 1967.

Wells, John Warren. *The Male Hustler.* N.Y: Lancer Books.

Wentworth, Harold, and Stuart Berg Flexner, eds. *A Dictionary of American Slang.* N.Y: T.Y. Crowell, 1960.

Westwood, Gordon. *A Minority.* Edinburgh: Longmans, Green & Co, Ltd, R & R Clark Ltd, 1960.

Wiener, Joan. "Cockettes." *Rags,* (Aug. 1970), 40-43.

Wright, Charles. *The Messenger.* N.Y: Crest Book Edition, 1964.

Bruce Rodgers spent 12 years collecting words for THE QUEEN'S VERNACULAR. He believes everyone should have at least one candid photograph of himself—preferably while asleep or as naked as lettuce.

BOOK DESIGN   JON GOODCHILD